This exclusive One Spirit collection brings together three of Paulo Coelho's enchanting works. *The Alchemist*, dazzling in its simplicity and wisdom, is Coelho's novel about an Andalusian shepherd boy named Santiago who travels from his homeland in Spain to the Egyptian desert in search of a treasure buried in the Pyramids. But what starts out as a journey to find worldly goods turns into a meditation on the treasures found within. Lush, evocative, and deeply humane, Santiago's story is an eternal testament to the transforming power of our dreams and the importance of listening to our hearts.

The Pilgrimage details Coelho's journey across Spain along the legendary road of San Tiago, where pilgrims have traveled since the Middle Ages. On this contemporary quest Coelho encounters a Chaucerian variety of mysterious guides and devilish opponents and learns to understand the nature of truth through the simplicity of life. *The Pilgrimage,* the author's first book, not only paves the way for *The Alchemist,* but it also fully expresses his humanist philosophy and the depth of his unique search for meaning.

A poetic story that reflects the depth of love and life, *By the River Piedra I Sat Down and Wept* describes what happens when, after eleven years, lovers come together again. Pilar has become an independent and strong young woman while her childhood friend has become a handsome spiritual leader. She has learned to bury her feelings and he has turned to religion as a refuge from his inner conflicts. Together they embark on a journey, and by the River Piedra, in a small village in the French Pyrenees, they discuss many of life's big questions and reevaluate their own special relationship.

PAULO COELHO is an internationally best-selling author whose books have sold more than 25 million copies in 117 countries and have been translated into 43 languages. Besides the works in this volume, he is also the author of *The Valkyries: An Encounter with Angels, Veronika Decides to Die,* and *The Fifth Mountain.* Coelho lives in Rio Janeiro, Brazil.

The Alchemist

The Pilgrimage

By the River Piedra I Sat Down and Wept

The Alchemist

The Pilgrimage

By the River Piedra I Sat Down and Wept

Paulo Coelho

Translated by Alan R. Clarke

One Spirit · New York

Printed in the United States of America

The Alchemist

A Fable About Following Your Dream

PROLOGUE

Translated by Clifford E. Landers

THE ALCHEMIST PICKED UP A BOOK THAT SOMEONE IN the caravan had brought. Leafing through the pages, he found a story about Narcissus.

The alchemist knew the legend of Narcissus, a youth who knelt daily beside a lake to contemplate his own beauty. He was so fascinated by himself that, one morning, he fell into the lake and drowned. At the spot where he fell, a flower was born, which was called the narcissus.

But this was not how the author of the book ended the story.

He said that when Narcissus died, the goddesses of the forest appeared and found the lake, which had been fresh water, transformed into a lake of salty tears.

"Why do you weep?" the goddesses asked.

"I weep for Narcissus," the lake replied.

"Ah, it is no surprise that you weep for Narcissus," they said, "for though we always pursued him in the forest, you alone could contemplate his beauty close at hand."

"But . . . was Narcissus beautiful?" the lake asked.

"Who better than you to know that?" the goddesses said in wonder. "After all, it was by your banks that he knelt each day to contemplate himself!"

The lake was silent for some time. Finally, it said:

"I weep for Narcissus, but I never noticed that Narcissus was beautiful. I weep because, each time he knelt beside my banks, I could see, in the depths of his eyes, my own beauty reflected."

"What a lovely story," the alchemist thought.

PART ONE

THE BOY'S NAME WAS SANTIAGO. DUSK WAS FALLING AS the boy arrived with his herd at an abandoned church. The roof had fallen in long ago, and an enormous sycamore had grown on the spot where the sacristy had once stood.

He decided to spend the night there. He saw to it that all the sheep entered through the ruined gate, and then laid some planks across it to prevent the flock from wandering away during the night. There were no wolves in the region, but once an animal had strayed during the night, and the boy had had to spend the entire next day searching for it.

He swept the floor with his jacket and lay down, using the book he had just finished reading as a pillow. He told himself that he would have to start reading thicker books: they lasted longer, and made more comfortable pillows.

It was still dark when he awoke, and, looking up, he could see the stars through the half-destroyed roof.

I wanted to sleep a little longer, he thought. He had had the same dream that night as a week ago, and once again he had awakened before it ended.

He arose and, taking up his crook, began to awaken the sheep that still slept. He had noticed that, as soon as he awoke, most of his animals also began to stir. It was as if some mysterious energy bound his life to that of the sheep, with whom he had spent the past two years, leading them through the countryside in search of food and water. "They are so used to me that they know my schedule," he muttered. Thinking about that for a moment, he realized that it could be the other way around: that it was he who had become accustomed to *their* schedule.

But there were certain of them who took a bit longer to awaken. The boy prodded them, one by one, with his crook, calling each by name. He had always believed that the sheep were able to understand what he said. So there were times when he read them parts of his books that had made an impression on him, or when he would tell them of the loneliness or the happiness of a shepherd in the fields. Sometimes he would comment to them on the things he had seen in the villages they passed.

But for the past few days he had spoken to them about only one thing: the girl, the daughter of a merchant who lived in the village they would reach in about four days. He had been to the village only once, the year before. The merchant was the proprietor of a dry goods shop, and he always demanded that the sheep be sheared in his presence, so that he would not be cheated. A friend had told the boy about the shop, and he had taken his sheep there.

"I NEED TO SELL SOME WOOL," THE BOY TOLD THE MERCHANT.

The shop was busy, and the man asked the shepherd to wait until the afternoon. So the boy sat on the steps of the shop and took a book from his bag.

"I didn't know shepherds knew how to read," said a girl's voice behind him.

The girl was typical of the region of Andalusia, with flowing black hair, and eyes that vaguely recalled the Moorish conquerors.

"Well, usually I learn more from my sheep than from books," he answered. During the two hours that they talked, she told him she was the merchant's daughter, and spoke of life in the village, where each day was like all the others. The shepherd told her of the Andalusian countryside, and related the news from the other towns where he had stopped. It was a pleasant change from talking to his sheep.

"How did you learn to read?" the girl asked at one point.

"Like everybody learns," he said. "In school."

"Well, if you know how to read, why are you just a shepherd?"

The boy mumbled an answer that allowed him to avoid responding to her question. He was sure the girl would never understand. He went on telling stories about his travels, and her bright, Moorish eyes went wide with fear and surprise. As the time passed, the boy found himself wishing that the day would never end, that her father would stay busy and keep him waiting for three days. He recognized that he was feeling something he had never experienced before: the desire to live in one place forever. With the girl with the raven hair, his days would never be the same again.

But finally the merchant appeared, and asked the boy to shear four sheep. He paid for the wool and asked the shepherd to come back the following year.

AND NOW IT WAS ONLY FOUR DAYS BEFORE HE WOULD BE back in that same village. He was excited, and at the same time uneasy: maybe the girl had already forgotten him. Lots of shepherds passed through, selling their wool.

"It doesn't matter," he said to his sheep. "I know other girls in other places."

But in his heart he knew that it did matter. And he knew that shepherds, like seamen and like traveling salesmen, always found a town where there was someone who could make them forget the joys of carefree wandering.

The day was dawning, and the shepherd urged his sheep in the direction of the sun. They never have to make any decisions, he thought. Maybe that's why they always stay close to me.

The only things that concerned the sheep were food and water. As long as the boy knew how to find the best pastures in Andalusia, they would be his friends. Yes, their days were all the same, with the seemingly endless hours between sunrise and dusk; and they had never read a book in their young lives, and didn't understand when the boy told them about the sights of the cities. They were content with just food and water, and, in exchange, they generously gave of their wool, their company, and—once in a while—their meat.

If I became a monster today, and decided to kill them, one by one, they would become aware only after most of the flock had been slaughtered, thought the boy. They trust me, and they've forgotten how to rely on their own instincts, because I lead them to nourishment.

The boy was surprised at his thoughts. Maybe the church, with the sycamore growing from within, had been haunted. It had caused him to have the same dream for a second time, and it was causing him to feel anger toward his faithful companions. He drank a bit from the wine that remained from his dinner of the night before, and he gathered his jacket closer to his body. He knew that a few hours from now, with the sun at its zenith, the heat would be so great that he would not be able to lead his flock across the fields. It was the time of day when all of Spain slept during the summer. The heat lasted until nightfall, and all that time he had to carry his jacket. But when he thought to complain about the burden of its weight, he remembered that, because he had the jacket, he had withstood the cold of the dawn.

We have to be prepared for change, he thought, and he was grateful for the jacket's weight and warmth.

The jacket had a purpose, and so did the boy. His purpose in life was to travel, and, after two years of walking the Andalusian terrain, he knew all the cities of the region. He was planning, on this visit, to explain to the girl how it was that a simple shepherd knew how to read. That he had attended a seminary until he was sixteen. His parents had wanted him to become a priest, and thereby a source of pride for a simple farm family. They worked hard just to have food and water, like the sheep. He had studied Latin, Spanish, and theology. But ever since he had been a child, he had wanted to know the world, and this was much more important to him than knowing God and learning about man's sins. One afternoon, on a visit to his family, he had summoned up the courage to tell his father that he didn't want to become a priest. That he wanted to travel.

✷

"PEOPLE FROM ALL OVER THE WORLD HAVE PASSED through this village, son," said his father. "They come in search of new things, but when they leave they are basically the same people they were when they arrived. They climb the mountain to see the castle, and they wind up thinking that the past was better than what we have now. They have blond hair, or dark skin, but basically they're the same as the people who live right here."

"But I'd like to see the castles in the towns where they live," the boy explained.

"Those people, when they see our land, say that they would like to live here forever," his father continued.

"Well, I'd like to see their land, and see how they live," said his son.

"The people who come here have a lot of money to spend, so they can afford to travel," his father said. "Amongst us, the only ones who travel are the shepherds."

"Well, then I'll be a shepherd!"

His father said no more. The next day, he gave his son a pouch that held three ancient Spanish gold coins.

"I found these one day in the fields. I wanted them to be a part of your inheritance. But use them to buy your flock. Take to the fields, and someday you'll learn that our countryside is the best, and our women the most beautiful."

And he gave the boy his blessing. The boy could see in his father's gaze a desire to be able, himself, to travel the world—a desire that was still alive, despite his father's having had to bury it, over dozens of years, under the burden of struggling for water to drink, food to eat, and the same place to sleep every night of his life.

THE HORIZON WAS TINGED WITH RED, AND SUDDENLY the sun appeared. The boy thought back to that conversation with his father, and felt happy; he had already seen many castles and met many women (but none the equal of the one who awaited him several days hence). He owned a jacket, a book that he could trade for another, and a flock of sheep. But, most important, he was able every day to live out his dream. If he were to tire of the Andalusian fields, he could sell his sheep and go to sea. By the time he had had enough of the sea, he would already have known other cities, other women, and other chances to be happy. I couldn't have found God in the seminary, he thought, as he looked at the sunrise.

Whenever he could, he sought out a new road to travel. He had never been to that ruined church before, in spite of having traveled through those parts many times. The world was huge and inexhaustible; he had only to allow his sheep to set the route for a while, and he would discover other interesting things. The problem is that they don't even realize that they're walking a new road every day. They don't see that the fields are new and the seasons change. All they think about is food and water.

Maybe we're all that way, the boy mused. Even me—I haven't thought of other women since I met the merchant's daughter. Looking at the sun, he calculated that he would reach Tarifa before midday. There, he could exchange his book for a thicker one, fill his wine bottle, shave, and have a haircut; he had to prepare himself for his meeting with the girl, and he didn't want to think about the possibility that some other shepherd, with a larger flock of sheep, had arrived there before him and asked for her hand.

It's the possibility of having a dream come true that makes life interesting, he thought, as he looked again at the position of the sun, and hurried his pace. He had suddenly remembered that, in Tarifa, there was an old woman who interpreted dreams.

THE OLD WOMAN LED THE BOY TO A ROOM AT THE BACK of her house; it was separated from her living room by a curtain of colored beads. The room's furnishings consisted of a table, an image of the Sacred Heart of Jesus, and two chairs.

The woman sat down, and told him to be seated as well. Then she took both of his hands in hers, and began quietly to pray.

It sounded like a Gypsy prayer. The boy had already had experience on the road with Gypsies; they also traveled, but they had no flocks of sheep. People said that Gypsies spent their lives tricking others. It was also said that they had a pact with the devil, and that they kidnapped children and, taking them away to their mysterious camps, made them their slaves. As a child, the boy had always been frightened to death that he would be captured by Gypsies, and this childhood fear returned when the old woman took his hands in hers.

But she has the Sacred Heart of Jesus there, he thought, trying to reassure himself. He didn't want his hand to begin trembling, showing the old woman that he was fearful. He recited an Our Father silently.

"Very interesting," said the woman, never taking her eyes from the boy's hands, and then she fell silent.

The boy was becoming nervous. His hands began to tremble, and the woman sensed it. He quickly pulled his hands away.

"I didn't come here to have you read my palm," he said, already regretting having come. He thought for a moment that it would be better to pay her fee and leave without learning a thing, that he was giving too much importance to his recurrent dream.

"You came so that you could learn about your dreams," said the old woman. "And dreams are the language of God. When he speaks in our language, I can interpret what he has said. But if he speaks in the language of the soul, it is only you who can understand. But, whichever it is, I'm going to charge you for the consultation."

Another trick, the boy thought. But he decided to take a chance. A shepherd always takes his chances with wolves and with drought, and that's what makes a shepherd's life exciting.

"I have had the same dream twice," he said. "I dreamed that I was in a field with my sheep, when a child appeared and began to play with the animals. I don't like people to do that, because the sheep are afraid of strangers. But children always seem to be able to play with them without frightening them. I don't know why. I don't know how animals know the age of human beings."

"Tell me more about your dream," said the woman. "I have to get back to my cooking, and, since you don't have much money, I can't give you a lot of time."

"The child went on playing with my sheep for quite a while," continued the boy, a bit upset. "And suddenly, the child took me by both hands and transported me to the Egyptian pyramids."

He paused for a moment to see if the woman knew what the Egyptian pyramids were. But she said nothing.

"Then, at the Egyptian pyramids,"—he said the last three words slowly, so that the old woman would understand—"the child said to me, 'If you come here, you will find a hidden treasure.' And, just as she was about to show me the exact location, I woke up. Both times."

The woman was silent for some time. Then she again took his hands and studied them carefully.

"I'm not going to charge you anything now," she said. "But I want one-tenth of the treasure, if you find it."

The boy laughed—out of happiness. He was going to be able to save the little money he had because of a dream about hidden treasure!

"Well, interpret the dream," he said.

"First, swear to me. Swear that you will give me one-tenth of your treasure in exchange for what I am going to tell you."

The shepherd swore that he would. The old woman asked him to swear again while looking at the image of the Sacred Heart of Jesus.

"It's a dream in the language of the world," she said. "I can interpret it, but the interpretation is very difficult. That's why I feel that I deserve a part of what you find.

"And this is my interpretation: you must go to the Pyramids in Egypt. I have never heard of them, but, if it was a child who showed them to you, they exist. There you will find a treasure that will make you a rich man."

The boy was surprised, and then irritated. He didn't need to seek out the old woman for this! But then he remembered that he wasn't going to have to pay anything.

"I didn't need to waste my time just for this," he said.

"I told you that your dream was a difficult one. It's the

simple things in life that are the most extraordinary; only wise men are able to understand them. And since I am not wise, I have had to learn other arts, such as the reading of palms."

"Well, how am I going to get to Egypt?"

"I only interpret dreams. I don't know how to turn them into reality. That's why I have to live off what my daughters provide me with."

"And what if I never get to Egypt?"

"Then I don't get paid. It wouldn't be the first time."

And the woman told the boy to leave, saying she had already wasted too much time with him.

So the boy was disappointed; he decided that he would never again believe in dreams. He remembered that he had a number of things he had to take care of: he went to the market for something to eat, he traded his book for one that was thicker, and he found a bench in the plaza where he could sample the new wine he had bought. The day was hot, and the wine was refreshing. The sheep were at the gates of the city, in a stable that belonged to a friend. The boy knew a lot of people in the city. That was what made traveling appeal to him—he always made new friends, and he didn't need to spend all of his time with them. When someone sees the same people every day, as had happened with him at the seminary, they wind up becoming a part of that person's life. And then they want the person to change. If someone isn't what others want them to be, the others become angry. Everyone seems to have a clear idea of how other people should lead their lives, but none about his or her own.

He decided to wait until the sun had sunk a bit lower in the sky before following his flock back through the fields. Three days from now, he would be with the merchant's daughter.

He started to read the book he had bought. On the very first page it described a burial ceremony. And the names of the people involved were very difficult to pronounce. If he ever wrote a book, he thought, he would present one person at a time, so that the reader wouldn't have to worry about memorizing a lot of names.

When he was finally able to concentrate on what he was reading, he liked the book better; the burial was on a snowy day, and he welcomed the feeling of being cold. As he read on, an old man sat down at his side and tried to strike up a conversation.

"What are they doing?" the old man asked, pointing at the people in the plaza.

"Working," the boy answered dryly, making it look as if he wanted to concentrate on his reading.

Actually, he was thinking about shearing his sheep in front of the merchant's daughter, so that she could see that he was someone who was capable of doing difficult things. He had already imagined the scene many times; every time, the girl became fascinated when he explained that the sheep had to be sheared from back to front. He also tried to remember some good stories to relate as he sheared the sheep. Most of them he had read in books, but he would tell them as if they were from his personal experience. She would never know the difference, because she didn't know how to read.

Meanwhile, the old man persisted in his attempt to strike up a conversation. He said that he was tired and thirsty, and asked if he might have a sip of the boy's wine. The boy offered his bottle, hoping that the old man would leave him alone.

But the old man wanted to talk, and he asked the boy what book he was reading. The boy was tempted to be rude, and move to another bench, but his father had taught him to be respectful of the elderly. So he held out the book to the man—for two reasons: first, that he, himself, wasn't sure how to pronounce the title; and second, that if the old man didn't know how to read, he would probably feel ashamed and decide of his own accord to change benches.

"Hmm . . ." said the old man, looking at all sides of the book, as if it were some strange object. "This is an important book, but it's really irritating."

The boy was shocked. The old man knew how to read, and had already read the book. And if the book was irritating, as the old man had said, the boy still had time to change it for another.

"It's a book that says the same thing almost all the other books in the world say," continued the old man. "It describes people's inability to choose their own Personal Legends. And it ends up saying that everyone believes the world's greatest lie."

"What's the world's greatest lie?" the boy asked, completely surprised.

"It's this: that at a certain point in our lives, we lose control of what's happening to us, and our lives become controlled by fate. That's the world's greatest lie."

"That's never happened to me," the boy said. "They wanted me to be a priest, but I decided to become a shepherd."

"Much better," said the old man. "Because you really like to travel."

"He knew what I was thinking," the boy said to himself. The old man, meanwhile, was leafing through the book, without seeming to want to return it at all. The boy noticed that the man's clothing was strange. He looked like an Arab, which was not unusual in those parts. Africa was only a few hours from Tarifa; one had only to cross the narrow straits by boat. Arabs often appeared in the city, shopping and chanting their strange prayers several times a day.

"Where are you from?" the boy asked.

"From many places."

"No one can be from many places," the boy said. "I'm a shepherd, and I have been to many places, but I come from only one place—from a city near an ancient castle. That's where I was born."

"Well then, we could say that I was born in Salem."

The boy didn't know where Salem was, but he didn't want to ask, fearing that he would appear ignorant. He looked at the people in the plaza for a while; they were coming and going, and all of them seemed to be very busy.

"So, what is Salem like?" he asked, trying to get some sort of clue.

"It's like it always has been."

No clue yet. But he knew that Salem wasn't in Andalusia. If it were, he would already have heard of it.

"And what do you do in Salem?" he insisted.

"What do I do in Salem?" The old man laughed. "Well, I'm the king of Salem!"

People say strange things, the boy thought. Sometimes it's better to be with the sheep, who don't say anything. And better still to be alone with one's books. They tell their incredible stories at the time when you want to hear them. But when you're talking to people, they say some things that are so strange that you don't know how to continue the conversation.

"My name is Melchizedek," said the old man. "How many sheep do you have?"

"Enough," said the boy. He could see that the old man wanted to know more about his life.

"Well, then, we've got a problem. I can't help you if you feel you've got enough sheep."

The boy was getting irritated. He wasn't asking for help. It was the old man who had asked for a drink of his wine, and had started the conversation.

"Give me my book," the boy said. "I have to go and gather my sheep and get going."

"Give me one-tenth of your sheep," said the old man, "and I'll tell you how to find the hidden treasure."

The boy remembered his dream, and suddenly everything was clear to him. The old woman hadn't charged him anything, but the old man—maybe he was her husband—was going to find a way to get much more money in exchange for information about something that didn't even exist. The old man was probably a Gypsy, too.

But before the boy could say anything, the old man leaned over, picked up a stick, and began to write in the sand of the plaza. Something bright reflected from his chest with such intensity that the boy was momentarily blinded. With a movement that was too quick for someone his age, the man covered whatever it was with his cape. When his vision returned to normal, the boy was able to read what the old man had written in the sand.

There, in the sand of the plaza of that small city, the boy read the names of his father and his mother and the name of the seminary he had attended. He read the name of the merchant's daughter, which he hadn't even known, and he read things he had never told anyone.

"I'M THE KING OF SALEM," THE OLD MAN HAD SAID.

"Why would a king be talking with a shepherd?" the boy asked, awed and embarrassed.

"For several reasons. But let's say that the most important is that you have succeeded in discovering your Personal Legend."

The boy didn't know what a person's "Personal Legend" was.

"It's what you have always wanted to accomplish. Everyone, when they are young, knows what their Personal Legend is.

"At that point in their lives, everything is clear and everything is possible. They are not afraid to dream, and to yearn for everything they would like to see happen to them in their lives. But, as time passes, a mysterious force begins to convince them that it will be impossible for them to realize their Personal Legend."

None of what the old man was saying made much sense to the boy. But he wanted to know what the "mysterious force" was; the merchant's daughter would be impressed when he told her about that!

"It's a force that appears to be negative, but actually shows you how to realize your Personal Legend. It prepares your spirit and your will, because there is one great truth on this planet: whoever you are, or whatever it is that you do, when you really want something, it's because that desire originated in the soul of the universe. It's your mission on earth."

"Even when all you want to do is travel? Or marry the daughter of a textile merchant?"

"Yes, or even search for treasure. The Soul of the World is nourished by people's happiness. And also by unhappiness, envy, and jealousy. To realize one's Personal Legend is a person's only real obligation. All things are one.

"And, when you want something, all the universe conspires in helping you to achieve it."

They were both silent for a time, observing the plaza and the townspeople. It was the old man who spoke first.

"Why do you tend a flock of sheep?"

"Because I like to travel."

The old man pointed to a baker standing in his shop window at one corner of the plaza. "When he was a child, that man wanted to travel, too. But he decided first to buy his bakery and put some money aside. When he's an old man, he's going to spend a month in Africa. He never realized that people are capable, at any time in their lives, of doing what they dream of."

"He should have decided to become a shepherd," the boy said.

"Well, he thought about that," the old man said. "But bakers are more important people than shepherds. Bakers have homes, while shepherds sleep out in the open. Parents would rather see their children marry bakers than shepherds."

The boy felt a pang in his heart, thinking about the merchant's daughter. There was surely a baker in her town.

The old man continued, "In the long run, what people think about shepherds and bakers becomes more important for them than their own Personal Legends."

The old man leafed through the book, and fell to reading a page he came to. The boy waited, and then interrupted the old man just as he himself had been interrupted. "Why are you telling me all this?"

"Because you are trying to realize your Personal Legend. And you are at the point where you're about to give it all up."

"And that's when you always appear on the scene?"

"Not always in this way, but I always appear in one form or another. Sometimes I appear in the form of a solution, or a good idea. At other times, at a crucial moment, I make it easier for things to happen. There are other things I do, too, but most of the time people don't realize I've done them."

The old man related that, the week before, he had been forced to appear before a miner, and had taken the form of a stone. The miner had abandoned everything to go mining for emeralds. For five years he had been working a certain river, and had examined hundreds of thousands of stones looking for an emerald. The miner was about to give it all up, right at the point when, if he were to examine just one more stone—just *one more*—he would find his emerald. Since the miner had sacrificed everything to his Personal Legend, the old man decided to become involved. He transformed himself into a stone that rolled up to the miner's foot. The miner, with all the anger and frustration of his five fruitless years, picked up the stone and threw it aside. But he had thrown it with such force that it broke the stone it fell upon, and there, embedded in the broken stone, was the most beautiful emerald in the world.

"People learn, early in their lives, what is their reason for being," said the old man, with a certain bitterness. "Maybe that's why they give up on it so early, too. But that's the way it is."

The boy reminded the old man that he had said something about hidden treasure.

"Treasure is uncovered by the force of flowing water, and it is buried by the same currents," said the old man. "If you want to learn about your own treasure, you will have to give me one-tenth of your flock."

"What about one-tenth of my treasure?"

The old man looked disappointed. "If you start out by promising what you don't even have yet, you'll lose your desire to work toward getting it."

The boy told him that he had already promised to give one-tenth of his treasure to the Gypsy.

"Gypsies are experts at getting people to do that," sighed the old man. "In any case, it's good that you've learned that everything in life has its price. This is what the Warriors of the Light try to teach."

The old man returned the book to the boy.

"Tomorrow, at this same time, bring me a tenth of your flock. And I will tell you how to find the hidden treasure. Good afternoon."

And he vanished around the corner of the plaza.

THE BOY BEGAN AGAIN TO READ HIS BOOK, BUT HE WAS no longer able to concentrate. He was tense and upset, because he knew that the old man was right. He went over to the bakery and bought a loaf of bread, thinking about whether or not he should tell the baker what the old man had said about him. Sometimes it's better to leave things as they are, he thought to himself, and decided to say nothing. If he were to say anything, the baker would spend three days thinking about giving it all up, even though he had gotten used to the way things were. The boy could certainly resist causing that kind of anxiety for the baker. So he began to wander through the city, and found himself at the gates. There was a small building there, with a window at which people bought tickets to Africa. And he knew that Egypt was in Africa.

"Can I help you?" asked the man behind the window.

"Maybe tomorrow," said the boy, moving away. If he sold just one of his sheep, he'd have enough to get to the other shore of the strait. The idea frightened him.

"Another dreamer," said the ticket seller to his assistant, watching the boy walk away. "He doesn't have enough money to travel."

While standing at the ticket window, the boy had remembered his flock, and decided he should go back to being a shepherd. In two years he had learned everything about shepherding: he knew how to shear sheep, how to care for pregnant ewes, and how to protect the sheep from wolves. He knew all the fields and pastures of Andalusia. And he knew what was the fair price for every one of his animals.

He decided to return to his friend's stable by the longest route possible. As he walked past the city's castle, he interrupted his return, and climbed the stone ramp that led to the top of the wall. From there, he could see Africa in the distance. Someone had once told him that it was from there that the Moors had come, to occupy all of Spain.

He could see almost the entire city from where he sat, including the plaza where he had talked with the old man. Curse the moment I met that old man, he thought. He had come to the town only to find a woman who could interpret his dream. Neither the woman nor the old man were at all impressed by the fact that he was a shepherd. They were solitary individuals who no longer believed in things, and didn't understand that shepherds become attached to their sheep. He knew everything about each member of his flock: he knew which ones were lame, which one was to give birth two months from now, and which were the laziest. He knew how to shear them, and how to slaughter them. If he ever decided to leave them, they would suffer.

The wind began to pick up. He knew that wind: people called it the levanter, because on it the Moors had come from the Levant at the eastern end of the Mediterranean.

The levanter increased in intensity. Here I am, between my flock and my treasure, the boy thought. He had to choose between something he had become accustomed to and something he wanted to have. There was also the merchant's daughter, but she wasn't as important as his flock, because she didn't depend on him. Maybe she didn't even remember him. He was sure that it made no difference to her on which day he appeared: for her, every day was the same, and when each day is the same as the next, it's because people fail to recognize the good things that happen in their lives every day that the sun rises.

I left my father, my mother, and the town castle behind. They have gotten used to my being away, and so have I. The sheep will get used to my not being there, too, the boy thought.

From where he sat, he could observe the plaza. People continued to come and go from the baker's shop. A young couple sat on the bench where he had talked with the old man, and they kissed.

"That baker . . ." he said to himself, without completing the thought. The levanter was still getting stronger, and he felt its force on his face. That wind had brought the Moors, yes, but it had also brought the smell of the desert and of veiled women. It had brought with it the sweat and the dreams of men who had once left to search for the unknown, and for gold and adventure—and for the Pyramids. The boy felt jealous of the freedom of the wind, and saw that he could have the same freedom. There was nothing to hold him back except himself. The sheep, the merchant's daughter, and the fields of Andalusia were only steps along the way to his Personal Legend.

The next day, the boy met the old man at noon. He brought six sheep with him.

"I'm surprised," the boy said. "My friend bought all the other sheep immediately. He said that he had always dreamed of being a shepherd, and that it was a good omen."

"That's the way it always is," said the old man. "It's called the principle of favorability. When you play cards the first time, you are almost sure to win. Beginner's luck."

"Why is that?"

"Because there is a force that wants you to realize your Personal Legend; it whets your appetite with a taste of success."

Then the old man began to inspect the sheep, and he saw that one was lame. The boy explained that it wasn't important, since that sheep was the most intelligent of the flock, and produced the most wool.

"Where is the treasure?" he asked.

"It's in Egypt, near the Pyramids."

The boy was startled. The old woman had said the same thing. But she hadn't charged him anything.

"In order to find the treasure, you will have to follow the omens. God has prepared a path for everyone to follow. You just have to read the omens that he left for you."

Before the boy could reply, a butterfly appeared and fluttered between him and the old man. He remembered something his grandfather had once told him: that butterflies were a good omen. Like crickets, and like expectations; like lizards and four-leaf clovers.

"That's right," said the old man, able to read the boy's thoughts. "Just as your grandfather taught you. These are good omens."

The old man opened his cape, and the boy was struck by what he saw. The old man wore a breastplate of heavy gold, covered with precious stones. The boy recalled the brilliance he had noticed on the previous day.

He really was a king! He must be disguised to avoid encounters with thieves.

"Take these," said the old man, holding out a white stone and a black stone that had been embedded at the center of the breastplate. "They are called Urim and Thummim. The black signifies 'yes,' and the white 'no.' When you are unable to read the omens, they will help you to do so. Always ask an objective question.

"But, if you can, try to make your own decisions. The treasure is at the Pyramids; that you already knew. But I had to insist on the payment of six sheep because I helped you to make your decision."

The boy put the stones in his pouch. From then on, he would make his own decisions.

"Don't forget that everything you deal with is only one thing and nothing else. And don't forget the language of omens. And, above all, don't forget to follow your Personal Legend through to its conclusion.

"But before I go, I want to tell you a little story.

"A certain shopkeeper sent his son to learn about the secret of happiness from the wisest man in the world. The lad wandered through the desert for forty days, and finally came upon a beautiful castle, high atop a mountain. It was there that the wise man lived.

"Rather than finding a saintly man, though, our hero, on entering the main room of the castle, saw a hive of activity: tradesmen came and went, people were conversing in the corners, a small orchestra was playing soft music, and there was a table covered with platters of the most delicious food in that part of the world. The wise man conversed with every one, and the boy had to wait for two hours before it was his turn to be given the man's attention.

"The wise man listened attentively to the boy's explanation of why he had come, but told him that he didn't have time just then to explain the secret of happiness. He suggested that the boy look around the palace and return in two hours.

"'Meanwhile, I want to ask you to do something,' said the wise man, handing the boy a teaspoon that held two drops of oil. 'As you wander around, carry this spoon with you without allowing the oil to spill.'

"The boy began climbing and descending the many stairways of the palace, keeping his eyes fixed on the spoon. After two hours, he returned to the room where the wise man was.

"'Well,' asked the wise man, 'did you see the Persian tapestries that are hanging in my dining hall? Did you see the garden that it took the master gardener ten years to create? Did you notice the beautiful parchments in my library?'

"The boy was embarrassed, and confessed that he had observed nothing. His only concern had been not to spill the oil that the wise man had entrusted to him.

"'Then go back and observe the marvels of my world,' said the wise man. 'You cannot trust a man if you don't know his house.'

"Relieved, the boy picked up the spoon and returned to his exploration of the palace, this time observing all of the works of art on the ceilings and the walls. He saw the gardens, the mountains all around him, the beauty of the flowers, and the taste with which everything had been selected. Upon returning to the wise man, he related in detail everything he had seen.

"'But where are the drops of oil I entrusted to you?' asked the wise man.

"Looking down at the spoon he held, the boy saw that the oil was gone.

"'Well, there is only one piece of advice I can give you,' said the wisest of wise men. 'The secret of happiness is to see all the marvels of the world, and never to forget the drops of oil on the spoon.' "

The shepherd said nothing. He had understood the story the old king had told him. A shepherd may like to travel, but he should never forget about his sheep.

The old man looked at the boy and, with his hands held together, made several strange gestures over the boy's head. Then, taking his sheep, he walked away.

At the highest point in Tarifa there is an old fort, built by the Moors. From atop its walls, one can catch a glimpse of Africa. Melchizedek, the king of Salem, sat on the wall of the fort that afternoon, and felt the levanter blowing in his face. The sheep fidgeted nearby, uneasy with their new owner and excited by so much change. All they wanted was food and water.

Melchizedek watched a small ship that was plowing its way out of the port. He would never again see the boy, just as he had never seen Abraham again after having charged him his one-tenth fee. That was his work.

The gods should not have desires, because they don't have Personal Legends. But the king of Salem hoped desperately that the boy would be successful.

It's too bad that he's quickly going to forget my name, he thought. I should have repeated it for him. Then when he spoke about me he would say that I am Melchizedek, the king of Salem.

He looked to the skies, feeling a bit abashed, and said, "I know it's the vanity of vanities, as you said, my Lord. But an old king sometimes has to take some pride in himself."

HOW STRANGE AFRICA IS, THOUGHT THE BOY.

He was sitting in a bar very much like the other bars he had seen along the narrow streets of Tangier. Some men were smoking from a gigantic pipe that they passed from one to the other. In just a few hours he had seen men walking hand in hand, women with their faces covered, and priests that climbed to the tops of towers and chanted—as everyone about him went to their knees and placed their foreheads on the ground.

"A practice of infidels," he said to himself. As a child in church, he had always looked at the image of Saint Santiago Matamoros on his white horse, his sword unsheathed, and figures such as these kneeling at his feet. The boy felt ill and terribly alone. The infidels had an evil look about them.

Besides this, in the rush of his travels he had forgotten a detail, just one detail, which could keep him from his treasure for a long time: only Arabic was spoken in this country.

The owner of the bar approached him, and the boy pointed to a drink that had been served at the next table. It turned out to be a bitter tea. The boy preferred wine.

But he didn't need to worry about that right now. What he had to be concerned about was his treasure, and how he was going to go about getting it. The sale of his sheep had left him with enough money in his pouch, and the boy knew that in money there was magic; whoever has money is never really alone. Before long, maybe in just a few days, he would be at the Pyramids. An old man, with a breastplate of gold, wouldn't have lied just to acquire six sheep.

The old man had spoken about signs and omens, and, as the boy was crossing the strait, he had thought about omens. Yes, the old man had known what he was talking about: during the time the boy had spent in the fields of Andalusia, he had become used to learning which path he should take by observing the ground and the sky. He had discovered that the presence of a certain bird meant that a snake was nearby, and that a certain shrub was a sign that there was water in the area. The sheep had taught him that.

If God leads the sheep so well, he will also lead a man, he thought, and that made him feel better. The tea seemed less bitter.

"Who are you?" he heard a voice ask him in Spanish.

The boy was relieved. He was thinking about omens, and someone had appeared.

"How come you speak Spanish?" he asked. The new arrival was a young man in Western dress, but the color of his skin suggested he was from this city. He was about the same age and height as the boy.

"Almost everyone here speaks Spanish. We're only two hours from Spain."

"Sit down, and let me treat you to something," said the boy. "And ask for a glass of wine for me. I hate this tea."

"There is no wine in this country," the young man said. "The religion here forbids it."

The boy told him then that he needed to get to the Pyramids. He almost began to tell about his treasure, but decided not to do so. If he did, it was possible that the Arab would want a part of it as payment for taking him there. He remembered what the old man had said about offering something you didn't even have yet.

"I'd like you to take me there if you can. I can pay you to serve as my guide."

"Do you have any idea how to get there?" the newcomer asked.

The boy noticed that the owner of the bar stood nearby, listening attentively to their conversation. He felt uneasy at the man's presence. But he had found a guide, and didn't want to miss out on an opportunity.

"You have to cross the entire Sahara desert," said the young man. "And to do that, you need money. I need to know whether you have enough."

The boy thought it a strange question. But he trusted in the old man, who had said that, when you really want something, the universe always conspires in your favor.

He took his money from his pouch and showed it to the young man. The owner of the bar came over and looked, as well. The two men exchanged some words in Arabic, and the bar owner seemed irritated.

"Let's get out of here," said the new arrival. "He wants us to leave."

The boy was relieved. He got up to pay the bill, but the owner grabbed him and began to speak to him in an angry stream of words. The boy was strong, and wanted to retaliate, but he was in a foreign country. His new friend pushed the owner aside, and pulled the boy outside with him. "He wanted your money," he said. "Tangier is not like the rest of Africa. This is a port, and every port has its thieves."

The boy trusted his new friend. He had helped him out in a dangerous situation. He took out his money and counted it.

"We could get to the Pyramids by tomorrow," said the other, taking the money. "But I have to buy two camels."

They walked together through the narrow streets of Tangier. Everywhere there were stalls with items for sale. They reached the center of a large plaza where the market was held. There were thousands of people there, arguing, selling, and buying; vegetables for sale amongst daggers, and carpets displayed alongside tobacco. But the boy never took his eye off his new friend. After all, he had all his money. He thought about asking him to give it back, but decided that would be unfriendly. He knew nothing about the customs of the strange land he was in.

"I'll just watch him," he said to himself. He knew he was stronger than his friend.

Suddenly, there in the midst of all that confusion, he saw the most beautiful sword he had ever seen. The scabbard was embossed in silver, and the handle was black and encrusted with precious stones. The boy promised himself that, when he returned from Egypt, he would buy that sword.

"Ask the owner of that stall how much the sword costs," he said to his friend. Then he realized that he had been distracted for a few moments, looking at the sword. His heart squeezed, as if his chest had suddenly compressed it. He was afraid to look around, because he knew what he would find. He continued to look at the beautiful sword for a bit longer, until he summoned the courage to turn around.

All around him was the market, with people coming and going, shouting and buying, and the aroma of strange foods . . . but nowhere could he find his new companion.

The boy wanted to believe that his friend had simply become separated from him by accident. He decided to stay right there and await his return. As he waited, a priest climbed to the top of a nearby tower and began his chant; everyone in the market fell to their knees, touched their foreheads to the ground, and took up the chant. Then, like a colony of worker ants, they dismantled their stalls and left.

The sun began its departure, as well. The boy watched it through its trajectory for some time, until it was hidden behind the white houses surrounding the plaza. He recalled that when the sun had risen that morning, he was on another continent, still a shepherd with sixty sheep, and looking forward to meeting with a girl. That morning he had known everything that was going to happen to him as he walked through the familiar fields. But now, as the sun began to set, he was in a different country, a stranger in a strange land, where he couldn't even speak the language. He was no longer a shepherd, and he had nothing, not even the money to return and start everything over.

All this happened between sunrise and sunset, the boy thought. He was feeling sorry for himself, and lamenting the fact that his life could have changed so suddenly and so drastically.

He was so ashamed that he wanted to cry. He had never even wept in front of his own sheep. But the marketplace was empty, and he was far from home, so he wept. He wept because God was unfair, and because this was the way God repaid those who believed in their dreams.

When I had my sheep, I was happy, and I made those around me happy. People saw me coming and welcomed me, he thought. But now I'm sad and alone. I'm going to become bitter and distrustful of people because one person betrayed me. I'm going to hate those who have found their treasure because I never found mine. And I'm going to hold on to what little I have, because I'm too insignificant to conquer the world.

He opened his pouch to see what was left of his possessions; maybe there was a bit left of the sandwich he had eaten on the ship. But all he found was the heavy book, his jacket, and the two stones the old man had given him.

As he looked at the stones, he felt relieved for some reason. He had exchanged six sheep for two precious stones that had been taken from a gold breastplate. He could sell the stones and buy a return ticket. But this time I'll be smarter, the boy thought, removing them from the pouch so he could put them in his pocket. This was a port town, and the only truthful thing his friend had told him was that port towns are full of thieves.

Now he understood why the owner of the bar had been so upset: he was trying to tell him not to trust that man. "I'm like everyone else—I see the world in terms of what I would like to see happen, not what actually does."

He ran his fingers slowly over the stones, sensing their temperature and feeling their surfaces. They were his treasure. Just handling them made him feel better. They reminded him of the old man.

"When you want something, all the universe conspires in helping you to achieve it," he had said.

The boy was trying to understand the truth of what the old man had said. There he was in the empty marketplace, without a cent to his name, and with not a sheep to guard through the night. But the stones were proof that he had met with a king—a king who knew of the boy's past.

"They're called Urim and Thummim, and they can help you to read the omens." The boy put the stones back in the pouch and decided to do an experiment. The old man had said to ask very clear questions, and to do that, the boy had to know what he wanted. So, he asked if the old man's blessing was still with him.

He took out one of the stones. It was "yes."

"Am I going to find my treasure?" he asked.

He stuck his hand into the pouch, and felt around for one of the stones. As he did so, both of them pushed through a hole in the pouch and fell to the ground. The boy had never even noticed that there was a hole in his pouch. He knelt down to find Urim and Thummim and put them back in the pouch. But as he saw them lying there on the ground, another phrase came to his mind.

"Learn to recognize omens, and follow them," the old king had said.

An omen. The boy smiled to himself. He picked up the two stones and put them back in his pouch. He didn't consider mending the hole—the stones could fall through any time they wanted. He had learned that there were certain things one shouldn't ask about, so as not to flee from one's own Personal Legend. "I promised that I would make my own decisions," he said to himself.

But the stones had told him that the old man was still with him, and that made him feel more confident. He looked around at the empty plaza again, feeling less desperate than before. This wasn't a strange place; it was a new one.

After all, what he had always wanted was just that: to know new places. Even if he never got to the Pyramids, he had already traveled farther than any shepherd he knew. Oh, if they only knew how different things are just two hours by ship from where they are, he thought. Although his new world at the moment was just an empty marketplace, he had already seen it when it was teeming with life, and he would never forget it. He remembered the sword. It hurt him a bit to think about it, but he had never seen one like it before. As he mused about these things, he realized that he had to choose between thinking of himself as the poor victim of a thief and as an adventurer in quest of his treasure.

"I'm an adventurer, looking for treasure," he said to himself.

HE WAS SHAKEN INTO WAKEFULNESS BY SOMEONE. He had fallen asleep in the middle of the marketplace, and life in the plaza was about to resume.

Looking around, he sought his sheep, and then realized that he was in a new world. But instead of being saddened, he was happy. He no longer had to seek out food and water for the sheep; he could go in search of his treasure, instead. He had not a cent in his pocket, but he had faith. He had decided, the night before, that he would be as much an adventurer as the ones he had admired in books.

He walked slowly through the market. The merchants were assembling their stalls, and the boy helped a candy seller to do his. The candy seller had a smile on his face: he was happy, aware of what his life was about, and ready to begin a day's work. His smile reminded the boy of the old man—the mysterious old king he had met. "This candy merchant isn't making candy so that later he can travel or marry a shopkeeper's daughter. He's doing it because it's what he wants to do," thought the boy. He realized that he could do the same thing the old man had done—sense whether a person was near to or far from his Personal Legend. Just by looking at them. It's easy, and yet I've never done it before, he thought.

When the stall was assembled, the candy seller offered the boy the first sweet he had made for the day. The boy thanked him, ate it, and went on his way. When he had gone only a short distance, he realized that, while they were erecting the stall, one of them had spoken Arabic and the other Spanish.

And they had understood each other perfectly well.

There must be a language that doesn't depend on words, the boy thought. I've already had that experience with my sheep, and now it's happening with people.

He was learning a lot of new things. Some of them were things that he had already experienced, and weren't really new, but that he had never perceived before. And he hadn't perceived them because he had become accustomed to them. He realized: If I can learn to understand this language without words, I can learn to understand the world.

Relaxed and unhurried, he resolved that he would walk through the narrow streets of Tangier. Only in that way would he be able to read the omens. He knew it would require a lot of patience, but shepherds know all about patience. Once again he saw that, in that strange land, he was applying the same lessons he had learned with his sheep.

"All things are one," the old man had said.

THE CRYSTAL MERCHANT AWOKE WITH THE DAY, AND FELT the same anxiety that he felt every morning. He had been in the same place for thirty years: a shop at the top of a hilly street where few customers passed. Now it was too late to change anything—the only thing he had ever learned to do was to buy and sell crystal glassware. There had been a time when many people knew of his shop: Arab merchants, French and English geologists, German soldiers who were always well-heeled. In those days it had been wonderful to be selling crystal, and he had thought how he would become rich, and have beautiful women at his side as he grew older.

But, as time passed, Tangier had changed. The nearby city of Ceuta had grown faster than Tangier, and business had fallen off. Neighbors moved away, and there remained only a few small shops on the hill. And no one was going to climb the hill just to browse through a few small shops.

But the crystal merchant had no choice. He had lived thirty years of his life buying and selling crystal pieces, and now it was too late to do anything else.

He spent the entire morning observing the infrequent comings and goings in the street. He had done this for years, and knew the schedule of everyone who passed. But, just before lunchtime, a boy stopped in front of the shop. He was dressed normally, but the practiced eyes of the crystal merchant could see that the boy had no money to spend. Nevertheless, the merchant decided to delay his lunch for a few minutes until the boy moved on.

A CARD HANGING IN THE DOORWAY ANNOUNCED THAT several languages were spoken in the shop. The boy saw a man appear behind the counter.

"I can clean up those glasses in the window, if you want," said the boy. "The way they look now, nobody is going to want to buy them."

The man looked at him without responding.

"In exchange, you could give me something to eat."

The man still said nothing, and the boy sensed that he was going to have to make a decision. In his pouch, he had his jacket—he certainly wasn't going to need it in the desert. Taking the jacket out, he began to clean the glasses. In half an hour, he had cleaned all the glasses in the window, and, as he was doing so, two customers had entered the shop and bought some crystal.

When he had completed the cleaning, he asked the man for something to eat. "Let's go and have some lunch," said the crystal merchant.

He put a sign on the door, and they went to a small café nearby. As they sat down at the only table in the place, the crystal merchant laughed.

"You didn't have to do any cleaning," he said. "The Koran requires me to feed a hungry person."

"Well then, why did you let me do it?" the boy asked.

"Because the crystal was dirty. And both you and I needed to cleanse our minds of negative thoughts."

When they had eaten, the merchant turned to the boy and said, "I'd like you to work in my shop. Two customers came in today while you were working, and that's a good omen."

People talk a lot about omens, thought the shepherd. But they really don't know what they're saying. Just as I hadn't realized that for so many years I had been speaking a language without words to my sheep.

"Do you want to go to work for me?" the merchant asked.

"I can work for the rest of today," the boy answered. "I'll work all night, until dawn, and I'll clean every piece of crystal in your shop. In return, I need money to get to Egypt tomorrow."

The merchant laughed. "Even if you cleaned my crystal

for an entire year . . . even if you earned a good commission selling every piece, you would still have to borrow money to get to Egypt. There are thousands of kilometers of desert between here and there."

There was a moment of silence so profound that it seemed the city was asleep. No sound from the bazaars, no arguments among the merchants, no men climbing to the towers to chant. No hope, no adventure, no old kings or Personal Legends, no treasure, and no Pyramids. It was as if the world had fallen silent because the boy's soul had. He sat there, staring blankly through the door of the café, wishing that he had died, and that everything would end forever at that moment.

The merchant looked anxiously at the boy. All the joy he had seen that morning had suddenly disappeared.

"I can give you the money you need to get back to your country, my son," said the crystal merchant.

The boy said nothing. He got up, adjusted his clothing, and picked up his pouch.

"I'll work for you," he said.

And after another long silence, he added, "I need money to buy some sheep."

PART TWO

THE BOY HAD BEEN WORKING FOR THE CRYSTAL MERCHANT for almost a month, and he could see that it wasn't exactly the kind of job that would make him happy. The merchant spent the entire day mumbling behind the counter, telling the boy to be careful with the pieces and not to break anything.

But he stayed with the job because the merchant, although he was an old grouch, treated him fairly; the boy received a good commission for each piece he sold, and had already been able to put some money aside. That morning he had done some calculating: if he continued to work every day as he had been, he would need a whole year to be able to buy some sheep.

"I'd like to build a display case for the crystal," the boy said to the merchant. "We could place it outside, and attract those people who pass at the bottom of the hill."

"I've never had one before," the merchant answered. "People will pass by and bump into it, and pieces will be broken."

"Well, when I took my sheep through the fields some of them might have died if we had come upon a snake. But that's the way life is with sheep and with shepherds."

The merchant turned to a customer who wanted three crystal glasses. He was selling better than ever . . . as if time had turned back to the old days when the street had been one of Tangier's major attractions.

"Business has really improved," he said to the boy, after the customer had left. "I'm doing much better, and soon you'll be able to return to your sheep. Why ask more out of life?"

"Because we have to respond to omens," the boy said, almost without meaning to; then he regretted what he had said, because the merchant had never met the king.

"It's called the principle of favorability, beginner's luck. Because life wants you to achieve your Personal Legend," the old king had said.

But the merchant understood what the boy had said. The boy's very presence in the shop was an omen, and, as time passed and money was pouring into the cash drawer, he had no regrets about having hired the boy. The boy was being paid more money than he deserved, because the merchant, thinking that sales wouldn't amount to much, had offered the boy a high commission rate. He had assumed he would soon return to his sheep.

"Why did you want to get to the Pyramids?" he asked, to get away from the business of the display.

"Because I've always heard about them," the boy answered, saying nothing about his dream. The treasure was now nothing but a painful memory, and he tried to avoid thinking about it.

"I don't know anyone around here who would want to cross the desert just to see the Pyramids," said the merchant. "They're just a pile of stones. You could build one in your backyard."

"You've never had dreams of travel," said the boy, turning to wait on a customer who had entered the shop.

Two days later, the merchant spoke to the boy about the display.

"I don't much like change," he said. "You and I aren't like Hassan, that rich merchant. If he makes a buying mistake, it doesn't affect him much. But we two have to live with our mistakes."

That's true enough, the boy thought, ruefully.

"Why did you think we should have the display?"

"I want to get back to my sheep faster. We have to take advantage when luck is on our side, and do as much to help it as it's doing to help us. It's called the principle of favorability. Or beginner's luck."

The merchant was silent for a few moments. Then he said, "The Prophet gave us the Koran, and left us just five obligations to satisfy during our lives. The most important is to believe only in the one true God. The others are to pray five times a day, fast during Ramadan, and be charitable to the poor."

He stopped there. His eyes filled with tears as he spoke of the Prophet. He was a devout man, and, even with all his impatience, he wanted to live his life in accordance with Muslim law.

"What's the fifth obligation?" the boy asked.

"Two days ago, you said that I had never dreamed of travel," the merchant answered. "The fifth obligation of every Muslim is a pilgrimage. We are obliged, at least once in our lives, to visit the holy city of Mecca.

"Mecca is a lot farther away than the Pyramids. When I was young, all I wanted to do was put together enough money to start this shop. I thought that someday I'd be rich, and could go to Mecca. I began to make some money, but I could never bring myself to leave someone in charge of the shop; the crystals are delicate things. At the same time, people were passing my shop all the time, heading for Mecca. Some of them were rich pilgrims, traveling in caravans with servants and camels, but most of the people making the pilgrimage were poorer than I.

"All who went there were happy at having done so. They placed the symbols of the pilgrimage on the doors of their houses. One of them, a cobbler who made his living mending boots, said that he had traveled for almost a year through the desert, but that he got more tired when he had to walk through the streets of Tangier buying his leather."

"Well, why don't you go to Mecca now?" asked the boy.

"Because it's the thought of Mecca that keeps me alive. That's what helps me face these days that are all the same, these mute crystals on the shelves, and lunch and dinner at that same horrible café. I'm afraid that if my dream is realized, I'll have no reason to go on living.

"You dream about your sheep and the Pyramids, but you're different from me, because you want to realize your dreams. I just want to dream about Mecca. I've already imagined a thousand times crossing the desert, arriving at the Plaza of the Sacred Stone, the seven times I walk around it before allowing myself to touch it. I've already imagined the people who would be at my side, and those in front of me, and the conversations and prayers we would share. But I'm afraid that it would all be a disappointment, so I prefer just to dream about it."

That day, the merchant gave the boy permission to build the display. Not everyone can see his dreams come true in the same way.

TWO MORE MONTHS PASSED, AND THE SHELF BROUGHT many customers into the crystal shop. The boy estimated that, if he worked for six more months, he could return to Spain and buy sixty sheep, and yet another sixty. In less than a year, he would have doubled his flock, and he would be able to do business with the Arabs, because he was now able to speak their strange language. Since that morning in the marketplace, he had never again made use of Urim and Thummim, because Egypt was now just as distant a dream for him as was Mecca for the merchant. Anyway, the boy had become happy in his work, and thought all the time about the day when he would disembark at Tarifa as a winner.

"You must always know what it is that you want," the old king had said. The boy knew, and was now working toward it. Maybe it was his treasure to have wound up in that strange land, met up with a thief, and doubled the size of his flock without spending a cent.

He was proud of himself. He had learned some important things, like how to deal in crystal, and about the language without words . . . and about omens. One afternoon he had seen a man at the top of the hill, complaining that it was impossible to find a decent place to get something to drink after such a climb. The boy, accustomed to recognizing omens, spoke to the merchant.

"Let's sell tea to the people who climb the hill."

"Lots of places sell tea around here," the merchant said.

"But we could sell tea in crystal glasses. The people will enjoy the tea and want to buy the glasses. I have been told that beauty is the great seducer of men."

The merchant didn't respond, but that afternoon, after saying his prayers and closing the shop, he invited the boy to sit with him and share his hookah, that strange pipe used by the Arabs.

"What is it you're looking for?" asked the old merchant.

"I've already told you. I need to buy my sheep back, so I have to earn the money to do so."

The merchant put some new coals in the hookah, and inhaled deeply.

"I've had this shop for thirty years. I know good crystal from bad, and everything else there is to know about crystal. I know its dimensions and how it behaves. If we serve tea in crystal, the shop is going to expand. And then I'll have to change my way of life."

"Well, isn't that good?"

"I'm already used to the way things are. Before you came, I was thinking about how much time I had wasted in the same place, while my friends had moved on, and either went bankrupt or did better than they had before. It made me very depressed. Now, I can see that it hasn't been too bad. The shop is exactly the size I always wanted it to be. I don't want to change anything, because I don't know how to deal with change. I'm used to the way I am."

The boy didn't know what to say. The old man continued, "You have been a real blessing to me. Today, I understand something I didn't see before: every blessing ignored becomes a curse. I don't want anything else in life. But you are forcing me to look at wealth and at horizons I have never known. Now that I have seen them, and now that I see how immense my possibilities are, I'm going to feel worse than I did before you arrived. Because I know the things I should be able to accomplish, and I don't want to do so."

It's good I refrained from saying anything to the baker in Tarifa, thought the boy to himself.

They went on smoking the pipe for a while as the sun began to set. They were conversing in Arabic, and the boy was proud of himself for being able to do so. There had been a time when he thought that his sheep could teach him everything he needed to know about the world. But they could never have taught him Arabic.

There are probably other things in the world that the sheep can't teach me, thought the boy as he regarded the old merchant. All they ever do, really, is look for food and water. And maybe it wasn't that they were teaching me, but that I was learning from them.

"*Maktub,*" the merchant said, finally.

"What does that mean?"

"You would have to have been born an Arab to understand," he answered. "But in your language it would be something like 'It is written.'"

And, as he smothered the coals in the hookah, he told the boy that he could begin to sell tea in the crystal glasses. Sometimes, there's just no way to hold back the river.

THE MEN CLIMBED THE HILL, AND THEY WERE TIRED when they reached the top. But there they saw a crystal shop that offered refreshing mint tea. They went in to drink the tea, which was served in beautiful crystal glasses.

"My wife never thought of this," said one, and he bought some crystal—he was entertaining guests that night, and the guests would be impressed by the beauty of the glassware. The other man remarked that tea was always more delicious when it was served in crystal, because the aroma was retained. The third said that it was a tradition in the Orient to use crystal glasses for tea because it had magical powers.

Before long, the news spread, and a great many people began to climb the hill to see the shop that was doing something new in a trade that was so old. Other shops were opened that served tea in crystal, but they weren't at the top of a hill, and they had little business.

Eventually, the merchant had to hire two more employees. He began to import enormous quantities of tea, along with his crystal, and his shop was sought out by men and women with a thirst for things new.

And, in that way, the months passed.

THE BOY AWOKE BEFORE DAWN. IT HAD BEEN ELEVEN months and nine days since he had first set foot on the African continent.

He dressed in his Arabian clothing of white linen, bought especially for this day. He put his headcloth in place and secured it with a ring made of camel skin. Wearing his new sandals, he descended the stairs silently.

The city was still sleeping. He prepared himself a sandwich and drank some hot tea from a crystal glass. Then he sat in the sun-filled doorway, smoking the hookah.

He smoked in silence, thinking of nothing, and listening to the sound of the wind that brought the scent of the desert. When he had finished his smoke, he reached into one of his pockets, and sat there for a few moments, regarding what he had withdrawn.

It was a bundle of money. Enough to buy himself a hundred and twenty sheep, a return ticket, and a license to import products from Africa into his own country.

He waited patiently for the merchant to awaken and

open the shop. Then the two went off to have some more tea.

"I'm leaving today," said the boy. "I have the money I need to buy my sheep. And you have the money you need to go to Mecca."

The old man said nothing.

"Will you give me your blessing?" asked the boy. "You have helped me." The man continued to prepare his tea, saying nothing. Then he turned to the boy.

"I am proud of you," he said. "You brought a new feeling into my crystal shop. But you know that I'm not going to go to Mecca. Just as you know that you're not going to buy your sheep."

"Who told you that?" asked the boy, startled.

"Maktub," said the old crystal merchant.

And he gave the boy his blessing.

The boy went to his room and packed his belongings. They filled three sacks. As he was leaving, he saw, in the corner of the room, his old shepherd's pouch. It was bunched up, and he had hardly thought of it for a long time. As he took his jacket out of the pouch, thinking to give it to someone in the street, the two stones fell to the floor. Urim and Thummim.

It made the boy think of the old king, and it startled him to realize how long it had been since he had thought of him.

For nearly a year, he had been working incessantly, thinking only of putting aside enough money so that he could return to Spain with pride.

"Never stop dreaming," the old king had said. "Follow the omens."

The boy picked up Urim and Thummim, and, once again, had the strange sensation that the old king was nearby. He had worked hard for a year, and the omens were that it was time to go.

I'm going to go back to doing just what I did before, the boy thought. Even though the sheep didn't teach me to speak Arabic.

But the sheep had taught him something even more important: that there was a language in the world that everyone understood, a language the boy had used throughout the time that he was trying to improve things at the shop. It was the language of enthusiasm, of things accomplished with love and purpose, and as part of a search for something believed in and desired. Tangier was no longer a strange city, and he felt that, just as he had conquered this place, he could conquer the world.

"When you want something, all the universe conspires to help you achieve it," the old king had said.

But the old king hadn't said anything about being robbed, or about endless deserts, or about people who know what their dreams are but don't want to realize them. The old king hadn't told him that the Pyramids were just a pile of stones, or that anyone could build one in his backyard. And he had forgotten to mention that, when you have enough money to buy a flock larger than the one you had before, you should buy it.

The boy picked up his pouch and put it with his other things. He went down the stairs and found the merchant waiting on a foreign couple, while two other customers walked about the shop, drinking tea from crystal glasses. It was more activity than usual for this time of the morning. From where he stood, he saw for the first time that the old merchant's hair was very much like the hair of the old king. He remembered the smile of the candy seller, on his first day in Tangier, when he had nothing to eat and nowhere to go—that smile had also been like the old king's smile.

It's almost as if he had been here and left his mark, he thought. *And yet, none of these people has ever met the old king. On the other hand, he said that he always appeared to help those who are trying to realize their Personal Legend.*

He left without saying good-bye to the crystal merchant. He didn't want to cry with the other people there. He was going to miss the place and all the good things he had learned. He was more confident in himself, though, and felt as though he could conquer the world.

"But I'm going back to the fields that I know, to take care of my flock again." He said that to himself with certainty, but he was no longer happy with his decision. He had worked for an entire year to make a dream come true, and that dream, minute by minute, was becoming less important. Maybe because that wasn't really his dream.

Who knows . . . maybe it's better to be like the crystal merchant: never go to Mecca, and just go through life wanting to do so, he thought, again trying to convince himself. But as he held Urim and Thummim in his hand, they had transmitted to him the strength and will of the old king. By coincidence—or maybe it was an omen, the boy thought—he came to the bar he had entered on his first day there. The thief wasn't there, and the owner brought him a cup of tea.

I can always go back to being a shepherd, the boy thought. I learned how to care for sheep, and I haven't forgotten how that's done. But maybe I'll never have another chance to get to the Pyramids in Egypt. The old man wore a breastplate of gold, and he knew about my past. He really was a king, a wise king.

The hills of Andalusia were only two hours away, but there was an entire desert between him and the Pyramids. Yet the boy felt that there was another way to regard his situation: he was actually two hours closer to his treasure . . . the fact that the two hours had stretched into an entire year didn't matter.

I know why I want to get back to my flock, he thought. I

understand sheep; they're no longer a problem, and they can be good friends. On the other hand, I don't know if the desert can be a friend, and it's in the desert that I have to search for my treasure. If I don't find it, I can always go home. I finally have enough money, and all the time I need. Why not?

He suddenly felt tremendously happy. He could always go back to being a shepherd. He could always become a crystal salesman again. Maybe the world had other hidden treasures, but he had a dream, and he had met with a king. That doesn't happen to just anyone!

He was planning as he left the bar. He had remembered that one of the crystal merchant's suppliers transported his crystal by means of caravans that crossed the desert. He held Urim and Thummim in his hand; because of those two stones, he was once again on the way to his treasure.

"I am always nearby, when someone wants to realize their Personal Legend," the old king had told him.

What could it cost to go over to the supplier's warehouse and find out if the Pyramids were really that far away?

THE ENGLISHMAN WAS SITTING ON A BENCH IN A STRUCTURE that smelled of animals, sweat, and dust; it was part warehouse, part corral. I never thought I'd end up in a place like this, he thought, as he leafed through the pages of a chemical journal. Ten years at the university, and here I am in a corral.

But he had to move on. He believed in omens. All his life and all his studies were aimed at finding the one true language of the universe. First he had studied Esperanto, then the world's religions, and now it was alchemy. He knew how to speak Esperanto, he understood all the major religions well, but he wasn't yet an alchemist. He had unraveled the truths behind important questions, but his studies had taken him to a point beyond which he could not seem to go. He had tried in vain to establish a relationship with an alchemist. But the alchemists were strange people, who thought only about themselves, and almost always refused to help him. Who knows, maybe they had failed to discover the secret of the Master Work—the Philosopher's Stone—and for this reason kept their knowledge to themselves.

He had already spent much of the fortune left to him by his father, fruitlessly seeking the Philosopher's Stone. He had spent enormous amounts of time at the great libraries of the world, and had purchased all the rarest and most important volumes on alchemy. In one he had read that, many years ago, a famous Arabian alchemist had visited Europe. It was said that he was more than two hundred years old, and that he had discovered the Philosopher's Stone and the Elixir of Life. The Englishman had been profoundly impressed by the story. But he would never have thought it more than just a myth, had not a friend of his—returning from an archaeological expedition in the desert—told him about an Arab that was possessed of exceptional powers.

"He lives at the Al-Fayoum oasis," his friend had said. "And people say that he is two hundred years old, and is able to transform any metal into gold."

The Englishman could not contain his excitement. He canceled all his commitments and pulled together the most important of his books, and now here he was, sitting inside a dusty, smelly warehouse. Outside, a huge caravan was being prepared for a crossing of the Sahara, and was scheduled to pass through Al-Fayoum.

I'm going to find that damned alchemist, the Englishman thought. And the odor of the animals became a bit more tolerable.

A young Arab, also loaded down with baggage, entered, and greeted the Englishman.

"Where are you bound?" asked the young Arab.

"I'm going into the desert," the man answered, turning back to his reading. He didn't want any conversation at this point. What he needed to do was review all he had learned over the years, because the alchemist would certainly put him to the test.

The young Arab took out a book and began to read. The book was written in Spanish. That's good, thought the Englishman. He spoke Spanish better than Arabic, and, if this boy was going to Al-Fayoum, there would be someone to talk to when there were no other important things to do.

"THAT'S STRANGE," SAID THE BOY, AS HE TRIED ONCE AGAIN to read the burial scene that began the book. "I've been trying for two years to read this book, and I never get past these first few pages." Even without a king to provide an interruption, he was unable to concentrate.

He still had some doubts about the decision he had made. But he was able to understand one thing: making a decision was only the beginning of things. When someone makes a decision, he is really diving into a strong current that will carry him to places he had never dreamed of when he first made the decision.

When I decided to seek out my treasure, I never imagined that I'd wind up working in a crystal shop, he thought. And joining this caravan may have been my decision, but where it goes is going to be a mystery to me.

Nearby was the Englishman, reading a book. He seemed unfriendly, and had looked irritated when the boy had entered. They might even have become friends, but the Englishman closed off the conversation.

The boy closed his book. He felt that he didn't want to do anything that might make him look like the Englishman. He took Urim and Thummim from his pocket, and began playing with them.

The stranger shouted, "Urim and Thummim!"

In a flash the boy put them back in his pocket.

"They're not for sale," he said.

"They're not worth much," the Englishman answered. "They're only made of rock crystal, and there are millions of rock crystals in the earth. But those who know about such things would know that those are Urim and Thummim. I didn't know that they had them in this part of the world."

"They were given to me as a present by a king," the boy said.

The stranger didn't answer; instead, he put his hand in his pocket, and took out two stones that were the same as the boy's.

"Did you say a king?" he asked.

"I guess you don't believe that a king would talk to someone like me, a shepherd," he said, wanting to end the conversation.

"Not at all. It was shepherds who were the first to recognize a king that the rest of the world refused to acknowledge. So, it's not surprising that kings would talk to shepherds."

And he went on, fearing that the boy wouldn't understand what he was talking about, "It's in the Bible. The same book that taught me about Urim and Thummim. These stones were the only form of divination permitted by God. The priests carried them in a golden breastplate."

The boy was suddenly happy to be there at the warehouse.

"Maybe this is an omen," said the Englishman, half aloud.

"Who told you about omens?" The boy's interest was increasing by the moment.

"Everything in life is an omen," said the Englishman, now closing the journal he was reading. "There is a universal language, understood by everybody, but already forgotten. I am in search of that universal language, among other things. That's why I'm here. I have to find a man who knows that universal language. An alchemist."

The conversation was interrupted by the warehouse boss.

"You're in luck, you two," the fat Arab said. "There's a caravan leaving today for Al-Fayoum."

"But I'm going to Egypt," the boy said.

"Al-Fayoum is in Egypt," said the Arab. "What kind of Arab are you?"

"That's a good luck omen," the Englishman said, after the fat Arab had gone out. "If I could, I'd write a huge encyclopedia just about the words luck and coincidence. It's with those words that the universal language is written."

He told the boy it was no coincidence that he had met him with Urim and Thummim in his hand. And he asked the boy if he, too, were in search of the alchemist.

"I'm looking for a treasure," said the boy, and he immediately regretted having said it. But the Englishman appeared not to attach any importance to it.

"In a way, so am I," he said.

"I don't even know what alchemy is," the boy was saying, when the warehouse boss called to them to come outside.

"I'M THE LEADER OF THE CARAVAN," SAID A DARK-EYED, bearded man. "I hold the power of life and death for every person I take with me. The desert is a capricious lady, and sometimes she drives men crazy."

There were almost two hundred people gathered there, and four hundred animals—camels, horses, mules, and fowl. In the crowd were women, children, and a number of men with swords at their belts and rifles slung on their shoulders. The Englishman had several suitcases filled with books. There was a babble of noise, and the leader had to repeat himself several times for everyone to understand what he was saying.

"There are a lot of different people here, and each has his own God. But the only God I serve is Allah, and in his name I swear that I will do everything possible once again to win out over the desert. But I want each and every one of you to swear by the God you believe in that you will follow my orders no matter what. In the desert, disobedience means death."

There was a murmur from the crowd. Each was swearing quietly to his or her own God. The boy swore to Jesus Christ. The Englishman said nothing. And the murmur lasted longer than a simple vow would have. The people were also praying to heaven for protection.

A long note was sounded on a bugle, and everyone mounted up. The boy and the Englishman had bought camels, and climbed uncertainly onto their backs. The boy felt sorry for the Englishman's camel, loaded down as he was with the cases of books.

"There's no such thing as coincidence," said the Englishman, picking up the conversation where it had been interrupted in the warehouse. "I'm here because a friend of mine heard of an Arab who . . ."

But the caravan began to move, and it was impossible to hear what the Englishman was saying. The boy knew what he was about to describe, though: the mysterious chain that links one thing to another, the same chain that had caused him to become a shepherd, that had caused his recurring dream, that had brought him to a city near Africa, to find a king, and to be robbed in order to meet a crystal merchant, and . . .

The closer one gets to realizing his Personal Legend, the more that Personal Legend becomes his true reason for being, thought the boy.

The caravan moved toward the east. It traveled during the morning, halted when the sun was at its strongest, and resumed late in the afternoon. The boy spoke very little with the Englishman, who spent most of his time with his books.

The boy observed in silence the progress of the animals and people across the desert. Now everything was quite different from how it was that day they had set out: then, there had been confusion and shouting, the cries of children and the whinnying of animals, all mixed with the nervous orders of the guides and the merchants.

But, in the desert, there was only the sound of the eternal wind, and of the hoofbeats of the animals. Even the guides spoke very little to one another.

"I've crossed these sands many times," said one of the camel drivers one night. "But the desert is so huge, and the horizons so distant, that they make a person feel small, and as if he should remain silent."

The boy understood intuitively what he meant, even without ever having set foot in the desert before. Whenever he saw the sea, or a fire, he fell silent, impressed by their elemental force.

I've learned things from the sheep, and I've learned things from crystal, he thought. I can learn something from the desert, too. It seems old and wise.

The wind never stopped, and the boy remembered the day he had sat at the fort in Tarifa with this same wind blowing in his face. It reminded him of the wool from his sheep . . . his sheep who were now seeking food and water in the fields of Andalusia, as they always had.

"They're not my sheep anymore," he said to himself, without nostalgia. "They must be used to their new shepherd, and have probably already forgotten me. That's good.

Creatures like the sheep, that are used to traveling, know about moving on."

He thought of the merchant's daughter, and was sure that she had probably married. Perhaps to a baker, or to another shepherd who could read and could tell her exciting stories—after all, he probably wasn't the only one. But he was excited at his intuitive understanding of the camel driver's comment: maybe he was also learning the universal language that deals with the past and the present of all people. "Hunches," his mother used to call them. The boy was beginning to understand that intuition is really a sudden immersion of the soul into the universal current of life, where the histories of all people are connected, and we are able to know everything, because it's all written there.

"Maktub," the boy said, remembering the crystal merchant.

The desert was all sand in some stretches, and rocky in others. When the caravan was blocked by a boulder, it had to go around it; if there was a large rocky area, they had to make a major detour. If the sand was too fine for the animals' hooves, they sought a way where the sand was more substantial. In some places, the ground was covered with the salt of dried-up lakes. The animals balked at such places, and the camel drivers were forced to dismount and unburden their charges. The drivers carried the freight themselves over such treacherous footing, and then reloaded the camels. If a guide were to fall ill or die, the camel drivers would draw lots and appoint a new one.

But all this happened for one basic reason: no matter how many detours and adjustments it made, the caravan moved toward the same compass point. Once obstacles were overcome, it returned to its course, sighting on a star that indicated the location of the oasis. When the people saw that star shining in the morning sky, they knew they were on the right course toward water, palm trees, shelter, and other people. It was only the Englishman who was unaware of all this; he was, for the most part, immersed in reading his books.

The boy, too, had his book, and he had tried to read it during the first few days of the journey. But he found it much more interesting to observe the caravan and listen to the wind. As soon as he had learned to know his camel better, and to establish a relationship with him, he threw the book away. Although the boy had developed a superstition that each time he opened the book he would learn something important, he decided it was an unnecessary burden.

He became friendly with the camel driver who traveled alongside him. At night, as they sat around the fire, the boy related to the driver his adventures as a shepherd.

During one of these conversations, the driver told of his own life.

"I used to live near El Cairum," he said. "I had my orchard, my children, and a life that would change not at all until I died. One year, when the crop was the best ever, we all went to Mecca, and I satisfied the only unmet obligation in my life. I could die happily, and that made me feel good.

"One day, the earth began to tremble, and the Nile overflowed its banks. It was something that I thought could happen only to others, never to me. My neighbors feared they would lose all their olive trees in the flood, and my wife was afraid that we would lose our children. I thought that everything I owned would be destroyed.

"The land was ruined, and I had to find some other way to earn a living. So now I'm a camel driver. But that disaster taught me to understand the word of Allah: people need not fear the unknown if they are capable of achieving what they need and want.

"We are afraid of losing what we have, whether it's our life or our possessions and property. But this fear evaporates when we understand that our life stories and the history of the world were written by the same hand."

Sometimes, their caravan met with another. One always had something that the other needed—as if everything were indeed written by one hand. As they sat around the fire, the camel drivers exchanged information about windstorms, and told stories about the desert.

At other times, mysterious, hooded men would appear; they were Bedouins who did surveillance along the caravan route. They provided warnings about thieves and barbarian tribes. They came in silence and departed the same way, dressed in black garments that showed only their eyes. One night, a camel driver came to the fire where the Englishman and the boy were sitting. "There are rumors of tribal wars," he told them.

The three fell silent. The boy noted that there was a sense of fear in the air, even though no one said anything. Once again he was experiencing the language without words . . . the universal language.

The Englishman asked if they were in danger.

"Once you get into the desert, there's no going back," said the camel driver. "And, when you can't go back, you have to worry only about the best way of moving forward. The rest is up to Allah, including the danger."

And he concluded by saying the mysterious word: *"Maktub."*

"You should pay more attention to the caravan," the boy said to the Englishman, after the camel driver had left. "We make a lot of detours, but we're always heading for the same destination."

"And you ought to read more about the world," answered the Englishman. "Books are like caravans in that respect."

The immense collection of people and animals began to travel faster. The days had always been silent, but now, even the nights—when the travelers were accustomed to talking around the fires—had also become quiet. And, one day, the leader of the caravan made the decision that the fires should no longer be lighted, so as not to attract attention to the caravan.

The travelers adopted the practice of arranging the animals in a circle at night, sleeping together in the center as protection against the nocturnal cold. And the leader posted armed sentinels at the fringes of the group.

The Englishman was unable to sleep one night. He called to the boy, and they took a walk along the dunes surrounding the encampment. There was a full moon, and the boy told the Englishman the story of his life.

The Englishman was fascinated with the part about the progress achieved at the crystal shop after the boy began working there.

"That's the principle that governs all things," he said. "In alchemy, it's called the Soul of the World. When you want something with all your heart, that's when you are closest to the Soul of the World. It's always a positive force."

He also said that this was not just a human gift, that everything on the face of the earth had a soul, whether mineral, vegetable, or animal—or even just a simple thought.

"Everything on earth is being continuously transformed, because the earth is alive . . . and it has a soul. We are part of that soul, so we rarely recognize that it is working for us. But in the crystal shop you probably realized that even the glasses were collaborating in your success."

The boy thought about that for a while as he looked at the moon and the bleached sands. "I have watched the caravan as it crossed the desert," he said. "The caravan and the desert speak the same language, and it's for that reason that the desert allows the crossing. It's going to test the caravan's every step to see if it's in time, and, if it is, we will make it to the oasis."

"If either of us had joined this caravan based only on personal courage, but without understanding that language, this journey would have been much more difficult."

They stood there looking at the moon.

"That's the magic of omens," said the boy. "I've seen how the guides read the signs of the desert, and how the soul of the caravan speaks to the soul of the desert."

The Englishman said, "I'd better pay more attention to the caravan."

"And I'd better read your books," said the boy.

THEY WERE STRANGE BOOKS. THEY SPOKE ABOUT MERCURY, salt, dragons, and kings, and he didn't understand any of it. But there was one idea that seemed to repeat itself throughout all the books: all things are the manifestation of one thing only.

In one of the books he learned that the most important text in the literature of alchemy contained only a few lines, and had been inscribed on the surface of an emerald.

"It's the Emerald Tablet," said the Englishman, proud that he might teach something to the boy.

"Well, then, why do we need all these books?" the boy asked.

"So that we can understand those few lines," the Englishman answered, without appearing really to believe what he had said.

The book that most interested the boy told the stories of the famous alchemists. They were men who had dedicated their entire lives to the purification of metals in their laboratories; they believed that, if a metal were heated for many years, it would free itself of all its individual properties, and what was left would be the Soul of the World. This Soul of the World allowed them to understand anything on the face of the earth, because it was the language with which all things communicated. They called that discovery the Master Work—it was part liquid and part solid.

"Can't you just observe men and omens in order to understand the language?" the boy asked.

"You have a mania for simplifying everything," answered the Englishman, irritated. "Alchemy is a serious discipline. Every step has to be followed exactly as it was followed by the masters."

The boy learned that the liquid part of the Master Work was called the Elixir of Life, and that it cured all illnesses; it also kept the alchemist from growing old. And the solid part was called the Philosopher's Stone.

"It's not easy to find the Philosopher's Stone," said the Englishman. "The alchemists spent years in their laboratories, observing the fire that purified the metals. They spent so much time close to the fire that gradually they gave up the vanities of the world. They discovered that the purification of the metals had led to a purification of themselves."

The boy thought about the crystal merchant. He had said that it was a good thing for the boy to clean the crystal pieces, so that he could free himself from negative thoughts. The boy was becoming more and more convinced that alchemy could be learned in one's daily life.

"Also," said the Englishman, "the Philosopher's Stone has a fascinating property. A small sliver of the stone can transform large quantities of metal into gold."

Having heard that, the boy became even more interested in alchemy. He thought that, with some patience, he'd be able to transform everything into gold. He read the lives of the various people who had succeeded in doing so: Helvétius, Elias, Fulcanelli, and Geber. They were fascinating stories: each of them lived out his Personal Legend to the end. They traveled, spoke with wise men, performed miracles for the incredulous, and owned the Philosopher's Stone and the Elixir of Life.

But when the boy wanted to learn how to achieve the Master Work, he became completely lost. There were just drawings, coded instructions, and obscure texts.

"Why do they make things so complicated?" he asked the Englishman one night. The boy had noticed that the Englishman was irritable, and missed his books.

"So that those who have the responsibility for understanding can understand," he said. "Imagine if everyone went around transforming lead into gold. Gold would lose its value.

"It's only those who are persistent, and willing to study things deeply, who achieve the Master Work. That's why I'm here in the middle of the desert. I'm seeking a true alchemist who will help me to decipher the codes."

"When were these books written?" the boy asked.

"Many centuries ago."

"They didn't have the printing press in those days," the boy argued. "There was no way for everybody to know about alchemy. Why did they use such strange language, with so many drawings?"

The Englishman didn't answer him directly. He said that for the past few days he had been paying attention to how the caravan operated, but that he hadn't learned anything new. The only thing he had noticed was that talk of war was becoming more and more frequent.

THEN ONE DAY THE BOY RETURNED THE BOOKS TO THE Englishman. "Did you learn anything?" the Englishman asked, eager to hear what it might be. He needed someone to talk to so as to avoid thinking about the possibility of war.

"I learned that the world has a soul, and that whoever understands that soul can also understand the language of things. I learned that many alchemists realized their Personal Legends, and wound up discovering the Soul of the World, the Philosopher's Stone, and the Elixir of Life.

"But, above all, I learned that these things are all so simple that they could be written on the surface of an emerald."

The Englishman was disappointed. The years of research, the magic symbols, the strange words and the laboratory equipment . . . none of this had made an impression on the boy. His soul must be too primitive to understand those things, he thought.

He took back his books and packed them away again in their bags.

"Go back to watching the caravan," he said. "That didn't teach me anything, either."

The boy went back to contemplating the silence of the desert, and the sand raised by the animals. "Everyone has his or her own way of learning things," he said to himself. "His way isn't the same as mine, nor mine as his. But we're both in search of our Personal Legends, and I respect him for that."

THE CARAVAN BEGAN TO TRAVEL DAY AND NIGHT. THE hooded Bedouins reappeared more and more frequently, and the camel driver—who had become a good friend of the boy's—explained that the war between the tribes had already begun. The caravan would be very lucky to reach the oasis.

The animals were exhausted, and the men talked among themselves less and less. The silence was the worst aspect of the night, when the mere groan of a camel—which before had been nothing but the groan of a camel—now frightened everyone, because it might signal a raid.

The camel driver, though, seemed not to be very concerned with the threat of war.

"I'm alive," he said to the boy, as they ate a bunch of dates one night, with no fires and no moon. "When I'm eating, that's all I think about. If I'm on the march, I just concentrate on marching. If I have to fight, it will be just as good a day to die as any other.

"Because I don't live in either my past or my future. I'm interested only in the present. If you can concentrate always on the present, you'll be a happy man. You'll see that there is life in the desert, that there are stars in the heavens, and that tribesmen fight because they are part of the human race. Life will be a party for you, a grand festival, because life is the moment we're living right now."

Two nights later, as he was getting ready to bed down, the boy looked for the star they followed every night. He thought that the horizon was a bit lower than it had been, because he seemed to see stars on the desert itself.

"It's the oasis," said the camel driver.

"Well, why don't we go there right now?" the boy asked.

"Because we have to sleep."

THE BOY AWOKE AS THE SUN ROSE. THERE, IN FRONT OF HIM, where the small stars had been the night before, was an endless row of date palms, stretching across the entire desert.

"We've done it!" said the Englishman, who had also awakened early.

But the boy was quiet. He was at home with the silence of the desert, and he was content just to look at the trees. He still had a long way to go to reach the pyramids, and someday this morning would just be a memory. But this was the present moment—the party the camel driver had mentioned—and he wanted to live it as he did the lessons of his past and his dreams of the future. Although the vision of the date palms would someday be just a memory, right now it signified shade, water, and a refuge from the war. Yesterday, the camel's groan signaled danger, and now a row of date palms could herald a miracle.

The world speaks many languages, the boy thought.

THE TIMES RUSH PAST, AND SO DO THE CARAVANS, thought the alchemist, as he watched the hundreds of people and animals arriving at the oasis. People were shouting at the new arrivals, dust obscured the desert sun, and the children of the oasis were bursting with excitement at the arrival of the strangers. The alchemist saw the tribal chiefs greet the leader of the caravan, and converse with him at length.

But none of that mattered to the alchemist. He had already seen many people come and go, and the desert remained as it was. He had seen kings and beggars walking the desert sands. The dunes were changed constantly by the wind, yet these were the same sands he had known since he was a child. He always enjoyed seeing the happiness that the travelers experienced when, after weeks of yellow sand and blue sky, they first saw the green of the date palms. Maybe God created the desert so that man could appreciate the date trees, he thought.

He decided to concentrate on more practical matters. He knew that in the caravan there was a man to whom he was to teach some of his secrets. The omens had told him so. He didn't know the man yet, but his practiced eye would recognize him when he appeared. He hoped that it would be someone as capable as his previous apprentice.

I don't know why these things have to be transmitted by word of mouth, he thought. It wasn't exactly that they were secrets; God revealed his secrets easily to all his creatures.

He had only one explanation for this fact: things have to be transmitted this way because they were made up from the pure life, and this kind of life cannot be captured in pictures or words.

Because people become fascinated with pictures and words, and wind up forgetting the Language of the World.

THE BOY COULDN'T BELIEVE WHAT HE WAS SEEING: THE oasis, rather than being just a well surrounded by a few palm trees—as he had seen once in a geography book—was much larger than many towns back in Spain. There were three hundred wells, fifty thousand date trees, and innumerable colored tents spread among them.

"It looks like *A Thousand and One Nights,*" said the Englishman, impatient to meet with the alchemist.

They were surrounded by children, curious to look at the animals and people that were arriving. The men of the oasis wanted to know if they had seen any fighting, and the women competed with one another for access to the cloth and precious stones brought by the merchants. The silence of the desert was a distant dream; the travelers in the caravan were talking incessantly, laughing and shouting, as if they had emerged from the spiritual world and found themselves once again in the world of people. They were relieved and happy.

They had been taking careful precautions in the desert, but the camel driver explained to the boy that oases were always considered to be neutral territories, because the majority of the inhabitants were women and children. There were oases throughout the desert, but the tribesmen fought in the desert, leaving the oases as places of refuge.

With some difficulty, the leader of the caravan brought all his people together and gave them his instructions. The group was to remain there at the oasis until the conflict between the tribes was over. Since they were visitors, they would have to share living space with those who lived there, and would be given the best accommodations. That was the law of hospitality. Then he asked that everyone, including his own sentinels, hand over their arms to the men appointed by the tribal chieftains.

"Those are the rules of war," the leader explained. "The oases may not shelter armies or troops."

To the boy's surprise, the Englishman took a chrome-plated revolver out of his bag and gave it to the men who were collecting the arms.

"Why a revolver?" he asked.

"It helped me to trust in people," the Englishman answered.

Meanwhile, the boy thought about his treasure. The closer he got to the realization of his dream, the more difficult things became. It seemed as if what the old king had called "beginner's luck" were no longer functioning. In his pursuit of the dream, he was being constantly subjected to tests of his persistence and courage. So he could not be hasty, nor impatient. If he pushed forward impulsively, he would fail to see the signs and omens left by God along his path.

God placed them along my path. He had surprised himself with the thought. Until then, he had considered the omens to be things of this world. Like eating or sleeping, or like seeking love or finding a job. He had never thought of them in terms of a language used by God to indicate what he should do.

"Don't be impatient," he repeated to himself. "It's like the camel driver said: 'Eat when it's time to eat. And move along when it's time to move along.'"

That first day, everyone slept from exhaustion, including the Englishman. The boy was assigned a place far from his friend, in a tent with five other young men of about his age. They were people of the desert, and clamored to hear his stories about the great cities.

The boy told them about his life as a shepherd, and was about to tell them of his experiences at the crystal shop when the Englishman came into the tent.

"I've been looking for you all morning," he said, as he led the boy outside. "I need you to help me find out where the alchemist lives."

First, they tried to find him on their own. An alchemist would probably live in a manner that was different from that of the rest of the people at the oasis, and it was likely that in his tent an oven was continuously burning. They searched everywhere, and found that the oasis was much larger than they could have imagined; there were hundreds of tents.

"We've wasted almost the entire day," said the Englishman, sitting down with the boy near one of the wells.

"Maybe we'd better ask someone," the boy suggested.

The Englishman didn't want to tell others about his reasons for being at the oasis, and couldn't make up his mind. But, finally, he agreed that the boy, who spoke better Arabic than he, should do so. The boy approached a woman who had come to the well to fill a goatskin with water.

"Good afternoon, ma'am. I'm trying to find out where the alchemist lives here at the oasis."

The woman said she had never heard of such a person, and hurried away. But before she fled, she advised the boy that he had better not try to converse with women who were dressed in black, because they were married women. He should respect tradition.

The Englishman was disappointed. It seemed he had made the long journey for nothing. The boy was also saddened; his friend was in pursuit of his Personal Legend. And, when someone was in such pursuit, the entire universe made an effort to help him succeed—that's what the old king had said. He couldn't have been wrong.

"I had never heard of alchemists before," the boy said. "Maybe no one here has, either."

The Englishman's eyes lit up. "That's it! Maybe no one here knows what an alchemist is! Find out who it is who cures the people's illnesses!"

Several women dressed in black came to the well for water, but the boy would speak to none of them, despite the Englishman's insistence. Then a man approached.

"Do you know someone here who cures people's illnesses?" the boy asked.

"Allah cures our illnesses," said the man, clearly frightened of the strangers. "You're looking for witch doctors." He spoke some verses from the Koran, and moved on.

Another man appeared. He was older, and was carrying a small bucket. The boy repeated his question.

"Why do you want to find that sort of person?" the Arab asked.

"Because my friend here has traveled for many months in order to meet with him," the boy said.

"If such a man is here at the oasis, he must be the very powerful one," said the old man after thinking for a few moments. "Not even the tribal chieftains are able to see him when they want to. Only when he consents.

"Wait for the end of the war. Then leave with the caravan. Don't try to enter into the life of the oasis," he said, and walked away.

But the Englishman was exultant. They were on the right track.

Finally, a young woman approached who was not dressed in black. She had a vessel on her shoulder, and her head was covered by a veil, but her face was uncovered. The boy approached her to ask about the alchemist.

At that moment, it seemed to him that time stood still, and the Soul of the World surged within him. When he looked into her dark eyes, and saw that her lips were poised between a laugh and silence, he learned the most important part of the language that all the world spoke—the language that everyone on earth was capable of understanding in their heart. It was love. Something older than humanity, more ancient than the desert. Something that exerted the same force whenever two pairs of eyes met, as had theirs here at the well. She smiled, and that was certainly an omen—the omen he had been awaiting, without even knowing he was, for all his life. The omen he had sought to find with his sheep and in his books, in the crystals and in the silence of the desert.

It was the pure Language of the World. It required no explanation, just as the universe needs none as it travels through endless time. What the boy felt at that moment was that he was in the presence of the only woman in his life, and that, with no need for words, she recognized the same thing. He was more certain of it than of anything in the world. He had been told by his parents and grandparents that he must fall in love and really know a person before becoming committed. But maybe people who felt that way had never learned the universal language. Because, when you know that language, it's easy to understand that someone in the world awaits you, whether it's in the middle of the desert or in some great city. And when two such people encounter each other, and their eyes meet, the past and the future become unimportant. There is only that moment, and the incredible certainty that everything under the sun has been written by one hand only. It is the hand that evokes love, and creates a twin soul for every person in the world. Without such love, one's dreams would have no meaning.

Maktub, thought the boy.

The Englishman shook the boy: "Come on, ask her!"

The boy stepped closer to the girl, and when she smiled, he did the same.

"What's your name?" he asked.

"Fatima," the girl said, averting her eyes.

"That's what some women in my country are called."

"It's the name of the Prophet's daughter," Fatima said. "The invaders carried the name everywhere." The beautiful girl spoke of the invaders with pride.

The Englishman prodded him, and the boy asked her about the man who cured people's illnesses.

"That's the man who knows all the secrets of the world," she said. "He communicates with the genies of the desert."

The genies were the spirits of good and evil. And the girl pointed to the south, indicating that it was there the strange man lived. Then she filled her vessel with water and left.

The Englishman vanished, too, gone to find the alchemist. And the boy sat there by the well for a long time, remembering that one day in Tarifa the levanter had brought to him the perfume of that woman, and realizing that he had loved her before he even knew she existed. He knew that his love for her would enable him to discover every treasure in the world.

The next day, the boy returned to the well, hoping to see the girl. To his surprise, the Englishman was there, looking out at the desert.

"I waited all afternoon and evening," he said. "He appeared with the first stars of evening. I told him what I was seeking, and he asked me if I had ever transformed lead into gold. I told him that was what I had come here to learn.

"He told me I should try to do so. That's all he said: 'Go and try.'"

The boy didn't say anything. The poor Englishman had traveled all this way, only to be told that he should repeat what he had already done so many times.

"So, then try," he said to the Englishman.

"That's what I'm going to do. I'm going to start now."

As the Englishman left, Fatima arrived and filled her vessel with water.

"I came to tell you just one thing," the boy said. "I want you to be my wife. I love you."

The girl dropped the container, and the water spilled.

"I'm going to wait here for you every day. I have crossed the desert in search of a treasure that is somewhere near the Pyramids, and for me, the war seemed a curse. But now it's a blessing, because it brought me to you."

"The war is going to end someday," the girl said.

The boy looked around him at the date palms. He reminded himself that he had been a shepherd, and that he could be a shepherd again. Fatima was more important than his treasure.

"The tribesmen are always in search of treasure," the girl said, as if she had guessed what he was thinking. "And the women of the desert are proud of their tribesmen."

She refilled her vessel and left.

The boy went to the well every day to meet with Fatima. He told her about his life as a shepherd, about the king, and about the crystal shop. They became friends, and except for the fifteen minutes he spent with her, each day seemed that it would never pass. When he had been at the oasis for almost a month, the leader of the caravan called a meeting of all of the people traveling with him.

"We don't know when the war will end, so we can't continue our journey," he said. "The battles may last for a long time, perhaps even years. There are powerful forces on both sides, and the war is important to both armies. It's not a battle of good against evil. It's a war between forces that are fighting for the balance of power, and, when that type of battle begins, it lasts longer than others—because Allah is on both sides."

The people went back to where they were living, and the boy went to meet with Fatima that afternoon. He told her about the morning's meeting. "The day after we met," Fatima said, "you told me that you loved me. Then, you taught me something of the universal language and the Soul of the World. Because of that, I have become a part of you."

The boy listened to the sound of her voice, and thought it to be more beautiful than the sound of the wind in the date palms.

"I have been waiting for you here at this oasis for a long time. I have forgotten about my past, about my traditions, and the way in which men of the desert expect women to behave. Ever since I was a child, I have dreamed that the desert would bring me a wonderful present. Now, my present has arrived, and it's you."

The boy wanted to take her hand. But Fatima's hands held to the handles of her jug.

"You have told me about your dreams, about the old king and your treasure. And you've told me about omens. So now, I fear nothing, because it was those omens that brought you to me. And I am a part of your dream, a part of your Personal Legend, as you call it.

"That's why I want you to continue toward your goal. If you have to wait until the war is over, then wait. But if you have to go before then, go on in pursuit of your dream. The dunes are changed by the wind, but the desert never changes. That's the way it will be with our love for each other.

"Maktub," she said. "If I am really a part of your dream, you'll come back one day."

The boy was sad as he left her that day. He thought of all the married shepherds he had known. They had a difficult time convincing their wives that they had to go off into distant fields. Love required them to stay with the people they loved.

He told Fatima that, at their next meeting.

"The desert takes our men from us, and they don't always return," she said. "We know that, and we are used to it. Those who don't return become a part of the clouds, a part of the animals that hide in the ravines and of the water that comes from the earth. They become a part of everything . . . they become the Soul of the World.

"Some do come back. And then the other women are happy because they believe that their men may one day return, as well. I used to look at those women and envy them their happiness. Now, I too will be one of the women who wait.

"I'm a desert woman, and I'm proud of that. I want my husband to wander as free as the wind that shapes the dunes. And, if I have to, I will accept the fact that he has become a part of the clouds, and the animals, and the water of the desert."

The boy went to look for the Englishman. He wanted to tell him about Fatima. He was surprised when he saw that the Englishman had built himself a furnace outside his tent. It was a strange furnace, fueled by firewood, with a transparent flask heating on top. As the Englishman stared out at the desert, his eyes seemed brighter than they had when he was reading his books.

"This is the first phase of the job," he said. "I have to separate out the sulfur. To do that successfully, I must have no fear of failure. It was my fear of failure that first kept me from attempting the Master Work. Now, I'm beginning what I could have started ten years ago. But I'm happy at least that I didn't wait twenty years."

He continued to feed the fire, and the boy stayed on until the desert turned pink in the setting sun. He felt the urge to go out into the desert, to see if its silence held the answers to his questions.

He wandered for a while, keeping the date palms of the oasis within sight. He listened to the wind, and felt the stones beneath his feet. Here and there, he found a shell, and realized that the desert, in remote times, had been a sea. He sat on a stone, and allowed himself to become hypnotized by the horizon. He tried to deal with the concept of love as distinct from possession, and couldn't separate them. But Fatima was a woman of the desert, and, if anything could help him to understand, it was the desert.

As he sat there thinking, he sensed movement above him. Looking up, he saw a pair of hawks flying high in the sky.

He watched the hawks as they drifted on the wind. Although their flight appeared to have no pattern, it made a certain kind of sense to the boy. It was just that he couldn't grasp what it meant. He followed the movement of the birds, trying to read something into it. Maybe these desert birds could explain to him the meaning of love without ownership.

He felt sleepy. In his heart, he wanted to remain awake, but he also wanted to sleep. "I am learning the Language of the World, and everything in the world is beginning to make sense to me . . . even the flight of the hawks," he said to himself. And, in that mood, he was grateful to be in love. When you are in love, things make even more sense, he thought.

Suddenly, one of the hawks made a flashing dive through the sky, attacking the other. As it did so, a sudden, fleeting image came to the boy: an army, with its swords at the ready, riding into the oasis. The vision vanished immediately, but it had shaken him. He had heard people speak of mirages, and had already seen some himself: they were desires that, because of their intensity, materialized over the sands of the desert. But he certainly didn't desire that an army invade the oasis.

He wanted to forget about the vision, and return to his meditation. He tried again to concentrate on the pink shades of the desert, and its stones. But there was something there in his heart that wouldn't allow him to do so.

"Always heed the omens," the old king had said. The boy recalled what he had seen in the vision, and sensed that it was actually going to occur.

He rose, and made his way back toward the palm trees. Once again, he perceived the many languages in the things about him: this time, the desert was safe, and it was the oasis that had become dangerous.

The camel driver was seated at the base of a palm tree, observing the sunset. He saw the boy appear from the other side of the dunes.

"An army is coming," the boy said. "I had a vision."

"The desert fills men's hearts with visions," the camel driver answered.

But the boy told him about the hawks: that he had been watching their flight and had suddenly felt himself to have plunged to the Soul of the World.

The camel driver understood what the boy was saying. He knew that any given thing on the face of the earth could reveal the history of all things. One could open a book to any page, or look at a person's hand; one could turn a card, or watch the flight of the birds . . . whatever the thing observed, one could find a connection with his experience of the moment. Actually, it wasn't that those things, in themselves, revealed anything at all; it was just that people, looking at what was occurring around them, could find a means of penetration to the Soul of the World.

The desert was full of men who earned their living based on the ease with which they could penetrate to the Soul of the World. They were known as seers, and they were held in fear by women and the elderly. Tribesmen were also wary of consulting them, because it would be impossible to be effective in battle if one knew that he was fated to die. The tribesmen preferred the taste of battle, and the thrill of not knowing what the outcome would be; the future was already written by Allah, and what he had written was always for the good of man. So the tribesmen lived only for the present, because the present was full of surprises, and they had to be aware of many things: Where was the enemy's sword? Where was his horse? What kind of blow should one deliver next in order to remain alive? The camel driver was not a fighter, and he had consulted with seers. Many of them had been right about what they said, while some had been wrong. Then, one day, the oldest seer he had ever sought out (and the one most to be feared) had asked why the camel driver was so interested in the future.

"Well . . . so I can do things," he had responded. "And so I can change those things that I don't want to happen."

"But then they wouldn't be a part of your future," the seer had said.

"Well, maybe I just want to know the future so I can prepare myself for what's coming."

"If good things are coming, they will be a pleasant surprise," said the seer. "If bad things are, and you know in advance, you will suffer greatly before they even occur."

"I want to know about the future because I'm a man," the camel driver had said to the seer. "And men always live their lives based on the future."

The seer was a specialist in the casting of twigs; he threw them on the ground, and made interpretations based on how they fell. That day, he didn't make a cast. He wrapped the twigs in a piece of cloth and put them back in his bag.

"I make my living forecasting the future for people," he said. "I know the science of the twigs, and I know how to use them to penetrate to the place where all is written. There, I can read the past, discover what has already been forgotten, and understand the omens that are here in the present.

"When people consult me, it's not that I'm reading the future; I am guessing at the future. The future belongs to God, and it is only he who reveals it, under extraordinary circumstances. How do I guess at the future? Based on the omens of the present. The secret is here in the present. If you pay attention to the present, you can improve upon it. And, if you improve on the present, what comes later will also be better. Forget about the future, and live each day according to the teachings, confident that God loves his children. Each day, in itself, brings with it an eternity."

The camel driver had asked what the circumstances were under which God would allow him to see the future.

"Only when he, himself, reveals it. And God only rarely reveals the future. When he does so, it is for only one reason: it's a future that was written so as to be altered."

God had shown the boy a part of the future, the camel driver thought. Why was it that he wanted the boy to serve as his instrument?

"Go and speak to the tribal chieftains," said the camel driver. "Tell them about the armies that are approaching."

"They'll laugh at me."

"They are men of the desert, and the men of the desert are used to dealing with omens."

"Well, then, they probably already know."

"They're not concerned with that right now. They believe that if they have to know about something Allah wants them to know, someone will tell them about it. It has happened many times before. But, this time, the person is you."

The boy thought of Fatima. And he decided he would go to see the chiefs of the tribes.

THE BOY APPROACHED THE GUARD AT THE FRONT OF THE huge white tent at the center of the oasis.

"I want to see the chieftains. I've brought omens from the desert."

Without responding, the guard entered the tent, where he remained for some time. When he emerged, it was with a young Arab, dressed in white and gold. The boy told the younger man what he had seen, and the man asked him to wait there. He disappeared into the tent.

Night fell, and an assortment of fighting men and merchants entered and exited the tent. One by one, the campfires were extinguished, and the oasis fell as quiet as the desert. Only the lights in the great tent remained. During all this time, the boy thought about Fatima, and he was still unable to understand his last conversation with her.

Finally, after hours of waiting, the guard bade the boy enter. The boy was astonished by what he saw inside. Never could he have imagined that, there in the middle of the desert, there existed a tent like this one. The ground was covered with the most beautiful carpets he had ever walked upon, and from the top of the structure hung lamps of hand-wrought gold, each with a lighted candle. The tribal chieftains were seated at the back of the tent in a semicircle, resting upon richly embroidered silk cushions. Servants came and went with silver trays laden with spices and tea. Other servants maintained the fires in the hookahs. The atmosphere was suffused with the sweet scent of smoke.

There were eight chieftains, but the boy could see immediately which of them was the most important: an Arab dressed in white and gold, seated at the center of the semicircle. At his side was the young Arab the boy had spoken with earlier.

"Who is this stranger who speaks of omens?" asked one of the chieftains, eyeing the boy.

"It is I," the boy answered. And he told what he had seen.

"Why would the desert reveal such things to a stranger, when it knows that we have been here for generations?" said another of the chieftains.

"Because my eyes are not yet accustomed to the desert," the boy said. "I can see things that eyes habituated to the desert might not see."

And also because I know about the Soul of the World, he thought to himself.

"The oasis is neutral ground. No one attacks an oasis," said a third chieftain.

"I can only tell you what I saw. If you don't want to believe me, you don't have to do anything about it."

The men fell into an animated discussion. They spoke in an Arabic dialect that the boy didn't understand, but, when he made to leave, the guard told him to stay. The boy became fearful; the omens told him that something was wrong. He regretted having spoken to the camel driver about what he had seen in the desert.

Suddenly, the elder at the center smiled almost imperceptibly, and the boy felt better. The man hadn't participated in the discussion, and, in fact, hadn't said a word up to that point. But the boy was already used to the Language of the World, and he could feel the vibrations of peace throughout the tent. Now his intuition was that he had been right in coming.

The discussion ended. The chieftains were silent for a few moments as they listened to what the old man was saying. Then he turned to the boy: this time his expression was cold and distant.

"Two thousand years ago, in a distant land, a man who believed in dreams was thrown into a dungeon and then sold as a slave," the old man said, now in the dialect the boy understood. "Our merchants bought that man, and brought him to Egypt. All of us know that whoever believes in dreams also knows how to interpret them."

The elder continued, "When the pharaoh dreamed of cows that were thin and cows that were fat, this man I'm speaking of rescued Egypt from famine. His name was Joseph. He, too, was a stranger in a strange land, like you, and he was probably about your age."

He paused, and his eyes were still unfriendly.

"We always observe the Tradition. The Tradition saved Egypt from famine in those days, and made the Egyptians the wealthiest of peoples. The Tradition teaches men how to cross the desert, and how their children should marry. The Tradition says that an oasis is neutral territory, because both sides have oases, and so both are vulnerable."

No one said a word as the old man continued.

"But the Tradition also says that we should believe the messages of the desert. Everything we know was taught to us by the desert."

The old man gave a signal, and everyone stood. The meeting was over. The hookahs were extinguished, and the guards stood at attention. The boy made ready to leave, but the old man spoke again:

"Tomorrow, we are going to break the agreement that says that no one at the oasis may carry arms. Throughout the entire day we will be on the lookout for our enemies. When the sun sets, the men will once again surrender their arms to me. For every ten dead men among our enemies, you will receive a piece of gold.

"But arms cannot be drawn unless they also go into battle. Arms are as capricious as the desert, and, if they are not used, the next time they might not function. If at least one of them hasn't been used by the end of the day tomorrow, one will be used on you."

When the boy left the tent, the oasis was illuminated only by the light of the full moon. He was twenty minutes from his tent, and began to make his way there.

He was alarmed by what had happened. He had succeeded in reaching through to the Soul of the World, and now the price for having done so might be his life. It was a frightening bet. But he had been making risky bets ever since the day he had sold his sheep to pursue his Personal Legend. And, as the camel driver had said, to die tomorrow was no worse than dying on any other day. Every day was there to be lived or to mark one's departure from this world. Everything depended on one word: *"Maktub."*

Walking along in the silence, he had no regrets. If he died tomorrow, it would be because God was not willing to change the future. He would at least have died after having crossed the strait, after having worked in a crystal shop, and after having known the silence of the desert and Fatima's eyes. He had lived every one of his days intensely since he had left home so long ago. If he died tomorrow, he would already have seen more than other shepherds, and he was proud of that.

Suddenly he heard a thundering sound, and he was thrown to the ground by a wind such as he had never known. The area was swirling in dust so intense that it hid the moon from view. Before him was an enormous white horse, rearing over him with a frightening scream.

When the blinding dust had settled a bit, the boy trembled at what he saw. Astride the animal was a horseman dressed completely in black, with a falcon perched on his left shoulder. He wore a turban and his entire face, except for his eyes, was covered with a black kerchief. He appeared to be a messenger from the desert, but his presence was much more powerful than that of a mere messenger.

The strange horseman drew an enormous, curved sword from a scabbard mounted on his saddle. The steel of its blade glittered in the light of the moon.

"Who dares to read the meaning of the flight of the hawks?" he demanded, so loudly that his words seemed to echo through the fifty thousand palm trees of Al-Fayoum.

"It is I who dared to do so," said the boy. He was reminded of the image of Santiago Matamoros, mounted on his white horse, with the infidels beneath his hooves. This man looked exactly the same, except that now the roles were reversed.

"It is I who dared to do so," he repeated, and he lowered his head to receive a blow from the sword. "Many lives will be saved, because I was able to see through to the Soul of the World."

The sword didn't fall. Instead, the stranger lowered it slowly, until the point touched the boy's forehead. It drew a droplet of blood.

The horseman was completely immobile, as was the boy.

It didn't even occur to the boy to flee. In his heart, he felt a strange sense of joy: he was about to die in pursuit of his Personal Legend. And for Fatima. The omens had been true, after all. Here he was, face-to-face with his enemy, but there was no need to be concerned about dying—the Soul of the World awaited him, and he would soon be a part of it. And, tomorrow, his enemy would also be a part of that Soul.

The stranger continued to hold the sword at the boy's forehead. "Why did you read the flight of the birds?"

"I read only what the birds wanted to tell me. They wanted to save the oasis. Tomorrow all of you will die, because there are more men at the oasis than you have."

The sword remained where it was. "Who are you to change what Allah has willed?"

"Allah created the armies, and he also created the hawks. Allah taught me the language of the birds. Everything has been written by the same hand," the boy said, remembering the camel driver's words.

The stranger withdrew the sword from the boy's forehead, and the boy felt immensely relieved. But he still couldn't flee.

"Be careful with your prognostications," said the stranger. "When something is written, there is no way to change it."

"All I saw was an army," said the boy. "I didn't see the outcome of the battle."

The stranger seemed satisfied with the answer. But he kept the sword in his hand. "What is a stranger doing in a strange land?"

"I am following my Personal Legend. It's not something you would understand."

The stranger placed his sword in its scabbard, and the boy relaxed.

"I had to test your courage," the stranger said. "Courage is the quality most essential to understanding the Language of the World."

The boy was surprised. The stranger was speaking of things that very few people knew about.

"You must not let up, even after having come so far," he continued. "You must love the desert, but never trust it completely. Because the desert tests all men: it challenges every step, and kills those who become distracted."

What he said reminded the boy of the old king.

"If the warriors come here, and your head is still on your shoulders at sunset, come and find me," said the stranger.

The same hand that had brandished the sword now held a whip. The horse reared again, raising a cloud of dust.

"Where do you live?" shouted the boy, as the horseman rode away.

The hand with the whip pointed to the south.

The boy had met the alchemist.

NEXT MORNING, THERE WERE TWO THOUSAND ARMED MEN scattered throughout the palm trees at Al-Fayoum. Before the sun had reached its high point, five hundred tribesmen appeared on the horizon. The mounted troops entered the oasis from the north; it appeared to be a peaceful expedition, but they all carried arms hidden in their robes. When they reached the white tent at the center of Al-Fayoum, they withdrew their scimitars and rifles. And they attacked an empty tent.

The men of the oasis surrounded the horsemen from the desert and within half an hour all but one of the intruders were dead. The children had been kept at the other side of a grove of palm trees, and saw nothing of what had happened. The women had remained in their tents, praying for the safekeeping of their husbands, and saw nothing of the battle, either. Were it not for the bodies there on the ground, it would have appeared to be a normal day at the oasis.

The only tribesman spared was the commander of the battalion. That afternoon, he was brought before the tribal chieftains, who asked him why he had violated the Tradition. The commander said that his men had been starving and thirsty, exhausted from many days of battle, and had decided to take the oasis so as to be able to return to the war.

The tribal chieftain said that he felt sorry for the tribesmen, but that the Tradition was sacred. He condemned the commander to death without honor. Rather than being killed by a blade or a bullet, he was hanged from a dead palm tree, where his body twisted in the desert wind.

The tribal chieftain called for the boy, and presented him with fifty pieces of gold. He repeated his story about Joseph of Egypt, and asked the boy to become the counselor of the oasis.

When the sun had set, and the first stars made their appearance, the boy started to walk to the south. He eventually sighted a single tent, and a group of Arabs passing by told the boy that it was a place inhabited by genies. But the boy sat down and waited.

Not until the moon was high did the alchemist ride into view. He carried two dead hawks over his shoulder.

"I am here," the boy said.

"You shouldn't be here," the alchemist answered. "Or is it your Personal Legend that brings you here?"

"With the wars between the tribes, it's impossible to cross the desert. So I have come here."

The alchemist dismounted from his horse, and signaled that the boy should enter the tent with him. It was a tent like many at the oasis. The boy looked around for the ovens and other apparatus used in alchemy, but saw none. There were only some books in a pile, a small cooking stove, and the carpets, covered with mysterious designs.

"Sit down. We'll have something to drink and eat these hawks," said the alchemist.

The boy suspected that they were the same hawks he had seen on the day before, but he said nothing. The alchemist lighted the fire, and soon a delicious aroma filled the tent. It was better than the scent of the hookahs.

"Why did you want to see me?" the boy asked.

"Because of the omens," the alchemist answered. "The wind told me you would be coming, and that you would need help."

"It's not I the wind spoke about. It's the other foreigner, the Englishman. He's the one that's looking for you."

"He has other things to do first. But he's on the right track. He has begun to try to understand the desert."

"And what about me?"

"When a person really desires something, all the universe conspires to help that person to realize his dream," said the alchemist, echoing the words of the old king. The boy understood. Another person was there to help him toward his Personal Legend.

"So you are going to instruct me?"

"No. You already know all you need to know. I am only going to point you in the direction of your treasure."

"But there's a tribal war," the boy reiterated.

"I know what's happening in the desert."

"I have already found my treasure. I have a camel, I have

my money from the crystal shop, and I have fifty gold pieces. In my own country, I would be a rich man."

"But none of that is from the Pyramids," said the alchemist.

"I also have Fatima. She is a treasure greater than anything else I have won."

"She wasn't found at the Pyramids, either."

They ate in silence. The alchemist opened a bottle and poured a red liquid into the boy's cup. It was the most delicious wine he had ever tasted.

"Isn't wine prohibited here?" the boy asked

"It's not what enters men's mouths that's evil," said the alchemist. "It's what comes out of their mouths that is."

The alchemist was a bit daunting, but, as the boy drank the wine, he relaxed. After they finished eating they sat outside the tent, under a moon so brilliant that it made the stars pale.

"Drink and enjoy yourself," said the alchemist, noticing that the boy was feeling happier. "Rest well tonight, as if you were a warrior preparing for combat. Remember that wherever your heart is, there you will find your treasure. You've got to find the treasure, so that everything you have learned along the way can make sense.

"Tomorrow, sell your camel and buy a horse. Camels are traitorous: they walk thousands of paces and never seem to tire. Then suddenly, they kneel and die. But horses tire bit by bit. You always know how much you can ask of them, and when it is that they are about to die."

The following night, the boy appeared at the alchemist's tent with a horse. The alchemist was ready, and he mounted his own steed and placed the falcon on his left shoulder. He said to the boy, "Show me where there is life out in the desert. Only those who can see such signs of life are able to find treasure."

They began to ride out over the sands, with the moon lighting their way. I don't know if I'll be able to find life in the desert, the boy thought. I don't know the desert that well yet.

He wanted to say so to the alchemist, but he was afraid of the man. They reached the rocky place where the boy had seen the hawks in the sky, but now there was only silence and the wind.

"I don't know how to find life in the desert," the boy said. "I know that there is life here, but I don't know where to look."

"Life attracts life," the alchemist answered.

And then the boy understood. He loosened the reins on his horse, who galloped forward over the rocks and sand. The alchemist followed as the boy's horse ran for almost half an hour. They could no longer see the palms of the oasis—only the gigantic moon above them, and its silver reflections from the stones of the desert. Suddenly, for no apparent reason, the boy's horse began to slow.

"There's life here," the boy said to the alchemist. "I don't know the language of the desert, but my horse knows the language of life."

They dismounted, and the alchemist said nothing. Advancing slowly, they searched among the stones. The alchemist stopped abruptly, and bent to the ground. There was a hole there among the stones. The alchemist put his hand into the hole, and then his entire arm, up to his shoulder. Something was moving there, and the alchemist's eyes—the boy could see only his eyes—squinted with his effort. His arm seemed to be battling with whatever was in the hole. Then, with a motion that startled the boy, he withdrew his arm and leaped to his feet. In his hand, he grasped a snake by the tail.

The boy leapt as well, but away from the alchemist. The snake fought frantically, making hissing sounds that shattered the silence of the desert. It was a cobra, whose venom could kill a person in minutes.

"Watch out for his venom," the boy said. But even though the alchemist had put his hand in the hole, and had surely already been bitten, his expression was calm. "The alchemist is two hundred years old," the Englishman had told him. He must know how to deal with the snakes of the desert.

The boy watched as his companion went to his horse and

withdrew a scimitar. With its blade, he drew a circle in the sand, and then he placed the snake within it. The serpent relaxed immediately.

"Not to worry," said the alchemist. "He won't leave the circle. You found life in the desert, the omen that I needed."

"Why was that so important?"

"Because the Pyramids are surrounded by the desert."

The boy didn't want to talk about the Pyramids. His heart was heavy, and he had been melancholy since the previous night. To continue his search for the treasure meant that he had to abandon Fatima.

"I'm going to guide you across the desert," the alchemist said.

"I want to stay at the oasis," the boy answered. "I've found Fatima, and, as far as I'm concerned, she's worth more than treasure."

"Fatima is a woman of the desert," said the alchemist. "She knows that men have to go away in order to return. And she already has her treasure: it's you. Now she expects that you will find what it is you're looking for."

"Well, what if I decide to stay?"

"Let me tell you what will happen. You'll be the counselor of the oasis. You have enough gold to buy many sheep and many camels. You'll marry Fatima, and you'll both be happy for a year. You'll learn to love the desert, and you'll get to know every one of the fifty thousand palms. You'll watch them as they grow, demonstrating how the world is always changing. And you'll get better and better at understanding omens, because the desert is the best teacher there is.

"Sometime during the second year, you'll remember about the treasure. The omens will begin insistently to speak of it, and you'll try to ignore them. You'll use your knowledge for the welfare of the oasis and its inhabitants. The tribal chieftains will appreciate what you do. And your camels will bring you wealth and power.

"During the third year, the omens will continue to speak of your treasure and your Personal Legend. You'll walk around, night after night, at the oasis, and Fatima will be unhappy because she'll feel it was she who interrupted your quest. But you will love her, and she'll return your love. You'll remember that she never asked you to stay, because a woman of the desert knows that she must await her man. So you won't blame her. But many times you'll walk the sands of the desert, thinking that maybe you could have left . . . that you could have trusted more in your love for Fatima. Because what kept you at the oasis was your own fear that you might never come back. At that point, the omens will tell you that your treasure is buried forever.

"Then, sometime during the fourth year, the omens will abandon you, because you've stopped listening to them. The tribal chieftains will see that, and you'll be dismissed from your position as counselor. But, by then, you'll be a rich merchant, with many camels and a great deal of merchandise. You'll spend the rest of your days knowing that you didn't pursue your Personal Legend, and that now it's too late.

"You must understand that love never keeps a man from pursuing his Personal Legend. If he abandons that pursuit, it's because it wasn't true love . . . the love that speaks the Language of the World."

The alchemist erased the circle in the sand, and the snake slithered away among the rocks. The boy remembered the crystal merchant who had always wanted to go to Mecca, and the Englishman in search of the alchemist. He thought of the woman who had trusted in the desert. And he looked out over the desert that had brought him to the woman he loved.

They mounted their horses, and this time it was the boy who followed the alchemist back to the oasis. The wind brought the sounds of the oasis to them, and the boy tried to hear Fatima's voice.

But that night, as he had watched the cobra within the circle, the strange horseman with the falcon on his shoulder had spoken of love and treasure, of the women of the desert and of his Personal Legend.

"I'm going with you," the boy said. And he immediately felt peace in his heart.

"We'll leave tomorrow before sunrise," was the alchemist's only response.

THE BOY SPENT A SLEEPLESS NIGHT. TWO HOURS BEFORE dawn, he awoke one of the boys who slept in his tent, and asked him to show him where Fatima lived. They went to her tent, and the boy gave his friend enough gold to buy a sheep.

Then he asked his friend to go to into the tent where Fatima was sleeping, and to awaken her and tell her that he was waiting outside. The young Arab did as he was asked, and was given enough gold to buy yet another sheep.

"Now leave us alone," said the boy to the young Arab. The Arab returned to his tent to sleep, proud to have helped the counselor of the oasis, and happy at having enough money to buy himself some sheep.

Fatima appeared at the entrance to the tent. The two walked out among the palms. The boy knew that it was a violation of the Tradition, but that didn't matter to him now.

"I'm going away," he said. "And I want you to know that I'm coming back. I love you because . . ."

"Don't say anything," Fatima interrupted. "One is loved because one is loved. No reason is needed for loving."

But the boy continued, "I had a dream, and I met with a king. I sold crystal and crossed the desert. And, because the tribes declared war, I went to the well, seeking the alchemist. So, I love you because the entire universe conspired to help me find you."

The two embraced. It was the first time either had touched the other.

"I'll be back," the boy said.

"Before this, I always looked to the desert with longing," said Fatima. "Now it will be with hope. My father went away one day, but he returned to my mother, and he has always come back since then."

They said nothing else. They walked a bit farther among the palms, and then the boy left her at the entrance to her tent.

"I'll return, just as your father came back to your mother," he said.

He saw that Fatima's eyes were filled with tears.

"You're crying?"

"I'm a woman of the desert," she said, averting her face. "But above all, I'm a woman."

Fatima went back to her tent, and, when daylight came, she went out to do the chores she had done for years. But everything had changed. The boy was no longer at the oasis, and the oasis would never again have the same meaning it had had only yesterday. It would no longer be a place with fifty thousand palm trees and three hundred wells, where the pilgrims arrived, relieved at the end of their long journeys. From that day on, the oasis would be an empty place for her.

From that day on, it was the desert that would be important. She would look to it every day, and would try to guess which star the boy was following in search of his treasure. She would have to send her kisses on the wind, hoping that the wind would touch the boy's face, and would tell him that she was alive. That she was waiting for him, a woman awaiting a courageous man in search of his treasure. From that day on, the desert would represent only one thing to her: the hope for his return.

"DON'T THINK ABOUT WHAT YOU'VE LEFT BEHIND," the alchemist said to the boy as they began to ride across the sands of the desert. "Everything is written in the Soul of the World, and there it will stay forever."

"Men dream more about coming home than about leaving," the boy said. He was already reaccustomed to the desert's silence.

"If what one finds is made of pure matter, it will never spoil. And one can always come back. If what you had found was only a moment of light, like the explosion of a star, you would find nothing on your return."

The man was speaking the language of alchemy. But the boy knew that he was referring to Fatima.

It was difficult not to think about what he had left behind. The desert, with its endless monotony, put him to dreaming. The boy could still see the palm trees, the wells, and the face of the woman he loved. He could see the Englishman at his experiments, and the camel driver who was a teacher without realizing it. Maybe the alchemist has never been in love, the boy thought.

The alchemist rode in front, with the falcon on his shoulder. The bird knew the language of the desert well, and whenever they stopped, he flew off in search of game. On the first day he returned with a rabbit, and on the second with two birds.

At night, they spread their sleeping gear and kept their fires hidden. The desert nights were cold, and were becoming darker and darker as the phases of the moon passed. They went on for a week, speaking only of the precautions they needed to follow in order to avoid the battles between the tribes. The war continued, and at times the wind carried the sweet, sickly smell of blood. Battles had been fought nearby, and the wind reminded the boy that there was the language of omens, always ready to show him what his eyes had failed to observe.

On the seventh day, the alchemist decided to make camp earlier than usual. The falcon flew off to find game, and the alchemist offered his water container to the boy.

"You are almost at the end of your journey," said the alchemist. "I congratulate you for having pursued your Personal Legend."

"And you've told me nothing along the way," said the boy. "I thought you were going to teach me some of the things you know. A while ago, I rode through the desert with a man who had books on alchemy. But I wasn't able to learn anything from them."

"There is only one way to learn," the alchemist answered. "It's through action. Everything you need to know you have learned through your journey. You need to learn only one thing more."

The boy wanted to know what that was, but the alchemist was searching the horizon, looking for the falcon.

"Why are you called the alchemist?"

"Because that's what I am."

"And what went wrong when other alchemists tried to make gold and were unable to do so?"

"They were looking only for gold," his companion answered. "They were seeking the treasure of their Personal Legend, without wanting actually to live out the Personal Legend."

"What is it that I still need to know?" the boy asked.

But the alchemist continued to look to the horizon. And finally the falcon returned with their meal. They dug a hole and lit their fire in it, so that the light of the flames would not be seen.

"I'm an alchemist simply because I'm an alchemist," he said, as he prepared the meal. "I learned the science from my grandfather, who learned from his father, and so on, back to the creation of the world. In those times, the Master Work could be written simply on an emerald. But men began to reject simple things, and to write tracts, interpretations, and philosophical studies. They also began to feel that they knew a better way than others had. Yet the Emerald Tablet is still alive today."

"What was written on the Emerald Tablet?" the boy wanted to know.

The alchemist began to draw in the sand, and completed his drawing in less than five minutes. As he drew, the boy thought of the old king, and the plaza where they had met that day; it seemed as if it had taken place years and years ago.

"This is what was written on the Emerald Tablet," said the alchemist, when he had finished.

The boy tried to read what was written in the sand.

"It's a code," said the boy, a bit disappointed. "It looks like what I saw in the Englishman's books."

"No," the alchemist answered. "It's like the flight of those two hawks; it can't be understood by reason alone. The Emerald Tablet is a direct passage to the Soul of the World.

"The wise men understood that this natural world is only an image and a copy of paradise. The existence of this world is simply a guarantee that there exists a world that is perfect. God created the world so that, through its visible objects, men could understand his spiritual teachings and the marvels of his wisdom. That's what I mean by action."

"Should I understand the Emerald Tablet?" the boy asked.

"Perhaps, if you were in a laboratory of alchemy, this would be the right time to study the best way to understand the Emerald Tablet. But you are in the desert. So immerse yourself in it. The desert will give you an understanding of the world; in fact, anything on the face of the earth will do that. You don't even have to understand the desert: all you have to do is contemplate a simple grain of sand, and you will see in it all the marvels of creation."

"How do I immerse myself in the desert?"

"Listen to your heart. It knows all things, because it came from the Soul of the World, and it will one day return there."

THEY CROSSED THE DESERT FOR ANOTHER TWO DAYS IN silence. The alchemist had become much more cautious, because they were approaching the area where the most violent battles were being waged. As they moved along, the boy tried to listen to his heart.

It was not easy to do; in earlier times, his heart had always been ready to tell its story, but lately that wasn't true. There had been times when his heart spent hours telling of its sadness, and at other times it became so emotional over the desert sunrise that the boy had to hide his tears. His heart beat fastest when it spoke to the boy of treasure, and more slowly when the boy stared entranced at the endless horizons of the desert. But his heart was never quiet, even when the boy and the alchemist had fallen into silence.

"Why do we have to listen to our hearts?" the boy asked, when they had made camp that day.

"Because, wherever your heart is, that is where you'll find your treasure."

"But my heart is agitated," the boy said. "It has its dreams, it gets emotional, and it's become passionate over a woman of the desert. It asks things of me, and it keeps me from sleeping many nights, when I'm thinking about her."

"Well, that's good. Your heart is alive. Keep listening to what it has to say."

During the next three days, the two travelers passed by a number of armed tribesmen, and saw others on the horizon. The boy's heart began to speak of fear. It told him stories it had heard from the Soul of the World, stories of men who sought to find their treasure and never succeeded. Sometimes it frightened the boy with the idea that he might not find his treasure, or that he might die there in the desert. At other times, it told the boy that it was satisfied: it had found love and riches.

"My heart is a traitor," the boy said to the alchemist, when they had paused to rest the horses. "It doesn't want me to go on."

"That makes sense," the alchemist answered. "Naturally it's afraid that, in pursuing your dream, you might lose everything you've won."

"Well, then, why should I listen to my heart?"

"Because you will never again be able to keep it quiet. Even if you pretend not to have heard what it tells you, it will always be there inside you, repeating to you what you're thinking about life and about the world."

"You mean I should listen, even if it's treasonous?"

"Treason is a blow that comes unexpectedly. If you know your heart well, it will never be able to do that to you. Because you'll know its dreams and wishes, and will know how to deal with them.

"You will never be able to escape from your heart. So it's better to listen to what it has to say. That way, you'll never have to fear an unanticipated blow."

The boy continued to listen to his heart as they crossed the desert. He came to understand its dodges and tricks, and to accept it as it was. He lost his fear, and forgot about his need to go back to the oasis, because, one afternoon, his heart told him that it was happy. "Even though I complain sometimes," it said, "it's because I'm the heart of a person, and people's hearts are that way. People are afraid to pursue their most important dreams, because they feel that they don't deserve them, or that they'll be unable to achieve them. We, their hearts, become fearful just thinking of loved ones who go away forever, or of moments that could have been good but weren't, or of treasures that might have been found but were forever hidden in the sands. Because, when these things happen, we suffer terribly."

"My heart is afraid that it will have to suffer," the boy told the alchemist one night as they looked up at the moonless sky.

"Tell your heart that the fear of suffering is worse than the suffering itself. And that no heart has ever suffered when it goes in search of its dreams, because every second of the search is a second's encounter with God and with eternity."

"Every second of the search is an encounter with God," the boy told his heart. "When I have been truly searching for my treasure, every day has been luminous, because I've known that every hour was a part of the dream that I would find it. When I have been truly searching for my treasure, I've discovered things along the way that I never would have seen had I not had the courage to try things that seemed impossible for a shepherd to achieve."

So his heart was quiet for an entire afternoon. That night, the boy slept deeply, and, when he awoke, his heart began to tell him things that came from the Soul of the World. It said that all people who are happy have God within them. And that happiness could be found in a grain of sand from the desert, as the alchemist had said. Because a grain of sand is a moment of creation, and the universe has taken millions of years to create it. "Everyone on earth has a treasure that awaits him," his heart said. "We, people's hearts, seldom say much about those treasures, because people no longer want to go in search of them. We speak of them only to children. Later, we simply let life proceed, in its own direction, toward its own fate. But, unfortunately, very few follow the path laid out for them—the path to their Personal Legends, and to happiness. Most people see the world as a threatening place, and, because they do, the world turns out, indeed, to be a threatening place.

"So, we, their hearts, speak more and more softly. We never stop speaking out, but we begin to hope that our words won't be heard: we don't want people to suffer because they don't follow their hearts."

"Why don't people's hearts tell them to continue to follow their dreams?" the boy asked the alchemist.

"Because that's what makes a heart suffer most, and hearts don't like to suffer."

From then on, the boy understood his heart. He asked it, please, never to stop speaking to him. He asked that, when he wandered far from his dreams, his heart press him and sound the alarm. The boy swore that, every time he heard the alarm, he would heed its message.

That night, he told all of this to the alchemist. And the alchemist understood that the boy's heart had returned to the Soul of the World.

"So what should I do now?" the boy asked.

"Continue in the direction of the Pyramids," said the alchemist. "And continue to pay heed to the omens. Your heart is still capable of showing you where the treasure is."

"Is that the one thing I still needed to know?"

"No," the alchemist answered. "What you still need to know is this: before a dream is realized, the Soul of the World tests everything that was learned along the way. It does this not because it is evil, but so that we can, in addition to realizing our dreams, master the lessons we've learned as we've moved toward that dream. That's the point at which most people give up. It's the point at which, as we say in the language of the desert, one 'dies of thirst just when the palm trees have appeared on the horizon.'

"Every search begins with beginner's luck. And every search ends with the victor's being severely tested."

The boy remembered an old proverb from his country. It said that the darkest hour of the night came just before the dawn.

On the following day, the first clear sign of danger appeared. Three armed tribesmen approached, and asked what the boy and the alchemist were doing there.

"I'm hunting with my falcon," the alchemist answered.

"We're going to have to search you to see whether you're armed," one of the tribesmen said.

The alchemist dismounted slowly, and the boy did the same.

"Why are you carrying money?" asked the tribesman, when he had searched the boy's bag.

"I need it to get to the Pyramids," he said.

The tribesman who was searching the alchemist's belongings found a small crystal flask filled with a liquid, and a yellow glass egg that was slightly larger than a chicken's egg.

"What are these things?" he asked.

"That's the Philosopher's Stone and the Elixir of Life. It's the Master Work of the alchemists. Whoever swallows that elixir will never be sick again, and a fragment from that stone turns any metal into gold."

The Arabs laughed at him, and the alchemist laughed along. They thought his answer was amusing, and they allowed the boy and the alchemist to proceed with all of their belongings.

"Are you crazy?" the boy asked the alchemist, when they had moved on. "What did you do that for?"

"To show you one of life's simple lessons," the alchemist answered. "When you possess great treasures within you, and try to tell others of them, seldom are you believed."

They continued across the desert. With every day that passed, the boy's heart became more and more silent. It no longer wanted to know about things of the past or future; it was content simply to contemplate the desert, and to drink with the boy from the Soul of the World. The boy and his heart had become friends, and neither was capable now of betraying the other.

When his heart spoke to him, it was to provide a stimulus to the boy, and to give him strength, because the days of silence there in the desert were wearisome. His heart told the boy what his strongest qualities were: his courage in having given up his sheep and in trying to live out his Personal Legend, and his enthusiasm during the time he had worked at the crystal shop.

And his heart told him something else that the boy had never noticed: it told the boy of dangers that had threatened him, but that he had never perceived. His heart said that one time it had hidden the rifle the boy had taken from his father, because of the possibility that the boy might wound himself. And it reminded the boy of the day when he had been ill and vomiting out in the fields, after which he had fallen into a deep sleep. There had been two thieves farther ahead who were planning to steal the boy's sheep and murder him. But, since the boy hadn't passed by, they had decided to move on, thinking that he had changed his route.

"Does a man's heart always help him?" the boy asked the alchemist.

"Mostly just the hearts of those who are trying to realize their Personal Legends. But they do help children, drunkards, and the elderly, too."

"Does that mean that I'll never run into danger?"

"It means only that the heart does what it can," the alchemist said.

One afternoon, they passed by the encampment of one of the tribes. At each corner of the camp were Arabs garbed in beautiful white robes, with arms at the ready. The men were smoking their hookahs and trading stories from the battlefield. No one paid any attention to the two travelers.

"There's no danger," the boy said, when they had moved on past the encampment.

The alchemist sounded angry: "Trust in your heart, but never forget that you're in the desert. When men are at war with one another, the Soul of the World can hear the screams of battle. No one fails to suffer the consequences of everything under the sun."

All things are one, the boy thought. And then, as if the desert wanted to demonstrate that the alchemist was right, two horsemen appeared from behind the travelers.

"You can't go any farther," one of them said. "You're in the area where the tribes are at war."

"I'm not going very far," the alchemist answered, looking straight into the eyes of the horsemen. They were silent for a moment, and then agreed that the boy and the alchemist could move along.

The boy watched the exchange with fascination. "You dominated those horsemen with the way you looked at them," he said.

"Your eyes show the strength of your soul," answered the alchemist.

That's true, the boy thought. He had noticed that, in the midst of the multitude of armed men back at the encampment, there had been one who stared fixedly at the two. He had been so far away that his face wasn't even visible. But the boy was certain that he had been looking at them.

Finally, when they had crossed the mountain range that

extended along the entire horizon, the alchemist said that they were only two days from the Pyramids.

"If we're going to go our separate ways soon," the boy said, "then teach me about alchemy."

"You already know about alchemy. It is about penetrating to the Soul of the World, and discovering the treasure that has been reserved for you."

"No, that's not what I mean. I'm talking about transforming lead into gold."

The alchemist fell as silent as the desert, and answered the boy only after they had stopped to eat.

"Everything in the universe evolved," he said. "And, for wise men, gold is the metal that evolved the furthest. Don't ask me why; I don't know why. I just know that the Tradition is always right.

"Men have never understood the words of the wise. So gold, instead of being seen as a symbol of evolution, became the basis for conflict."

"There are many languages spoken by things," the boy said. "There was a time when, for me, a camel's whinnying was nothing more than whinnying. Then it became a signal of danger. And, finally, it became just a whinny again."

But then he stopped. The alchemist probably already knew all that.

"I have known true alchemists," the alchemist continued.

"They locked themselves in their laboratories, and tried to evolve, as gold had. And they found the Philosopher's Stone, because they understood that when something evolves, everything around that thing evolves as well.

"Others stumbled upon the stone by accident. They already had the gift, and their souls were readier for such things than the souls of others. But they don't count. They're quite rare.

"And then there were the others, who were interested only in gold. They never found the secret. They forgot that lead, copper, and iron have their own Personal Legends to fulfill. And anyone who interferes with the Personal Legend of another thing never will discover his own."

The alchemist's words echoed out like a curse. He reached over and picked up a shell from the ground.

"This desert was once a sea," he said.

"I noticed that," the boy answered.

The alchemist told the boy to place the shell over his ear. He had done that many times when he was a child, and had heard the sound of the sea.

"The sea has lived on in this shell, because that's its Personal Legend. And it will never cease doing so until the desert is once again covered by water."

They mounted their horses, and rode out in the direction of the Pyramids of Egypt.

THE SUN WAS SETTING WHEN THE BOY'S HEART SOUNDED a danger signal. They were surrounded by gigantic dunes, and the boy looked at the alchemist to see whether he had sensed anything. But he appeared to be unaware of any danger. Five minutes later, the boy saw two horsemen waiting ahead of them. Before he could say anything to the alchemist, the two horsemen had become ten, and then a hundred. And then they were everywhere in the dunes.

They were tribesmen dressed in blue, with black rings surrounding their turbans. Their faces were hidden behind blue veils, with only their eyes showing.

Even from a distance, their eyes conveyed the strength of their souls. And their eyes spoke of death.

THE TWO WERE TAKEN TO A NEARBY MILITARY CAMP. A soldier shoved the boy and the alchemist into a tent where the chief was holding a meeting with his staff.

"These are the spies," said one of the men.

"We're just travelers," the alchemist answered.

"You were seen at the enemy camp three days ago. And you were talking with one of the troops there."

"I'm just a man who wanders the desert and knows the stars," said the alchemist. "I have no information about troops or about the movement of the tribes. I was simply acting as a guide for my friend here."

"Who is your friend?" the chief asked.

"An alchemist," said the alchemist. "He understands the forces of nature. And he wants to show you his extraordinary powers."

The boy listened quietly. And fearfully.

"What is a foreigner doing here?" asked another of the men.

"He has brought money to give to your tribe," said the alchemist, before the boy could say a word. And seizing the boy's bag, the alchemist gave the gold coins to the chief.

The Arab accepted them without a word. There was enough there to buy a lot of weapons.

"What is an alchemist?" he asked, finally.

"It's a man who understands nature and the world. If he wanted to, he could destroy this camp just with the force of the wind."

The men laughed. They were used to the ravages of war, and knew that the wind could not deliver them a fatal blow. Yet each felt his heart beat a bit faster. They were men of the desert, and they were fearful of sorcerers.

"I want to see him do it," said the chief.

"He needs three days," answered the alchemist. "He is going to transform himself into the wind, just to demonstrate his powers. If he can't do so, we humbly offer you our lives, for the honor of your tribe."

"You can't offer me something that is already mine," the chief said, arrogantly. But he granted the travelers three days.

The boy was shaking with fear, but the alchemist helped him out of the tent.

"Don't let them see that you're afraid," the alchemist said. "They are brave men, and they despise cowards."

But the boy couldn't even speak. He was able to do so only after they had walked through the center of the camp. There was no need to imprison them: the Arabs simply confiscated their horses. So, once again, the world had demonstrated its many languages: the desert only moments ago had been endless and free, and now it was an impenetrable wall.

"You gave them everything I had!" the boy said. "Everything I've saved in my entire life!"

"Well, what good would it be to you if you had to die?" the alchemist answered. "Your money saved us for three days. It's not often that money saves a person's life."

But the boy was too frightened to listen to words of wisdom. He had no idea how he was going to transform himself into the wind. He wasn't an alchemist!

The alchemist asked one of the soldiers for some tea, and poured some on the boy's wrists. A wave of relief washed over him, and the alchemist muttered some words that the boy didn't understand.

"Don't give in to your fears," said the alchemist, in a strangely gentle voice. "If you do, you won't be able to talk to your heart."

"But I have no idea how to turn myself into the wind."

"If a person is living out his Personal Legend, he knows everything he needs to know. There is only one thing that makes a dream impossible to achieve: the fear of failure."

"I'm not afraid of failing. It's just that I don't know how to turn myself into the wind."

"Well, you'll have to learn; your life depends on it."

"But what if I can't?"

"Then you'll die in the midst of trying to realize your Personal Legend. That's a lot better than dying like millions of other people, who never even knew what their Personal Legends were.

"But don't worry," the alchemist continued. "Usually the threat of death makes people a lot more aware of their lives."

THE FIRST DAY PASSED. THERE WAS A MAJOR BATTLE NEARBY, and a number of wounded were brought back to the camp. The dead soldiers were replaced by others, and life went on. Death doesn't change anything, the boy thought.

"You could have died later on," a soldier said to the body of one of his companions. "You could have died after peace had been declared. But, in any case, you were going to die."

At the end of the day, the boy went looking for the alchemist, who had taken his falcon out into the desert.

"I still have no idea how to turn myself into the wind," the boy repeated.

"Remember what I told you: the world is only the visible aspect of God. And that what alchemy does is to bring spiritual perfection into contact with the material plane."

"What are you doing?"

"Feeding my falcon."

"If I'm not able to turn myself into the wind, we're going to die," the boy said. "Why feed your falcon?"

"You're the one who may die," the alchemist said. "I already know how to turn myself into the wind."

On the second day, the boy climbed to the top of a cliff near the camp. The sentinels allowed him to go; they had already heard about the sorcerer who could turn himself into the wind, and they didn't want to go near him. In any case, the desert was impassable.

He spent the entire afternoon of the second day looking out over the desert, and listening to his heart. The boy knew the desert sensed his fear.

They both spoke the same language.

On the third day, the chief met with his officers. He called the alchemist to the meeting and said, "Let's go see the boy who turns himself into the wind."

"Let's," the alchemist answered.

The boy took them to the cliff where he had been on the previous day. He told them all to be seated.

"It's going to take a while," the boy said.

"We're in no hurry," the chief answered. "We are men of the desert."

The boy looked out at the horizon. There were mountains in the distance. And there were dunes, rocks, and plants that insisted on living where survival seemed impossible. There was the desert that he had wandered for so many months; despite all that time, he knew only a small part of it. Within that small part, he had found an Englishman, caravans, tribal wars, and an oasis with fifty thousand palm trees and three hundred wells.

"What do you want here today?" the desert asked him. "Didn't you spend enough time looking at me yesterday?"

"Somewhere you are holding the person I love," the boy said. "So, when I look out over your sands, I am also looking at her. I want to return to her, and I need your help so that I can turn myself into the wind."

"What is love?" the desert asked.

"Love is the falcon's flight over your sands. Because for

him, you are a green field, from which he always returns with game. He knows your rocks, your dunes, and your mountains, and you are generous to him."

"The falcon's beak carries bits of me, myself," the desert said. "For years, I care for his game, feeding it with the little water that I have, and then I show him where the game is. And, one day, as I enjoy the fact that his game thrives on my surface, the falcon dives out of the sky, and takes away what I've created."

"But that's why you created the game in the first place," the boy answered. "To nourish the falcon. And the falcon then nourishes man. And, eventually, man will nourish your sands, where the game will once again flourish. That's how the world goes."

"So is that what love is?"

"Yes, that's what love is. It's what makes the game become the falcon, the falcon become man, and man, in his turn, the desert. It's what turns lead into gold, and makes the gold return to the earth."

"I don't understand what you're talking about," the desert said.

"But you can at least understand that somewhere in your sands there is a woman waiting for me. And that's why I have to turn myself into the wind."

The desert didn't answer him for a few moments.

Then it told him, "I'll give you my sands to help the wind

to blow, but, alone, I can't do anything. You have to ask for help from the wind."

A breeze began to blow. The tribesmen watched the boy from a distance, talking among themselves in a language that the boy couldn't understand.

The alchemist smiled.

The wind approached the boy and touched his face. It knew of the boy's talk with the desert, because the winds know everything. They blow across the world without a birthplace, and with no place to die.

"Help me," the boy said. "One day you carried the voice of my loved one to me."

"Who taught you to speak the language of the desert and the wind?"

"My heart," the boy answered.

The wind has many names. In that part of the world, it was called the sirocco, because it brought moisture from the oceans to the east. In the distant land the boy came from, they called it the levanter, because they believed that it brought with it the sands of the desert, and the screams of the Moorish wars. Perhaps, in the places beyond the pastures where his sheep lived, men thought that the wind came from Andalusia. But, actually, the wind came from no place at all, nor did it go to any place; that's why it was stronger than the desert. Someone might one day plant trees in the desert, and even raise sheep there, but never would they harness the wind.

"You can't be the wind," the wind said. "We're two very different things."

"That's not true," the boy said. "I learned the alchemist's secrets in my travels. I have inside me the winds, the deserts, the oceans, the stars, and everything created in the universe. We were all made by the same hand, and we have the same soul. I want to be like you, able to reach every corner of the world, cross the seas, blow away the sands that cover my treasure, and carry the voice of the woman I love."

"I heard what you were talking about the other day with the alchemist," the wind said. "He said that everything has its own Personal Legend. But people can't turn themselves into the wind."

"Just teach me to be the wind for a few moments," the boy said. "So you and I can talk about the limitless possibilities of people and the winds."

The wind's curiosity was aroused, something that had never happened before. It wanted to talk about those things, but it didn't know how to turn a man into the wind. And look how many things the wind already knew how to do! It created deserts, sank ships, felled entire forests, and blew through cities filled with music and strange noises. It felt that it had no limits, yet here was a boy saying that there were other things the wind should be able to do.

"This is what we call love," the boy said, seeing that the wind was close to granting what he requested. "When you are loved, you can do anything in creation. When you are loved, there's no need at all to understand what's happening, because everything happens within you, and even men can turn themselves into the wind. As long as the wind helps, of course."

The wind was a proud being, and it was becoming irritated with what the boy was saying. It commenced to blow harder, raising the desert sands. But finally it had to recognize that, even making its way around the world, it didn't know how to turn a man into the wind. And it knew nothing about love.

"In my travels around the world, I've often seen people speaking of love and looking toward the heavens," the wind said, furious at having to acknowledge its own limitations. "Maybe it's better to ask heaven."

"Well then, help me do that," the boy said. "Fill this place with a sandstorm so strong that it blots out the sun. Then I can look to heaven without blinding myself."

So the wind blew with all its strength, and the sky was filled with sand. The sun was turned into a golden disk.

At the camp, it was difficult to see anything. The men of the desert were already familiar with that wind. They called it the *simum,* and it was worse than a storm at sea. Their horses cried out, and all their weapons were filled with sand.

On the heights, one of the commanders turned to the chief and said, "Maybe we had better end this!"

They could barely see the boy. Their faces were covered with the blue cloths, and their eyes showed fear.

"Let's stop this," another commander said.

"I want to see the greatness of Allah," the chief said, with respect. "I want to see how a man turns himself into the wind."

But he made a mental note of the names of the two men who had expressed their fear. As soon as the wind stopped, he was going to remove them from their commands, because true men of the desert are not afraid.

"The wind told me that you know about love," the boy said to the sun. "If you know about love, you must also know about the Soul of the World, because it's made of love."

"From where I am," the sun said, "I can see the Soul of the World. It communicates with my soul, and together we cause the plants to grow and the sheep to seek out shade. From where I am—and I'm a long way from the earth—I learned how to love. I know that if I came even a little bit closer to the earth, everything there would die, and the Soul of the World would no longer exist. So we contemplate each other, and we want each other, and I give it life and warmth, and it gives me my reason for living."

"So you know about love," the boy said.

"And I know the Soul of the World, because we have talked at great length to each other during this endless trip through the universe. It tells me that its greatest problem is that, up until now, only the minerals and vegetables understand that all things are one. That there's no need for iron to be the same as copper, or copper the same as gold. Each performs its own exact function as a unique being, and everything would be a symphony of peace if the hand that wrote all this had stopped on the fifth day of creation.

"But there was a sixth day," the sun went on.

"You are wise, because you observe everything from a distance," the boy said. "But you don't know about love. If there hadn't been a sixth day, man would not exist; copper would always be just copper, and lead just lead. It's true that everything has its Personal Legend, but one day that Personal Legend will be realized. So each thing has to transform itself into something better, and to acquire a new Personal Legend, until, someday, the Soul of the World becomes one thing only."

The sun thought about that, and decided to shine more brightly. The wind, which was enjoying the conversation, started to blow with greater force, so that the sun would not blind the boy.

"This is why alchemy exists," the boy said. "So that everyone will search for his treasure, find it, and then want to be better than he was in his former life. Lead will play its role until the world has no further need for lead; and then lead will have to turn itself into gold.

"That's what alchemists do. They show that, when we strive to become better than we are, everything around us becomes better, too."

"Well, why did you say that I don't know about love?" the sun asked the boy.

"Because it's not love to be static like the desert, nor is it love to roam the world like the wind. And it's not love to see everything from a distance, like you do. Love is the force that transforms and improves the Soul of the World. When I first reached through to it, I thought the Soul of the World was perfect. But later, I could see that it was like other aspects of creation, and had its own passions and wars. It is we who nourish the Soul of the World, and the world we live in will be either better or worse, depending on whether we become better or worse. And that's where the power of love comes in. Because when we love, we always strive to become better than we are."

"So what do you want of me?" the sun asked.

"I want you to help me turn myself into the wind," the boy answered.

"Nature knows me as the wisest being in creation," the sun said. "But I don't know how to turn you into the wind."

"Then, whom should I ask?"

The sun thought for a minute. The wind was listening closely, and wanted to tell every corner of the world that the sun's wisdom had its limitations. That it was unable to deal with this boy who spoke the Language of the World.

"Speak to the hand that wrote all," said the sun.

The wind screamed with delight, and blew harder than ever. The tents were being blown from their ties to the earth, and the animals were being freed from their tethers. On the cliff, the men clutched at each other as they sought to keep from being blown away.

The boy turned to the hand that wrote all. As he did so, he sensed that the universe had fallen silent, and he decided not to speak.

A current of love rushed from his heart, and the boy began to pray. It was a prayer that he had never said before, because it was a prayer without words or pleas. His prayer didn't give thanks for his sheep having found new pastures; it didn't ask that the boy be able to sell more crystal; and it didn't beseech that the woman he had met continue to await his return. In the silence, the boy understood that the desert, the wind, and the sun were also trying to understand the signs written by the hand, and were seeking to follow their paths, and to understand what had been written on a single emerald. He saw that omens were scattered throughout the earth and in space, and that there was no reason or significance attached to their appearance; he could see that not the deserts, nor the winds, nor the sun, nor people knew why they had been created. But that the hand had a reason for all of this, and that only the hand could perform miracles, or transform the sea into a desert . . . or a man into the wind. Because only the hand understood that it was a larger design that had moved the universe to the point at which six days of creation had evolved into a Master Work.

The boy reached through to the Soul of the World, and saw that it was a part of the Soul of God. And he saw that the Soul of God was his own soul. And that he, a boy, could perform miracles.

THE *SIMUM* BLEW THAT DAY AS IT HAD NEVER BLOWN before. For generations thereafter, the Arabs recounted the legend of a boy who had turned himself into the wind, almost destroying a military camp, in defiance of the most powerful chief in the desert.

When the *simum* ceased to blow, everyone looked to the place where the boy had been. But he was no longer there; he was standing next to a sand-covered sentinel, on the far side of the camp.

The men were terrified at his sorcery. But there were two people who were smiling: the alchemist, because he had found his perfect disciple, and the chief, because that disciple had understood the glory of God.

The following day, the general bade the boy and the alchemist farewell, and provided them with an escort party to accompany them as far as they chose.

✱

THEY RODE FOR THE ENTIRE DAY. TOWARD THE END OF the afternoon, they came upon a Coptic monastery. The alchemist dismounted, and told the escorts they could return to the camp.

"From here on, you will be alone," the alchemist said. "You are only three hours from the Pyramids."

"Thank you," said the boy. "You taught me the Language of the World."

"I only invoked what you already knew."

The alchemist knocked on the gate of the monastery. A monk dressed in black came to the gates. They spoke for a few minutes in the Coptic tongue, and the alchemist bade the boy enter.

"I asked him to let me use the kitchen for a while," the alchemist smiled.

They went to the kitchen at the back of the monastery. The alchemist lighted the fire, and the monk brought him some lead, which the alchemist placed in an iron pan. When the lead had become liquid, the alchemist took from his pouch the strange yellow egg. He scraped from it a sliver as thin as a hair, wrapped it in wax, and added it to the pan in which the lead had melted.

The mixture took on a reddish color, almost the color of blood. The alchemist removed the pan from the fire, and set it aside to cool. As he did so, he talked with the monk about the tribal wars.

"I think they're going to last for a long time," he said to the monk.

The monk was irritated. The caravans had been stopped at Giza for some time, waiting for the wars to end. "But God's will be done," the monk said.

"Exactly," answered the alchemist.

When the pan had cooled, the monk and the boy looked at it, dazzled. The lead had dried into the shape of the pan, but it was no longer lead. It was gold.

"Will I learn to do that someday?" the boy asked.

"This was my Personal Legend, not yours," the alchemist answered. "But I wanted to show you that it was possible."

They returned to the gates of the monastery. There, the alchemist separated the disk into four parts.

"This is for you," he said, holding one of the parts out to the monk. "It's for your generosity to the pilgrims."

"But this payment goes well beyond my generosity," the monk responded.

"Don't say that again. Life might be listening, and give you less the next time."

The alchemist turned to the boy. "This is for you. To make up for what you gave to the general."

The boy was about to say that it was much more than he had given the general. But he kept quiet, because he had heard what the alchemist said to the monk.

"And this is for me," said the alchemist, keeping one of

the parts. "Because I have to return to the desert, where there are tribal wars."

He took the fourth part and handed it to the monk.

"This is for the boy. If he ever needs it."

"But I'm going in search of my treasure," the boy said. "I'm very close to it now."

"And I'm certain you'll find it," the alchemist said.

"Then why this?"

"Because you have already lost your savings twice. Once to the thief, and once to the general. I'm an old, superstitious Arab, and I believe in our proverbs. There's one that says, 'Everything that happens once can never happen again. But everything that happens twice will surely happen a third time.'" They mounted their horses.

"I WANT TO TELL YOU A STORY ABOUT DREAMS," SAID THE alchemist.

The boy brought his horse closer.

"In ancient Rome, at the time of Emperor Tiberius, there lived a good man who had two sons. One was in the military, and had been sent to the most distant regions of the empire. The other son was a poet, and delighted all of Rome with his beautiful verses.

"One night, the father had a dream. An angel appeared to him, and told him that the words of one of his sons would be learned and repeated throughout the world for all generations to come. The father woke from his dream grateful and crying, because life was generous, and had revealed to him something any father would be proud to know.

"Shortly thereafter, the father died as he tried to save a child who was about to be crushed by the wheels of a chariot. Since he had lived his entire life in a manner that was correct and fair, he went directly to heaven, where he met the angel that had appeared in his dream.

"'You were always a good man,' the angel said to him. 'You lived your life in a loving way, and died with dignity. I can now grant you any wish you desire.'

"'Life was good to me,' the man said. 'When you appeared in my dream, I felt that all my efforts had been rewarded, because my son's poems will be read by men for generations to come. I don't want anything for myself. But any father would be proud of the fame achieved by one whom he had cared for as a child, and educated as he grew up. Sometime in the distant future, I would like to see my son's words.'

"The angel touched the man's shoulder, and they were both projected far into the future. They were in an immense setting, surrounded by thousands of people speaking a strange language.

"The man wept with happiness.

"'I knew that my son's poems were immortal,' he said to

the angel through his tears. 'Can you please tell me which of my son's poems these people are repeating?'

"The angel came closer to the man, and, with tenderness, led him to a bench nearby, where they sat down.

"'The verses of your son who was the poet were very popular in Rome,' the angel said. 'Everyone loved them and enjoyed them. But when the reign of Tiberius ended, his poems were forgotten. The words you're hearing now are those of your son in the military.'

"The man looked at the angel in surprise.

"'Your son went to serve at a distant place, and became a centurion. He was just and good. One afternoon, one of his servants fell ill, and it appeared that he would die. Your son had heard of a rabbi who was able to cure illnesses, and he rode out for days and days in search of this man. Along the way, he learned that the man he was seeking was the Son of God. He met others who had been cured by him, and they instructed your son in the man's teachings. And so, despite the fact that he was a Roman centurion, he converted to their faith. Shortly thereafter, he reached the place where the man he was looking for was visiting.'

"'He told the man that one of his servants was gravely ill, and the rabbi made ready to go to his house with him. But the centurion was a man of faith, and, looking into the eyes of the rabbi, he knew that he was surely in the presence of the Son of God.'

"'And this is what your son said,' the angel told the man. 'These are the words he said to the rabbi at that point, and they have never been forgotten: "My Lord, I am not worthy that you should come under my roof. But only speak a word and my servant will be healed."'"

The alchemist said, "No matter what he does, every person on earth plays a central role in the history of the world. And normally he doesn't know it."

The boy smiled. He had never imagined that questions about life would be of such importance to a shepherd.

"Good-bye," the alchemist said.

"Good-bye," said the boy.

The boy rode along through the desert for several hours, listening avidly to what his heart had to say. It was his heart that would tell him where his treasure was hidden.

"Where your treasure is, there also will be your heart," the alchemist had told him.

But his heart was speaking of other things. With pride, it told the story of a shepherd who had left his flock to follow a dream he had on two different occasions. It told of Personal Legend, and of the many men who had wandered in search of distant lands or beautiful women, confronting the people of their times with their preconceived notions. It spoke of journeys, discoveries, books, and change.

As he was about to climb yet another dune, his heart whispered, "Be aware of the place where you are brought to tears. That's where I am, and that's where your treasure is."

The boy climbed the dune slowly. A full moon rose again in the starry sky: it had been a month since he had set forth from the oasis. The moonlight cast shadows through the dunes, creating the appearance of a rolling sea; it reminded the boy of the day when that horse had reared in the desert, and he had come to know the alchemist. And the moon fell on the desert's silence, and on a man's journey in search of treasure.

When he reached the top of the dune, his heart leapt. There, illuminated by the light of the moon and the brightness of the desert, stood the solemn and majestic Pyramids of Egypt.

The boy fell to his knees and wept. He thanked God for making him believe in his Personal Legend, and for leading him to meet a king, a merchant, an Englishman, and an alchemist. And above all for his having met a woman of the desert who had told him that love would never keep a man from his Personal Legend.

If he wanted to, he could now return to the oasis, go back to Fatima, and live his life as a simple shepherd. After all, the alchemist continued to live in the desert, even though he understood the Language of the World, and knew how to transform lead into gold. He didn't need to demonstrate his science and art to anyone. The boy told himself that, on the way toward realizing his own Personal Legend, he had learned all he needed to know, and had experienced everything he might have dreamed of.

But here he was, at the point of finding his treasure, and he reminded himself that no project is completed until its objective has been achieved. The boy looked at the sands around him, and saw that, where his tears had fallen, a scarab beetle was scuttling through the sand. During his time in the desert, he had learned that, in Egypt, the scarab beetles are a symbol of God.

Another omen! The boy began to dig into the dune. As he did so, he thought of what the crystal merchant had once said: that anyone could build a pyramid in his backyard. The boy could see now that he couldn't do so if he placed stone upon stone for the rest of his life.

Throughout the night, the boy dug at the place he had chosen, but found nothing. He felt weighted down by the centuries of time since the Pyramids had been built. But he didn't stop. He struggled to continue digging as he fought the wind, which often blew the sand back into the excavation. His hands were abraded and exhausted, but he listened to his heart. It had told him to dig where his tears fell.

As he was attempting to pull out the rocks he encountered, he heard footsteps. Several figures approached him. Their backs were to the moonlight, and the boy could see neither their eyes nor their faces.

"What are you doing here?" one of the figures demanded.

Because he was terrified, the boy didn't answer. He had found where his treasure was, and was frightened at what might happen.

"We're refugees from the tribal wars, and we need money," the other figure said. "What are you hiding there?"

"I'm not hiding anything," the boy answered.

But one of them seized the boy and yanked him back out of the hole. Another, who was searching the boy's bags, found the piece of gold.

"There's gold here," he said.

The moon shone on the face of the Arab who had seized him, and in the man's eyes the boy saw death.

"He's probably got more gold hidden in the ground."

They made the boy continue digging, but he found nothing. As the sun rose, the men began to beat the boy. He was bruised and bleeding, his clothing was torn to shreds, and he felt that death was near.

"What good is money to you if you're going to die? It's not often that money can save someone's life," the alchemist had said. Finally, the boy screamed at the men, "I'm digging for treasure!" And, although his mouth was bleeding and swollen, he told his attackers that he had twice dreamed of a treasure hidden near the Pyramids of Egypt.

The man who appeared to be the leader of the group

spoke to one of the others: "Leave him. He doesn't have anything else. He must have stolen this gold."

The boy fell to the sand, nearly unconscious. The leader shook him and said, "We're leaving."

But before they left, he came back to the boy and said, "You're not going to die. You'll live, and you'll learn that a man shouldn't be so stupid. Two years ago, right here on this spot, I had a recurrent dream, too. I dreamed that I should travel to the fields of Spain and look for a ruined church where shepherds and their sheep slept. In my dream, there was a sycamore growing out of the ruins of the sacristy, and I was told that, if I dug at the roots of the sycamore, I would find a hidden treasure. But I'm not so stupid as to cross an entire desert just because of a recurrent dream."

And they disappeared.

The boy stood up shakily, and looked once more at the Pyramids. They seemed to laugh at him, and he laughed back, his heart bursting with joy.

Because now he knew where his treasure was.

EPILOGUE

THE BOY REACHED THE SMALL, ABANDONED CHURCH JUST as night was falling. The sycamore was still there in the sacristy, and the stars could still be seen through the half-destroyed roof. He remembered the time he had been there with his sheep; it had been a peaceful night . . . except for the dream.

Now he was here not with his flock, but with a shovel.

He sat looking at the sky for a long time. Then he took from his knapsack a bottle of wine, and drank some. He remembered the night in the desert when he had sat with the alchemist, as they looked at the stars and drank wine together. He thought of the many roads he had traveled, and of the strange way God had chosen to show him his treasure. If he hadn't believed in the significance of recurrent dreams, he would not have met the Gypsy woman, the king, the thief, or . . . "Well, it's a long list. But the path was written in the omens, and there was no way I could go wrong," he said to himself.

He fell asleep, and when he awoke the sun was already high. He began to dig at the base of the sycamore.

"You old sorcerer," the boy shouted up to the sky. "You knew the whole story. You even left a bit of gold at the monastery so I could get back to this church. The monk laughed when he saw me come back in tatters. Couldn't you have saved me from that?"

"No," he heard a voice on the wind say. "If I had told you, you wouldn't have seen the Pyramids. They're beautiful, aren't they?"

The boy smiled, and continued digging. Half an hour later, his shovel hit something solid. An hour later, he had before him a chest of Spanish gold coins. There were also precious stones, gold masks adorned with red and white feathers, and stone statues embedded with jewels. The spoils of a conquest that the country had long ago forgotten, and that some conquistador had failed to tell his children about.

The boy took out Urim and Thummim from his bag. He had used the two stones only once, one morning when he was at a marketplace. His life and his path had always provided him with enough omens.

He placed Urim and Thummim in the chest. They were also a part of his new treasure, because they were a reminder of the old king, whom he would never see again.

It's true; life really is generous to those who pursue their Personal Legend, the boy thought. Then he remembered that he had to get to Tarifa so he could give one-tenth of his treasure to the Gypsy woman, as he had promised. "Those Gypsies are really smart, he thought. Maybe it was because they moved around so much.

The wind began to blow again. It was the levanter, the

wind that came from Africa. It didn't bring with it the smell of the desert, nor the threat of Moorish invasion. Instead, it brought the scent of a perfume he knew well, and the touch of a kiss—a kiss that came from far away, slowly, slowly, until it rested on his lips.

The boy smiled. It was the first time she had done that.

"I'm coming, Fatima," he said.

The Pilgrimage

A Contemporary Quest for Ancient Wisdom

Contents

Contents

Prologue

"And now, before the sacred countenance of RAM, you must touch with your hands the Word of Life and acquire such power as you need to become a witness to that Word throughout the world."

The Master raised high my new sword, still sheathed in its scabbard. The flames of the bonfire crackled—a good omen, indicating that the ritual should continue. I knelt and, with my bare hands, began to dig into the earth.

It was the night of January 2, 1986, and we were in Itatiaia, high on one of the peaks in the Serra do Mar, close to the formation known as the Agulhas Negras (Black Needles) in Brazil. My Master and I were accompanied by my wife, one of my disciples, a local guide, and a representative of the great fraternity that is comprised of esoteric orders from all over the world—the fraternity known as "the Tradition." The five of us—and the guide, who had been told what was to happen—were participating in my ordination as a Master of the Order of RAM.

I finished digging a smooth, elongated hole in the dirt. With great solemnity, I placed my hands on the earth and spoke the ritual words. My wife drew near and handed me the sword I had used for more than ten years; it had been a great help to me during hundreds of magical operations. I placed it in the hole I had dug, covered it with dirt, and smoothed the surface. As I did so, I thought of the many tests I had endured, of all I had learned, and of the strange phenomena I had been able to invoke simply because I had had that ancient and friendly sword with me. Now it was to be devoured by the earth, the iron of its blade and the wood of its hilt returning to nourish the source from which its power had come.

The Master approached me and placed my new sword on the earth that now covered the grave of my ancient one. All of us spread our arms wide, and the Master, invoking his power, created a strange light that surrounded us; it did not illuminate, but it was clearly visible, and it caused the figures of those who were there to take on a color that was different from the yellowish tinge cast by the fire. Then, drawing his own sword, he touched it to my shoulders and my forehead as he said, "By the power and the love of RAM, I anoint you Master and Knight of the Order, now and for all the days of your life. R for rigor, A for adoration, and M for mercy; R for *regnum,* A for *agnus,* and M for *mundi.* Let not your sword remain for long in its scabbard, lest it rust. And when you draw your sword, it must never be replaced without having performed an act of goodness, opened a new path, or tasted the blood of an enemy."

With the point of his sword, he lightly cut my forehead. From then on, I was no longer required to remain silent. No longer did I have to hide my capabilities nor maintain secrecy regarding the marvels I had learned to accomplish on the road of the Tradition. From that moment on, I was a Magus.

I reached out to take my new sword of indestructible steel and wood, with its black and red hilt and black scabbard. But as my hands touched the scabbard and as I prepared to pick it up, the Master came forward and stepped on my fingers with all his might. I screamed and let go of the sword.

I looked at him, astonished. The strange light had disappeared, and his face had taken on a phantasmagoric appearance, heightened by the flames of the bonfire.

He returned my gaze coldly, called to my wife, and gave her the sword, speaking a few words that I could not hear. Turning to me, he said, "Take away your hand; it has deceived you. The road of the Tradition is not for the chosen few. It is everyone's road. And the power that you think you have is worthless, because it is a power that is shared by all. You should have refused the sword. If you had done so, it would have been given to you, because you would have shown that your heart was pure. But just as I feared, at the supreme moment you stumbled and fell. Because of your avidity, you will now have to seek again for your sword. And because of your pride, you will have to seek it among simple people. Because of your fascination with miracles, you will have to struggle to recapture what was about to be given to you so generously."

The world seemed to fall away from me. I knelt there unable to think about anything. Once I had returned my old sword to the earth, I could not retrieve it. And since the new one had not been given to me, I now had to begin my quest for it all over again, powerless and defenseless. On the day of my Celestial Ordination, my Master's violence had brought me back to earth.

The guide smothered the fire, and my wife helped me up. She had my new sword in her hands, but according to the rules of the Tradition, I could not touch it without permission from my Master. We descended through the forest in silence, following the guide's lantern, until we reached the narrow dirt road where the cars were parked.

Nobody said good-bye. My wife put the sword in the trunk of the car and started the engine. We were quiet for a long time as she carefully navigated around the bumps and holes in the road.

"Don't worry," she said, trying to encourage me. "I'm sure you'll get it back."

I asked her what the Master had said to her.

"He said three things to me. First, that he should have brought along something warm to wear, because it was much colder up there than he had expected. Second, that he wasn't surprised at anything that had happened up there, that this has happened many times before with others who have reached the same point as you. And third, that your sword would be waiting for you at the right time, on the right day, at some point on the road that you will have to travel. I don't know either the day or the time. He only told me where I should hide it."

"And what road was he talking about?" I asked nervously.

"Ah, well, that he didn't explain very well. He just said that you should look on the map of Spain for a medieval route known as the Strange Road to Santiago."

THE ROAD TO SANTIAGO

FRANCE
BISCAY
SAINT-JEAN-PIED-DE-PORT
DOMINGO
ESTELLA
RONCESVALLES
PAMPLONA
PUENTE DE LA REINA
LOGROÑO
S DE OCA
BARCELONA
MEDITERRANEAN SEA

Arrival

THE CUSTOMS AGENT SPENT MORE TIME THAN USUAL examining the sword that my wife had brought into the country and then asked what we intended to do with it. I said that a friend of ours was going to assess its value so that we could sell it at auction. This lie worked: the agent gave us a declaration stating that we had entered the country with the sword at the Bajadas airport, and he told us that if we had any problems trying to leave the country with it, we need only show the declaration to the customs officials.

We went to the car rental agency and confirmed our two vehicles. Armed with the rental documents, we had a bite together at the airport restaurant prior to going our separate ways.

We had spent a sleepless night on the plane—the result of both a fear of flying and a sense of apprehension about what was going to happen once we arrived—but now we were excited and wide awake.

"Not to worry," she said for the thousandth time. "You're supposed to go to France and, at Saint-Jean-Pied-de-Port, seek out Mme Lourdes. She is going to put you in touch with someone who will guide you along the Road to Santiago."

"And what about you?" I asked, also for the thousandth time, knowing what her answer would be.

"I'm going where I have to go, and there I'll leave what has been entrusted to me. Afterward, I'll spend a few days in Madrid and then return to Brazil. I can take care of things back there as well as you would."

"I know you can," I answered, wanting to avoid the subject. I felt an enormous anxiety about the business matters I had left behind in Brazil. I had learned all I needed to know about the Road to Santiago in the fifteen days following the incident in the Agulhas Negras, but I had vacillated for another seven months before deciding to leave everything behind and make the trip. I had put it off until one morning when my wife had said that the time was drawing near and that if I did not make a decision, I might as well forget about the road of the Tradition and the Order of RAM. I had tried to explain to her that my Master had assigned me an impossible task, that I couldn't simply shrug off my livelihood. She had smiled and said that my excuse was dumb, that during the entire seven months I had done nothing but ask myself night and day whether or not I should go. And with the most casual of gestures, she had held out the two airline tickets, with the flight already scheduled.

"We're here because of your decision," I said glumly now in the airport restaurant. "I don't know if this will even work, since I let another person make the decision for me to seek out my sword."

My wife said that if we were going to start talking nonsense, we had better say good-bye and go our separate ways.

"You have never in your life let another person make an important decision for you. Let's go. It's getting late." She rose, picked up her suitcase, and headed for the parking lot. I didn't stop her. I stayed seated, observing the casual way in which she carried my sword; at any moment it seemed that it could slip from under her arm.

She stopped suddenly, came back to the table, and kissed me desperately. She looked at me for some time without saying a word. This suddenly made me realize that now I was actually in Spain and that there was no going back. In spite of the knowledge that there were many ways in which I could fail, I had taken the first step. I hugged her passionately, trying to convey all the love I felt for her at that moment. And while she was still in my arms, I prayed to everything and everyone I believed in, imploring that I be given the strength to return to her with the sword.

"That was a beautiful sword, wasn't it?" said a woman's voice from the next table, after my wife had left.

"Don't worry," a man said. "I'll buy one just like it for you. The tourist shops here in Spain have thousands of them."

After I had driven for an hour or so, I began to feel the fatigue accumulated from the night before. The August heat was so powerful that even on the open highway, the car began to overheat. I decided to stop in a small town identified by the road signs as Monumento Nacional. As I climbed the steep road that led to it, I began to review all that I had learned about the Road to Santiago.

Just as the Muslim tradition requires that all members of the faith, at least once in their life, make the same pilgrimage that Muhammad made from Mecca to Medina, so Christians in the first millennium considered three routes to be sacred. Each of them offered a series of blessings and indulgences to those who traveled its length. The first led to the tomb of Saint Peter in Rome; its travelers, who were called wanderers, took the cross as their symbol. The second led to the Holy Sepulcher of Christ in Jerusalem; those who took this road were called palmists, since they had as their symbol the palm branches with which Jesus was greeted when he entered that city. There was a third road, which led to the mortal remains of the apostle, San Tiago—Saint James in English, Jacques in French, Giacomo in Italian, Jacob in Latin. He was buried at a place on the Iberian peninsula where, one night, a shepherd had seen a brilliant star above a field. The legend says that not only San Tiago but also the Virgin Mary went there shortly after the death of Christ, carrying the word of the Evangelist and exhorting the people to convert. The site came to be known as Compostela—the star field—and there a city had arisen that drew travelers from every part of the Christian world. These travelers were called pilgrims, and their symbol was the scallop shell.

At the height of its fame, during the fourteenth century, the Milky Way—another name for the third road, since at night the pilgrims plotted their course using this galaxy—was traveled each year by more than a million people from every corner of Europe. Even today, mystics, devotees, and researchers traverse on foot the seven hundred kilometers that separate the French city of Saint-Jean-Pied-de-Port from the cathedral of Santiago de Compostela in Spain.[1]

Thanks to the French priest, Aymeric Picaud, who walked to Compostela in 1123, the route followed by the pilgrims today is exactly the same as the medieval path taken by Charlemagne, Saint Francis of Assisi, Isabella of Castile, and, most recently, by Pope John XXIII.

Picaud wrote five books about his experience. They were presented as the work of Pope Calixtus II—a devotee of San Tiago—and they were later known as the Codex Calixtinus. In Book Five of the codex, Picaud identified the natural features, fountains, hospitals, shelters, and cities found along the road. A special society—"Les Amis de Saint-Jacques"—was then formed with the charge of maintaining all of the natural markings on the route and helping to guide the pilgrims, using Picaud's annotations.

[1]The Road to Santiago, on the French side, was comprised of several routes that joined at a Spanish city called Puente de la Reina. The city of Saint-Jean-Pied-de-Port is located on one of those three routes; it is neither the only one nor the most important.

Also in the twelfth century, Spain began to capitalize on the legend of San Tiago as the country fought against the Moors who had invaded the peninsula. Several militant religious orders were established along the Road to Santiago, and the apostle's ashes became a powerful symbol in the fight against the Muslims. The Muslims, in turn, claimed that they had with them one of Muhammad's arms and took that as their guiding symbol. By the time Spain had regained control of the country, the militant orders had become so strong that they posed a threat to the nobility, and the Catholic kings had to intervene directly to prevent the orders from mounting an insurgency. As a result, the Road to Santiago was gradually forgotten, and were it not for sporadic artistic manifestations—in paintings such as Buñuel's *The Milky Way* and Juan Manoel Serrat's *Wanderer*—no one today would remember that millions of the people who would one day settle the New World had passed along that route.

The town that I reached by car was completely deserted. After searching on foot for quite some time, I finally found a small bar open for business in an old, medieval-style house. The owner, who did not even look up from the television program he was watching, advised me that it was siesta time and suggested that I must be crazy to be out walking in such heat.

I asked for a soft drink and tried to watch television, but I was unable to concentrate. All I could think of was that in two days, I was going to relive, here in the latter part of the twentieth century, something of the great human adventure that had brought Ulysses from Troy, that had been a part of Don Quixote's experience, that had led Dante and Orpheus into hell, and that had directed Columbus to the Americas: the adventure of traveling toward the unknown.

By the time I returned to my car, I was a bit calmer. Even if I were not able to find my sword, the pilgrimage along the Road to Santiago was going to help me to find myself.

Saint-Jean-Pied-de-Port

A PARADE OF MASKED PEOPLE ACCOMPANIED BY A BAND—all of them dressed in red, green, and white, the colors of the French Basque region—filled the main street of Saint-Jean-Pied-de-Port. It was Sunday. I had spent the last two days driving, and now I was enjoying the festivities. But it was time for my meeting with Mme Lourdes. Forcing my way through the crowd by car, I heard some shouted insults in French, but I finally made it through to the fortified sector that constituted the oldest part of the city, where Mme Lourdes lived. Even this high in the Pyrenees, it was hot during the day, and I was soaked with perspiration as I got out of the car.

I knocked at the gate. I knocked again, but there was no response. A third time, and still nothing happened. I felt confused and worried. My wife had said that I had to arrive there exactly on that day, but no one answered when I called out. I thought that perhaps Mme Lourdes had gone out to watch the parade, but it was also possible that I had arrived too late and that she had decided not to meet with me. My journey along the Road to Santiago seemed to have ended even before it had begun.

Suddenly, the gate opened, and a child jumped through it. I was startled, and in halting French I asked for Mme Lourdes. The child smiled at me and pointed toward the house. It was only then that I saw my mistake: the gate led onto an immense courtyard, around which were situated medieval houses with balconies. The gate had been open, and I hadn't even thought to try its handle.

I ran across the courtyard and up to the house that the child had indicated. Inside, an elderly, obese woman yelled something in Basque at a small boy with sad, brown eyes. I waited for a few moments, giving the argument a chance to end; it finally did, with the poor boy being sent to the kitchen under a hail of insults from the old woman. It was only then that she turned to me and, without even asking what it was that I wanted, led me—with delicate gestures and slight shoves—to the second floor of the small house. This floor consisted of just one room: a small, crowded office filled with books, objects, statues of San Tiago, and memorabilia from the Road. She took a book from its shelf and sat down behind the only table in the room, leaving me standing.

"You must be another pilgrim to Santiago," she said, without preamble. "I need to enter your name in the register of those who walk the Road."

I gave her my name, and she wanted to know if I had brought "the Scallops." She was referring to the shells adopted as a symbol by pilgrims to the tomb of the apostle; they served as a means of identification for the pilgrims when they met.[1]

Before leaving for Spain, I had made a pilgrimage to a place in Brazil called Aparecida do Norte. There, I had purchased an image of Our Lady of the Visitation, mounted on three scallop shells. I took it from my knapsack and offered it to Mme Lourdes.

"Pretty but not very practical," she said, handing it back to me. "It could break during your pilgrimage."

"It's not going to break. And I am going to leave it at the tomb of the apostle."

Mme Lourdes appeared not to have much time for me. She gave me a small card that would help me to get lodging at the monasteries along the Road, stamped it with the seal of Saint-Jean-Pied-de-Port to indicate that I had started the pilgrimage there, and said that I could leave with God's blessing.

"But where is my guide?" I asked.

"What guide?" she answered, a bit surprised but also with a gleam in her eye.

[1]The Road to Santiago has made only one mark on French culture, and that has been on that country's national pride, gastronomy, through the name "Coquilles Saint-Jacques."

I realized that I had forgotten something very important. In my eagerness to arrive and be attended to, I had neglected to say the Ancient Word—a kind of password that identifies those who belong to the orders of the Tradition. I immediately corrected my mistake and said the word to her. In response, Mme Lourdes quickly snatched from my hands the card she had given me a few moments earlier.

"You won't be needing this," she said, as she moved a pile of old newspapers that were sitting on top of a cardboard box. "Your road and your stopping places will depend on decisions made by your guide."

Mme Lourdes took a hat and a cape from the box. They seemed to be very old but well preserved. She asked me to stand in the middle of the room, and she began silently to pray. Then she placed the cape on my shoulders and the hat on my head. I could see that scallop shells had been sewn onto both the hat and the shoulders of the cape. Without interrupting her prayers, the old woman seized a shepherd's crook from the corner of the room and made me take it in my right hand. A small water gourd hung from the crook. There I stood: dressed in Bermuda shorts and a T-shirt that read "I LOVE NY," covered by the medieval garb of the pilgrims to Compostela.

The old woman approached me and stopped only a foot away. Then, in a kind of trance, placing the palms of her hands on my head, she said, "May the apostle San Tiago be with you, and may he show you the only thing that you need to discover; may you walk neither too slowly nor too fast but always according to the laws and the requirements of the Road; may you obey the one who is your guide, even though he may issue an order that is homicidal, blasphemous, or senseless. You must swear total obedience to your guide."

I so swore.

"The Spirit of the ancient pilgrims of the Tradition must be with you during your journey. The hat will protect you from the sun and from evil thoughts; the cape will protect you from the rain and from evil words; the gourd will protect you from enemies and from evil deeds. May the blessing of God, of San Tiago, and of the Virgin Mary be with you through all of your nights and days. Amen."

Having said this, she returned to her normal manner: hurriedly and with a bit of irritation, she took back the articles of clothing, placed them in the box, and returned the crook with the gourd to the corner of the room; then, after teaching me the password, she asked me to leave, since my guide was waiting for me two kilometers outside of Saint-Jean-Pied-de-Port.

"He hates band music," she said. But even two kilometers away he must have been able to hear it; the Pyrenees are an excellent echo chamber.

Before I left, I asked what I should do with the car, and she said I should leave the keys with her; someone would come to pick it up. Then, without another word, she descended the stairs and went to the kitchen to inflict more torment on the boy with the sad eyes. I opened the trunk of the car, took out my small blue knapsack with my sleeping bag tied to it, and placed the image of Our Lady of the Visitation in its most protected corner. I put the knapsack on my back and went back to give the keys to Mme Lourdes.

"Leave Pied-de-Port by following this street to the city gates at the end of the wall," she told me. "And when you get to Santiago de Compostela, say a Hail Mary for me. I have walked the Road so many times that now I content myself with reading in other pilgrims' eyes the excitement that I still feel; I just can't put it into practice anymore because of my age. Tell that to San Tiago. And tell him also that any time now I will join him, following a different road that's more direct and less exhausting."

I left the small city, passing through the wall at the Spanish Gate. In the past, the city had been on the preferred route for the Roman invaders, and through that gate had also passed the armies of Charlemagne and Napoleon. I walked along, hearing the band music in the distance, and suddenly, in the ruins of a village not far from the city, I was overwhelmed by emotion, and my eyes filled with tears: there in the ruins, the full impact of the fact that I was walking the Strange Road to Santiago finally hit me.

The view of the Pyrenees surrounding the valley, lit by the morning sun and intensified by the sound of the music, gave me the sensation that I was returning to something primitive, something that had been forgotten by most other human beings, something that I was unable to identify. But it was a strange and powerful feeling, and I decided to quicken my pace and arrive as soon as possible at the place where Mme Lourdes had said my guide would be waiting for me. Without stopping, I took off my shirt and put it in my knapsack. The straps cut into my bare shoulders a bit, but at least my old sneakers were broken in enough that they caused me no discomfort. After almost forty minutes, at a curve in the road that circled around a gigantic rock, I came upon an old abandoned well. There, sitting on the ground, was a man of about fifty; he had black hair and the look of a gypsy, and he was searching for something in his knapsack.

"*Hola,*" I said in Spanish, with the same timidity that I show whenever I meet anyone new. "You must be waiting for me. My name is Paulo."

The man interrupted his search through the knapsack and looked me up and down. His gaze was cold, and he seemed not at all surprised by my arrival. I also had the vague impression that I knew him.

"Yes, I was waiting for you, but I didn't know that I was going to meet you so soon. What do you want?"

I was a little disconcerted by his question and answered

that it was I whom he was to guide along the Milky Way in search of my sword.

"That's not necessary," said the man. "If you want me to, I can find it for you. But you have to decide right now whether you want me to."

This conversation with the stranger seemed increasingly weird to me. But since I had sworn complete obedience, I tried to respond. If he could find my sword for me, it would save an enormous amount of time, and I could return immediately to my friends and my business in Brazil; they were always on my mind. This could also be a trick, but there was no harm in giving him an answer.

As I was about to say yes, I heard a voice behind me say, in heavily accented Spanish, "You don't have to climb a mountain to find out whether or not it's high."

It was the password! I turned and saw a man of about forty, in khaki Bermudas and a white, sweaty T-shirt, staring at the gypsy. He was gray-haired, and his skin was darkened by the sun. In my haste, I had forgotten the most elementary rules of self-protection and had thrown myself body and soul into the arms of the first stranger I had met.

"The ship is safest when it's in port, but that's not what ships were built for," I said, as the correct response. Meanwhile, the man looked directly at the gypsy and the gypsy stared at the man. Both confronted each other, with no sign of fear or challenge, for some time. Then the gypsy left the knapsack on the ground, smiled disdainfully, and walked off in the direction of Saint-Jean-Pied-de-Port.

"My name is Petrus,"[2] said the new arrival as soon as the gypsy had disappeared behind the huge stone that I had circled a few minutes earlier. "Next time, be more cautious."

I heard a sympathetic tone in his voice; it was different from the tone of the gypsy and of Mme Lourdes. He lifted the knapsack from the ground, and I noticed that it had the scallop shell on its back. He produced a bottle of wine, took a swallow, and offered it to me. After I had taken a drink, I asked him who the gypsy was.

"This is a frontier route often used by smugglers and terrorist refugees from the Spanish Basque country," said Petrus. "The police hardly ever come near here."

"But you're not answering me. You two looked at each other like old acquaintances. And I had the feeling that I knew him, too. That's why I was so much at ease."

Petrus smiled and said that we should move along. I picked up my things, and we began to walk in silence. From Petrus's smile I knew that he was thinking the same thing I was.

We had met with a devil.

[2]Actually, Petrus told me his real name. I have changed it in order to protect his privacy, but this is one of the few times that names have been changed in this book.

We walked along without talking for a while, and I could see that Mme Lourdes had been right: from almost three kilometers away, we could still hear the sound of the band. I wanted to ask some questions of Petrus—about his life, his work, and what had brought him here. I knew, though, that we still had seven hundred kilometers to cover together and that the appropriate moment would come for having all of my questions answered. But I could not get the gypsy out of my mind, and finally I broke the silence.

"Petrus, I think that the gypsy was the devil."

"Yes, he was the devil." When he confirmed this, I felt a mixture of terror and relief. "But he isn't the devil that you know from the Tradition."

In the Tradition, the devil is a spirit that is neither good nor evil; he is considered to be the guardian of most of the secrets that are accessible to human beings and to have strength and power over material things. Since he is a fallen angel, he is identified with the human race, and he is always ready to make deals and exchange favors. I asked what was the difference between the gypsy and the devil of the Tradition.

"We are going to meet others along the Road," he smiled. "You will see for yourself. But just to give you an idea, try to remember your entire conversation with the gypsy."

I reviewed the two phrases I had heard from him. He had said that he was waiting for me and had affirmed that he would seek out the sword for me.

Then Petrus said that those two phrases fit perfectly well in the mouth of a thief who had been surprised in the act of robbing a knapsack: they were aimed at gaining time and at winning favor while he quickly figured out a means of escape. On the other hand, the two phrases could mean exactly what they said.

"Which is right?"

"Both are true. That poor thief, while he defended himself, picked out of the air the very words that needed to be said to you. He thought that he was being intelligent, but he was really acting as the instrument of a greater power. If he had fled when I arrived, we wouldn't be having this conversation now. But he confronted me, and I read in his eyes the name of a devil that you are going to meet somewhere along the Road."

For Petrus, the meeting had been a favorable omen, since the devil had revealed himself so early.

"Meanwhile, don't worry about him because, as I have already told you, he won't be the only one. He may be the most important one, but he won't be the only one."

We continued walking, passing from a desertlike area to one where small trees were scattered here and there. Once in a while Petrus broke the silence to tell me some historic fact or other about the places we were passing. I saw the house where a queen had spent the last night of her life and a small chapel encrusted with rocks, which had been the hermitage of a saintly man who the few inhabitants of the area swore could perform miracles.

"Miracles are very important, don't you think?" Petrus said.

I agreed but said that I had never witnessed a great miracle. My apprenticeship in the Tradition had been much more on the intellectual plane. I believed that when I recovered my sword, then, yes, I would be capable of doing the great deeds that my Master did.

"But what my Master performs are not miracles, because they don't contradict the laws of nature. What my Master does is utilize these forces to . . ."

I couldn't finish the sentence because I couldn't explain how my Master had been able to materialize spirits, move objects from one place to another without touching them, or, as I had witnessed more than once, create patches of blue sky on a cloudy afternoon.

"Maybe he does those things simply to convince you that he has the knowledge and the power," answered Petrus.

"Yes, maybe so," I said, without much conviction.

We sat down on a stone because Petrus told me that he hated to smoke cigarettes while he was walking. According to him, the lungs absorbed much more nicotine if one smoked while walking, and the smoke nauseated him.

"That was why the Master refused to let you have the sword," Petrus continued. "Because you didn't understand why he performs his prodigious feats. Because you forgot that the path to knowledge is a path that's open to everyone, to the common people. During our journey, I'm going to teach you some exercises and some rituals that are known as the practices of RAM. All of us, at some time in our lives, have made use of at least one of them. Every one of these practices, without exception, can be discovered by anyone who is willing to seek them out, with patience and perspicacity, among the lessons that life itself teaches us.

"The RAM practices are so simple that people like you, who are used to making life too complicated, ascribe little value to them. But it is they that make people capable of achieving anything, absolutely anything, that they desire.

"Jesus glorified the Father when his disciples began to perform miracles and cures; he thanked God for having kept such things secret from wise people and for revealing them to simple folk. When all is said and done, if we believe in God, we have to believe also that God is just."

Petrus was absolutely right. It would be a divine injustice to allow only those people who were learned and who had the time and money to buy expensive books to have access to true knowledge.

"The true path to wisdom can be identified by three things," said Petrus. "First, it must involve agape, and I'll tell you more about this later; second, it has to have practical application in your life. Otherwise, wisdom becomes a useless thing and deteriorates, like a sword that is never used.

"And finally, it has to be a path that can be followed by anyone. Like the road you are walking now, the Road to Santiago."

We walked for the rest of the afternoon, and only when the sun began to disappear behind the mountains did Petrus decide to stop again. All around us the highest peaks of the Pyrenees still shone in the last light of day.

Petrus told me to clear a small area on the ground and to kneel there.

"The first RAM practice will help you to achieve rebirth. You will have to do the exercise for seven consecutive days, each time trying to experience in some different way your first contact with the world. You know how difficult it was for you to make the decision to drop everything and come here to walk the Road to Santiago in search of a sword. But this was difficult only because you were a prisoner of the past. You had been defeated before, and you were afraid that it could happen again. You had already achieved things, and you were afraid you might lose them. But at the same time, something stronger than any of that prevailed: the desire to find your sword. So you decided to take the risk."

I said that he was right but that I still had the worries he described.

"That doesn't matter. The exercise, little by little, will free you from the burdens that you have created in your life."

And Petrus taught me the first RAM practice: the Seed Exercise.

"Do it now for the first time," he said.

I lowered my head between my knees, breathed deeply, and began to relax. My body obeyed without question, perhaps because we had walked so far during the day and I was exhausted. I began to listen to the sound of the earth, muffled and harsh, and bit by bit I transformed myself into a seed. I didn't think. Everything was dark, and I was asleep at the center of the earth. Suddenly, something moved. It was a part of me, a minuscule part of me that wanted to awaken, that said that I had to leave this place because there was something else "up there." I wanted to sleep, but this part insisted. I began to move my fingers, and my fingers began to move my arms—but they were neither fingers nor arms. They were a small shoot that was fighting to overcome the force of the earth and to move in the direction of that "something up there." I felt my body begin to follow the movement of my arms. Each second seemed like an eternity, but the seed needed to be born; it needed to know what that "something up there" was. With immense difficulty, my head, then my body, began to rise. Everything was too slow, and I had to fight against the force that was pushing me down toward the center of the earth where before I had been tranquil, dreaming an eternal dream. But I was winning, I was winning, and finally I broke through something and was upright. The force that had been pressing down on me suddenly ceased. I had broken through the earth and was surrounded by that "something up there."

The "something up there" was the field. I sensed the heat of the sun, the hum of the mosquitoes, the sound of a river that ran in the distance. I arose slowly, with my eyes closed, and felt that at any moment I was going to become dizzy and fall to the ground. But meanwhile I continued to grow. My arms were spreading and my body stretching. There I was, being reborn, wanting to be bathed both inside and out by the immense sun that was shining and that was asking me to continue to grow more, stretch more, and embrace it with all of my branches. I was stretching my arms more and more, and the muscles throughout my body began to hurt. I felt that I was a thousand meters tall and that I could embrace mountains. And my body was expanding, expanding until the pain in my muscles became so intense that I couldn't bear it, and I screamed.

The Seed Exercise

Kneel on the ground. Then seat yourself on your heels and bend forward so that your head touches your knees. Stretch your arms behind you. You are now in a fetal position. Relax, releasing all of your tensions. Breathe calmly and deeply. Little by little you will perceive that you are a tiny seed, cradled in the comfort of the earth. Everything around you is warm and delicious. You are in a deep, restful sleep.

•

Suddenly, a finger moves. The shoot no longer wants to be a seed; it wants to grow. Slowly you begin to move your arms, and then your body will begin to rise, straightening up until you are seated on your heels. Now you begin to lift your body up, and slowly, slowly you become erect, still kneeling on the ground.

•

The moment has come to break completely through the earth. You begin to rise slowly, placing one foot on the ground, then the other, fighting against the disequilibrium just as a shoot battles to make its own space, until finally you are standing. Imagine the area about you, the sun, the water, the wind, and the birds. Now you are a shoot that is beginning to grow. Slowly raise your arms toward the sky. Then stretch yourself more and more, more and more, as if you want to grasp the enormous sun that shines above you, giving you strength and attracting you. Your body begins to become more and more rigid, all of your muscles strain, and you feel yourself to be growing, growing, growing—you become huge. The tension increases more and more until it becomes painful, unbearable. When you can no longer stand it, scream and open your eyes.

•

Repeat this exercise for seven consecutive days, always at the same time.

•

I opened my eyes, and Petrus was there in front of me, smiling and smoking a cigarette. The light of day had not yet disappeared, but I was surprised to see that the sun was not as bright as I had imagined. I asked if he wanted me to describe the sensations, and he said no.

"This is a very personal thing, and you should keep it to yourself. How can I judge it? The sensations are yours, not mine."

Petrus said that we were going to sleep right there. We built a small fire, drank what was left of his wine, and I made some sandwiches with a foie gras that I had bought before I reached Saint-Jean. Petrus went to the stream that ran nearby and caught some fish, which he fried over the fire. And then we crawled into our sleeping bags.

Among the greatest sensations that I have experienced in my life were those I felt on that unforgettable first night on the Road to Santiago. It was cold, despite its being summer, but I could still taste the warmth of the wine that Petrus had brought. I looked up at the sky; the Milky Way spread across it, reflecting the immensity of the Road we would have to travel. This immensity made me very anxious; it created a terrible fear that I would not be able to succeed—that I was too small for this task. Yet today I had been a seed and had been reborn. I had discovered that although the earth and my sleep were full of comfort, the life "up there" was much more beautiful. And I could always be reborn, as many times as I wanted, until my arms were long enough to embrace the earth from which I had come.

The Creator and the Created

For seven days we continued walking through the Pyrenees, climbing and descending the mountains, and each evening, as the rays of the sun reflected from the tallest peaks, Petrus had me perform the Seed Exercise. On the third day of our trek, we passed a cement marker, painted yellow, indicating that we had crossed the frontier; from then on we would be walking through Spain. Little by little, Petrus began to reveal some things about his private life; I learned that he was Italian and that he worked in industrial design.[1]

I asked him whether he was worried about the many things he had been forced to abandon in order to guide a pilgrim in search of his sword.

[1]It has been said that there is no such thing as coincidence in this world, and the following story confirms the truth of this assertion once again. One afternoon, I was leafing through some magazines in the lobby of the hotel where I was staying in Madrid, when I noticed a piece about the Prince of Asturias Prize; a Brazilian journalist, Roberto Marinho, had been one of the prize winners. A closer study of the photograph of those at the awards dinner startled me, though. At one of the tables, elegantly dressed in his tuxedo, was Petrus, described in the caption as "one of the most famous European designers of the moment."

"Let me explain something to you," he answered. "I am not guiding you to your sword. It is your job, solely and exclusively, to find it. I am here to lead you along the Road to Santiago and to teach you the RAM practices. How you apply this to your search for your sword is your problem."

"But you didn't answer my question."

"When you travel, you experience, in a very practical way, the act of rebirth. You confront completely new situations, the day passes more slowly, and on most journeys you don't even understand the language the people speak. So you are like a child just out of the womb. You begin to attach much more importance to the things around you because your survival depends upon them. You begin to be more accessible to others because they may be able to help you in difficult situations. And you accept any small favor from the gods with great delight, as if it were an episode you would remember for the rest of your life.

"At the same time, since all things are new, you see only the beauty in them, and you feel happy to be alive. That's why a religious pilgrimage has always been one of the most objective ways of achieving insight. The word *peccadillo,* which means a "small sin," comes from *pecus,* which means "defective foot," a foot that is incapable of walking a road. The way to correct the peccadillo is always to walk forward, adapting oneself to new situations and receiving in return all of the thousands of blessings that life generously offers to those who seek them.

"So why would you think that I might be worried about a half-dozen projects that I left behind in order to be here with you?"

Petrus looked around him, and I followed his eyes. On the uplands of one of the peaks, some goats were grazing. One of them, more daring than the others, stood on an outcropping of a high boulder, and I could not figure out how he had reached that spot or how he would get down. But as I was thinking this, the goat leapt and, alighting in a place I couldn't even see, rejoined his companions. Everything in our surroundings reflected an uneasy peace, the peace of a world that was still in the process of growing and being created—a world that seemed to know that, in order to grow, it had to continue moving along, always moving along. Great earthquakes and killer storms might make nature seem cruel, but I could see that these were just the vicissitudes of being on the road. Nature itself journeyed, seeking illumination.

"I am very glad to be here," said Petrus, "because the work I did not finish is not important and the work I will be able to do after I get back will be so much better."

When I had read the works of Carlos Castaneda, I had wanted very much to meet the old medicine man, Don Juan. Watching Petrus look at the mountains, I felt that I was with someone very much like him.

On the afternoon of the seventh day, after having passed through some pine woods, we reached the top of a mountain.

There, Charlemagne had said his prayers for the first time on Spanish soil, and now an ancient monument urged in Latin that all who passed by should say a Salve Regina. We both did as the monument asked. Then Petrus had me do the Seed Exercise for the last time.

There was a strong wind, and it was cold. I argued that it was still early—at the latest, it was only three in the afternoon—but he told me not to talk about it, just do exactly as he ordered.

I knelt on the ground and began to perform the exercise. Everything went as usual until the moment when I extended my arms and began to imagine the sun. When I reached that point, with the gigantic sun shining there in front of me, I felt myself entering into a state of ecstasy. My memories of human life began slowly to dim, and I was no longer doing an exercise: I had become a tree. I was happy about this. The sun shone and revolved, which had never happened before. I remained there, my branches extended, my leaves trembling in the wind, not wanting ever to change my position—until something touched me, and everything went dark for a fraction of a second.

I immediately opened my eyes. Petrus had slapped me across the face and was holding me by the shoulders.

"Don't lose sight of your objective!" he said, enraged. "Don't forget that you still have a great deal to learn before you find your sword!"

I sat down on the ground, shivering in the cold wind.

"Does that always happen?" I asked.

"Almost always," he said. "Mainly with people like you, who are fascinated by details and forget what they are after."

Petrus took a sweater from his knapsack and put it on. I put my overshirt on, covering my "I LOVE NY" T-shirt. I would never have imagined that in "the hottest summer of the decade," according to the newspapers, it could be so cold. The two shirts helped to cut the wind, but I asked Petrus if we couldn't move along more quickly so that I could warm up.

The Road now made for an easy descent. I thought that the extreme cold I had experienced was due to the fact that we had eaten very frugally, just fish and the fruits of the forest.[2]

Petrus said that it wasn't the lack of food and explained that it was cold because we had reached the highest point in that range of mountains.

We had not gone more than five hundred meters when, at a curve in the Road, the scene changed completely. A tremendous, rolling plain extended into the distance. And to the left, on the Road down, less than two hundred meters away, a beautiful little village awaited us with its chimneys smoking.

I began to walk faster, but Petrus held me back.

[2]There is a red fruit whose name I do not know, but just the sight of it today makes me nauseated from having eaten so much of it while walking through the Pyrenees.

"I think that this is a good time to teach you the second RAM practice," he said, sitting down on the ground and indicating that I should do the same.

I was irritated, but I did as he asked. The sight of the small village with its inviting chimney smoke had really upset me. Suddenly I realized that we had been out in the woods for a week; we had seen no one and had been either sleeping on the ground or walking throughout the day. I had run out of cigarettes, so I had been smoking the horrible roller tobacco that Petrus used. Sleeping in a sleeping bag and eating unseasoned fish were things that I had loved when I was twenty, but here on the Road to Santiago, they were sacrifices. I waited impatiently for Petrus to finish rolling his cigarette, while I thought about the warmth of a glass of wine in the bar I could see less than five minutes down the Road.

Petrus, bundled up in his sweater, was relaxed and looked out over the immense plain.

"What do you think about this crossing of the Pyrenees?" he asked, after a while.

"Very nice," I answered, not wanting to prolong the conversation.

"It must have been nice, because it took us six days to go a distance we could have gone in one."

I could not believe what he was saying. He pulled out the map and showed me the distance: seventeen kilometers. Even walking at a slow pace because of the ups and downs, the Road could have been hiked in six hours.

"You are so concerned about finding your sword that you forgot the most important thing: you have to get there. Looking only for Santiago—which you can't see from here, in any case—you didn't see that we passed by certain places four or five times, approaching them from different angles."

Now that Petrus mentioned it, I began to realize that Mount Itchasheguy—the highest peak in the region had sometimes been to my right and sometimes to my left. Although I had noticed this, I had not drawn the only possible conclusion: that we had gone back and forth many times.

"All I did was to follow different routes, using the paths made through the woods by the smugglers. But it was your responsibility to have seen that. This happened because the process of moving along did not exist for you. The only thing that existed was your desire to arrive at your goal."

"Well, what if I had noticed?"

"We would have taken seven days anyway, because that is what the RAM practices call for. But at least you would have approached the Pyrenees in a different way."

I was so surprised that I forgot about the village and the temperature.

"When you are moving toward an objective," said Petrus, "it is very important to pay attention to the road. It is the road that teaches us the best way to get there, and the road enriches us as we walk its length. You can compare it to a sexual relationship: the caresses of foreplay determine the intensity of the orgasm. Everyone knows that.

"And it is the same thing when you have an objective in your life. It will turn out to be better or worse depending on the route you choose to reach it and the way you negotiate that route. That's why the second RAM practice is so important; it extracts from what we are used to seeing every day the secrets that because of our routine, we never see."

And then Petrus taught me the Speed Exercise.

"In the city, amid all the things we have to do every day, this exercise should be done for twenty minutes. But since we are on the Strange Road to Santiago, we should wait an hour before getting to the village."

The Speed Exercise

Walk for twenty minutes at half the speed at which you normally walk. Pay attention to the details, people, and surroundings. The best time to do this is after lunch.

•

Repeat the exercise for seven days.

•

The cold—about which I had already forgotten—returned, and I looked at Petrus with desperation. But he paid no attention; he got up, grabbed his knapsack, and began to walk the two hundred meters to the village with an exasperating slowness. At first, I looked only in the direction of the tavern, a small, ancient, two-story building with a wooden sign hanging above the door. We were so close that I could even read the year when the tavern had been built: 1652. We were moving, but it seemed as if we had not left our original spot. Petrus placed one foot in front of the other very slowly, and I did the same. I took my watch from my knapsack and strapped it on my wrist.

"It's going to be worse that way," he said, "because time isn't something that always proceeds at the same pace. It is we who determine how quickly time passes."

I began to look at my watch every minute and found that he was right. The more I looked at it, the more slowly the minutes passed. I decided to take his advice, and I put the watch back in my knapsack. I tried to pay more attention to the Road, the plain, and the stones I stepped on, but I kept looking ahead to the tavern—and I was convinced that we hadn't moved at all. I thought about telling myself some stories, but the exercise was making me anxious, and I couldn't concentrate. When I couldn't resist any longer and took my watch out again, only eleven minutes had passed.

"Don't make a torture out of this exercise, because it

wasn't meant to be that," said Petrus. "Try to find pleasure in a speed that you're not used to. Changing the way you do routine things allows a new person to grow inside of you. But when all is said and done, you're the one who must decide how you handle it."

The kindness expressed in his final phrase calmed me down a bit. If it was I who decided what I would do, then it was better to take advantage of the situation. I breathed deeply and tried not to think. I put myself into a strange state, one in which time was something distant and of no interest to me. I calmed myself more and more and began to perceive the things that surrounded me through new eyes. My imagination, which was unavailable when I was tense, began to work to my advantage. I looked at the small village there in front of me and began to create a story about it: how it had been built, the pilgrims that had passed through it, the delight in finding people and lodging after the cold wind of the Pyrenees. At one point, I sensed that there was in the village a strong, mysterious, and all-knowing presence. My imagination peopled the plain with knights and battles. I could see their swords shining in the sun and hear the cries of war. The village was no longer just a place where I could warm my soul with wine and my body with a blanket; it was a historic monument, the work of heroic people who had left everything behind to become a part of that solitary place. The world was there around me, and I realized that seldom had I paid attention to it.

When I regained my everyday awareness, we were at the door of the tavern, and Petrus was inviting me to enter.

"I'll buy the wine," he said. "And let's get to sleep early, because tomorrow I have to introduce you to a great sorcerer."

Mine was a deep and dreamless sleep. As soon as daylight began to show itself in the two streets of the village of Roncesvalles, Petrus knocked on my door. We were in rooms on the top floor of the tavern, which also served as a hotel.

We had some coffee and some bread with olive oil, and we left, plodding through the dense fog that had fallen over the area. I could see that Roncesvalles wasn't exactly a village, as I had thought at first. At the time of the great pilgrimages along the Road, it had been the most powerful monastery in the region, with direct influence over the territory that extended all the way to the Navarra border. And it still retained some of its original character: its few buildings had been part of a religious brotherhood. The only construction that had any lay characteristics was the tavern where we had stayed.

We walked through the fog to the Collegiate Church. Inside, garbed in white, several monks were saying the first morning mass in unison. I couldn't understand a word they were saying, since the mass was being celebrated in Basque. Petrus sat in one of the pews to the side and indicated that I should join him.

The church was enormous and filled with art objects of incalculable value. Petrus explained to me in a whisper that it had been built through donations from the kings and queens of Portugal, Spain, France, and Germany, on a site selected by the emperor Charlemagne. On the high altar, the Virgin of Roncesvalles—sculpted in massive silver, with a face of precious stone—held in her hands a branch of flowers made of jewels. The smell of incense, the Gothic construction, and the chanting monks in white began to induce in me a state similar to the trances I had experienced during the rituals of the Tradition.

"And the sorcerer?" I asked, remembering what he had said on the previous afternoon.

Petrus indicated with a nod of his head a monk who was middle-aged, thin, and bespectacled, sitting with the other brothers on the narrow benches beside the high altar. A sorcerer, and at the same time a monk! I was eager for the mass to be over, but as Petrus had said to me the day before, it is we who determine the pace of time: my anxiety caused the religious ceremony to last for more than an hour.

When the mass was over, Petrus left me alone in the pew and went out through the door that the monks had used as an exit. I remained there for a while, gazing about the church and feeling that I should offer some kind of prayer, but I wasn't able to concentrate. The images appeared to be in the distance, locked in a past that would never return, like the Golden Age of the Road to Santiago.

Petrus appeared in the doorway and, without a word, signaled that I should follow him.

We came to an inside garden of the monastery, surrounded by a stone veranda. At the center of the garden there was a fountain, and seated at its edge, waiting for us, was the bespectacled monk.

"Father Jordi, this is the pilgrim," said Petrus, introducing me.

The monk held out his hand, and I shook it. No one said anything else. I was waiting for something to happen, but I heard only the crowing of roosters in the distance and the cries of the hawks taking off for their daily hunt. The monk looked at me expressionlessly, in a way that reminded me of Mme Lourdes's manner after I had spoken the Ancient Word.

Finally, after a long and uncomfortable silence, Father Jordi spoke.

"It looks to me like you rose through the levels of the Tradition a bit early, my friend."

I answered that I was thirty-eight and had been quite successful in all of the trials.[3]

"Except for one, the last and most important," he said, continuing to look at me without expression. "And without that one, nothing you have learned has any significance."

[3]Trials are ritual tests in which importance is given not only to the disciple's dedication but also to the auguries that emerge during their execution. This usage of the term originated during the Inquisition.

"That is why I am walking the Road to Santiago."

"Which guarantees nothing. Come with me."

Petrus stayed in the garden, and I followed Father Jordi. We crossed the cloisters, passed the place where a king was buried—Sancho the Strong—and went to a small chapel set among the group of main buildings that made up the monastery of Roncesvalles.

There was almost nothing inside: only a table, a book, and a sword—a sword that wasn't mine.

Father Jordi sat at the table, leaving me standing. He took some herbs and lit them, filling the place with their perfume. More and more, the situation reminded me of my encounter with Mme Lourdes.

"First, I want to tell you something," said Father Jordi. "The Jacobean route is only one of four roads. It is the Road of the Spades, and it may give you power, but that is not enough."

"What are the other three?"

"You know at least two others: the Road to Jerusalem, which is the Road of the Hearts, or of the Grail, and which endows you with the ability to perform miracles; and the Road to Rome, which is the Road of the Clubs; it allows you to communicate with other worlds."

"So what's missing is the Road of the Diamonds to complete the four suits of the deck," I joked. And the father laughed.

"Exactly. That's the secret Road. If you take it someday, you won't be helped by anybody. For now, let us leave that one aside. Where are your scallop shells?"

I opened my knapsack and took out the shells on which stood the image of Our Lady of the Visitation. He put the figure on the table. He held his hands over it and began to concentrate. He told me to do the same. The perfume in the air was growing stronger. Both the monk and I had our eyes open, and suddenly I could sense that the same phenomenon was occurring as had taken place at Itatiaia: the shells glowed with a light that did not illuminate. The brightness grew and grew, and I heard a mysterious voice, emanating from Father Jordi's throat, saying, "Wherever your treasure is, there will be your heart."

It was a phrase from the Bible. But the voice continued, "And wherever your heart is, there will be the cradle of the Second Coming of Christ; like these shells, the pilgrim is only an outer layer. When that layer, which is a stratum of life, is broken, life appears, and that life is comprised of agape."

He drew back his hands, and the shells lost their glow. Then he wrote my name in the book that was on the table. Along the Road to Santiago, I saw only three books where my name was written: Mme Lourdes's, Father Jordi's, and the Book of Power, where later I was to write my own name.

"That's all," he said. "You can go with the blessing of the Virgin of Roncesvalles and of San Tiago of the Sword.

"The Jacobean route is marked with yellow pointers, painted all the way across Spain," said the monk, as we returned to the place where Petrus was waiting. "If you should lose your way at any time, look for the markers—on trees, on stones, and on traffic signs—and you will be able to find a safe place."

"I have a good guide."

"But try to depend mainly on yourself—so that you aren't coming and going for six days in the Pyrenees."

So the monk already knew the story.

We found Petrus and then said good-bye. As we left Roncesvalles that morning, the fog had disappeared completely. A straight, flat road extended in front of us, and I began to see the yellow markers Father Jordi had mentioned. The knapsack was a bit heavier, because I had bought a bottle of wine at the tavern, despite the fact that Petrus had told me that it was unnecessary. After Roncesvalles, hundreds of small villages dotted the route, and I was to sleep outdoors very seldom.

"Petrus, Father Jordi spoke about the Second Coming of Christ as if it were something that were happening now."

"It is always happening. That is the secret of your sword."

"And you told me that I was going to meet with a sorcerer, but I met with a monk. What does magic have to do with the Catholic Church?"

Petrus said just one word:

"Everything."

Cruelty

"RIGHT THERE. THAT'S THE EXACT SPOT WHERE LOVE WAS murdered," said the old man, pointing to a small church built into the rocks.

We had walked for five days in a row, stopping only to eat and sleep. Petrus continued to be guarded about his private life but asked many questions about Brazil and about my work. He said that he really liked my country, because the image he knew best was that of Christ the Redeemer on Corcovado, standing open armed rather than suffering on the cross. He wanted to know everything, and he especially wanted to know if the women were as pretty as the ones here in Spain. The heat of the day was almost unbearable, and in all of the bars and villages where we stopped, the people complained about the drought. Because of the heat, we adopted the Spanish custom of the siesta and rested between two and four in the afternoon when the sun was at its hottest.

That afternoon, as we sat in an olive grove, the old man had come up to us and offered us a taste of wine. In spite of the heat, the habit of drinking wine had been part of life in that region for centuries.

"What do you mean, love was murdered there?" I asked, since the old man seemed to want to strike up a conversation.

"Many centuries ago, a princess who was walking the Road to Santiago, Felicia of Aquitaine, decided, on her way back from Compostela, to give up everything and live here. She was love itself, because she divided all of her wealth among the poor people of the region and began to care for the sick."

Petrus had lit one of his horrible rolled cigarettes, but despite his air of indifference, I could see that he was listening carefully to the old man's story.

"Her brother, Duke Guillermo, was sent by their father to bring her home. But Felicia refused to go. In desperation, the duke fatally stabbed her there in that small church that you can see in the distance; she had built it with her own hands in order to care for the poor and offer praise to God.

"When he came to his senses and realized what he had done, the duke went to Rome to ask the pope's forgiveness. As penitence, the pope ordered him to walk to Compostela. Then a curious thing happened: on his way back, when he arrived here, he had the same impulse as his sister, and he stayed on, living in that little church that his sister had built, caring for the poor until the last days of his long life."

"That's the law of retribution at work," Petrus laughed. The old man did not understand, but I knew what Petrus was saying. His concept of the law of retribution was similar to that of karma, or of the concept that as one sows, so shall they reap.

As we had been walking, we had gotten involved in some long theological discussions about the relationship between God and humanity. I had argued that in the Tradition, there was always an involvement with God, but that it was a complex one. The path to God, for me, was quite different from the one we were following on the Road to Santiago, with its priests who were sorcerers, its gypsies who were devils, and its saints who performed miracles. All of these things seemed to me to be primitive, and too much connected with Christianity; they lacked the fascination, the elegance and the ecstasy that the rituals of the Tradition evoked in me. Petrus, on the other hand, argued that the guiding concept along the Road to Santiago was its simplicity. That the Road was one along which any person could walk, that its significance could be understood by even the least sophisticated person, and that, in fact, only such a road as that could lead to God. So Petrus thought my relationship to God was based too much on concept, on intellect and on reasoning; I felt that his was too simplistic and intuitive.

"You believe that God exists, and so do I," Petrus had said at one point. "So God exists for both of us. But if someone doesn't believe in him, that doesn't mean God ceases to exist. Nor does it mean that the nonbeliever is wrong."

"Does that mean that the existence of God depends on a person's desire and power?"

"I had a friend once who was drunk all the time but who

said three Hail Marys every night. His mother had conditioned him to do so ever since he was a child. Even when he came home helplessly drunk, and even though he did not believe in God, my friend always said his three Hail Marys. After he died, I was at a ritual of the Tradition, and I asked the spirit of the ancients where my friend was. The spirit answered that he was fine and that he was surrounded by light. Without ever having had the faith during his life, the three prayers he had said ritualistically every day had brought him salvation.

"God was manifest in the caves and in the thunderstorms of prehistory. After people began to see God's hand in the caves and thunderstorms, they began to see him in the animals and in special places in the forest. During certain difficult times, God existed only in the catacombs of the great cities. But through all of time, he never ceased to live in the human heart in the form of love.

"In recent times, some thought that God was merely a concept, subject to scientific proof. But, at this point, history has been reversed, or rather is starting all over again. Faith and love have resumed their importance. When Father Jordi cited that quotation from Jesus, saying that wherever your treasure is, there also would your heart be, he was referring to the importance of love and good works. Wherever it is that you want to see the face of God, there you will see it. And if you don't want to see it, that doesn't matter, so long as you are performing good works. When Felicia of Aquitaine built her small church and began to help the poor, she forgot about the God of the Vatican. She became God's manifestation by becoming wiser and by living a simpler life—in other words, through love. It is in that respect that the old man was absolutely right in saying that love had been murdered."

Now Petrus said, "The law of retribution was operating when Felicia's brother felt forced to continue the good works he had interrupted. Anything is permissable but the interruption of a manifestation of love. When that happens, whoever tried to destroy it is responsible for its re-creation."

I explained that in my country the law of return said that people's deformities and diseases were punishments for mistakes committed in previous incarnations.

"Nonsense," said Petrus. "God is not vengeance, God is love. His only form of punishment is to make someone who interrupts a work of love continue it."

The old man excused himself, saying that it was late and that he had to get back to work. Petrus thought it was a good time for us to get up, too, and get back on the Road.

"Let's forget all of our discussion about God," he said, as we made our way through the olive trees. "God is in everything around us. He has to be felt and lived. And here I am trying to transform him into a problem in logic so that you can understand him. Keep doing the exercise of walking slowly, and you will learn more and more about his presence."

Two days later, we had to climb a mountain called the Peak of Forgiveness. The climb took several hours, and at the top, I was shocked to find a group of tourists sunbathing and drinking beer; their car radios blasted music at top volume. They had driven up a nearby road to get to the top of the mountain.

"That's the way it is," said Petrus. "Did you expect that you were going to find one of El Cid's warriors up here, watching for the next Moorish attack?"

As we descended, I performed the Speed Exercise for the last time. Before us was another immense plain with sparse vegetation burned by the drought; it was bordered by blue mountains. There were almost no trees, only the rocky ground and some cactus. At the end of the exercise, Petrus asked me about my work, and it was only then that I realized that I hadn't thought about it for some time. My worries about business and about the things I had left undone had practically disappeared. Now I thought of these things only at night, and even then I didn't give them much importance. I was happy to be there, walking the Road to Santiago.

I told Petrus how I was feeling, and he joked, "Any time now you are going to do the same thing as Felicia of Aquitaine." Then he stopped and asked me to put my knapsack on the ground.

"Look around you, and choose some point to fixate on," he said.

I chose the cross on a church that I could see in the distance.

"Keep your eyes fixed on that point, and try to concentrate only on what I am going to tell you. Even if you feel something different, don't become distracted. Do as I am telling you."

I stood there, relaxed, with my eyes fixed on the cross, as Petrus took a position behind me and pressed a finger into the base of my neck.

"The Road you are traveling is the Road of power, and only the exercises having to do with power will be taught to you. The journey, which prior to this was torture because all you wanted to do was get there, is now beginning to become a pleasure. It is the pleasure of searching and the pleasure of an adventure. You are nourishing something that's very important—your dreams.

"We must never stop dreaming. Dreams provide nourishment for the soul, just as a meal does for the body. Many times in our lives we see our dreams shattered and our desires frustrated, but we have to continue dreaming. If we don't, our soul dies, and agape cannot reach it. A lot of blood has been shed in those fields out there; some of the cruelest battles of Spain's war to expel the Moors were fought on them. Who was in the right or who knew the truth does not matter; what's important is knowing that both sides were fighting the good fight.

"The good fight is the one we fight because our heart asks it of us. In the heroic ages—at the time of the knights in armor—this was easy. There were lands to conquer and much to do. Today, though, the world has changed a lot, and the good fight has shifted from the battlefields to the fields within ourselves.

"The good fight is the one that's fought in the name of our dreams. When we're young and our dreams first explode inside us with all of their force, we are very courageous, but we haven't yet learned how to fight. With great effort, we learn how to fight, but by then we no longer have the courage to go into combat. So we turn against ourselves and do battle within. We become our own worst enemy. We say that our dreams were childish, or too difficult to realize, or the result of our not having known enough about life. We kill our dreams because we are afraid to fight the good fight."

The pressure of Petrus's finger on my neck became stronger. I perceived that the cross on the church had been transformed; now its outline seemed to be that of a winged being, an angel. I blinked my eyes, and the cross became a cross again.

"The first symptom of the process of our killing our dreams is the lack of time," Petrus continued. "The busiest people I have known in my life always have time enough to do everything. Those who do nothing are always tired and pay no attention to the little amount of work they are required to do. They complain constantly that the day is too short. The truth is, they are afraid to fight the good fight.

"The second symptom of the death of our dreams lies in our certainties. Because we don't want to see life as a grand adventure, we begin to think of ourselves as wise and fair and correct in asking so little of life. We look beyond the walls of our day-to-day existence, and we hear the sound of lances breaking, we smell the dust and the sweat, and we see the great defeats and the fire in the eyes of the warriors. But we never see the delight, the immense delight in the hearts of those who are engaged in the battle. For them, neither victory nor defeat is important; what's important is only that they are fighting the good fight.

"And, finally, the third symptom of the passing of our dreams is peace. Life becomes a Sunday afternoon; we ask for nothing grand, and we cease to demand anything more than we are willing to give. In that state, we think of ourselves as being mature; we put aside the fantasies of our youth, and we seek personal and professional achievement. We are surprised when people our age say that they still want this or that out of life. But really, deep in our hearts, we know that what has happened is that we have renounced the battle for our dreams—we have refused to fight the good fight."

The tower of the church kept changing; now it appeared to be an angel with its wings spread. The more I blinked, the longer the figure remained. I wanted to speak to Petrus, but I sensed that he hadn't finished.

"When we renounce our dreams and find peace," he said after a while, "we go through a short period of tranquillity. But the dead dreams begin to rot within us and to infect our entire being. We become cruel to those around us, and then we begin to direct this cruelty against ourselves. That's when illnesses and psychoses arise. What we sought to avoid in combat—disappointment and defeat—came upon us because of our cowardice. And one day, the dead, spoiled dreams make it difficult to breathe, and we actually seek death. It's death that frees us from our certainties, from our work, and from that terrible peace of our Sunday afternoons."

Now I was sure that I was really seeing an angel, and I couldn't pay attention to what Petrus was saying. He must have sensed this, because he removed his finger from my neck and stopped talking. The image of the angel remained for a few moments and then disappeared. In its place, the tower of the church returned.

We were silent for a few minutes. Petrus rolled himself a cigarette and began to smoke. I took the bottle of wine from my knapsack and had a swallow. It was warm, but it was still delicious.

"What did you see?" he asked me.

I told him about the angel. I said that at the beginning, the image would disappear when I blinked.

"You, too, have to learn how to fight the good fight. You have already learned to accept the adventures and challenges that life provides, but you still want to deny anything that is extraordinary."

Petrus took a small object from his knapsack and handed it to me. It was a golden pin.

"This was a present from my grandmother. In the Order of RAM, all of the ancients have an object such as this. It's called "the Point of Cruelty." When you saw the angel appear on the church tower, you wanted to deny it, because it wasn't something that you are used to. In your view of the world, churches are churches, and visions occur only during the ecstasy created by the rituals of the Tradition."

I said that my vision must have been caused by the pressure he was applying to my neck.

"That's right, but that doesn't change anything. The fact is that you rejected the vision. Felicia of Aquitaine must have seen something similar, and she bet her entire life on what she saw. And the result of her having done that transformed her work into a work of love. The same thing probably happened to her brother. And the same thing happens to everyone every day: we always know which is the best road to follow, but we follow only the road that we have become accustomed to."

Petrus began to walk again, and I followed along. The rays of the sun made the pin in my hand glisten.

"The only way we can rescue our dreams is by being generous with ourselves. Any attempt to inflict self-punishment—no matter how subtle it may be—should be dealt with rigorously. In order to know when we are being cruel to ourselves, we have to transform any attempt at causing spiritual pain—such as guilt, remorse, indecision, and cowardice—into physical pain. By transforming a spiritual pain into a physical one, we can learn what harm it can cause us."

And then Petrus taught me the Cruelty Exercise.

The Cruelty Exercise

Every time a thought comes to mind that makes you feel bad about yourself—jealousy, self-pity, envy, hatred, and so on—do the following:

•

Dig the nail of your index finger into the cuticle of the thumb of the same hand until it becomes quite painful. Concentrate on the pain: it is a physical reflection of the suffering you are going through spiritually. Ease the pressure only when the cruel thought has gone.

•

Repeat this as many times as necessary until the thought has left you, even if this means digging your fingernail into your thumb over and over. Each time, it will take longer for the cruel thought to return, and eventually it will disappear altogether, so long as you do not fail to perform the exercise every time it comes to mind.

•

"In ancient times, they used a golden pin for this," he said. "Nowadays, things have changed, just as the sights along the Road to Santiago change."

Petrus was right. Seen from down at this level, the plain appeared to be a series of mountains in front of me.

"Think of something cruel that you did to yourself today, and perform the exercise."

I couldn't think of anything.

"That's the way it always is. We are only able to be kind to ourselves at the few times when we need severity."

Suddenly I remembered that I had called myself an idiot for having laboriously climbed the Peak of Forgiveness while the tourists had driven up in their cars. I knew that this was unfair and that I had been cruel to myself; the tourists, after all, were only looking for a place to sunbathe, while I was looking for my sword. I wasn't an idiot, even if I had felt like one. I dug the nail of my index finger forcefully into the cuticle of my thumb. I felt intense pain, and as I concentrated on it, the feeling of having been an idiot dissipated.

I described this to Petrus, and he laughed without saying anything.

That night, we stayed in a comfortable hotel in the village where the church I had focused on was located. After dinner, we decided to take a walk through the streets, as an aid to digestion.

"Of all the ways we have found to hurt ourselves, the

worst has been through love. We are always suffering because of someone who doesn't love us, or someone who has left us, or someone who won't leave us. If we are alone, it is because no one wants us; if we are married, we transform the marriage into slavery. What a terrible thing!" he said angrily.

We came to a square, and there was the church I had seen. It was small and lacked any architectural distinction. Its bell tower reached up toward the sky. I tried to see the angel again, but I couldn't.

"When the Son of God descended to earth, he brought love to us. But since people identified love only with suffering and sacrifice, they felt they had to crucify Jesus. Had they not done so, no one would have believed in the love that Jesus brought, since people were so used to suffering every day with their own problems."

We sat on the curb and stared at the church. Once again, it was Petrus who broke the silence.

"Do you know what Barabbas means, Paulo? *Bar* means son, and *abba* means father."

He gazed at the cross on the bell tower. His eyes shone, and I sensed that he was moved by something—perhaps by the love he had spoken so much about, but I couldn't be certain.

"The intentions of the divine glory were so wise!" he said, his voice echoing in the empty square. "When Pontius Pilate made the people choose, he actually gave them no choice at all. He presented them with one man who had been whipped and was falling apart, and he presented them with another man who held his head high—Barabbas, the revolutionary. God knew that the people would put the weaker one to death so that he could prove his love."

He concluded, "And regardless of which choice they made, it was the Son of God who was going to be crucified."

The Messenger

"AND HERE ALL ROADS TO SANTIAGO BECOME ONE."

It was early in the morning when we reached Puente de la Reina, where the name of the village was etched into the base of a statue of a pilgrim in medieval garb: three-cornered hat, cape, scallop shells, and in his hand a shepherd's crook with a gourd—a memorial to the epic journey, now almost forgotten, that Petrus and I were reliving.

We had spent the previous night at one of the many monasteries along the Road. The brother of the gate who had greeted us had warned us that we were not to speak a word within the walls of the abbey. A young monk had led each of us to an alcove, furnished only with the bare necessities: a hard bed, old but clean sheets, a pitcher of water and a basin for personal hygiene. There was no plumbing or hot water, and the schedule for meals was posted behind the door.

At the time indicated, we had come down to the dining hall. Because of the vow of silence, the monks communicated only with their glances, and I had the impression that their eyes gleamed with more intensity than those of other people. The supper was served early at narrow tables where we sat with the monks in their brown habits. From his seat, Petrus had given me a signal, and I had understood perfectly what he meant: he was dying to light a cigarette, but it looked like he was going to have to go through the entire night without one. The same was true for me, and I dug a nail into the cuticle of my thumb, which was already like raw meat. The moment was too beautiful for me to commit any kind of cruelty toward myself.

The meal was served: vegetable soup, bread, fish, and wine. Everyone prayed, and we recited the invocation with them. Afterward, as we ate, a monk read from an Epistle of Saint Paul.

"But God hath chosen the foolish things of the world to put to shame the wise, and God hath chosen the weak things of the world to put to shame the things which are mighty," read the monk in a thin, tuneless voice. "We are fools for Christ's sake. We are made as the filth of the world and are the offscouring of all things unto this day. But the kingdom of God is not in word but in power."

The admonitions of Paul to the Corinthians echoed off the bare walls of the dining hall throughout the meal.

As we entered Puente de la Reina we had been talking about the monks of the previous night. I confessed to Petrus that I had smoked in my room, in mortal fear that someone would smell my cigarette burning. He laughed, and I could tell that he had probably done the same thing.

"Saint John the Baptist went into the desert, but Jesus went among the sinners, and he traveled endlessly," Petrus said. "That's my preference, too."

In fact, aside from the time he had spent in the desert, Jesus had spent all of his life among people.

"Actually, his first miracle was not the saving of someone's soul nor the curing of a disease, and it wasn't an expulsion of the devil; it was the transformation of water into an excellent wine at a wedding because the wine supply of the owner of the house had run out."

After Petrus said this, he suddenly stopped walking. It was so abrupt that I became alarmed and stopped, too. We were at the bridge that gave its name to the village. Petrus, though, wasn't looking at the road in front of us. His eyes were fastened on two boys who were playing with a rubber ball at the edge of the river. They were eight or ten years old and seemed not to have noticed us. Instead of crossing the bridge, Petrus scrambled down the bank and approached the two boys. As always, I followed him without question.

The boys continued to ignore us. Petrus sat down to watch them at play, until the ball fell close to where he was seated. With a quick movement, he grabbed the ball and threw it to me.

I caught the ball in the air and waited to see what would happen.

One of the boys—the elder of the two—approached me. My first impulse was to throw him the ball, but Petrus's behavior had been so unusual that I decided that I would try to understand what was happening.

"Give me the ball, Mister," said the boy.

I looked at the small figure two meters away from me. I sensed that there was something familiar about him. It was the same feeling I had had about the gypsy.

The lad asked for the ball several times, and when he got no response from me, he bent down and picked up a stone.

"Give me the ball, or I'll throw a stone at you," he said.

Petrus and the other boy were watching me silently. The boy's aggressiveness irritated me.

"Throw the stone," I answered. "If it hits me, I'll come over there and whack you one."

I sensed that Petrus gave a sigh of relief. Something in the back of my mind told me that I had already lived through this scene.

The boy was frightened by what I said. He let the stone fall and tried a different approach.

"There's a relic here in Puente de la Reina. It used to belong to a rich pilgrim. I see by your shell and your knapsack that you are pilgrims. If you give me my ball, I'll give you the relic. It's hidden in the sand here along the river."

"I want to keep the ball," I answered, without much conviction. Actually, I wanted the relic. The boy seemed to be telling the truth. But maybe Petrus needed the ball for some reason, and I didn't want to disappoint him. He was my guide.

"Look, Mister, you don't need the ball," the boy said, now with tears in his eyes. "You're strong, and you've been around, and you know the world. All I know is the edge of this river, and that ball is my only toy. Please give it back."

The boy's words got to me. But the strangely familiar surroundings and my feeling that I had already read about or lived through the situation made me refuse again.

"No. I need the ball. I'll give you enough money to buy another one, even better than this one, but this one is mine."

When I said that, time seemed to stop. The surroundings began to change, even without Petrus's finger at my neck; for a fraction of a second, it seemed that we had been transported to a broad, terrifying, ashen desert. Neither Petrus nor the other boy was there, just myself and the boy in front of me. He was older, and his features were kinder and friendlier. But there was a light in his eyes that frightened me.

The vision didn't last more than a second. Then I was back at Puente de la Reina, where the many Roads to Santiago, coming from all over Europe, became one. There in front of me, a boy was asking for his ball, with a sweet, sad look in his eye.

Petrus approached me, took the ball from my hand, and gave it to the boy.

"Where is the relic hidden?" he asked the boy.

"What relic?" he said, as he grabbed his friend's hand, jumped away, and threw himself into the water.

We climbed the bank and crossed the bridge. I began to ask questions about what had happened, and I described my vision of the desert, but Petrus changed the subject and said that we should talk about it when we had traveled further from that spot.

Half an hour later, we came to a stretch of the Road that still showed vestiges of Roman paving. Here was another bridge, this one in ruins, and we sat down to have the breakfast that had been given to us by the monks: rye bread, yogurt, and goat's cheese.

"Why did you want the kid's ball?" Petrus asked me.

I told him that I hadn't wanted the ball—that I had acted that way because Petrus himself had behaved so strangely, as if the ball were very important to him.

"In fact, it was. It allowed you to win out over your personal devil."

My personal devil? This was the most ridiculous thing I had heard during the entire trip. I had spent six days coming and going in the Pyrenees, I had met a sorcerer priest who had performed no sorcery, and my finger was raw meat because every time I had a cruel thought about myself—from hypochondria, to feelings of guilt, to an inferiority complex—I had to dig my fingernail into my wounded thumb. But about one thing Petrus was right: my negative thinking had diminished considerably. Still, this story about having a personal devil was something I had never heard—and I wasn't going to swallow it easily.

"Today, before crossing the bridge, I had a strong feeling of the presence of someone, someone who was trying to give us a warning. But the warning was more for you than for me. A battle is coming on very soon, and you will have to fight the good fight.

"When you do not know your personal devil, he usually manifests himself in the nearest person. I looked around, and I saw those boys playing—and I figured that it was there that he would probably give his warning. But I was only following a hunch. I became sure that it was your personal devil when you refused to give the ball back."

I repeated that I had done so because I thought it was what Petrus wanted.

"Why me? I never said a word."

I began to feel a little dizzy. Maybe it was the food, which I was devouring voraciously after almost an hour of walking and feeling hungry. Still, I could not escape the feeling that the boy had seemed familiar.

"Your personal devil tried three classical approaches: a threat, a promise, and an attack on your weak side. Congratulations: you resisted bravely."

Now I remembered that Petrus had asked the boy about the relic. At the time, I had thought that the boy's response showed that he had tried to fool me. But he must really have had a relic hidden there—a devil never makes false promises.

"When the boy could not remember about the relic, your personal devil had gone away."

Then he added without blinking, "It is time to call him back. You are going to need him."

We were sitting on the ruins of the old bridge. Petrus carefully gathered the remains of the meal and put them into the paper bag that the monks had given us. In the fields in front of us, the workers began to arrive for the day's plowing, but they were so far away that I couldn't hear what they were saying. It was rolling land, and the cultivated patches created unusual designs across the landscape. Under our feet, the water course, almost nonexistent due to the drought, made very little noise.

"Before he went out into the world, Christ went into the desert to talk with his personal devil," Petrus began. "He learned what he needed to know about people, but he did not let the devil dictate the rules of the game; that is how he won.

"Once, a poet said that no man is an island. In order to fight the good fight, we need help. We need friends, and when the friends aren't nearby, we have to turn solitude into our main weapon. We need the help of everything around us in order to take the necessary steps toward our goal. Everything has to be a personal manifestation of our will to win the good fight. If we don't understand that, then we don't recognize that we need everything and everybody, and we become arrogant warriors. And our arrogance will defeat us in the end, because we will be so sure of ourselves that we won't see the pitfalls there on the field of battle."

His comments about warriors and battles reminded me again of Carlos Castaneda's Don Juan. I asked myself whether the old medicine man would have given lessons early in the morning, before his disciple had even been able to digest his breakfast. But Petrus continued:

"Over and above the physical forces that surround us and help us, there are basically two spiritual forces on our side: an angel and a devil. The angel always protects us and is a divine gift—you do not have to invoke him. Your angel's face is always visible when you look at the world with eyes that are receptive. He is this river, the workers in the field, and that blue sky. This old bridge that helps us to cross the stream was built here by the hands of anonymous Roman legionnaires, and the bridge, too, is the face of your angel. Our grandparents called him the guardian angel.

"The devil is an angel, too, but he is a free, rebellious force. I prefer to call him the messenger, since he is the main link between you and the world. In antiquity, he was represented by Mercury and by Hermes Trismegistus, the messenger of the gods. His arena is only on the material plane. He is present in the gold of the Church, because the gold comes from the earth, and the earth is your devil. He is present in our work and in our ways of dealing with money. When we let him loose, his tendency is to disperse himself. When we exorcise him, we lose all of the good things that he has to teach us; he knows a great deal about the world and about human beings. When we become fascinated by his power, he owns us and keeps us from fighting the good fight.

"So the only way to deal with our messenger is to accept him as a friend—by listening to his advice and asking for his help when necessary, but never allowing him to dictate the rules of the game. Like you did with the boy. To keep the messenger from dictating the rules of the game, it is necessary first that you know what you want and then that you know his face and his name."

"How can I know them?" I asked.

And then Petrus taught me the Messenger Ritual.

"Wait until night to perform it, when it is easier," Petrus said. "Today, at your first meeting, he will tell you his name. This name is secret and should never be told to anyone, not even me. Whoever knows the name of your messenger can destroy you."

Petrus got up, and we began to walk. Shortly, we reached the field where the farmers were working. We said "*Buenos días*" to them and went on down the road.

"If I had to use a metaphor, I would say that your angel is your armor, and your messenger is your sword. Armor protects you under any set of circumstances, but a sword can fall to the ground in the midst of a battle, or it can kill a friend, or be turned against its owner. A sword can be used for almost anything . . . except as something to sit on," he said, laughing.

We stopped in a town for lunch, and the young waiter who served us was clearly in a bad mood. He didn't answer any of our questions, he served the meal sloppily, and he even succeeded in spilling coffee on Petrus's shorts. I watched my guide go through a transformation: furious, he went to find the owner and complained loudly about the waiter's rudeness. He wound up going to the men's room and taking off his shorts; the owner cleaned them and spread them out to dry.

As we waited for the two o'clock sun to dry Petrus's shorts, I was thinking about everything we had talked about that morning. It was true that most of what Petrus had said about the boy by the river made sense. After all, I had had a vision of the desert and of a face. But that story about "the messenger" seemed a little primitive to me. For a person with any intelligence here in the the twentieth century, the concepts of hell, of sin, and of the devil did not make much sense. In the Tradition, whose teachings I had followed for much longer than I had followed the Road to Santiago, the messenger was a spirit that ruled the forces of the earth and was always a friend. He was often used in magical operations but never as an ally or counselor with regard to daily events. Petrus had led me to believe that I could use the friendship of the messenger as a means to improve my work and my dealings with the world. Beside being profane, this idea seemed to me to be childish.

The Messenger Ritual

1. Sit down and relax completely. Let your mind wander and your thinking flow without restraint. After a while, begin to repeat to yourself, "Now I am relaxed, and I am in the deepest kind of sleep."
2. When you feel that your mind is no longer concerned with anything, imagine a billow of fire to your right. Make the flames lively and brilliant. Then quietly say, "I order my subconscious to show itself. I order it to open and reveal its magic secrets." Wait a bit, and concentrate only on the fire. If an image appears, it will be a manifestation of your subconscious. Try to keep it alive.
3. Keeping the fire always to your right, now begin to imagine another billow of fire to your left. When the flames are lively, say the following words quietly: "May the power of the Lamb, which manifests itself in everything and everyone, manifest itself also in me when I invoke my messenger. (Name of messenger) will appear before me now."
4. Talk with your messenger, who should appear between the two fires. Discuss your specific problems, ask for advice, and give him the necessary orders.
5. When your conversation has ended, dismiss the messenger with the following words: "I thank the Lamb for the miracle I have performed. May (name of messenger) return whenever he is invoked, and when he is far away, may he help me to carry on my work."

•

Note: On the first invocation—or during the first invocations, depending on the ability of the person performing the ritual to concentrate—do not say the name of the messenger. Just say "he." If the ritual is well performed, the messenger should immediately reveal his name telepathically. If not, insist until you learn his name, and only then begin the conversation. The more the ritual is repeated, the stronger the presence of the messenger will be and the more rapid his actions.

•

But I had sworn to Mme Lourdes that I would give total obedience to my guide. Once again, I had to dig my nail into my red, raw thumb.

"I should not have put him down," Petrus said about the waiter after we had left. "I mean, after all, he didn't spill that coffee on me but on the world that he hated. He knows that there is a huge world out there that extends well beyond the borders of his imagination. And his participation in that world is limited to getting up early, going to the bakery, waiting on whoever comes by, and masturbating every night, dreaming about the women he will never get to know."

It was the time of day when we usually stopped for our siesta, but Petrus had decided to keep walking. He said that it was a way of doing penance for his intolerance. And I, who had not done a thing, had to trudge along with him under the hot sun. I was thinking about the good fight and the millions of souls who, right then, were scattered all over the planet, doing things they didn't want to do. The Cruelty Exercise, in spite of having made my thumb raw, was helping me. It had helped me to see how my mind could betray me, pushing me into situations I wanted no part of and into feelings that were no help to me. Right then, I began to hope that Petrus was right: that a messenger really did exist and that I could talk to him about practical matters and ask him for help with my day-to-day problems. I was anxious for night to fall.

Meanwhile, Petrus could not stop talking about the waiter. Finally, he wound up convincing himself that he had acted properly; once again, he used a Christian argument to make his case.

"Christ forgave the adulterous woman but cursed the grower who would not give him a fig. And I am not here, either, just to be a nice guy."

That was it. In his view, the matter was settled. Once again, the Bible had saved him.

We reached Estella at almost nine o'clock at night. I took a bath, and we went down to eat. The author of the first guide for the Jacobean route, Aymeric Picaud, had described Estella as a "fertile place, with good bread and great wine, meat, and fish. Its river, the Ega, has good, fresh, clean water." I didn't drink the river water, but as far as the menu at our restaurant was concerned, Picaud's assessment was still right, even after eight centuries. It offered braised leg of lamb, artichoke hearts, and a Rioja wine from a very good year. We sat at the table for a long time, talking about inconsequential things and enjoying the wine. But finally Petrus said that it was a good time for me to have my first contact with my messenger.

We went out to look around the city. Some alleys led directly to the river—as they do in Venice—and I decided to sit down in one of them. Petrus knew that from that point on it was I who would conduct the ceremony, so he hung back.

I looked at the river for a long time. Its water and its sound began to take me out of this world and to create a profound serenity in me. I closed my eyes and imagined the first billow of fire. It was not easy to imagine at first, but finally it appeared.

I pronounced the ritual words, and another billow of fire appeared to my left. The space between the two billows, illuminated by the fires, was completely empty. I kept looking at that space for a while, trying not to think, so that the messenger would manifest himself. But instead of his appearing, various exotic scenes began to appear—the entrance to a pyramid, a woman dressed in pure gold, some black men dancing around a fire. The images came and went in rapid succession, and I let them flow uncontrolled. There also appeared some stretches of the Road that I had traversed with Petrus—byways, restaurants, forests—until, with no warning, the ashen desert that I had seen that morning appeared between the two fires. And there, looking at me, was the friendly man with the traitorous look in his eyes.

He laughed, and I smiled in my trance. He showed me a closed bag, then opened it and looked inside—but in such a way that I could not see into it. Then a name came to my mind: Astrain.[1]

I began to envision the name and make it dance between the two fires, and the messenger gave a nod of approval; I had learned his name.

It was time to end the exercise. I said the ritual words and extinguished the fires—first on the left and then on the right. I opened my eyes, and there was the river Ega in front of me.

"It was much less difficult than I had imagined," I said to Petrus, after I had told him about everything that had occurred between the two fires.

"This was your first contact—a meeting to establish mutual recognition and mutual friendship. Your conversations with the messenger will be productive if you invoke him every day and discuss your problems with him. But you have to know how to distinguish between what is real assistance and what is a trap. Keep your sword ready every time you meet with him."

"But I don't have my sword yet," I answered.

"Right, so he can't cause you much damage. But even so, don't make it easy for him."

[1]This is not the real name.

The ritual having ended, I left Petrus and went back to the hotel. In bed, I thought about the poor young waiter who had served us lunch. I felt like going back there and teaching him the Messenger Ritual, telling him that he could change everything if he wanted to. But it was useless to try to save the world: I hadn't even been able to save myself yet.[2]

[2]This description of my first experience with the Messenger Ritual is incomplete. Actually, Petrus explained the meaning of the visions, of the memories, and of the bag that Astrain showed me. But since each meeting with the messenger is different for every person, I do not want to insist on my own personal experience as it might influence the experience of others.

Love

"Talking with your messenger doesn't mean asking questions about the world of the spirits," Petrus said the next day. "The messenger performs only one function for you: he helps you with regard to the material world. And he will give you this help only if you know exactly what it is that you want."

We had stopped in a town to have something to drink. Petrus had ordered a beer, and I asked for a soft drink. My fingers made abstract designs in the water on the table, and I was worried.

"You told me that the messenger had manifested himself in the boy because he needed to tell me something."

"Something urgent," he confirmed.

We talked some more about messengers, angels, and devils. It was difficult for me to accept such a practical application of the mysteries of the Tradition. Petrus said that we are always seeking some kind of reward. But I reminded him that Jesus had said that the rich man would not enter into the kingdom of heaven.

"But Jesus rewarded the man who knew how to make his master more adept. People did not believe in Jesus just because he was an outstanding orator: he had to perform miracles and reward those who followed him."

"No one is going to blaspheme Jesus in my bar," said the owner, who had been listening to our conversation.

"No one is blaspheming Jesus," Petrus answered. "People speak poorly of Jesus when they commit the sin of taking his name in vain. Like all of you did out there in the plaza."

The owner hesitated for a moment. But then he answered, "I had nothing to do with that. I was only a child at the time."

"The guilty ones are always the others," Petrus mumbled. The owner went into the kitchen, and I asked Petrus what he was talking about.

"Fifty years ago, in this twentieth century of ours, a gypsy was burned at the stake out there in the plaza. He was accused of sorcery and of blaspheming the sacred host. The case was lost amid the news of the Spanish civil war, and no one remembers it today. Except the people who live here."

"How do you know about it, Petrus?"

"Because I have already walked the Road to Santiago."

We went on drinking there in the empty bar. The sun was hot, and it was our siesta time. A few minutes later, the owner reappeared, accompanied by the town priest.

"Who are you people?" asked the priest.

Petrus showed him the scallop shells sewn to his knapsack. For twelve hundred years, pilgrims had passed along the Road in front of the bar, and the tradition was that every pilgrim was respected and welcomed under any circumstance. The priest changed his tone.

"How can it be that pilgrims on the Road to Santiago are speaking poorly of Jesus?" he asked, in a tone that was appropriate to a catechism.

"Nobody here was speaking poorly of Jesus. We were speaking poorly of the crimes committed in the name of Jesus. Like the gypsy that was burned at the stake there in the square."

The shells on Petrus's knapsack had also changed the owner's attitude. Now he addressed us with some respect.

"The curse of the gypsy is still with us today," he said, and the priest looked at him reprovingly.

Petrus wanted to know how. The priest said that these were stories told by the villagers and that the church did not approve of them. But the owner of the bar went on:

"Before the gypsy died, he said that the youngest child in the village was going to receive and incorporate his devils. And that when that child became old and died, the devils would pass on to another child. And so on, for all the centuries to come."

"The soil here is the same as the soil in the other towns around here," said the priest. "When the other towns have a drought, we do, too. When it rains and there's a good harvest, we fill our barns, too. Nothing has happened here with us that has not happened in the neighboring towns, too. This whole story is a fantasy."

"Nothing has happened because we isolated the curse," said the owner.

"Well, then, let's see it," answered Petrus. The priest laughed and said that that was no way to talk. The owner of the bar made the sign of the cross. But neither of them moved.

Petrus got the check and insisted that someone take us to the person who had inherited the curse. The priest excused himself, saying that he had been interrupted at something important and had to get back to his church. And he left before anyone could say anything.

The owner of the bar looked at Petrus fearfully.

"Not to worry," said my guide. "Just show us the house where the curse resides. We are going to try to rid the town of it."

The owner of the bar went out into the dusty street with us. The hot sun of the afternoon beat down everywhere. We walked to the outskirts of the town, and he pointed to a house set off by itself at the side of the Road.

"We always send meals, clothing, everything they need," he apologized. "But not even the priest goes in there."

We said good-bye to him and walked toward the house. The owner of the bar waited there, perhaps thinking that we would pass it by. But Petrus went up to the house and knocked on the door, and when I looked around, the bar owner had disappeared.

A woman of about seventy came to the door. At her side was an enormous black dog, wagging his tail and apparently happy to see company. The woman asked what we wanted; she said she was busy washing clothes and had left some pots on the fire. She did not seem surprised by our visit. I figured that many pilgrims, not knowing about the curse, must have knocked on the door seeking shelter.

"We are pilgrims on the Road to Compostela, and we need some hot water," Petrus said. "I knew that you would not refuse us."

With a show of irritation, the woman opened the door. We went into a small room, clean but poorly furnished. There was a sofa with its stuffing coming out, a bureau, and a Formica-topped table with two chairs. On the bureau was an image of the Sacred Heart of Jesus, some saints, and a crucifix made of mirrors. Through one of the two doors in the room, I could see the bedroom. The woman led Petrus through the other door into the kitchen.

"I have some water boiling," she said. "Let me get you a container, and you can both get going."

I was there in the living room, alone with the huge dog. He wagged his tail, docile and contented. The woman came back with an old can, filled it with water, and held it out to Petrus.

"There. Go with God's blessing."

But Petrus did not move. He took a tea bag from his

knapsack, put it in the can, and said that he would like to share the little he had with her in appreciation for her welcome.

The woman, clearly upset now, brought two cups and sat down at the table with Petrus. I kept looking at the dog as I listened to their conversation.

"They told me in the village that there was a curse on this house," Petrus commented boldly. The dog's eyes seemed to light up, as if he had understood what had been said. The old woman stood up immediately.

"That's a lie. It's an old superstition. Please finish your tea, because I have lots of things to do."

The dog sensed the woman's sudden mood change. He remained still but alert. But Petrus continued to do what he was doing. He slowly poured the tea into the cup, raised it to his lips, and put it down on the table without drinking a drop.

"That's really hot," he said. "I think I will wait until it cools off a bit."

The woman did not sit down again. She was visibly uncomfortable with us there and clearly regretted having opened the door. She noticed that I was staring fixedly at the dog and called him to her. The animal obeyed, but when he reached her side, he turned to look at me.

"This is why he did it, my friend," Petrus said, looking at me. "This is why your messenger appeared yesterday in the child."

Suddenly I realized that I was not just looking at the dog. As soon as I had come in, the animal had hypnotized me and had kept my eyes fastened on him. The dog was staring at me and making me do as he wanted. I began to feel weak, as if I would like to lie down and sleep on the torn couch; it was really hot outside, and I did not feel much like walking. The feelings all seemed strange to me, and I had the impression that I was falling into a trap. The dog continued to look fixedly at me, and the more he looked at me, the more tired I felt.

"Let's go," said Petrus, getting up and offering me the cup of tea. "Drink a bit of tea, because the lady wants us to get going."

I hesitated, but I took the cup, and the hot tea revived me. I wanted to say something, ask what the animal's name was, but I could not get my voice to work. Something inside me had been aroused, something that Petrus had not taught me but that nevertheless began to manifest itself. I felt an uncontrollable desire to say strange words, the meaning of which I didn't even know. I thought that Petrus had put something in the tea. Everything began to blur, and I heard only very faintly the woman repeat to Petrus that we had to leave. I was in a state of euphoria, and I decided to speak the strange words that were coming to my mind.

All I could see in the room was the dog. When I began to say those strange words, the dog started to growl. He understood what I was saying. I became more excited and continued to speak, louder and louder. The dog rose and bared his teeth. He was no longer the docile animal I had seen on arrival but something awful and threatening that could attack me at any moment. I knew that the words were protecting me, and I began to speak even louder, focusing all of my energies on the dog. I felt that I had a different power within me and that it could keep the animal from attacking me.

From that point on, everything began to happen in slow motion. I saw the woman come toward me, shrieking and trying to push me out of the house. And I saw Petrus holding the woman back. The dog paid no attention at all to their struggle. Snarling and baring his teeth, he continued to stare at me. I was trying to understand the strange language I was speaking, but each time I stopped to think about it, my power would weaken and the dog would start coming toward me; he was growing stronger. I began to scream, giving up my attempt at understanding, and the woman began to scream, too. The dog barked and threatened me, but so long as I continued speaking, I was safe. I heard raucous laughter, but I did not know if it was really occurring or if it was in my imagination.

Suddenly, a strong wind swept through the house, and the dog howled and leapt on me. I raised my arm to protect my face, shouted something, and waited to see what the impact would be.

The dog had thrown himself upon me with all his strength, and I fell to the couch. For a few moments, our eyes were locked on each other's; in the next second, he ran from the house.

I began to cry hysterically. I thought of my family, my wife, and my friends. I experienced an enormous feeling of love and, at the same time, an absurd happiness, because all of a sudden I understood everything about the dog.

Petrus took me by the arm and led me outside, as the woman pushed us both from behind. I looked around, and there was no sign of the dog. I hugged Petrus and continued to cry as we walked along in the sunlight.

The next part of the journey is a blank; I only came to my senses later at a fountain, where Petrus was throwing water in my face and on the back of my neck. I asked for some to drink, and he said that if I drank anything then, I would vomit. I was a little nauseated, but I felt good. An immense love for everything and everybody had invaded my being. I looked around me and sensed the trees along the edge of the Road, the small fountain where we had stopped, the fresh breeze, and the bird song from the forest. I was seeing the face of my angel, as Petrus had told me I would. I asked how far we were from the woman's house, and he said we had been walking for about fifteen minutes.

"You probably want to know what happened," he said.

Actually that was not important to me at all. I was just

happy about the feelings of love that permeated me. The dog, the woman, the owner of the bar, everything was a distant memory that seemed to have nothing to do with what I was feeling now. I told Petrus that I would like to go on walking because I was feeling so well.

I got up, and we returned to the Road to Santiago. Throughout the rest of the afternoon, I said almost nothing, delighting in the agreeable feeling that seemed to fill me. I still thought that perhaps Petrus had put something in the tea, but this was no longer important.

We arrived at a hotel at eight o'clock that night, and I was still in this state of beatitude, although it had diminished somewhat. The owner asked me for my passport so that I could register, and I gave it to him.

"You're from Brazil? I've been there. I stayed at a hotel on Ipanema Beach."

That absurd message brought me back to reality. There, along the Jacobean route, in a town that had been built centuries ago was a hotel keeper who had been to Ipanema Beach.

"I'm ready to talk," I told Petrus. "I have to know what happened today."

The sense of beatitude had passed. Reason took its place, and my fear of the unknown, along with an urgent need to get my feet back on the ground, had returned.

"After we eat," said Petrus.

Petrus asked the hotel owner to turn on the television but to leave the sound off. He said that this was the best way for me to hear everything he said without asking a lot of questions, because part of me would be watching the television screen. He asked me how much I remembered of what had happened. I answered that I remembered everything except the part where we had walked to the fountain.

"That part is not important to the story," he answered. On the television screen, a film having something to do with coal mines began. The actors were dressed in turn-of-the-century clothing.

"Yesterday, when I sensed the urgency in your messenger, I knew that a battle along the Road to Santiago was about to begin. You are here to find your sword and learn the RAM practices. But every time a guide leads a pilgrim, there is at least one situation that goes beyond the control of both of them. It represents a kind of practical test of what is being taught. In your case, this was the encounter with the dog.

"The details of the battle and the explanation for the many devils that can be present in an animal I will explain later. What is important now is that you understand that the woman was already used to the curse. She had accepted it as normal, and the attitudes of the world were fine with her. She had learned to be satisfied with very little.

"When you exorcised the poor old woman's demons, you also unbalanced her universe. The other day we talked about the cruelty that people are capable of inflicting on themselves. Often, when we try to demonstrate that life is good and generous, such people reject the idea as if it came from the devil. People don't like to ask too much of life because they are afraid they will be defeated. But if someone wants to fight the good fight, that person must view the world as if it were a marvelous treasure waiting to be discovered and won."

Petrus asked me if I knew what I was doing there on the Road to Santiago.

"I am searching for my sword," I answered.

"And what do you want your sword for?"

"I want it because it will bring me the power and the wisdom of the Tradition."

I felt that he was not too happy with my response. But he continued, "You are here, searching for a reward. You are daring to dream, and you are doing everything possible to make your dream come true. You need to have a better idea of what it is that you are going to do with your sword; this has to be clearer to you before we can find it. But there is one thing in your favor: you are looking for a reward. You are walking the Road to Santiago only because you want to be rewarded for your effort. I have noticed that you have applied everything I have taught you; you have been looking for a practical outcome. That is very positive.

"The only thing missing is your learning how to combine the RAM practices with your own intuition. The language of your heart is what is going to determine the best way to find and use your sword. If you can't bring the two together, the exercises and the RAM practices will become simply a part of the useless wisdom of the Tradition."

Petrus had told me this before, in a different way, and although I agreed with him, it wasn't what I wanted to hear about. There were two aspects of the experience that I could not understand: the strange language I had spoken and my feeling of love and happiness after having evicted the dog.

"The sensation of happiness occurred because your action was suffused with agape."

"You talk a lot about agape, but you haven't really explained to me what it is. I have a feeling we are dealing with something that relates to a higher form of love."

"That's exactly right. In a little while, the time will come for you to experience that intense love—the love that consumes the one who loves. Meanwhile, be happy knowing that this love has manifested itself freely in you."

"I have had this sensation before, but it was brief, and it was different somehow. It always happened after a professional triumph, a win, or when I felt that Lady Luck was being generous with me. But when the feeling arose, I always pulled back; I felt frightened of experiencing it too intensely—as if the happiness could cause envy in others or as if I were unworthy of it."

"All of us, before we learn about agape, act that way," he said, with his gaze on the television screen.

I asked him about the strange language I had spoken.

"That was a surprise to me. That is not a practice of the Road to Santiago. It is a divine grace, and it is one of the RAM practices for the Road to Rome."

I had already heard some things about the divine graces, but I asked Petrus to explain them to me.

"They are gifts from the Holy Ghost that manifest themselves in people. There are a number of different kinds: the gift of curing, the gift of miracles, the gift of prophecy, among others. You experienced the gift of tongues, which is what the apostles experienced at Pentecost.

"The gift of tongues is related to direct communication with the Holy Ghost. It is used in powerful oratory, in exorcisms—as was your case—and in wisdom. Your days on the Road and the RAM practices not only led to the danger that the dog represented for you but also by chance gave rise to the gift of tongues. It won't happen again, unless you find your sword and decide to walk the Road to Rome. In any case, it was a good omen."

I watched the silent television screen. The story of the coal mines had been transformed into a succession of men and women talking and arguing. Every so often, an actor and an actress would kiss.

"One other thing," said Petrus. "It may be that you are going to meet up with that dog again. Next time, don't try to invoke the gift of tongues, because it won't come back. Trust in what your intuition is going to tell you. I am going to teach you another RAM practice that will enhance your intuition. With it, you will begin to learn the secret language of your mind, and that language will be very useful to you for the rest of your life."

Petrus turned the television off, just as I was beginning to get involved in the story. He went to the bar and asked for a bottle of mineral water. We each drank a little, and he took what was left outdoors.

We felt the fresh air, and for a few moments neither of us said anything. The night was quiet, and the Milky Way overhead reminded me again that my goal was to find my sword.

After some time, Petrus taught me the Water Exercise.

"I'm tired; I'm going to bed," he said. "But do this exercise now. Call up your intuition again, your secret side. Don't be concerned about logic, because water is a fluid element, and it does not allow itself to be controlled easily. But water, little by little and in a nonviolent way, is going to build a new relationship between you and your universe."

And before he went through the door of the hotel, he added, "It is not often that someone gets help from a dog."

I continued to enjoy the freshness and the silence of the night. The hotel was out in the country, and there was no one there with me. I remembered the owner, who had been to Ipanema; he must find it absurd to see me there in that arid place, burned by the sun that shone down with such ferocity day after day.

The Arousal of Intuition

(The Water Exercise)

Make a puddle of water on a smooth, nonabsorbent surface. Look into the puddle for a while. Then, begin to play with it, without any particular commitment or objective. Make designs that mean absolutely nothing.

•

Do this exercise for a week, allowing at least ten minutes each time.

•

Don't look for practical results from this exercise; it is simply calling up your intuition, little by little. When this intuition begins to manifest itself at other times of the day, always trust in it.

•

I was getting sleepy, so I decided to do the exercise right away. I emptied the remaining water onto the cement and a small puddle formed. I did not have any image or shape in mind, and I wasn't seeking one. I swirled my fingers through the cold water, and I experienced the same kind of hypnosis that one feels when staring into the flames of a fire. I thought about nothing; I was just playing—playing with a puddle of water. I made some streaks at the edge of the puddle, and it seemed to become a wet sun; but the streaks quickly rejoined the puddle and disappeared. With the palm of my hand, I batted at the center of the puddle; the water splashed away, covering the cement with droplets, black stars on a gray background. I was completely lost in that absurd exercise, an exercise that had not the slightest purpose but was delightful to do. I felt that my mind had stopped working almost completely, a feeling I had previously achieved only after long periods of meditation and relaxation. At the same time, something told me that down deep, in places that my mind could not reach, a force was being born and becoming ready to manifest itself.

I stayed there for quite a while playing with the puddle, and it was difficult to give up the exercise. If Petrus had taught me the water exercise at the beginning of the journey, there is no doubt that I would have found it to be a waste of time. But now, having spoken in strange tongues and having exorcised devils, that puddle of water established a contact—however fragile—with the Milky Way above me. It reflected the stars, created designs I could not understand, and gave me the feeling not that I was wasting time but that I was creating a new code for communicating with the world. It was the soul's secret code—the language that we know but so seldom hear.

When I came back to myself, it was late. The lights at the door had been turned off, and I entered the hotel quietly. In my room, once again I invoked Astrain. He appeared more clearly, and I spoke to him for a while about my sword and about my goals in life. For now, he made no answer, but Petrus had told me that as the invocations continued, Astrain would become a live and powerful presence at my side.

Marriage

LOGROÑO IS ONE OF THE LARGEST CITIES THROUGH WHICH pilgrims traveling the Jacobean route pass. The only other city of any size that we had entered had been Pamplona—but we had not spent the night there. On the afternoon that we arrived in Logroño, though, the city was preparing for a great festival, and Petrus suggested that we stay there, at least for one night.

I was used to the silence and freedom of the countryside, so the idea did not much appeal to me. It had been five days since the incident with the dog, and every night since then, I had invoked Astrain and performed the Water Exercise. I was feeling very calm, and I was more and more aware of the importance of the Road to Santiago in my life and of the question of what I was going to do after the pilgrimage had ended. The area we walked through was like a desert, the meals were seldom very good, and the long days on the Road were exhausting, but I was living my dream.

All of these feelings disappeared the day we arrived at Logroño. Instead of the warm, pure air of the fields, we found a city crowded with cars, journalists, and television equipment. Petrus went into the first bar we saw to ask what was happening.

"You didn't know? Today is the wedding of Colonel M.'s daughter," said the bartender. "We are going to have a huge public banquet in the square, and I am closing early today."

It was impossible to find rooms at a hotel, but eventually we were given lodging at the home of an elderly couple who had noticed the shells on Petrus's knapsack. We showered, I put on the only trousers that I had brought, and we left for the town square.

Dozens of workers, perspiring in their black suits, were putting the finishing touches on the tables that had been placed all over the square. National television crews were filming the preparations. We went down a narrow street that led to the church of the Royal Santiago parish, where the ceremony was about to begin.

Flocking to the church were great numbers of well-dressed people. The women's makeup was running in the heat, and their children, dressed in white, were irritable. Some fireworks were exploding overhead as a long black limousine stopped at the main gate. It was the groom arriving. There was no room for Petrus and me in the church, so we decided to go back to the square.

Petrus wanted to scout around, but I sat down on one of the benches, waiting for the ceremony to end and the banquet to begin. Nearby, a popcorn vendor, hoping for a windfall profit, awaited the crowd from the church.

"Are you one of the invited guests?" he asked me.

"No," I answered. "We are pilgrims on our way to Compostela."

"There's a train that goes there straight from Madrid, and if you leave on a Friday, you get your hotel free."

"Yes, but we are doing a pilgrimage."

The vendor looked at me and said respectfully, "Pilgrimages are made by saints."

I decided not to get into that discussion. He said that his daughter had already been married but was now separated from her husband.

"In Franco's time, there was more respect," he said. "Nowadays, no one cares about the family."

Despite my being in a strange country, where it is never advisable to talk politics, I could not let this pass without a response. I said that Franco had been a dictator and that nothing during his time could have been better than now.

The vendor's face turned red.

"Who do you think you are, talking like that?"

"I know this country's history. I know the war the people fought for their freedom. I have read about the crimes of the Franco forces during the Spanish civil war."

"Well, I fought in that war. I was there when my family's blood was spilled. Whatever stories you have read don't interest me; what I'm concerned about is what happens to my family. I fought against Franco, but when he won the war, life was better for me. I'm not a beggar, and I have my little popcorn stand. It wasn't this socialist government we have now that helped me. I'm worse off now than I was before."

I remembered what Petrus had said about people being content with very little. I decided not to press my point of view, and I moved to another bench.

When Petrus came back, I told him about my exchange with the popcorn vendor.

"Conversation is useful," he said, "when people want to convince themselves that what they are saying is right. I am a member of the Italian Communist Party. But I didn't know about this fascist side of you."

"What do you mean, fascist side?" I asked him angrily.

"Well, you helped the popcorn man to convince himself that Franco was good. Maybe he never knew why. Now he knows."

"Well, I'm just as surprised to learn that the ICP believes in the gifts of the Holy Ghost."

"Well, I have to be careful about what the neighbors will think," he said, laughing.

The fireworks started up again, as musicians climbed to the bandstand and tuned their instruments. The festival was about to begin.

I looked up at the sky. It was growing dark, and the stars were beginning to appear. Petrus went over to one of the waiters and brought back two plastic cups full of wine.

"It is good luck to have a drink before the party begins,"

he said, handing me one of the cups. "Have some of this. It will help you forget about the popcorn man."

"I wasn't even thinking about him anymore."

"Well, you should. Because what happened with him is an example of mistaken behavior. We are always trying to convert people to a belief in our own explanation of the universe. We think that the more people there are who believe as we do, the more certain it will be that what we believe is the truth. But it doesn't work that way at all.

"Look around. Here is a huge party about to begin. A commemoration. Many different things are being celebrated simultaneously: the father's hope that his daughter would marry, the daughter's wish for the same thing, the groom's dreams. That's good, because they believe in their dreams and want to demonstrate to everyone that they have achieved their goals. It is not a party that is being held to convince anyone of anything, so it's going to be a lot of fun. From what I can see, they are people who have fought the good fight of love."

"But you are trying to convince me, Petrus, by guiding me along the Road to Santiago."

He gave me a cold look.

"I am only teaching you the RAM practices. But you will find your sword only if you discover that the Road and the truth and the life are in your heart."

Petrus pointed to the sky, where the stars were now clearly visible.

"There is no religion that is capable of bringing all of the stars together, because if this were to happen, the universe would become a gigantic, empty space and would lose its reason for existence. Every star—and every person—has their own space and their own special characteristics. There are green stars, yellow stars, blue stars, and white stars, and there are comets, meteors and meteorites, nebulas and rings. What appear from down here to be a huge number of bodies that are similar to each other are really a million different things, spread over a space that is beyond human comprehension."

A rocket from the fireworks burst, and its light obscured the sky for a moment. A shower of brilliant green streamers fell to the ground.

"Earlier, we only heard their noise because of the daylight. Now we can see their light," Petrus said. "That's the only change people can aspire to."

The bride came out of the church, and people shouted and threw their handfuls of rice. She was a thin girl of about sixteen, and she held the arm of a boy in a tuxedo. The congregation appeared and began to move toward the square.

"Look, there's the colonel. . . . Oh, look at the bride's dress. How beautiful," said some boys near us. The guests took their places at the tables, the waiters served the wine, and the band began to play. The popcorn vendor was surrounded by a mob of screaming boys who made their purchases and then scattered the empty bags on the ground. I imagined that for the townspeople of Logroño, at least that night, the rest of the world—with its threat of nuclear war, unemployment, and murders—did not exist. It was a festival night, the tables had been placed in the square for the people, and everyone felt important.

A television crew came toward us, and Petrus averted his face. But the men passed us by, heading for one of the guests who sat near us. I recognized immediately who he was: Antonio, the man who had led the Spanish fans in their cheers at the World Cup in Mexico in 1986. When the interview was over, I went up to him and told him that I was a Brazilian; feigning anger, he complained about a goal of which Spain had been robbed in the opening round of the Cup.[1]

But then he gave me a hug, and said that Brazil would soon once again have the best players in the world.

"How do you manage to see the game when your back is always to the field and you are inciting the fans," I asked. It was something I had noticed over and over again during the television transmissions of the World Cup games.

[1]In the game between Spain and Brazil at that World Cup in Mexico, a Spanish goal was nullified because the referee had not seen the ball hit behind the goal line before ricocheting out. Brazil wound up winning that game 1–0.

"That's what gives me satisfaction. Helping the fans believe in victory."

And then, as if he too were a guide on the Road to Santiago, he said, "Fans who lack the faith can make a team lose a game it is already winning."

Manolo was then grabbed by others who wanted to interview him, but I stood there thinking about what he had said. Even without ever having walked the Road to Santiago, he knew what it was to fight the good fight.

I found Petrus hiding behind some trees, obviously uncomfortable with the presence of the television cameras. It was only after their lights had been turned off that he emerged from the trees and relaxed a bit. We asked for two more cups of wine, I fixed myself a plate of canapés, and Petrus found a table where we could sit with some of the guests.

The newlyweds cut into a huge wedding cake. People cheered.

"They must really love each other," I said.

"Of course they do," said a dark-suited man sitting with us. "Have you ever heard of anyone marrying for any other reason?"

I kept my answer to myself, remembering what Petrus had said about the popcorn vendor. But my guide didn't let it pass.

"Which kind of love are you talking about: eros, philos, or agape?"

The man looked at him blankly. Petrus got up, filled his cup, and asked me to walk with him.

"There are three Greek words that mean love," he began. "Today, you are seeing a manifestation of eros, the feeling of love that exists between two people."

The bride and groom were smiling for the photographers and accepting congratulations.

"It appears that these two really do love each other," he said, looking at the couple. "And they believe that their love will grow. But shortly, they will be alone with each other, struggling to earn a living, build a house, and share their adventure. This is what ennobles love and dignifies it. He will do his time in the army. She is probably a good cook and will be an excellent housewife, because she has been trained since she was a child for that role. She will be good company for him, they'll have children, and they will feel that they are building something together. They'll be fighting the good fight. So even if they have problems, they will never be really unhappy.

"However, this story that I am telling you could go a very different way. He might begin to feel that he's not free enough to express all of the eros, all of the love that he has for other women. She might begin to feel that she gave up a brilliant career in order to be with her husband. So instead of creating something together, each could begin to feel robbed of a means of expressing love. Eros, the spirit that unites them, would begin to reveal only its negative side. And what God had provided to humans as their noblest sentiment would become a source of hatred and destructiveness."

I looked around me. Eros was present in many of the relationships there. The Water Exercise had awakened the language of my heart, and I was seeing people in a different way. Maybe it was the days of solitude on the road, or maybe it was the RAM practices, but I could feel the presence of good eros and evil eros, just as Petrus had described.

"It's strange," Petrus said, sensing the same thing. "Whether it's good or evil, the face of eros is never the same for any two people. Just like the stars I was talking about half an hour ago. And no one can escape eros. Everyone needs its presence, despite the fact that many times, eros makes us feel apart from the world, trapped in our solitude."

The band began to play a waltz. The guests went to a small cement section in front of the bandstand and started to dance. The alcohol was making itself felt, and people were perspiring more and smiling more. I noticed a girl dressed in blue who looked as if she had waited for this wedding just to have the chance to dance the waltz—she wanted to dance with someone who would embrace her in the way she had dreamed of since adolescence. She was watching a well-dressed boy, who wore a white suit and stood among his friends. They were all talking and had not noticed that the waltz had begun. Nor did they see that a few yards away, a girl in a blue dress looked longingly at one of them.

I thought about small towns and marriage to the boy one has dreamed of since childhood.

The girl in blue saw that I was watching her and tried to conceal herself among her girlfriends. As she did, the boy searched for her with his eyes. When he saw that she was there with her friends, he went back to his conversation with his own group.

I pointed out the two of them to Petrus. He watched the game of glances for a while and then went back to his cup of wine.

"They act as if it were shameful to make any show of love," was all he said.

A girl near us was staring at Petrus and me. She must have been half our age. Petrus held up his cup of wine and made a toast in her direction. The girl laughed in embarrassment and pointed toward her parents, as if to explain why she did not come closer.

"That's the beautiful side of love," Petrus said. "The love that dares, the love for two older strangers who have come from nowhere and will be gone tomorrow—gone into a world where she would like to travel, too."

I could hear in his voice that the wine was having an effect on him.

"Today, we will talk of love!" said my guide, a bit loudly. "Let us speak of true love, which grows and grows, and makes the world go round, and makes people wise!"

A well-dressed woman near us seemed not to be paying any attention at all to the party. She went from table to table, straightening the cups, the china, and the silverware.

"See that woman there?" asked Petrus. "The one who's straightening things up? Well, as I said, eros has many faces, and that's another of them. That's frustrated love, with its own kind of unhappiness. She is going to kiss the bride and groom, but inside she'll be saying that a knot has been tied around them. She's trying to neaten up the world because she herself is in complete disorder. And there"—he pointed toward another couple, the wife wearing excessive makeup and an elaborate coiffure—"is eros accepted. Social love, without a vestige of passion. She has accepted her role and has severed any connection with the world or with the good fight."

"You're being very bitter, Petrus. Isn't there anyone here who can be saved?"

"Of course there is. The girl who was watching us, the adolescents that are dancing—they know only about good eros. If they don't allow themselves to be influenced by the hypocrisy of the love that dominated the past generation, the world will certainly be a different place."

He pointed to an elderly couple sitting at one of the tables.

"And those two, also. They haven't let themselves be

infected by hypocrisy like the others. They look like working people. Hunger and need have required them to work together. They learned the practices you are learning without ever having heard of RAM. They find the power of love in the work they do. It's there that eros shows its most beautiful face, because it's united with that of philos."

"What is philos?"

"Philos is love in the form of friendship. It's what I feel toward you and others. When the flame of eros stops burning, it is philos that keeps a couple together."

"And agape?"

"Today's not the day to talk about agape. Agape is in both eros and philos—but that's just a phrase. Let's enjoy the rest of the party without talking about the love that consumes." And Petrus poured some more wine into his plastic cup.

The happiness around us was contagious. Petrus was getting drunk, and at first I was a little surprised. But I remembered what he had said one afternoon: that the RAM practices made sense only if they could be performed by the common people.

That night, Petrus seemed to be a person like any other. He was companionable and friendly, patting people on the back and talking to anyone who paid him any attention. A little later, he was so drunk that I had to help him back to the hotel.

On the way, I took stock of my situation. Here I was, guiding my guide. I realized that at no time during the entire journey had Petrus made any effort to appear wiser, holier, or in any way better than I. All he had done was to transmit to me his experience with the RAM practices. Beyond that, he had made a point of showing that he was just like anyone else—that he experienced eros, philos, and agape.

This realization made me feel stronger. Petrus was just another pilgrim on the Road to Santiago.

Enthusiasm

"Though I speak with the tongues of men and of angels . . . and though I have the gift of prophecy . . . and have all faith so that I could remove mountains . . . and have not love, I am nothing."

Petrus was once again quoting from Saint Paul. My guide felt that the apostle Paul was the major occult interpreter of Christ's message. We were fishing that afternoon after having walked for the whole morning. No fish had yet perished on the hook, but Petrus didn't care about that at all. According to him, fishing was basically a symbol of the human being's relationship with the world: we know why we are fishing, and we will catch something if we stay with it, but whether we do or not depends on God's help.

"It's a good idea always to do something relaxing prior to making an important decision in your life," he said. "The Zen monks listen to the rocks growing. I prefer fishing."

But at that time of day, because of the heat, even the fat, lazy fish on the bottom ignored the hook. Whether the bait was up or down, the result was the same. I decided to give it up and take a walk through the nearby woods. I went as far as an old, abandoned cemetery close to the river—it had a gate that was totally disproportionate to the size of the burial ground—and then came back to where Petrus was fishing. I asked about the cemetery.

"The gate was part of an ancient hospital for pilgrims," he said. "But the hospital was abandoned, and later, someone had the idea of using the facade and building the cemetery."

"Which has also been abandoned."

"That's right. The things of this life don't last very long."

I said that he had been nasty the night before in his judgments of the people at the party, and he was surprised at me. He said that what we had talked about was no more or less than we had ourselves experienced in our personal lives. All of us seek eros, and then when eros wants to turn itself into philos, we think that love is worthless. We don't see that it is philos that leads us to the highest form of love, agape.

"Tell me more about agape," I said.

Petrus answered that agape cannot really be discussed; it has to be lived. That afternoon, if possible, he wanted to show me one of the faces of agape. But in order for this to happen, the universe, as in the business of fishing, would have to collaborate so that everything went well.

"The messenger helps you, but there is one thing that is beyond the messenger's control, beyond his desires, and beyond you, as well."

"What is that?"

"The divine spark. What we call luck."

When the sun had begun to set, we resumed our walking.

The Jacobean route passed through some vineyards and fields that were completely deserted at that time of day. We crossed the main road—also deserted—and started again through the woods. In the distance, I could see the Saint Lorenzo peak, the highest point in the kingdom of Castile. I had changed a great deal since I had met Petrus for the first time near Saint-Jean-Pied-de-Port. Brazil and the business deals that I had been worried about had practically vanished from my mind. The only important thing for me now was my objective. I discussed it every night with Astrain, who was becoming clearer and clearer for me. I was able to see him, seated at my side, any time I tried. I learned that he had a nervous tic in his right eye and that he had the habit of smiling disdainfully every time I repeated something as evidence that I had understood what he was saying. A few weeks earlier—during the first days of the pilgrimage—I had been afraid that I would never complete it. When we had passed through Roncesvalles, I had been very disillusioned about everything to do with the journey. I had wanted to get to Santiago immediately, recover my sword, and get back to fighting what Petrus called the good fight.[1] But right now, with my connection to civilization severed, what was most important was the sun on my head and the possibility that I might experience agape.

[1]I found out later that the term had actually been created by Saint Paul.

We went down the bank of an arroyo, crossed the dry bed, and had to struggle to climb up the other side. An impressive river must have flowed there once, washing away the bottom in its search for the depths and secrets of the earth. Now the riverbed was so dry that it could be crossed on foot. But the river's major accomplishment, the valley it had created, was still there, and it took a major effort to climb out of it. "Nothing in this life endures," Petrus had said a few hours before.

"Petrus, have you ever been in love?"

The question was a spontaneous one, and I was surprised at my courage. Up until then, I had known only the bare outline of my guide's private life.

"I have known a lot of women, if that is what you mean. And I have really loved each of them. But I experienced agape only with two."

I told him that I had been in love many times but had been worried about whether I could ever become serious with anyone. If I had continued that way, it would have led to a solitary old age, and I had been very fearful of this.

"I don't think you look to love as a means to a comfortable retirement."

It was almost nine o'clock before it began to get dark. The vineyards were behind us, and we were walking through an arid landscape. I looked around and could see in the distance a small hermitage in the rocks, similar to many others we had passed on our pilgrimage. We walked on for a while, and then, detouring from the yellow markers, we approached the small building.

When we were close enough, Petrus called out a name that I didn't understand, and he stopped to listen for an answer. We heard nothing. Petrus called again, but no one answered.

"Let's go, anyway," he said. And we moved forward.

The hermitage consisted of just four whitewashed walls. The door was open—or rather, there really was no door, just a small entry panel, half a meter high, which hung precariously by one hinge. Within, there was a stone fireplace and some basins stacked on the floor. Two of them were filled with wheat and potatoes.

We sat down in the silence. Petrus lit a cigarette and said we should wait. My legs were hurting, but something in that hermitage, rather than calming me, made me feel excited. It would also have frightened me a little if Petrus had not been there.

"Where does whoever lives here sleep?" I asked, just to break the uneasy silence.

"There, where you are sitting," Petrus said, pointing to the bare earth. I said something about moving to another spot, but he told me to stay exactly where I was. The temperature must have been dropping, because I began to feel cold.

We waited for almost an hour. Petrus called out the

strange name several more times and then gave up. Just when I expected us to get up and leave, he began to speak.

"Present here is one of the two manifestations of agape," he said, as he stubbed out his third cigarette. "It is not the only one, but it is the purest. Agape is total love. It is the love that consumes the person who experiences it. Whoever knows and experiences agape learns that nothing else in the world is important—just love. This was the kind of love that Jesus felt for humanity, and it was so great that it shook the stars and changed the course of history. His solitary life enabled him to accomplish things that kings, armies, and empires could not.

"During the millennia of Christian civilization, many individuals have been seized by this love that consumes. They had so much to give—and their world demanded so little—that they went out into the deserts and to isolated places, because the love they felt was so great that it transformed them. They became the hermit saints that we know today.

"For you and for me, who experience a different form of agape, this life may seem terrible. But the love that consumes makes everything else—absolutely everything—lose its importance. Those men lived just to be consumed by their love."

Petrus told me that a monk named Alfonso lived there. Petrus had met him on his first pilgrimage to Compostela, as he was picking fruit to eat. His guide, a much more enlightened man than he, was a friend of Alfonso's, and the three of them had together performed the Ritual of Agape, the Blue Sphere Exercise. Petrus said that it had been one of the most important experiences of his life and that even today when he performed the exercise, he remembered the hermitage and Alfonso. There was more emotion in his voice than I had ever heard from him.

"Agape is the love that consumes," he repeated, as if that were the phrase that best defined this strange kind of love. "Martin Luther King once said that when Christ spoke of loving one's enemies, he was referring to agape. Because according to him, it was 'impossible to like our enemies, those who were cruel to us, those who tried to make our day-to-day suffering even worse.' But agape is much more than liking. It is a feeling that suffuses, that fills every space in us, and turns our aggression to dust.

"You have learned how to be reborn, how to stop being cruel to yourself, and how to communicate with your messenger. But everything you do from now on and every good result that you take with you from the Road to Santiago will make sense only when you have also experienced the love that consumes."

I reminded Petrus that he had said that there were two forms of agape. And that he probably had not experienced this first form, since he had not become a hermit.

"You're right. You and I and most pilgrims who walk the Road to Santiago, learning the RAM practices, experience agape in its other form: enthusiasm.

"For the ancients, enthusiasm meant trance, or ecstasy—a connection with God. Enthusiasm is agape directed at a particular idea or a specific thing. We have all experienced it. When we love and believe from the bottom of our heart, we feel ourselves to be stronger than anyone in the world, and we feel a serenity that is based on the certainty that nothing can shake our faith. This unusual strength allows us always to make the right decision at the right time, and when we achieve our goal, we are amazed at our own capabilities. Because when we are involved in the good fight, nothing else is important; enthusiasm carries us toward our goal.

"Enthusiasm normally manifests itself with all of its force during the first years of our lives. At that time, we still have strong links with the divinity, and we throw ourselves into our play with our toys with such a will that dolls take on life and our tin soldiers actually march. When Jesus said that the kingdom of heaven belonged to the children, he was referring to agape in the form of enthusiasm. Children were attracted to him, not because they understood his miracles, his wisdom, or his Pharisees and apostles. They went to him in joy, moved by enthusiasm."

I told Petrus that on that very afternoon, I had realized that I was completely absorbed by the Road to Santiago. Those days and nights in Spain had almost made me forget about my sword, and they were a unique experience. Most other things had lost their importance.

"This afternoon, we were trying to fish, but the fish would not bite," said Petrus. "Normally, we allow enthusiasm to elude us when we are involved in such mundane activities, those that have no importance at all in the overall scale of our existence. We lose our enthusiasm because of the small and unavoidable defeats we suffer during the good fight. And since we don't realize that enthusiasm is a major strength, able to help us win the ultimate victory, we let it dribble through our fingers; we do this without recognizing that we are letting the true meaning of our lives escape us. We blame the world for our boredom and for our losses, and we forget that it was we ourselves who allowed this enchanting power, which justifies everything, to diminish—the manifestation of agape in the form of enthusiasm."

I remembered the cemetery near the river. That strange, unusually large portal was a perfect representation of what had been lost. And beyond it, only the dead.

As if he had guessed what I was thinking, Petrus began to talk about something that was similar.

"A few days ago, you must have been surprised when I got so angry with that poor waiter who had spilled coffee on my shorts—shorts that were already filthy with the dust and dirt of the road. Actually, I was nervous because I saw in the boy's eyes that his enthusiasm was draining away like the blood that runs from wrists that have been slashed. I saw that boy, so strong and full of life, beginning to die because inside him, moment by moment, agape was perishing. I have been around for a long time, and I have learned to live with these things, but that lad, with the way he behaved and with all the good things I felt that he could bring to humanity, left me shocked and sad. But I know that my anger wounded him a bit and stemmed the death of agape.

"In the same vein, when you exorcised that woman's dog, you felt agape in its purest form. It was a noble deed, and it made me proud to be here serving as your guide. So for the first time in our experience on the Road, I am going to participate in an exercise with you."

And Petrus taught me the Ritual of Agape, the Blue Sphere Exercise.

"I am going to help you to arouse your enthusiasm, to create a power that is going to expand like a blue sphere that encloses the entire planet," he said, "to show that I respect you and what you are doing."

Up until then, Petrus had never expressed an opinion, either favorable or unfavorable, regarding the way in which I performed the exercises. He had helped me to interpret my first contact with the messenger, and he had rescued me from the trance of the Seed Exercise, but he had never expressed any interest in the results I had achieved. More than once I had asked him why he did not want to know about my feelings, and he had answered that his only obligation as my guide was to show me the Road and to teach me the RAM practices. It was up to me whether I enjoyed the results or found them to be unpleasant.

When he said that he was going to participate with me in the exercise, I suddenly felt unworthy of his praise. I knew my faults, and many times I had doubted whether he could succeed in guiding me along the Road. I wanted to say all this to him, but he interrupted me before I could begin.

"Don't be cruel with yourself, or you will not have learned the lesson I taught you before. Be kind. Accept the praise that you deserve."

Tears came to my eyes. Petrus led me outside. The night was darker than usual. I sat down next to him, and we began to sing. The melody came from within me, and he accompanied me with no effort. I began to clap my hands softly, as I rocked forward and back. My clapping increased in its intensity, and the music flowed from me, a psalm of praise to the darkness of the sky, the deserted plateau, and the lifeless stones around us. I began to see the saints that I had believed in as a child, and I could sense that life had gotten away from me because of my having killed a great deal of my agape. But now the love that consumes returned, and the saints smiled from the heavens with the same look and intensity that I had seen in them when I was small.

I spread my arms so that agape could flow, and a mysterious current of bright blue light began to wash through me, cleansing my soul and pardoning my sins. The light spread first to our surroundings and then enveloped the world, and I started to weep. I wept because I was re-experiencing the enthusiasm of my childhood; I was once again a child, and nothing in the world could cause me harm. I felt a presence draw near and sit down to my right. I imagined that it was my messenger and that he was the only one who could perceive the strong blue light that was entering me and leaving me, spreading throughout the world.

The Blue Sphere Exercise

Seat yourself comfortably, and relax. Try not to think about anything.

1. Feel how good it is to be alive. Let your heart feel free and affectionate; let it rise above and beyond the details of the problems that may be bothering you. Begin to sing softly a song from your childhood. Imagine that your heart is growing, filling the room—and later your home—with an intense, shining blue light.
2. When you reach this point, begin to sense the presence of the saints (or other beings) in which you placed your faith when you were a child. Notice that they are present, arriving from everywhere, smiling and giving you faith and confidence.
3. Picture the saints approaching you, placing their hands on your head and wishing you love, peace, and communion with the world—the communion of the saints.

4. When this sensation becomes strong, feel that the blue light is a current that enters you and leaves you like a shining, flowing river. This blue light begins to spread through your house, then through your neighborhood, your city, and your country; it eventually envelops the world in an immense blue sphere. This is the manifestation of the great love that goes beyond the day-to-day struggle; it reinforces and invigorates, as it provides energy and peace.
5. Keep the light spread around the world for as long as possible. Your heart is open, spreading love. This phase of the exercise should last for a minimum of five minutes.
6. Come out of your trance, bit by bit, and return to reality. The saints will remain near. The blue light will continue to spread around the world.

This ritual can and should be done with more than one person. When this is the case, the participants should hold hands while they do the exercise.

•

The light was increasing in its intensity, and I felt that as it enclosed the world, it penetrated into every door and every back alley, touching every person alive for at least a fraction of a second.

I felt my hands being held open and extended to the heavens. At that moment, the flow of the blue light increased and became so strong that I thought I was going to pass out. But I was able to keep the light alive for a few moments more, until I reached the end of the song I was singing.

I was exhausted but relaxed; I felt free and content with life and with what I had just done. The hands that held mine released me. I saw that one of them was Petrus's, and I knew in my heart who it was that held the other.

I opened my eyes, and there at my side was the monk, Alfonso. He smiled and said, "*Buenas noches.*" I smiled, too, and I seized his hand and held it tightly to my breast. He allowed me to do this for a moment and then gently removed his hand.

None of us spoke. Some time later, Alfonso arose and continued his trek along the rocky plateau. I watched him until he was completely hidden by the darkness.

Petrus broke the silence then, but he made no mention of Alfonso.

"Do this exercise whenever you can, and soon agape will live once again within you. Repeat it before you embark on any project, during the first days of any trip, or when you have been greatly affected by something. If possible, do it with someone you like. It is an exercise that should be shared."

So there was the old Petrus: coach, instructor, and guide, the man about whom I knew so little. The emotion that he had shown in the hermitage had already passed away. But when he had touched my hand during the exercise, I had felt the greatness of his soul.

We returned to the hermitage where we had left our things.

"The occupant won't be back today, so I think we can sleep here," said Petrus, lying down. I unrolled my sleeping bag, took a swallow of wine, and lay down. I was exhausted by the love that consumes. But it was a tiredness that was free of tension, and before I closed my eyes, I thought of the thin, bearded monk who had sat beside me and wished me good night. Somewhere out there he was being consumed by the divine flame. Maybe that was why the night was so unusually dark—he had taken all the light of the world into himself.

Death

"Are you pilgrims?" asked the old woman who served us our breakfast. We were in Azofra, a village of small houses, each with a medieval shield embossed on its facade. We had filled our canteens at the village fountain a few moments earlier.

I said that we were, and the woman's eyes glowed with respect and pride.

"When I was a girl, at least one pilgrim passed through here every day, bound for Compostela. After the war and after Franco, I don't know what happened, but the pilgrimages stopped. Someone must have built a highway. Nowadays, people only want to travel by car."

Petrus said nothing. He had awakened in a bad mood. I nodded in agreement with the old woman and pictured a new, paved expressway, climbing the mountains and running across the valleys, automobiles with scallop shells painted on their hoods, and souvenir shops at the gates of the monasteries. I finished my coffee and bread dipped in olive oil. Looking at Aymeric Picaud's guide, I estimated that we should arrive that afternoon in Santo Domingo de la Calzada, and I was planning to sleep at the Parador Nacional.[1]

[1]The Paradores Nacionales are ancient castles and historic monuments that have been turned into first-class hotels by the Spanish government.

I was spending much less money than I had planned, even eating three meals a day. It was time for an extravagance, time to give my body the same treatment I had been giving my stomach.

I had awakened with a strange feeling of being in a hurry and of wanting to be in Santo Domingo already. I had experienced the same feeling two days earlier, when we had walked to the hermitage. Petrus was more melancholy and quiet than usual; was this the result of our meeting with Alfonso two days ago? I felt a strong need to invoke Astrain so that we could discuss the matter. But I had never summoned him in the morning, and I was not sure that I could. I decided against it.

We finished our coffee and began to walk. We passed a medieval house with its coat of arms, the ruins of an ancient hostel for pilgrims, and a park on the outskirts of the village. As I once again readied myself to move out across the countryside, I felt a strong presence to my left side. I walked on, but Petrus stopped me.

"There is no use running away," he said. "Stop and deal with it."

I wanted to get away from Petrus and keep going. I had a disagreeable feeling, a kind of colic near my stomach. For a few moments, I tried to believe that it was caused by the bread with olive oil, but I knew that I had felt it earlier in the day and I could not fool myself. It was tension—tension and fear.

"Look behind you." Petrus's voice had an urgency to it. "Look before it's too late!"

I spun around quickly. To my left was an abandoned house, its vegetation burned by the sun. An olive tree raised its twisted branches to the sky. And between the tree and the house, looking fixedly at me, was a dog.

A black dog, the same dog that I had banished from the woman's house a few days earlier.

I forgot all about Petrus and looked squarely into the dog's eyes. Something inside me—perhaps it was the voice of Astrain or of my guardian angel—told me that if I averted my eyes, the dog would attack me. We remained that way, staring at each other, for some time. Here I was, I thought, after having experienced the wonder of the love that consumes, once again about to be confronted by the daily and constant threats to my existence that the world would always present. I wondered why the animal had followed me for such a great distance and what it was that he wanted; after all, I was just a pilgrim in quest of my sword, and I had neither the desire nor the patience for problems with people or animals. I tried to say this to him with my eyes—remembering the monks at the convent who communicated through their eyes—but the dog did not move. He continued to stare at me, without emotion, but he appeared ready to attack should I become distracted or show fear.

Fear! I could sense that my fear had vanished. I thought the situation too stupid for fear. My stomach was knotted up, and I felt like vomiting, but I wasn't frightened. If I had been, something told me that my eyes would have given me away, and the animal would try to overcome me, as he had before. I did not want to avert my eyes, even when I sensed that a figure was approaching along a narrow road to my right.

The figure stopped for an instant and then came directly toward us. It crossed my line of sight as I stared at the dog, and this person said something I could not understand in a feminine voice. Its presence was good—friendly and positive.

In the fraction of a second during which the image had crossed my line of sight, my stomach relaxed. I felt that I had a powerful friend who was there to help me through this absurd, unnecessary conflict. When the figure had passed by, the dog lowered his eyes. Then he jumped, ran behind the abandoned house, and disappeared from view.

It was only then that my heart began to react. The tachycardia was so strong that I felt dizzy and faint. As the scene around me spun, I looked along the road that Petrus and I had walked only a few minutes earlier, seeking the figure that had given me the strength to defeat the dog. It was a nun. Her back was to me, and she was walking toward Azofra. I could not see her face, but I remembered her voice, and I guessed that she was in her early twenties. I looked in the direction from which she had come: she had appeared from a narrow path that seemed to lead nowhere.

"It was she . . . it was she who helped me," I murmured, as my dizziness grew worse.

"Don't start creating fantasies in a world that is already extraordinary," said Petrus, supporting me by the arm. "She comes from a convent in Cañas, three or four miles from here. You can't see it from here."

My heart was still pounding, and I was sure I was going to be sick. I was too upset to speak or ask for an explanation. I sat down on the ground, and Petrus threw some water on my forehead and on the nape of my neck. I remembered that he had done the same thing after we had left the woman's house—but that day I had cried for joy. Now the sensation was just the opposite.

Petrus let me rest a bit. The water brought me around, and the nausea began to subside. Things slowly returned to normal. When I felt restored, Petrus said we should walk a little, and I obeyed. We walked for about fifteen minutes, but the exhaustion returned. We sat down at the foot of a *rollo,* a medieval column supporting a cross. Such columns marked a number of stretches along the Jacobean route.

"Your fear has hurt you much more than the dog did," said Petrus, as I rested.

I wanted to understand that absurd encounter.

"In the life on the Road to Santiago, certain things happen that are beyond our control. When we first met, I told you that I had read in the gypsy's eyes the name of the demon you would have to confront. I was surprised to learn that the demon was a dog, but I did not say anything to you about it at the time. Only after we arrived at that woman's house—when for the first time, you showed the love that consumes—did I see your enemy.

"When you chased away that woman's dog, you did not place him anywhere. You didn't hurl the spirits into a drove of pigs that was thrown over a precipice, as Jesus did. You simply chased the dog away. Now his force wanders along behind you, without a destination. Before finding your sword, you are going to have to decide whether you want to be enslaved by that force or whether you will dominate it."

My fatigue began to pass. I took a deep breath and felt the cold stone of the *rollo* against my back. Petrus gave me some more water and went on:

"Cases of obsession occur when people lose their mastery over the forces of the earth. The gypsy's curse had frightened that woman, and her fear had opened a breach that the messenger of death was then able to penetrate. This doesn't always happen, but neither is it rare. Your confidence and your sense of mastery depend a great deal on how you react to threats made by others."

This time it was I who remembered a passage from the Bible. A verse in the Book of Job says, "For the thing that I greatly feared is come upon me."

"A threat leads to nothing if it is not accepted. In fighting the good fight, you should never forget that. Just as you should never forget that both attacking and fleeing are part of the fight. What isn't a part of the fight is becoming paralyzed by fear."

I had not felt fear when the dog was there. This had surprised me, and I told Petrus about it.

"I could see that you felt no fear. If you had, the dog would have attacked you. And without a doubt, he would have won the fight. Because the dog was not afraid either. The strangest thing, though, was the arrival of that nun. When you sensed the presence of something positive, your imagination concluded that someone had arrived to help you. And this, your faith, saved you. Even though it was based on an assumption that was absolutely false."

Petrus was right. He laughed at me, and I laughed, too. We got up to resume our walking. I was already feeling better.

"There is one thing you have to know, though," said Petrus as we moved on. "The duel with the dog will end only with a victory for you or for him. He will be back, and the next time you must try to take the fight through to the end. If you don't, his presence will worry you for the rest of your life."

In the encounter with the gypsy, Petrus had told me, he had learned the name of the demon. I asked him what it was.

"Legion," he answered. "Because he is many."

We passed through fields that the farmers were preparing for sowing. Here and there, some peasants operated crude water pumps in the centuries-old fight against the arid soil. Along the edge of the Road to Santiago, stones had been piled into endless walls, crisscrossing the fields. I thought about how, in spite of all the centuries during which that soil had been worked, stones still surfaced—stones that could break the blade of a plow, render a horse lame, and leave calluses on the peasants' hands. It was a battle every year, a battle that would never end.

Petrus was quieter than usual, and I realized that he had said almost nothing since morning. After our conversation at the medieval *rollo,* he had been mute, not answering any of the questions I had asked. I wanted to know more about the "many demons," because he had already explained to me that each person has only one messenger. But Petrus was not interested in talking about it, and I decided to wait for a better time.

We climbed a small rise, and from the top we could see the main tower of the church at Santo Domingo de la Calzada. I was glad to see it; I began to think about the magical comfort of the Parador Nacional. From what I had read about it, the building had been constructed by Santo Domingo himself as a shelter for pilgrims. Saint Francis of Assisi had stayed there on his way to Compostela. Everything about it excited me.

At about seven o'clock that evening, Petrus said we should stop. I was reminded of Roncesvalles and of the slow pace we had taken when I had needed some wine to warm me, and I was afraid that he was preparing something like that.

"A messenger would never help you to defeat someone else. Messengers are neither good nor bad, as I have already told you, but they have a sense of loyalty among themselves. Don't rely on your messenger to help you defeat the dog."

Now it was my turn not to want to talk about messengers. I wanted to get to Santo Domingo.

"The messengers of people who have died can occupy the body of someone who is dominated by fear. That is why, in the case of the dog, he is many. Messengers were invited in by the woman's fear—not just the murdered gypsy's messenger but all of the many messengers who wander in space, seeking a way to establish contact with the forces of the earth."

He was finally answering my question, but there was something in the way he spoke that seemed artificial, as if this were not what he really wanted to say. My instincts told me to be wary.

"What do you want, Petrus?" I asked him, a bit irritated.

My guide did not answer. He walked into the field toward an ancient, almost leafless tree that stood about thirty yards from us. It was the only tree visible on the entire horizon. Since he had not given me the signal to follow, I stood where I was. And I saw a strange thing happen: Petrus walked around the tree several times and said something out loud, while he looked at the ground. When he had finished, he gestured for me to come over.

"Sit here," he said. There was a different tone to his voice, and I couldn't tell whether it was friendliness or irritation. "Stay here. I will see you tomorrow in Santo Domingo de la Calzada."

Before I could say a word, Petrus continued, "One of these days—and I guarantee you that it will not be today—you are going to have to confront the most important enemy you will meet on the Road to Santiago: the dog. When that day comes, you can be sure that I will be close at hand and will give you the strength you need to fight him. But today you are going to confront a different type of enemy, an unreal enemy that may destroy you or may turn out to be your best friend: death.

"Human beings are the only ones in nature who are aware that they will die. For that reason and only for that reason, I have a profound respect for the human race, and I believe that its future is going to be much better than its present. Even knowing that their days are numbered and that everything will end when they least expect it, people make of their lives a battle that is worthy of a being with eternal life. What people regard as vanity—leaving great works, having children, acting in such a way as to prevent one's name from being forgotten—I regard as the highest expression of human dignity.

"Still, being fragile creatures, humans always try to hide from themselves the certainty that they will die. They do not see that it is death itself that motivates them to do the best things in their lives. They are afraid to step into the dark, afraid of the unknown, and their only way of conquering that fear is to ignore the fact that their days are numbered. They do not see that with an awareness of death, they would be able to be even more daring, to go much further in their daily conquests, because then they would have nothing to lose—for death is inevitable."

The possibility of spending the night in Santo Domingo was looking more and more remote. But now I was interested in what Petrus was saying. The sun itself was dying beyond the horizon there in front of us.

"Death is our constant companion, and it is death that gives each person's life its true meaning. But in order to see the real face of our death, we first have to know all of the anxieties and terrors that the simple mention of its name is able to evoke in any human being."

Petrus sat down beside me under the tree. He said that he had circled its trunk a few minutes before because it reminded him of everything that had happened to him when he had been a pilgrim bound for Santiago. Then he took from his knapsack two sandwiches that he had bought at lunchtime.

"Here, where you are now, there is no danger," he said, giving me the sandwiches. "There are no poisonous snakes, and the dog will return to attack you only after he has forgotten this morning's defeat. And there are no bandits or criminals around here. You are in a spot that is absolutely safe, with one exception: the danger created by your own fear."

Petrus pointed out to me that two days earlier, I had experienced a sensation that had been as intense and as violent as death itself—that of the love that consumes. And that at one point I had vacillated and been afraid. He said that I had been afraid because I knew nothing about universal love. He explained to me that although all of us have some idea of death, we do not see that death is only another manifestation of agape. I answered that with all of my years of training in magic, I had practically lost my fear of death. Actually, I was more frightened by the way in which I would die than by death itself.

"Well, then, tonight take a look at the most frightening way to die."

And at that point, Petrus taught me the Buried Alive Exercise.

"You should do this exercise only once," he said. I was thinking of an exercise from the theater that was quite similar. "It is important that you be as truthful with yourself as possible and that you be as fearful as necessary for the exercise to get at the roots of your soul; it has to strip away the scary mask that hides the gentle face of your death."

Petrus stood up, and I saw his silhouette against the background of the setting sun. From where I was seated, he seemed to be a gigantic and powerful figure.

"Petrus, I have one more question."

"What is it?"

"This morning you were close-mouthed and strange. You sensed before I did that the dog was going to appear. How was that possible?"

The Buried Alive Exercise

Lie down on the floor and relax. Cross your arms over your chest in the posture of death.

•

Imagine all of the details of your burial, as if it were to be carried out tomorrow, the only difference being that you are being buried alive. As the situation develops in your mind—the chapel, the procession to the cemetery, the lowering of the casket, the worms in the grave—you begin tensing all of your muscles more and more in a desperate attempt to escape. But you cannot do so. Keep trying until you cannot stand it any longer, and then, using a movement that involves your entire body, throw aside the confines of the coffin, breathe deeply, and find yourself free. This movement will have a greater effect if you scream at the same time; it should be a scream that emanates from the depths of your body.

•

"When we both experienced the love that consumes, we shared in the Absolute. The Absolute shows each of us who we really are; it is an enormous web of cause and effect, where every small gesture made by one person affects the life of someone else. This morning, that slice of the Absolute was still very much alive in my soul. I was seeing not only you but everything there is in the world, unlimited by space or time. Now, the effect is much weaker and will only return in its full strength the next time that I do the exercise of the love that consumes."

I remembered Petrus's bad mood of that morning. If what he said was true, the world was going through a very bad phase.

"I will be waiting for you there at the Parador," he said, as he prepared to leave. "I will leave your name at the desk."

I watched him walk away until I could no longer see him. In the fields to my left, the peasants had finished their day's labors and gone home. I decided that I would do the exercise as soon as darkness had fallen.

I was content. It was the first time I had been completely alone since I had started along the Strange Road to Santiago. I stood up and explored my immediate surroundings, but night was falling fast, and I decided to go back to the tree before I got lost. Before it became completely dark, I made a mental estimate of the distance between the tree and the road. Even in darkness, I would be able to see the way perfectly well and make my way to Santo Domingo with just the help of the frail new moon that had risen in the sky.

Up until that point, I had not been at all frightened; I felt that it would take a lot of imagination to make me fearful of any kind of horrible death. But no matter how long we have lived, when night falls it arouses the hidden fears that have been there in our souls since we were children. The darker it grew, the less comfortable I became.

There I was, alone in the fields; if I were to scream, no one would even hear me. I remembered that I had almost passed out completely that morning. Never in my life had I felt my heart to be so out of control.

And what if I had died? My life would have ended, obviously. Through my experiences with the Tradition, I had already communicated with many spirits. I was absolutely certain that there was a life after death, but it had never occurred to me to wonder just how the transition was made. To pass from one dimension to another, no matter how well prepared one is, must be terrible. If I had died that morning, for example, I would have known nothing else about the rest of the Road to Santiago, about my years of study, about my family's grief for me, or about the money hidden in my belt. I thought about a plant on my desk in Brazil. The plant would go on, as would other plants, as would the streetcars, as would the man on the corner who charges more for his vegetables than anyone else, as would the woman at directory assistance who provides me with telephone numbers that are not listed in the book. All these things—which would have disappeared if I had died that morning—took on an enormous importance for me. I realized that those were the things, rather than the stars or wisdom, that told me I was alive.

The night was quite dark, and on the horizon I could see the faint lights of the city. I lay down on the ground and looked at the branches of the tree overhead. I began to hear strange sounds, sounds of all kinds. They were the sounds of the nocturnal animals, setting out on the hunt. Petrus could not know everything; he was just another human being like me. How was I to know if his guarantee about the absence of poisonous snakes was true? And the wolves, those eternal European wolves—wasn't it possible that they had decided to show up there that night, sniffing out my presence? A louder noise, similar to the breaking of a branch, frightened me, and my heart once again started pounding.

I was growing scared. The best thing to do would be to complete the exercise right away and then head for the hotel. I began to relax and crossed my arms over my chest in the posture of death. Something nearby made a sound. I jumped up immediately.

It was nothing. The night had aroused my greatest fears. I lay down again, deciding that this time I would turn any source of fear into a stimulus for the exercise. I noticed that even though the temperature had fallen quite a bit, I was perspiring.

I imagined my coffin being closed, and the screws being

turned. I was immobile, but I was alive, and I wanted to tell my family that I was seeing everything. I wanted to tell them all that I loved them, but not a sound came out of my mouth. My father and mother were weeping, my wife and my friends were gathered around, but I was completely alone! With all of the people dear to me standing there, no one was able to see that I was alive and that I had not yet accomplished all that I wanted to do in this world. I tried desperately to open my eyes, to give a sign, to beat on the lid of the coffin. But I could not move any part of my body.

I felt the coffin being carried toward the grave. I could hear the sound of the handles grinding against their fittings, the steps of those in the procession, and conversations from this side and that. Someone said that he had a date for dinner later on, and another observed that I had died early. The smell of flowers all around me began to suffocate me.

I remembered how I had given up trying to establish a relationship with two or three women, fearing their rejection. I remembered also the number of times I had failed to do what I wanted to do, thinking I could always do it later. I felt very sorry for myself, not only because I was about to be buried alive but also because I had been afraid to live. Why be fearful of saying no to someone or of leaving something undone when the most important thing of all was to enjoy life fully? There I was, trapped in a coffin, and it was already too late to go back and show the courage I should have had.

There I was, having played the role of my own Judas, having betrayed myself. There I was, powerless to move a muscle, screaming for help, while the others were involved in their lives, worrying about what they were going to do that night, admiring statues and buildings that I would never see again. I began to feel how unfair it was to have to be buried while others continued to live. I would have felt better if there had been a catastrophe and all of us had been in the same boat, heading for the same abyss toward which they were carrying me now. Help! I tried to cry out. I'm still alive. I haven't died. My mind is still functioning!

They placed my coffin at the edge of the grave. They are going to bury me! My wife is going to forget all about me; she will marry someone else and spend the money we have struggled to save for all these years! But who cares about that. I want to be with her now, because I'm alive!

I hear sobs, and I feel tears falling from my eyes, too. If my friends were to open my coffin now, they would see my tears and save me. But instead all I feel is the lowering of the coffin into the ground. Suddenly, everything is dark. A moment ago, there was a ray of light at the edge of the coffin, but now the darkness is complete. The grave diggers' shovels are filling in the grave, and I'm alive! Buried alive! I sense that the air is being cut off, and the fragrance of the flowers is awful. I hear the mourners' departing footsteps. My terror is total. I'm not able to do anything; if they go away now, it will soon be night, and no one will hear me knocking on the lid of my coffin!

The footsteps fade, nobody hears my screams, and I am alone in the darkness; the air is heavy, and the smell of the flowers is driving me crazy. Suddenly, I hear a sound. It's the worms, coming to eat me alive. I try with all my strength to move the parts of my body, but I am inert. The worms begin to climb over my body. They are sticky and cold. They creep over my face and crawl into my shorts. One of them enters through my anus, and another begins to sneak into a nostril. Help! I'm being eaten alive, and nobody can hear me; nobody says a word to me. The worm that entered my nostril has reached my throat. I feel another invading my ear. I have to get out! Where is God; why doesn't he help me? They are beginning to eat at my throat, and soon I won't be able to scream! They are coming into me everywhere: through my ear, the corner of my mouth, the opening in my penis. I feel those disgusting, oily things inside me, and I have to scream; I have to get away! I am shut up in this cold, dark grave, alone and being eaten alive! The air is giving out, and the worms are eating me! I have to move. I have to break out of this coffin! God, help me gather all of my strength, because I have to escape! I HAVE TO GET OUT OF HERE; I HAVE TO . . . I'M GOING TO GET OUT! I'M GOING TO GET OUT!

I DID IT!

The boards of the coffin flew in all directions, the grave

disappeared, and I filled my lungs with the fresh air of the Road to Santiago. My body was trembling from head to foot and bathed in perspiration. I moved a bit and felt that my insides had been twisted around. But none of this was important: I was alive.

The shaking continued, and I made no effort whatsoever to control it. A great sense of calm came over me, and I felt a kind of presence alongside me. I looked over and saw the face of my death. This was not the death that I had experienced a few minutes before, the death I had created with my fears and my imagination; it was my true death, my friend and counselor, who was never again going to allow me to act like such a coward. Starting then, he was going to be of more help to me than Petrus's guiding hand and advice. He was not going to allow me to put off until tomorrow what I should be enjoying today. He was not going to let me flee from life's battles, and he was going to help me fight the good fight. Never again, ever, was I going to feel ridiculous about doing anything. Because he was there, saying that when he took me in hand to travel with me to other worlds, I should leave behind the greatest sin of all: regret. With the certainty of his presence and the gentleness of his face, I was sure that I was going to be able to drink from the fountain of life.

The night held no further secrets or terrors. It was a joyful night, filled with peace. When the trembling ceased, I got up and walked to the pumps in the fields. I washed my shorts and put on a fresh pair from my knapsack. Then I returned to the tree and ate the two sandwiches that Petrus had left for me. They seemed like the most delicious food in the world, because I was alive and because death frightened me no longer.

I decided to sleep right there. The darkness had never been so reassuring.

Personal Vices

We were in the middle of a level field of wheat that stretched all the way to the horizon. The only object that stood out in the scene was another medieval column supporting a cross, one of the road markers for pilgrims. As we approached the column, Petrus stopped, placed his knapsack on the ground, and knelt down. He told me to do the same.

"We are going to say a prayer concerning the only thing that can defeat you as a pilgrim after you find your sword: your personal vices. No matter how much you learn from your Master about how to handle the sword, one of your hands will always be your potential enemy. Let us pray that, if you are successful in finding your sword, you will always wield it with the hand that does not bring scandal down upon you."

It was two o'clock in the afternoon, and there wasn't a sound to be heard as Petrus began to pray aloud:

"Pity us, O Lord, for we are pilgrims on the road to Compostela, and our being here may be a vice. In your infinite pity, help us never to turn our knowledge against ourselves.

"Have pity on those who pity themselves and who see themselves as good people treated unfairly by life—who feel that they do not deserve what has befallen them. Such people will never be able to fight the good fight. And pity those who are cruel to themselves and who see only the evil in their own actions, feeling that they are to blame for the injustice in the world. Because neither of these kinds of people know thy law that says, 'But the very hairs of your head are numbered.'

"Have pity on those who command and those who serve during long hours of work, and who sacrifice themselves in exchange merely for a Sunday off, only to find that there is nowhere to go, and everything is closed. But also have pity on those who sanctify their efforts, and who are able to go beyond the bounds of their own madness, winding up indebted, or nailed to the cross by their very brothers. Because neither of these kinds of people know thy law that says, 'Be ye therefore as wise as the serpents and as harmless as the doves.'

"Have pity on those who may conquer the world but never join the good fight within themselves. But pity also those who have won the good fight within themselves, and now find themselves in the streets and the bars of life because they were unable to conquer the world. Because neither of these kinds of people know thy law that says, 'He who heeds my words I will liken to a wise man who built his house on rock.'

"Have pity on those who are fearful of taking up a pen, or a paintbrush, or an instrument, or a tool because they are afraid that someone has already done so better than they could, and who feel themselves to be unworthy to enter the marvelous mansion of art. But have even more pity on those who, having taken up the pen, or the paintbrush, or the instrument, or the tool, have turned inspiration into a paltry thing, and yet feel themselves to be better than others. Neither of these kinds of people know thy law that says, 'For there is nothing covered that will not be revealed, nor hidden that will not be known.'

"Pity those who eat and drink and sate themselves, but are unhappy and alone in their satiety. But pity even more those who fast, and who censure and prohibit, and who thereby see themselves as saints, preaching your name in the streets. For neither of these types of people know thy law that says, 'If I bear witness of myself, my witness is not true.'

"Pity those who fear death, and are unaware of the many kingdoms through which they have already passed, and the many deaths they have already suffered, and who are unhappy because they think that one day their world will end. But have even more pity for those who already know their many deaths, and today think of themselves as immortal. Neither of these kinds of people know thy law that says, 'Except that one is born again, he cannot see the kingdom of God.'

"Have pity on those who bind themselves with the silken ties of love, and think of themselves as masters of others, and who feel envy, and poison themselves, and who torture themselves because they cannot see that love and all things change like the wind. But pity even more those who die of their fear of loving and who reject love in the name of a greater love that they know not. Neither of these kinds of people know thy law that says, 'Whoever drinks of the water that I shall give him will never thirst.'

"Pity those who reduce the cosmos to an explanation, God to a magic potion, and humanity to beings with basic needs that must be satisfied, because they never hear the music of the spheres. But have even more pity on those who have blind faith, and who in their laboratories transform mercury into gold, and who are surrounded by their books about the secrets of the Tarot and the power of the pyramids. Neither of these kinds of people know thy law that says, 'Whoever does not receive the kingdom of God as a little child will by no means enter it.'

"Pity those who see no one but themselves, and for whom others are a blurred and distant scenario as they pass through the streets in their limousines and lock themselves in their air-conditioned penthouse offices, as they suffer in silence the solitude of power. But pity even more those who will do anything for anybody, and are charitable, and seek to win out over evil only through love. For neither of these kinds of people know thy law that says, 'Let he who has no sword sell his garment and buy one.'

"Have pity, Lord, on we who seek out and dare to take up the sword that you have promised, and who are a saintly and sinful lot scattered throughout the world. Because we do not recognize even ourselves, and often think that we are dressed, but we are nude; we believe that we have committed a crime, when in reality we have saved someone's life. And do not forget in your pity for all of us that we hold the sword with the hand of an angel and the hand of a devil, and that they are both the same hand. Because we are of the world, and we continue to be of the world, and we have need of thee. We will always be in need of thy law that says, 'When I sent you without money bag, knapsack, and sandals, you lacked nothing.'"

Petrus ended his prayer. As silence prevailed, he gazed out over the field of wheat that surrounded us.

Conquest

We arrived one afternoon at the ruins of an old castle of the Order of the Knights Templar. We sat down to rest, and while Petrus smoked his usual cigarette, I drank a bit of the wine left over from lunch. I studied the view that surrounded us: a few peasant houses, the tower of the castle, the undulating fields ready for sowing. To my right appeared a shepherd, guiding his flock past the walls of the castle, bound for home. The sky was red, and the dust raised by the animals blurred the view, making it look like a dream or a magic vision. The shepherd waved to us, and we waved back.

The sheep passed in front of us and continued down the road. Petrus got to his feet. It was an impressive scene, and I would like to have stayed, but Petrus said, "Let's go, right away. We've got to hurry."

"Why?"

"Because I said so. Don't you think we have spent enough time on the Road to Santiago?"

But something told me that his haste had something to do with the magic scene of the shepherd and his sheep.

Two days later we were close to some mountains to the south; their elevation was a relief to the monotony of the immense wheat fields. The area had some natural elevations, but it was well punctuated by the yellow markers that Father Jordi had mentioned. At that point, Petrus, without explanation, began to stray from the markers and to plunge more and more in a northerly direction. When I pointed this out to him, he answered brusquely, saying that he was the guide and that he knew where he was leading me.

After half an hour or so along the new path, I began to hear the sound of tumbling water. All about us were the sun-drenched fields, and I tried to imagine what the sound could be. As we continued, the sound grew louder, and there was no doubt that it was produced by a waterfall. But I could see neither mountains nor falls near us.

Then, as we crested a small rise, we were confronted with one of nature's most extravagant works: a basin opened up in the plateau, deep enough to contain a five-story building, and a stream hurtled to its floor. The immense crater was bordered by luxuriant vegetation, completely different in appearance from the flora we had been passing until then, and it framed the falling water.

"Let's climb down here," Petrus said.

We began a descent that put me in mind of Jules Verne; it was as if we were descending to the center of the earth. The way was steep and difficult to navigate, and so as not to fall, we were forced to grasp at thorny branches and sharp rocks. When I reached the bottom, my arms and legs were lacerated.

"Isn't this beautiful," said Petrus, taking no notice of my discomfort.

I agreed. It was an oasis in the desert. The plant life and the rainbow formed by the droplets of water made the basin as beautiful seen from below as from above.

"This is where nature really shows its power," he said.

"True," I nodded.

"And it gives us a chance to show our own strength. Let's climb the falls," said my guide. "Through the water!"

I looked again at the scene. Now I no longer saw it as an oasis, nor as one of nature's more sophisticated caprices. Instead, I was looking at a wall more than fifty feet high over which the water fell with a deafening force. The small lagoon formed by the cataract was no deeper than a man's height, since the river ran to an opening that probably took it underground. On the wall, there were no protrusions that I could make use of in a climb, and the depth of the pool was not sufficient to break a fall. I was looking at an absolutely impossible task.

I thought of an event from five years ago, during a ritual that had required—like this situation—an extremely dangerous climb. My Master had given me a choice as to whether I wanted to continue or not. I was younger and fascinated by his powers and by the miracles of the Tradition, so I decided to go on. I needed to demonstrate my courage and my bravery.

After I had climbed the mountain for nearly an hour and as I was approaching the most difficult stretch, a wind of unexpected force arose, and to keep myself from falling, I had had to cling with all my strength to the small ledge that supported me. I closed my eyes, expecting the worst, and dug my nails into the rock. A minute later, I was surprised to find that someone had helped me to assume a safer and more comfortable position. I opened my eyes to see that my Master was there at my side.

He made some gestures in the air, and the wind suddenly ceased. With an absolutely mysterious agility, at times seeming to require an exercise in levitation, he descended the mountain and told me to do likewise.

I arrived at the base with my legs trembling and asked him angrily why he hadn't caused the wind to abate before it threatened me.

"Because it was I who ordered the wind to blow," he answered.

"So it would kill me?"

"No, in order to save you. It would have been impossible for you to climb this mountain. When I asked if you wanted to, I was not testing your courage. I was testing your wisdom.

"You made it into an order, when I had not given one," said the Master. "If you were able to levitate yourself, you would not have had a problem. But you wanted to be brave, when it was enough to have been intelligent."

That day, he told me about Magi who had become insane during the process of illumination and who could no longer distinguish between their own powers and those of their disciples. During my lifetime, I have known some great men in the Tradition. I had gotten to know three great Masters—including my own—who were able to dominate material objects in ways that went far beyond what anyone could imagine. I had witnessed miracles, exact predictions of the future, and knowledge of past incarnations. My Master had spoken of the Falklands War two months before Argentina had invaded the islands. He had described everything in detail and had explained the reasons, on an astral level, for the conflict.

But after that day, I had begun to notice that there were Magi who, in the Master's words, had been "crazed by the process of illumination." They were individuals who in almost every way were the equal of their Masters, even with respect to their powers: I saw one of them make a seed germinate in twenty minutes of extreme concentration. But that man and some others had already led many disciples to madness and despair; some of those disciples had had to be committed to mental hospitals, and there was at least one confirmed case of suicide. Those Masters were on the "blacklist" of the Tradition, but it was impossible to control them, and I know that many of them continue their work even today.

All of this passed through my mind in a fraction of a second as I looked at the waterfall that seemed impossible to scale. I thought of the length of time that Petrus and I had traveled together, of the dog's attack that had left me unhurt, of Petrus's lack of control with the boy who had waited on us in the restaurant, and of Petrus's drinking bout at the wedding celebration. Those events were all I could remember.

"Petrus, there's no way I'm going to climb that waterfall. And for a very simple reason: it's impossible."

He didn't say a word. He sat down in the grass, and I did the same. We sat there in silence for fifteen minutes. His silence disarmed me, and I took the initiative by beginning to speak.

"Petrus, I don't want to climb because I'll fall. I know that I'm not going to die, because when I saw the face of my death, I also saw the day it will happen. But I could fall and be crippled for the rest of my life."

"Paulo, Paulo . . . " He looked at me and smiled. "You have completely changed. There is in your voice a bit of the love that consumes, and your eyes are shining."

"Are you going to say that I'm breaking a vow of obedience that I made before setting out on the Road?"

"You are not breaking that vow. You are not afraid, and you are not lazy. Nor should you be thinking that I have given you a useless order. You don't want to climb the falls because you are thinking about the Black Magi.[1] You have not broken a vow just because you have used your decision-making ability. A pilgrim is never prevented from using that ability."

[1]This is the name given, in the Tradition, to those Masters who have lost their magical contact with their disciples, as just described. This expression is also used to describe Masters who interrupted their learning process after having established dominion only over earthly forces.

I looked again at the cataract and again at Petrus. I was weighing my chances of success in making the climb, and they didn't weigh very much.

"Now, pay attention," he continued. "I'm going to climb before you do, without using any gift. And I'm going to make it. If I succeed just by knowing where to place my feet, you will have to climb, too. I am nullifying your freedom to make a decision. If you refuse, after you have seen me make the climb, then you will be breaking your vow."

Petrus began to take off his sneakers. He was at least ten years older than I, and if he succeeded in the climb, I would have no further excuse. I studied the waterfall and felt my stomach seize up.

But he didn't move. Even though he had taken off his sneakers, he remained seated in the same place. He looked at the sky and said, "A few kilometers from here, in 1502, the Virgin appeared to a shepherd. Today is the feast day commemorating that event—the Feast of the Virgin of the Road—and I am going to offer my victory to her. I would advise you to do the same thing. Offer a victory to her. Don't offer the pain in your feet or the cuts on your hands from the rocks. Everybody in the world offers only pain as penance. There is nothing wrong with that, but I think she would be happier if, rather than just pain, people would also offer her their joys."

I was in no condition to speak. I still doubted whether Petrus could climb the wall. I thought the whole thing was a farce, that I was being drawn in by the way he spoke and that he would then convince me to do something I really did not want to do. In the face of these doubts, I closed my eyes for a moment and prayed to the Virgin of the Road. I promised that if Petrus and I were able to climb the wall, I would one day return to this place.

"Everything you have learned up to now makes sense only if it is applied in real life. Don't forget that I described the Road to Santiago to you as the road of the common person; I have said that a thousand times. On the Road to Santiago and in life itself, wisdom has value only if it helps us to overcome some obstacle.

"A hammer would make no sense in the world if there were not nails to be driven. And even given the existence of nails, the hammer would be useless if it only thought, 'I can drive those nails with two blows.' The hammer has to act. To put itself into the hands of the carpenter and to be used in its proper function."

I remembered my Master's words at Itatiaia: "Whoever has the sword must constantly put it to the test, so it doesn't rust in its scabbard."

"The waterfall is the place where you will put into practice everything you have learned so far," said my guide. "There is one thing working in your favor: you know the day on which you are going to die so that fear will not paralyze you when you have to decide quickly where to find a hold.

But remember that you are going to have to work with the water and use it to provide what you need. Remember that you have to dig a nail into your thumb if a bad thought takes over. And most important, that you have to find support for yourself in the love that consumes during every minute of the climb, because it is that love which directs and justifies your every step."

Petrus fell silent. He took off his shirt and his shorts and was completely naked. He went into the cold water of the lagoon, wet himself completely, and spread his arms to the sky. I could see that he was happy; he was enjoying the coldness of the water and the rainbows created by the mist that surrounded us.

"One more thing," he said, before going in under the falls. "This waterfall will teach you how to be a Master. I am going to make the climb, but there will be a veil of water between you and me. I will climb without your being able to see where I place my hands and feet.

"In the same way, a disciple such as you can never imitate his guide's steps. You have your own way of living your life, of dealing with problems, and of winning. Teaching is only demonstrating that it is possible. Learning is making it possible for yourself."

He said nothing else as he disappeared through the veil of the cascade and began to climb. I could see only his outline, as if perceived through frosted glass. But I could see that he was climbing. Slowly and inexorably he moved toward the top. The closer he got to the crest, the more fearful I became, because my time was coming. Finally, the most terrible moment arrived: the moment when he had to come up through the falling water without holding onto the sides. The force of the water would surely plunge him back to the ground. But Petrus's head emerged there at the top, and the falling water became his silver mantle. I saw him for just an instant because, with a rapid motion, he threw his body upward and secured himself somehow on top of the plateau, still immersed in the stream of water. Then, I lost sight of him for some moments.

Finally, Petrus appeared on the bank. He was bathed in moisture, brilliant in the sunlight, and laughing.

"Let's go," he yelled, waving his hands. "It's your turn."

It really was my turn. Either I did it, or I forever renounced my sword.

I took all of my clothes off and prayed again to the Virgin of the Road. Then I dived into the lagoon. It was freezing, and my body went rigid with its impact; but I then felt a pleasant sensation, a sensation of being really alive. Without thinking about it, I went straight to the waterfall.

The weight of the water on my head brought me back to a sense of reality, the sense that weakens us at the moment when we most need to have faith in our powers. I could see that the falls had much more force than I had thought and that if the water continued to fall directly onto the top of my head, it would defeat me, even if I kept both feet firmly planted on the bottom of the lagoon. I passed through the falls and stood between the water and the rock, in a space into which my body just fit, glued to the wall. From there, I could see that the task was easier than I had thought.

The water did not beat down here, and what had appeared to me to be a wall with a polished surface was actually a wall with a great many cavities. I was dumbfounded to think that I might have renounced my sword out of fear of the smoothness of the wall when it turned out to be the kind of rock that I had climbed dozens of times. I seemed to hear Petrus's voice saying, "Didn't I tell you? Once a problem is solved, its simplicity is amazing."

I began to climb, with my face against the humid rock. In ten minutes I was almost to the top. Only one hurdle remained: the final phase, the place where the water fell over the crest on its trajectory toward the lagoon. The victory I had won in making the climb would be worth nothing if I were not able to negotiate the last stretch that separated me from the open air. This was where the danger lay, and I had not been able to see how Petrus had succeeded. I prayed again to the Virgin of the Road, a Virgin I had never heard of but who was now the object of all my faith and all my hopes for success. I began tentatively to put first my hair and then my entire head up through the water that was rushing over and past me.

The water covered me completely and blurred my vision. I began to feel its impact and held firmly to the rock. I bent my head to create an air pocket that would allow me to breathe. I trusted completely in my hands and feet. My hands had, after all, already held an ancient sword, and my feet had trod the Road to Santiago. They were my friends, and they were helping me. But the noise of the water was deafening, and I began to have trouble breathing. I was determined to put my head through the flow, and for several seconds everything went black. I fought with all my strength to keep my hands and feet anchored to their holds, but the noise of the water seemed to take me to another place. It was a mysterious and distant place where nothing that was happening at that moment was at all important, and it was a place that I could get to if I had the strength. In that place, there would no longer be any need for the superhuman effort it took to keep my hands and feet holding to the rock; there would be only rest and peace.

But my hands and feet did not obey this impulse to surrender. They had resisted a mortal temptation. And my head began to emerge from the stream as gradually as it had entered it. I was overcome by a profound love for my body. It was there, helping me in this crazy adventure of climbing through a waterfall in search of a sword.

When my head came completely through the surface, I saw the bright sun above me and took a deep breath. This renewed my strength, and as I looked about, I could see, just a few inches away, the plateau we had originally walked along—the end of the journey. I had an impulse to throw myself up and grab for something to hold, but I could see nothing to grab through the flowing water. The impulse was strong, but the moment of victory had not yet come, and I had to control myself. I was at the most difficult point in the ascent, with the water beating on my chest, and the pressure was threatening to throw me back to the place below that I had dared to leave in pursuit of my dream.

It was no time to be thinking about Masters or friends, and I could not look to the side to see if Petrus would be able to save me if I should slip. "He has probably made this climb a million times," I thought, "and he knows that here is where I most desperately need help." But he had abandoned me. Or maybe he hadn't abandoned me, but he was there somewhere behind me, and I couldn't turn to look for him without losing my balance. I had to do it all. I, alone, had to win my victory.

I kept my feet and one hand holding to the rock, while the other hand let go and sought to become one with the water. I didn't want to exert any more effort, because I was already using all of my strength. My hand, knowing this, became a fish that gives itself up but knows where it wants to go. I remembered films from my childhood in which I had seen salmon jumping over waterfalls because they had a goal and they simply had to achieve it.

The arm rose slowly, using the force of the water to its advantage. It finally burst free, and it took on the task of finding a hold and deciding the fate of the rest of my body. Like a salmon in the film, the hand dived into the water atop the crest, searching for a place, a point that would support me in the final leap.

The rock had been polished by centuries of running water. But there must be a handhold: if Petrus had been able to find one, I could, too. I began to feel great pain, because now I knew that I was only one step from success; this is the moment when one's strength begins to flag, and one loses confidence in oneself. On a few occasions in my life I had lost at the last minute—swum across an ocean and drowned in the surf of regret. But I was on the Road to Santiago, and that old experience must not be allowed to repeat itself—I had to win.

My free hand slid along the smooth stone, and the pressure was becoming stronger and stronger. I felt that my other limbs could not hold out and that I was going to begin to cramp. The water was beating on my genitals, too, and the pain was unbearable. Then my free hand suddenly found a hold in the rock. It wasn't a large one, and it was off to the side of where I wanted to rise, but it would serve as a support for my other hand when its turn came. I marked its location mentally, and my free hand returned to its search for my salvation. A few inches from the first hold, I found another.

There it was! There was the place that for centuries had served as a hold for the pilgrims bound for Santiago. I could see this, and I held on with all my strength. The other hand came free, was thrown back by the force of the water, but, in an arc across the sky, reached and found the handhold. With a quick movement, my entire body followed the path opened by my arms, and I threw myself upward.

The biggest and final step had been taken. My whole body came up through the water, and a moment later the savage waterfall had become just a trickle of water, hardly moving. I crawled to the bank and gave in to exhaustion. The sun fell on my body, warming me, and I told myself again that I had won, that I was alive as before when I had stood below in the lagoon. Over the sound of the water, I heard Petrus's approaching footsteps.

I wanted to get up and show how happy I was, but my exhausted body refused.

"Relax, rest a little," he said. "Try to breathe slowly."

I did so and fell into a deep, dreamless sleep. When I awoke, the sun had moved across the sky, and Petrus, already fully dressed, handed me my clothes and said we had to move on.

"I'm very tired," I answered.

"Don't worry. I am going to show you how to draw energy from everything around you."

And Petrus taught me the RAM Breathing Exercise.

I did the exercise for five minutes and felt better. I arose, dressed, and grabbed my knapsack.

"Come here," Petrus said. I went to the edge of the cliff. At my feet, the waterfall rushed by.

"Looking at it from here, it looks a lot easier than it did from down there," I said.

"Exactly. And if I had shown it to you from here before, you would have been misled. You would have made a poor analysis of your chances."

I still felt weak, and I repeated the exercise. Shortly, the entire universe about me fell into harmony with me and came into my heart. I asked Petrus why he had not taught me RAM breathing before, since many times I had felt lazy and tired on the Road to Santiago.

"Because you never looked like you felt that way," he said, laughing. Then he asked me if I still had any of the delicious butter cookies I had bought in Astorga.

The Ram Breathing Exercise

Expel all of the air from your lungs, emptying them as much as you can. Then, inhale slowly as you raise your arms as high as possible. As you inhale, concentrate on allowing love, peace, and harmony with the universe to enter into your body.

•

Hold the air you have taken in and keep your arms raised for as long as you can, enjoying the harmony between your inner sensations and the outer world. When you reach your limit, exhale all of the air rapidly, as you say the word, "RAM."

•

Repeat this process for five minutes each time you do the exercise.

Madness

For three days we had been making a kind of forced march. Petrus would wake me before daybreak, and we would not end our day's hike before nine in the evening. The only rest stops granted were for quick meals, since my guide had abolished our siesta. He gave the impression that he was keeping to some mysterious schedule that he hadn't shared with me.

What's more, his behavior had changed completely. At first, I thought it had something to do with my hesitation at the waterfall, but later I could see that it was not that. He was irritable with everyone, and he looked at his watch frequently during the day. I reminded him that it was he who had told me that we ourselves create the pace of time.

"You are becoming wiser every day," he answered. "Let's see if you can put all of this wisdom into play when it is needed."

On one afternoon, I was so tired from the pace of our hiking that I simply could not get up. Petrus told me to take my shirt off and settle my spine along the trunk of a nearby tree. I held that position for several minutes and felt much better. He began to explain to me that vegetation, and especially mature trees, are able to transmit harmony when one rests one's nerve centers against a tree trunk. For hours he discoursed on the physical, energetic, and spiritual properties of plants.

Since I had already read all of this somewhere, I didn't worry about taking notes. But Petrus's discourse helped to diminish my feeling that he was irritated with me. Afterward, I treated his silence with greater respect, and he, perhaps guessing correctly at my apprehension, tried to be friendlier whenever his constant bad mood allowed him to do so.

We arrived one morning at an immense bridge, totally out of proportion to the modest stream that coursed below it. It was early on a Sunday morning, and, since the bars and taverns nearby were all closed, we sat down there to eat our breakfast.

"People and nature are equally capricious," I said, trying to start a conversation. "We build beautiful bridges, and then Mother Nature changes the course of the rivers they cross."

"It's the drought," he said. "Finish your sandwich, because we have to move along."

I decided to ask him why we were in such a hurry.

"We have been on the Road to Santiago for a long time. I have already told you that I left a lot of things unattended in Italy, and I have got to get back."

I wasn't convinced. What he was saying might well be true, but it wasn't the only issue. When I started to question what he had said, he changed the subject.

"What do you know about this bridge?"

"Nothing," I answered. "But even with the drought, it's too big. I think the river must have changed its course."

"As far as that goes, I have no idea," he said. "But it is known along the Road to Santiago as the 'honorable passage.' These fields around us were the site of some bloody battles between the Suevians and the Visigoths, and later between Alphonse III's soldiers and the Moors. Maybe the bridge is oversize to allow all that blood to run past without flooding the city."

He was making an attempt at macabre humor. I didn't laugh, and he was put off for a moment, but then he continued, "However, it wasn't the Visigoth hordes or the triumphant cries of Alphonse III that gave this bridge its name. It was another story of love and death.

"During the first centuries of the Road to Santiago, pilgrims, priests, nobles, and even kings came from all over Europe to pay homage to the saint. Because of this, there was also an influx of assailants and robbers. History has recorded innumerable cases of robbery of entire caravans of pilgrims and of horrible crimes committed against lone travelers."

Just like today, I thought.

"Because of the crimes, some of the nobility decided to provide protection for the pilgrims, and each of the nobles involved took responsibility for protecting one segment of the Road. But just as rivers change their course, people's ideals are subject to alteration. In addition to frightening the malefactors, the knights began to compete with each other to determine who was the strongest and most courageous on the

Road. It wasn't long before they began to do battle with each other, and the bandits returned to the Road with impunity.

"This developed over a long period of time until, in 1434, a noble from the city of León fell in love with a woman. The man was Don Suero de Quiñones; he was powerful and rich, and he did everything in his power to win his lady's hand in marriage. But this woman—history has forgotten her name—did not even want to know about his grand passion and rejected his request."

I was dying of curiosity to know what an unrequited love had to do with battles among the knights. Petrus saw that I was interested and said that he would relate the rest of the story only if I finished my sandwich and we began to move along.

"You are just like my mother when I was a child," I said. But I gulped down the last morsel of bread, picked up my knapsack, and we began to make our way through the sleepy city.

Petrus continued, "Our gentleman, whose pride had been offended, resolved to do what all men do when they feel themselves to have been rejected: he began a private war. He promised himself that he was going to perform such an important feat that the woman would never forget his name. For months he sought a noble idea that would consecrate his spurned love. And then he heard of the crimes and the battles along the Road to Santiago. That gave him an idea.

"He called together ten of his friends, and they set themselves up in the small city we are passing through right now. He spread the word by means of the pilgrims that he was prepared to remain there for thirty days—and break thirty lances—in order to prove that he was the strongest and boldest of all the knights of the Road. He established himself with his banners, his standards, his pages, and servants, and waited for challengers."

I could imagine what a picnic that must have been: roast boar, endless supplies of wine, music, stories, and battles. A lively picture came to my mind as Petrus related the rest of the story.

"The bouts began on the tenth of July with the arrival of the first challengers. Quiñones and his companions fought during the day and held huge feasts every night. The contests were always held on the bridge so that no one could flee. During one period, so many challengers came that fires were built along the entire length of the bridge so that the bouts could go on until dawn. All of the vanquished knights were required to swear that they would never again do battle with the others and that from then on, their only mission would be to protect the pilgrims going to Compostela.

"On the ninth of August, the combat ended, and Don Suero de Quiñones was recognized as the bravest and most valiant of all the knights of the Road to Santiago. From that day forward, no one dared to issue challenges of bravery, and the nobles returned to their battle against the only enemy in common, the bandits who assaulted the pilgrims. This epic was later to give rise to the Military Order of Santiago of the Sword."

We had crossed the small city. I wanted to go back and take another look at the "honorable passage," the bridge on which all of that had taken place. But Petrus said that we had to move on.

"And what happened to Don Quiñones?" I asked.

"He went to Santiago de Compostela and placed a golden necklace at San Tiago's shrine; even today it adorns the bust of San Tiago the Lesser."

"I was asking whether he wound up marrying the lady."

"Oh, I don't know," Petrus answered. "In those days, history was written only by men. With such a battlefield close at hand, who was going to be interested in a love story?"

After telling me the story of Don Suero de Quiñones, my guide went back to his now habitual silence, and we went along for two more days without a word. We hardly stopped to rest. On the third day, though, Petrus began to walk more slowly than usual. He said that he was a bit tired from the efforts of the week and that he was too old to continue at that pace. Again I was sure that he was not telling the truth; his face, rather than showing fatigue, revealed an intense preoccupation, as if something very important was about to occur.

We arrived that afternoon at Foncebadon, a large village that was completely in ruins. The houses, built of stone, had slate roofs that had been destroyed by time and the rotting of the wood that supported them. One side of the village gave onto a precipice, and in front of us, behind a mountain peak, was one of the most important landmarks of the Road to Santiago: the Iron Cross. This time it was I who was impatient; I wanted to get to that strange monument, comprised of an immense wooden base, almost thirty feet tall, topped by the Iron Cross. The cross had been left there during the epoch of Caesar's invasion, in homage to Mercury. Observing the pagan tradition, the pilgrims along the Jacobean route were accustomed to leaving stones brought from elsewhere at the base of the cross. I took advantage of the abundance of stones in the abandoned village and picked up a piece of slate.

It was only when I had resolved to move along more quickly that I saw that Petrus was walking more slowly. He examined the ruined houses and the fallen tree trunks and finally decided to sit down in the middle of one of the plazas where there was a wooden cross.

"Let's rest a bit," he said.

It was early afternoon, so even if we stayed there for an hour there would still be time to reach the Iron Cross before nightfall.

I sat down beside him and gazed at the empty surroundings. Just as rivers change their course, humans also change where they live. The houses were solid and must have lasted for a long time before falling into ruin. It was a pretty place, with mountains in the distance and a valley in front of us. I asked myself what could have happened to cause the people to leave such a place.

"Do you think that Don Suero de Quiñones was crazy?" Petrus asked.

I did not even remember who Don Suero was, and he had to remind me about the "honorable passage."

"I don't think he was crazy," I answered. But I wasn't sure about my answer.

"Well, he was, just as Alfonso, the monk that you met, was. Just as I am, as you can see from the plans that I make. Or you, seeking your sword. Every one of us has the flame of madness burning inside, and it is fed by agape.

"Crazy doesn't mean you want to conquer America or talk to the birds like Saint Francis of Assisi. Even a vegetable vendor on the street corner can show this flame of madness if he likes what he is doing. Agape is grander than our ordinary human concepts, and everyone thirsts for it."

Petrus told me that I knew how to invoke agape by means of the Blue Sphere Exercise. But in order for agape to flourish, I must not be afraid to change my life. If I liked what I was doing, very well. But if I did not, there was always the time for a change. If I allowed change to occur, I would be transforming myself into a fertile field and allowing the Creative Imagination to sow its seeds in me.

"Everything I have taught you, including agape, makes sense only if you are satisfied with yourself. If you are not, then the exercises you have learned are inevitably going to make you seek change. And if you do not want all of those exercises to work against you, you have to allow change to happen.

"This is the most difficult moment in a person's life—when the person witnesses the good fight and is unable to change and join the battle. When this happens, knowledge turns against the person who holds it."

I looked at the deserted city of Foncebadon. Maybe all of those people, collectively, had felt the need for a change. I asked whether Petrus had chosen this place purposely in order to say all of this to me.

"I don't know what happened here," he answered. "Often people have to accept the changes that destiny forces upon them, but that's not what I'm talking about. I am speaking of an act of will, a concrete desire to do battle against everything that is unsatisfying in one's everyday life.

"On the road of our lives, we always run into problems that are hard to solve—like, for example, passing through a waterfall without letting it make us fall. So you have to allow the Creative Imagination to do its work. In your case, the waterfall was a life-and-death situation, and there wasn't time to consider many options; agape showed you the only way.

"But there are problems in our lives that require us to choose between one way and another. Everyday problems, like a business decision, the breakup of a relationship, a social obligation. Each of these small decisions we have to make, throughout our lives, might represent a choice between life and death. When you leave the house in the morning on your way to work, you might choose one means of transportation that will drop you off safe and sound or another that is going to crash and kill its passengers. This is a radical example of how a simple decision may affect us for the rest of our lives."

I began to think about myself as Petrus spoke. I had chosen to walk the Road to Santiago in search of my sword. It was the sword that was most important to me now, and I needed somehow to find it. I had to make the right decision.

"The only way to make the right decision is to know what the wrong decision is," he said after I had mentioned my concern. "You have to examine the other path, without fear and without being morbid, and then decide."

It was then that Petrus taught me the Shadows Exercise.

"Your problem is your sword," he said after he had explained the exercise.

I agreed.

The Shadows Exercise

Relax completely.

•

For five minutes, study the shadows of all of the objects and people around you. Try to identify exactly which part of the object or person is casting a shadow.

•

For the next five minutes, continue to do this, but at the same time, focus on the problem you are trying to solve. Look for all of the possible wrong solutions to the problem.

•

Finally, spend five more minutes studying the shadows and thinking about what correct solutions remain. Eliminate them, one by one, until only the single correct solution is left.

•

"So do the exercise now. I'm going to take a walk. When I come back, I know that you will have the right solution."

I remembered how much of a hurry Petrus had been in during the past few days, yet now we were having a prolonged conversation in this abandoned city. It seemed to me that he was trying to gain some time so that he, too, could make a decision regarding something. This made me excited, and I began to do the exercise.

I did a bit of RAM breathing to put me in harmony with my surroundings. Then I noted on my watch when fifteen minutes would have passed, and I began to look at the shadows all around me—shadows of ruined houses, stones, wood, and the cross behind me. As I studied the shadows, I saw that it was difficult to know exactly what part was casting any given shadow. I had never noticed this before. Some house beams that were straight were transformed into shadows with sharp angles, and an irregular stone cast a shadow with a smoothly rounded form. I did this for ten minutes. The exercise was so fascinating that it was not difficult to concentrate on it. Then I began to think of the wrong solutions to the problem of finding my sword. Many ideas came to mind—I thought about taking a bus to Santiago, and then I thought about phoning my wife and using some sort of emotional trickery to find out where she had placed it.

When Petrus returned, I was smiling.

"So?" he asked.

"I found out how Agatha Christie wrote her mystery novels," I joked. "She transformed the hunch that was most wrong into the one that was correct. She must have known about the Exercise of the Shadows."

Petrus asked where my sword was.

"First I'm going to tell you the most erroneous guess that I came up with as I looked at the shadows: that the sword is somewhere other than on the Road to Santiago."

"You are a genius. You figured out that we have been walking all this way in order to find your sword. I thought they had told you that already in Brazil."

"It's being kept in a safe place that my wife could not enter," I continued. "I deduced that it's in an absolutely open place but that it has been assimilated so well into its surroundings that it can't be seen."

This time Petrus didn't smile. I went on:

"And since the most absurd thing would be that it is in a place where there are lots of people, it has to be in some locale that is practically deserted. And most important, and so that the few people who see it don't notice the difference between it and a typical Spanish sword, it must be in a place where no one knows how to distinguish between styles of swords."

"Do you think it is here?" he asked.

"No, it's not here. The thing that would be most wrong would be to do this exercise at the place where my sword is. I discarded that hunch right away. It must be in a city that is similar to this one, but it cannot be in an abandoned city, because a sword in an abandoned city would attract a lot of attention from pilgrims and passersby. It would wind up as a decoration on the wall of a bar."

"Very good," he said, and I could see that he was proud of me—or of the exercise he had taught me.

"There's another thing," I said.

"What's that?"

"The place that would be most wrong for the sword of a Magus to be left is a profane place. It has to be in a sacred place. Like a church, for example, where no one would dare to steal it. So, in a church in a small city near Santiago, visible to everyone but embedded in its surroundings—that's where my sword is. Starting now, I'm going to visit every church on the Road."

"You don't have to," he said. "When the moment comes, you will know it."

I had been right!

"Listen, Petrus, why did we hurry for such a long while, when now we're spending so much time in this abandoned city?"

"What would be the answer that is most wrong?"

I glanced at the shadows. He was right. We were there for some reason.

The sun was hidden behind the mountain, but nightfall was still some hours away. I was thinking that the sun was probably shining just then on the Iron Cross. The cross was only a few hundred yards distant, and I really wanted to see it. I also wanted to know why we were waiting around. We had moved along so rapidly for the entire week, and now it seemed to me that the only reason for that must have been that we had to be at this place, on this day, and at this time.

I tried to make conversation to pass the time, but I could see that Petrus was tense and preoccupied. I had already seen

Petrus in a bad mood many times, but I could not remember having seen him so tense. And then I remembered that I *had* seen him like this once. It was at breakfast one morning in a small town whose name I could not remember, just before we had run into . . .

I looked to my left. There he was: the dog! The ferocious dog that had thrown me to the ground, the coward of a dog that had immediately fled afterward. Petrus had promised to help me if we ran into him again, and I turned to my guide. But he had disappeared.

I kept my gaze fixed on the dog's eyes while I frantically tried to think of a way to deal with the situation. Neither of us moved, and I was reminded for a moment of the duel scenes in the ghost towns of Western movies. In those films, no one would ever have dreamed of pitting a man against a dog; it just wouldn't have worked. Yet here I was, confronted with a reality that fiction would have considered too far out.

And there was Legion, so named because he was so many. Nearby stood a deserted house. If I were to bolt suddenly, I could climb to its roof, and Legion could not follow. It seemed absurd that I felt trapped by the physical presence of a dog and all that his presence implied.

As I kept my eyes on him, I immediately rejected the possibility of taking flight. Many times along the Road I had feared this moment, and now here it was. Before I could find my sword, I had to meet with the Enemy and either vanquish him or be defeated by him. I had no choice but to go up against him. If I fled now, I would be falling into a trap. It might be that the dog would not appear again, but I would travel the Road to Santiago de Compostela gripped by fear and apprehension. Ever afterward, I would dream about the dog, fearing his reappearance at any minute and living with dread for the rest of my life.

As I thought about all this, the dog started toward me. I stopped thinking immediately and concentrated only on the battle that was about to begin. Petrus had left, and I was alone. I was frightened. And as I experienced that fear, the dog began to move closer, making a low growling sound. The growl was much more threatening than a loud bark would have been, and I became even more terrified. Seeing the weakness in my eyes, the dog leapt on me.

It was as if a boulder had been thrown at my chest. I fell to the ground, and he began to bite at me. I remembered vaguely that I already knew about my death and that it was not to be like this, but even so, my fear grew, and I was unable to control it. I began to fight just to protect my face and throat. An intense pain in my leg caused me to curl up, and I could see that some flesh had been torn away. I took my hands from my head and throat, reaching toward the wound. The dog, seeing this, began an assault on my face. At that moment, one of my hands felt a rock at my side. I grasped it and began to beat on the dog with all my strength.

He backed off a bit, more surprised than hurt, and I was able to stand. The dog continued to retreat, and the bloody stone gave me courage. I was paying too much respect to the strength of my enemy, and this was a trap. He could not be any stronger than I. He might be more agile, but he could not be stronger, because I weighed more and was taller than he. My fear had lessened, but I wasn't in control of myself yet, and with the rock in my hand, I began to shout at the dog. He withdrew a little further and then suddenly stopped.

It seemed as if he were reading my mind. In my desperation I was beginning to feel strong, and I began to think that it was ridiculous to be fighting a dog. A sense of power suddenly came to me, and a hot wind began to blow across the deserted city. Then I began to be tired of the whole thing; when all was said and done, I had only to batter him once on the head with the stone, and I would have won. I wanted it to be over immediately so that I could dress my wound and put an end to this absurd business of swords and the Strange Road to Santiago.

But this was another trap. The dog hurled himself at me and again pushed me to the ground. This time he evaded the rock easily, biting my hand and causing me to let it go. I began to punch him with my hands, but I was not causing any serious damage. The only thing my blows accomplished was to keep him from biting me even more. His sharp claws began to tear my clothing and my arms, and I saw that it was only a matter of time before he took charge completely.

All of a sudden, I heard a voice from within me. The voice said that if the dog established dominion over me, the fight would be over, and I would be saved: defeated but alive. My leg was aching, and my entire body stung from its lacerations. The voice insisted that I give up, and I recognized whose voice it was: it was Astrain, my messenger, speaking to me. The dog stopped for a moment, as if he had heard the same voice, and once again I felt like leaving the whole thing behind. Astrain had told me in our conversations that many people fail to find the sword in their lives, and what difference did it make? What I wanted to do was go home, be with my wife, have my children, and work at what I liked. Enough of these absurdities, fighting with dogs and climbing waterfalls. This was the second time that this thought had come to me, but the desire to give up was even stronger now, and I was certain that I would surrender.

A sound from the streets of the abandoned city caught the animal's attention. I looked in the direction of the sound and saw a shepherd returning from the fields with his flock. I remembered that I had seen this scene before, in the ruins of an old castle. When the dog spotted the sheep, he jumped away from me and made ready to attack them. This was my salvation.

The shepherd started to yell, and the sheep scattered. Before the dog got completely away, I decided to engage him for another moment or two, just to provide enough time for the animals to flee. I grabbed one of the dog's legs. I had the absurd hope that the shepherd might come to my assistance, and for a moment, my hopes about the sword and the power of RAM returned.

The dog tried to pull away from me. I was no longer the enemy; I was a hindrance. What he wanted now was there in front of him: the sheep. But I continued to grasp the animal's leg, awaiting a shepherd who would not come and suddenly hoping that the sheep would *not* take flight.

That is what saved my soul. An immense feeling of strength infused me. It was no longer the illusion of power, which causes one to become weary of the battle and to want to give in. Astrain whispered to me again, but this time it was something different. He said that I should always confront the world with the same weapons that were used to challenge me. And that I could confront a dog only by transforming myself into a dog.

This was the same craziness that Petrus had talked about that day. I began to feel that I was a dog. I bared my teeth and sounded a low growl, and hatred flowed from the sounds I made. I saw the frightened face of the shepherd off to the side and could sense that the sheep were as terrified of me as they were of the dog.

Legion also saw this and became fearful. Then I attacked him. It was the first time I had done this in our fight. I attacked him with my teeth and my nails, trying to bite the dog in the throat, exactly as I had feared he would do to me. Inside, I felt only a tremendous desire for victory. Nothing else was important. I threw myself on top of the animal and pressed him to the ground. He fought to free himself from the weight of my body, and he clawed at my skin, but I too was biting and scratching. I could sense that if he got out from under me, he would run away, and I did not want that to happen ever again. Today I was going to beat him.

The animal began to show fear in his eyes. Now I was the dog, and he seemed to have been transformed into a man. My old fear was operating in him now. It was so strong that he was able to work his way out from under me, but I corralled him in the basement of one of the abandoned houses. Behind its low slate wall was the precipice, and he had no escape. Right there, he was going to see the face of his death.

I suddenly began to realize that there was something wrong. My thinking was becoming cloudy, and I began to see a gypsy's face with vague images dancing around it. I had turned myself into Legion. This was the source of my power. The many devils had abandoned the poor, frightened dog that a moment from now was going to fall into an abyss, and now they were in me. I felt a terrible desire to destroy the defenseless animal. "You are the Prince, and they are Legion," whispered Astrain. But I did not want to be a Prince, and I heard from a distance the voice of my Master. He said insistently that there was a sword to be won. I had to resist for one more minute. I should not kill that dog.

I looked over at the shepherd. His look confirmed what I was thinking. He, too, was now more frightened of me than of the dog.

I began to feel dizzy, and the scene began to spin. I could not allow myself to faint. If I fainted now, Legion would have won. I had to find a solution. I was no longer fighting against an animal but against the force that possessed me. I felt my legs beginning to weaken, and I leaned against a wall, but it gave way under my weight. Among the stones and bits of wood, I fell with my face in the dirt.

The earth. Legion was the earth and the fruits of the earth—the good fruits of the earth and the bad, but of the earth. His house was in the earth, and there he ruled the earth or was ruled by it. Agape exploded within me, and I dug my nails into the earth. I screamed, and the scream was the same as I had heard the first time the dog and I had met. I felt Legion pass through my body and descend into the earth. Within me was agape, and Legion did not want to be eaten by the love that consumes. This was my will, the will that had made me fight with my remaining strength against fainting; it was the will of agape residing in my soul and resisting. My entire body trembled.

Legion plummeted into the earth. I began to vomit, but I felt that it was agape, growing and exiting through all of my pores. My body continued to tremble, and a long time later I sensed that Legion had returned to his realm.

I could feel his last vestige pass out through my fingers. I sat on the ground, wounded and exhausted, and looked at the absurd scene in front of me: a dog, bleeding and waving his tail, and a terrified shepherd staring at me.

"It must have been something you ate," said the shepherd, not wanting to believe what he had seen. "But now that you've vomited, you will feel better."

I nodded my head. He thanked me for having controlled "my" dog and went his way down the road with his sheep.

Petrus appeared but said nothing. He tore off a strip of his shirt and made a tourniquet for my leg, which was bleeding badly. He told me to check the rest of my body, and I replied that there was nothing serious.

"You look awful," he said, smiling. His good mood seemed to have returned. "We can't visit the Iron Cross with you looking like that. There are probably tourists there, and they would be frightened."

I didn't pay any attention to him. I got up, brushed off the dust, and saw that I could walk. Petrus suggested that I do the RAM Breathing Exercise, and he picked up my knapsack. I did the exercise and returned once again to a sense of harmony with the world. In half an hour, I would be at the Iron Cross.

And someday, Foncebadon was going to rise from its ruins. Legion had left a lot of power there.

Command and Obedience

PETRUS WAS CARRYING ME AS WE ARRIVED AT THE IRON Cross; my leg wound prevented me from walking. When he realized the extent of the damage done by the dog, he decided that I should rest until the wound had healed enough for us to continue along the Strange Road to Santiago. Nearby there was a village that provided shelter for pilgrims who were overtaken by nightfall before crossing the mountains, and Petrus found us two rooms in the home of a blacksmith.

My haven had a small veranda, an architectural feature we hadn't seen previously along the Road. From it, I could see the range of mountains we would have to cross sooner or later in order to reach Santiago. I fell into bed and slept until the following day; although I felt slightly feverish when I awoke, I also felt better.

Petrus brought some water from the fountain that the villagers called "the bottomless well," and he bathed my wounds. In the afternoon, he came to my room with an old woman who lived nearby. They placed several different types of herbs on the wounds and lacerations, and the woman made me drink some bitter tea. Petrus insisted that I lick the wounds until they had completely closed. I can still remember the sweet, metallic flavor of my blood; it nauseated me, but my guide told me that my saliva was a powerful disinfectant.

The fever returned during the second day. Petrus and the old woman again plied me with the tea, and they again put the herbs on my wounds. But the fever, although it was not high, continued. My guide decided to go to a military base nearby to see if he could get some bandages, since there was no place in the entire village where gauze or adhesive tape was available.

Several hours later, Petrus returned with the bandages. He was accompanied by a young medical officer, who insisted on knowing where the animal was that had attacked me.

"From the type of bite you have, the animal was rabid," he told me.

"No, no," I said. "I was just playing with him, and it got out of control. I have known the dog for a long time."

The medical officer was not convinced. He insisted that I take an antirabies vaccine, and I was forced to let him administer at least one dose or else I would have been transferred to the base hospital. Afterward, he again asked where the animal was.

"In Foncebadon," I answered.

"Foncebadon is a city in ruins. There are no dogs there," he said, with an air of having found out the lie.

I began to moan as though I were in pain, and Petrus led the young officer out of the room. But he left everything we would need: clean bandages, adhesive tape, and a styptic compound.

Petrus and the old woman refused to use the compound. They bound the wounds with gauze and herbs instead. This made me happy, because it meant that I would no longer have to lick the places where the dog had bitten me. During the night, they both knelt at my bedside and, with their hands placed on my body, prayed aloud for me. I asked Petrus what he was doing, and he made a vague reference to the divine graces and the Road to Rome. I wanted him to tell me more, but he said nothing else.

Two days later, I had recuperated completely. That morning, I looked out my window and saw some soldiers conducting a search of the houses nearby and of the hills around the village. I asked one of them what was happening.

"There is a rabid dog somewhere around here," he answered.

That afternoon, the blacksmith in whose rooms we were staying came to me and asked that I leave the town as soon as I was able to travel. The story had spread among the townspeople, and they were fearful that I would become rabid and transmit the disease to others. Petrus and the old woman began to argue with the blacksmith, but he was adamant. At one point, he even asserted that he had seen a trickle of foam at the corner of my mouth while I was sleeping.

There was no way to convince him that all of us drool a bit in our sleep. That night, Petrus and the woman prayed incessantly over me, and the next day, limping somewhat, I was once again on the Strange Road to Santiago.

I asked Petrus if he had been worried about my recovery.

"There is an understanding about the Road to Santiago that I have not told you about before," he said. "Once a pilgrimage has begun, the only acceptable excuse for interrupting it is illness. If you had not been able to recover from your wounds and your fever had continued, it would have been an omen, telling us that our pilgrimage had to end there."

But he added, with some pride, that his prayers had been answered. And I was certain that the outcome had been as important for him as it was for me.

The Road was downhill now, and Petrus pointed out that it would be that way for the next two days. We had returned to our usual schedule, with a siesta every afternoon at the time when the sun was fiercest. Because of my bandages, Petrus carried my knapsack. We were no longer in a hurry: the encounter we had been rushing toward was over.

My disposition improved with every hour, and I was quite proud of myself; I had climbed a waterfall and defeated the demon of the Road. All that remained was the most important task: to find my sword. I mentioned this to Petrus.

"Your victory was beautiful, but you failed in the most critical sense," he said, throwing a deluge of cold water over me.

"What do you mean?"

"Knowing the right moment for the encounter. I had to hurry us along, setting a pace that was demanding, and the only thing you could think about was that we were after your sword. What good is a sword if you don't know where you are going to run into your enemy?"

"The sword is the instrument of my power," I answered.

"You are too preoccupied with your power," he said. "The waterfall, the RAM practices, the dialogues with your messenger—they all made you forget that there was your enemy to vanquish. And forget that you had an impending encounter with him. Before your hand can wield the sword, you have to discover where your enemy is and how to deal with him. The sword only strikes a blow, but the hand is already victorious or defeated before the blow is delivered.

"You defeated Legion without your sword. There is a secret in this search, and it is a secret you have not yet learned. If you do not do so, you will never find what you are looking for."

I didn't answer him. Every time I began to feel that I was getting close to my objective, Petrus insisted on reminding me that I was just a simple pilgrim and that there was always something else I needed in order to find what I was looking for. The happiness I had been feeling a few minutes before we began the conversation now disappeared completely.

Once again I was starting out on the Strange Road to Santiago, and I was totally discouraged. Along the same Road that I was walking, millions of souls had passed during the past twelve centuries, going to and returning from Santiago de Compostela. In their case, getting to where they had wanted to go had only been a matter of time. In my case, the traps set by the Tradition were forever placing another obstacle in my path and creating new tests for me.

I told Petrus that I was growing tired, and we sat down in the shade. There were huge wooden crosses along the side of the road. Petrus put the two knapsacks on the ground and spoke again: "Our enemy always represents our weaker side. This may be a fear of physical pain, but it may also be a premature sense of victory or the desire to abandon the fight because we define it as not being worth the effort.

"Our enemy joins the battle only because he knows that he can hurt us—and hurt us in exactly the spot where our pride tells us that we are most invincible. During the fight, we always try to protect our weak spot, so the enemy strikes at the unguarded side—the side in which we have the most confidence. And we wind up defeated because we allow what should never be allowed: we let the enemy choose how the battle will be waged."

Everything Petrus was describing had happened during my fight with the dog. Yet I told him that I could not accept the idea that I had enemies and that I had to do battle with them. I said that when Petrus had spoken of the good fight, I had thought that he had been talking about fighting for achievements in one's life.

"That's right," he said. "But that is not all the good fight is. Going to war is not a sin. It is an act of love. The enemy develops us and sharpens us, as the dog did with you."

"OK, I understand that. But let's get back to what we were talking about before. Why is it that you never seem to be satisfied with what I do? I have the impression that you always think I am going about things the wrong way. And weren't you about to tell me the secret of my sword?"

Petrus said that this was something I should have learned before beginning the pilgrimage. And he went on about the enemy.

"Our enemy is part of agape, there to test our grip, our will, and our handling of the sword. He was placed in our lives—and we in his—with a purpose. And that purpose has to be met. So to flee from the battle is the worst thing that could happen. It is worse than losing the fight, because we can always learn something from defeat; if we flee, all we do is declare that our enemy has won."

I said I was surprised to hear him say that; it amazed me to hear a man who seemed to feel so close to Jesus talk about violence in this way.

"Think about why Jesus needed Judas so," he said. "He had to choose an enemy, or his battle here on earth could not have been glorified."

The wooden crosses along the road testified to how that glory had been achieved: with blood, treason, and desertion. I got up and said I was ready to move on.

As we walked, I asked him what, in a battle situation, was a person's greatest source of strength in trying to defeat the enemy.

"Your present. We defend ourselves best through what we are doing right now, because that is where agape and the will to win, through enthusiasm, are.

"And there's another thing I want to make very clear: the enemy rarely represents evil. He is an everyday presence, and it is he that keeps our sword from rusting in its scabbard."

I remembered that once, when we were building a summer house, my wife had decided suddenly to change the location of one of the rooms. It had been my job to give this disagreeable news to the builder. I had called him, a man of about seventy years of age, and told him what I wanted. He had looked at the plan, thought about it, and come up with an even better solution, using a wall that he had already begun to raise. My wife had loved the idea.

Maybe it was this that Petrus was trying to describe in a more complicated way: that we have to use the thrust of what we are doing right now to defeat the enemy.

I told him the story about the builder.

"Life always teaches us more than the Road to Santiago does," he answered. "But we don't have much faith in what life teaches us."

There were crosses all along this part of the Jacobean route. They were made of such massive, heavy wood that the pilgrim who put them there must have had an almost superhuman strength. A cross had been placed every thirty meters for as far as I could see. I asked Petrus what their significance was.

"An ancient and obsolete instrument of torture," he said.

"But why are they here?"

"They must have been some kind of pledge. How should I know?"

We stopped in front of one of them that had toppled over.

"Maybe the wood rotted," I said.

"It's the same wood as all the others. And none of the others rotted."

"Then it must not have been sunk into the earth firmly enough."

Petrus stopped and looked around. He put his knapsack on the ground and sat down. We had stopped to rest only a few minutes before, so I couldn't understand what he was doing. Instinctively, I looked around, expecting to see the dog.

"You defeated the dog," he said, knowing what I was thinking. "Don't worry about the ghosts of the dead."

"Well, then, why are we stopping?"

Petrus made a gesture that told me to be quiet, and I did not say anything for several minutes. I felt the old fear of the dog and decided to remain standing, hoping Petrus would say something.

"What do you hear?" he asked me.

"Nothing. The silence."

"We are not smart enough to be able to listen to the silence! We are just human beings, and we don't even know how to listen to our own ramblings. You have never asked me how I knew that Legion was about to arrive. Now I will tell you how: by listening. The sound began many days before, when we were still in Astorga. Starting then, I began to move along more quickly, because all the indications were that we were going to meet up with him in Foncebadon. You heard the same sound as I, but you were not listening.

"Everything is contained in sounds—the past, the present, and the future. The person who does not know how to listen will never hear the advice that life offers us all the time. And only the person who listens to the sounds of the moment is able to make the right decisions."

Petrus bade me sit down and forget about the dog. He said that he was going to teach me one of the easiest and most important practices of the Road to Santiago.

And he explained the Listening Exercise to me.

"Do it right now," he said.

I began to perform the exercise. I heard the wind and a woman's voice far in the distance, and at one point I sensed that a branch was being broken. It was not a difficult exercise, and I was fascinated by its simplicity. I put my ear to the ground and began to listen to the muted sounds of the earth. After a few moments, I began to separate the sounds from each other: the sound of the leaves rustling, the sound of the voice in the distance, and the noise of the beating of the wings of birds. An animal grunted, but I could not identify what kind of beast it was. The fifteen minutes I spent on the exercise flew by.

The Listening Exercise

Relax. Close your eyes.

•

Try for several minutes to concentrate on all of the sounds you hear in your surroundings, as if you were hearing an orchestra playing its instruments.

•

Little by little, try to separate each sound from the others. Concentrate on each one, as if it were the only instrument playing. Try to eliminate the other sounds from your awareness.

•

When you do this exercise every day, you will begin to hear voices. First, you will think that they are imaginary. Later, you will discover that they are voices of people from your past, present, and future, all of them participating with you in the remembrance of time.

•

This exercise should be performed only when you already know the voice of your messenger.

•

Do this exercise for ten minutes at a time.

•

"After a while, you will see that this exercise will help you to make the right decision," Petrus said, without asking me what I had heard. "Agape speaks to you through the Blue Sphere Exercise, but it also speaks to you through your sight, your sense of touch, through scents, and your heart, and your hearing. A week from now, at the most, you will begin to hear voices. At first, they will be timid, but before long they are going to begin to tell you things that are important. Be careful, though, with your messenger. He is going to try to confuse you. However, you already know the sound of his voice, so he will no longer be a threat."

Petrus asked if I had heard the joyful call of an enemy, or an invitation offered by a woman, or the secret of my sword.

"I just heard the voice of a woman in the distance," I said. "But it was a farmer's wife calling to her child."

"Well, look at that cross there, and see if you can raise it with your thoughts."

I asked him what such an exercise would mean.

"It means having faith in your thoughts," he responded.

I sat down on the ground in a yoga position. I was certain that after everything I had accomplished with the dog and with the waterfall, I was going to be able to do this, too. I fixated on the cross. I imagined myself leaving my body, grasping the cross, and raising it using my astral body. On the road of the Tradition, I had already performed some of these small "miracles." I had been able to shatter glasses and porcelain statues and to move objects along the surface of a table. It was an easy magic trick, and even though it did not signify any great power, it was useful in winning over nonbelievers. I had never tried it, though, with an object the size and weight of the cross. But if Petrus had commanded that I do so, I felt I would know how to make it happen.

For half an hour I tried everything I could. I used astral displacement and suggestion. I remembered the power my Master had over the force of gravity, and I tried to repeat the words that he always used on such occasions. Nothing happened. I was concentrating completely, but the cross did not budge. I invoked Astrain, and he appeared between the columns of fire. But when I spoke to him about the cross, he said that he detested crosses.

Petrus finally shook me to bring me out of my trance.

"Come on, this is becoming irritating," he said. "Since you can't do it by thinking, put the cross upright with your hands."

"With my hands?"

"Do it!"

I was startled. Suddenly the man in front of me had become nasty, very different from the person who had cared for my wounds. I didn't know what to say or do.

"Do it!" he repeated. "I am ordering you to do it!"

There I was, with my arms and hands wrapped in bandages because of the dog's attack. I had just been through the

Listening Exercise, but I couldn't believe what I was hearing from Petrus. Without saying anything, I showed him my bandages. But he continued to look coldly at me, not changing his expression in the least. He expected me to obey him. The guide and friend who had accompanied me all this time, who had taught me the RAM practices and told me the beautiful stories about the Road to Santiago, seemed no longer to be there. In his place I saw a man who regarded me as a slave and had ordered me to do something that was stupid.

"What are you waiting for?" he asked.

I remembered the waterfall experience. I recalled that on that day I had had some doubts about Petrus but that then he had been generous with me. He had demonstrated his love and had kept me from giving up on my sword. I could not understand how the same person who had been so kind could be so harsh now. He suddenly seemed to represent the very thing that the human race was trying to put behind it—the oppression of one person by another.

"Petrus, I . . ."

"Do it, or the Road to Santiago ends right here!"

I was scared again. At that moment, I was more frightened than I had been at the waterfall; I was more fearful of him than of the dog that had terrorized me for so long. I prayed that a signal would come to me from somewhere in our surroundings, that I would see or hear something that would explain his senseless command. But we were engulfed in silence. I either had to obey Petrus or forget about the sword. Once again, I raised my bandaged arms, but he sat down on the ground, waiting for me to carry out his orders.

So I decided to obey him.

I went to the cross and tried to budge it with my foot to test its weight. It hardly moved. Even if my hands had been in good shape, I would have had a very difficult time trying to lift it, and I knew that with my hands bound as they were, the task would be almost impossible. But I was going to comply. I was going to die in the attempt, if that was necessary; I was going to sweat blood, as Jesus had when he had had to carry the same kind of burden. But Petrus was going to perceive the seriousness of my effort, and perhaps that would touch him in some way and he would free me from the test.

The cross had broken at its base, but it was still attached to it. I had no knife with which to cut through the fibers. Forgetting about my pain, I put my arms around the cross and tried to wrench it from the shattered base, without using my hands. The wood abraded the lacerations on my arms, and I cried out in pain. I looked at Petrus, and he was completely impassive. I resolved that I would not cry out again. From that moment on, I would stifle any such demonstration.

I knew that my immediate problem was not to move the cross but to free it from its base. Afterward, I would have to dig a hole and push the cross into it. I found a stone with an edge to it and, ignoring the pain, began to pound at the wooden fibers.

The pain was terrible and grew worse with every blow, and the fibers were parting very slowly. I had to give up that approach right away, before my wounds reopened and the whole effort became impossible. I decided to work at it more slowly so that I could accomplish the task without succumbing to the pain. I took off my shirt, wrapped it around my hand, and went back to the job with this additional protection. The idea was a good one: the first fiber parted, and then the second. The stone was losing its edge, so I looked around for another. Each time I paused, I had the feeling that I would not be able to start again. I gathered several sharp stones and used them, one after the other, so that the pain in the hand I was working with was bearable. Almost all of the fibers had been cut, but the main one still held firm. The pain in my hand was increasing, and abandoning the idea of working slowly, I began to strike at the wood frantically. I knew that I was coming close to the point where the pain would make it impossible to continue. It was just a matter of time until this happened, and I had to make good use of that time. I was sawing and pounding now, and something sticky between my skin and the bandages was making the work even more difficult. It is probably blood, I thought, but then I put it out of my mind. I gritted my teeth, struck harder at the fiber, and it seemed about to break. I was so excited that I stood up and delivered a blow with all my strength to the wood that was causing all my suffering.

With a groan, the cross fell to the side, freed from its base.

My joy lasted only for a few moments. My hand was throbbing violently, and I had only begun the job. I looked over at Petrus and saw that he was sleeping. I stood there for a time, trying to figure out some way of fooling him, of putting the cross upright without his noticing it.

But that was exactly what Petrus wanted: that I raise the cross. And there was no way to deceive him, because the task depended solely on me.

I looked at the ground—the dry, yellow earth. Once again, stones would be my only tools. I could not work anymore with my right hand because it hurt too much, and there was that sticky substance under the bandage that worried me. I carefully unwrapped the shirt from the bandages; blood was staining the gauze—and this was a wound that had almost healed. Petrus was a monster!

I found a different kind of stone, one that was heavier and more resistant. Rolling the shirt around my left hand, I began to beat at the earth, trying to dig a hole at the foot of the cross. My initial progress was good, but it was soon slowed by the hardness and dryness of the ground. I kept digging, but the hole seemed to stay the same depth. I decided that I would not make the hole very wide so that the cross would fit into it without wobbling, but this made it more difficult to remove the dirt from the excavation. My right hand had stopped hurting as much as it had, but the coagulated blood made me nauseated and anxious. I was not used to working with my left hand, and the stone kept slipping from my grip.

I dug forever! Every time the stone beat on the ground, and every time I put my hand into the hole to remove some dirt, I thought of Petrus. I looked over at him, dozing peacefully, and I hated him from the bottom of my heart. Neither the noise nor my hatred appeared to disturb him. "He must have his reasons," I said to myself, but I could not understand the debasement and humiliation he was inflicting on me. I saw his face in the earth I was pounding, and the rage I was feeling helped me to dig the hole deeper. Again, it was just a matter of time: sooner or later I was going to win.

As I thought about this, the rock hit something solid and sprang back. This was my worst fear. After all that work, I had run into a stone that was too big for me to continue.

I stood up, wiping the sweat from my face, and began to think. I didn't have enough strength to move the cross to another place. I couldn't start again from the beginning because my left hand, now that I had stopped, felt dead. This was worse than pain, and it really scared me. I looked at my fingers, and I was able to move them, but instinct told me that I shouldn't punish the hand anymore.

I looked at the hole. It wasn't deep enough to hold the cross erect.

"The wrong answer will indicate the right one." I remembered the Shadows Exercise and what Petrus had said then. It was also then that he had told me that the RAM practices would make sense only if I could apply them in my daily life. Even in a situation as absurd as the present one, the RAM practices should be of some use.

"The wrong answer will indicate the right one." The impossible solution would be to try to drag the cross to a different place; I no longer had the strength to do that. It was also impossible to try digging deeper into the ground.

So if the impossible answer was to go deeper into the earth, the possible answer was to raise the earth. But how?

And suddenly, all of my love for Petrus was restored. He was right. I could raise the earth!

I began to collect all the stones nearby and placed them around the hole, mixing them with the earth I had removed. With great effort, I lifted the foot of the cross a little and supported it with stones to raise it higher off the ground. In half an hour, the ground was higher, and the hole was deep enough.

Now I just had to get the cross into the hole. It was the last step, and I had to make it work. One of my hands was numb, and the other was giving me a great deal of pain. My arms were wrapped in bandages. But my back was all right; it had just a few scratches. If I could lie down beneath the cross and raise it bit by bit, I would be able to slide it into the hole.

I stretched out on the ground, feeling the dust in my nose and eyes. With the hand that was numb, I raised the cross a fraction and slid underneath it. Carefully, I adjusted my position so that its trunk rested squarely on my back. I felt its weight and knew that it would be heavy to lift but not impossible. I thought about the Seed Exercise, and very slowly I squirmed into a fetal position, balancing the cross on my back. Several times I thought it was going to fall, but I was working slowly; I was able to sense the direction it might take and correct for it by repositioning my body. I finally achieved the position I wanted, with my knees in front of me and the cross balanced. For a moment, the foot of the cross shook on the pile of stones, but it did not fall out of place.

"It's a good thing I don't have to save the universe," I thought, oppressed by the weight of the cross and everything it represented. A profoundly religious feeling took possession of me. I remembered that another person had carried the cross on his shoulders and that his damaged hands had not been able to free themselves from the wood or the pain as mine could. This religious feeling was loaded down with pain, but I forgot about it immediately because the cross began to shake again.

Then, slowly raising myself up, I began a rebirth. I couldn't look behind me, and sound was my only means of orientation. But just a while ago I had learned how to listen to the world, as if Petrus had guessed that I was going to need this kind of knowledge. I felt the weight of the cross and sensed that the stones were accommodating each other. The cross rose bit by bit, as if to help me in this test. It was as if the cross, itself, wanted to return to its position, framing that section of the Road to Santiago.

One final push was all that was needed. If I could get into a seated position, the trunk of the cross would slide down my back into the hole. One or two of the stones had been dislodged, but the cross was now helping me, since its foot remained in place where I had built up the wall. Finally, a pull on my back indicated that the base was free. It was the final moment, just as at the waterfall when I had had to fight my way through the current: the most difficult moment, because it is then that we fear failure and want to give up before it occurs. Once again I sensed how absurd the task was, trying to raise a cross when all I really wanted to do was find my sword. But none of these thoughts was important. With a sudden thrust, I raised my back, and the cross slid into place. At that moment I recognized once again that fate had been directing the work I had done.

I stood there expecting the cross to fall in the other direction, scattering the stones I had placed. Then I thought that maybe my push had not been strong enough and that the cross was going to fall back on top of me. But what I heard was the muffled sound of something hitting against the bottom of the hole.

I turned carefully. The cross was upright, and it was still trembling from the impact. Some stones were rolling down their slope, but the cross was not going to fall. I quickly put the stones back in place and embraced the cross so that it would stop wavering. I felt alive and hot, certain that the cross had been my friend throughout all of my work. I stepped away slowly, improving the placement of the stones with my feet.

I stood there admiring my work for a long time, until my wounds began to hurt. Petrus was still asleep. I went over to him and nudged him with my foot.

He awoke with a start and looked at the cross.

"Very good," was all that he said. "In Ponferrada, we will change the bandages."

The Tradition

"I WOULD RATHER HAVE LIFTED A TREE. THAT CROSS ON MY back had me thinking that my search for wisdom was going to be the death of me."

Looking at my surroundings, my words rang a bit hollow. The cross episode was already history, as if it had happened a long time ago and not just the previous day. It had no relation to the black marble bathroom, the warmth of the water in the hot tub, or the crystal goblet of Rioja wine that I was enjoying. I could not see Petrus, who was in his own bedroom in the luxury suite we had rented in a first-class hotel.

"Why the cross?" I insisted.

"It wasn't easy to convince the man at the front desk that you weren't a beggar," he yelled from his room.

He was changing the subject, and I knew from experience that it would do no good to press the matter. I got up and put on trousers, a clean shirt, and fresh bandages. I had removed the old ones very carefully, expecting to find open wounds, but the scabs had only broken away from the skin slightly and allowed some blood to ooze out. A new scab had already formed, and I was feeling restored and happy.

We had dinner at the hotel restaurant. Petrus asked for the specialty of the house—a Valencia paella—which we ate in silence. After dinner, he suggested a walk.

We left the hotel and walked in the direction of the railroad station. He was in his now habitual laconic state and said nothing throughout our entire stroll. We came to a train yard, filthy and smelling of oil, and he sat down on the steps of a gigantic locomotive.

"Let's stop here," he said.

I didn't want to get oil stains on my pants, so I decided to stand. I asked him if he wouldn't prefer to walk to the main square of Ponferrada.

"The Road to Santiago is about to end," said my guide, "and since our reality is a lot more similar to these railroad cars, stinking of oil, than to the bucolic retreats we have encountered during our journey, it is better that today's conversation happen here."

Petrus told me to take off my sneakers and my shirt. Then he loosened the bandages on my arms, leaving them freer to move. But he left those on my hands as they were.

"Don't worry," he said. "You are not going to need your hands for this, at least not to hold anything."

He was more serious than usual, and his tone of voice surprised me. Something important was about to happen.

Petrus sat down again on the steps of the locomotive and looked at me for a long time. Then he said, "I am not going to say anything about yesterday's episode. You will discover for yourself what it means, and this will happen only if someday you decide to walk the Road to Rome—the Road of the graces and miracles. I want to tell you just one thing: people who consider themselves to be wise are often indecisive when command is called for and rebellious when they are called upon to obey. They are ashamed to give orders and consider it dishonorable to receive them. Don't ever be that way.

"In the room, you said that the path to wisdom leads to sacrifice. That is wrong. Your learning period did not end yesterday: you still have to find your sword and learn its secret. The RAM practices allow us to engage in the good fight and to have a better chance at winning in life. The experience you had yesterday was only one of the tests along the Road—it was part of the preparation for the Road to Rome. It saddens me that you thought that it might have been the death of you."

He really sounded saddened. I realized that throughout all the time we had spent together, I had always expressed doubt regarding what he was teaching me. I was not a strong, humble Castaneda receiving his teachings from Don Juan; I was an arrogant and fractious man in my approach to the simple RAM practices. I wanted to say this to Petrus, but I knew that it was too late.

"Close your eyes," Petrus said. "Do the RAM Breathing Exercise, and try to harmonize yourself with this iron, this machinery, and this smell of oil. This is our world. You should open your eyes only when I have completed teaching you an exercise."

I closed my eyes, concentrated on the RAM breathing, and felt my body begin to relax. I could hear the noises of the city, some dogs barking in the distance, and the sound of voices in argument not far from where we were. Suddenly, I began to hear Petrus's voice singing an Italian song recorded by Pepino Di Capri that had been a hit when I was a teenager. I didn't understand the words, but the melody brought back happy memories and helped me to reach a state of tranquillity.

"Some time ago," he began, when he had stopped singing, "as I was working on a project that I had to deliver to the mayor's office in Milan, I received a message from my Master. Someone had gone all the way to the end of the road of the Tradition and had not received his sword. I was supposed to guide him along the Road to Santiago.

"I was not surprised at this: I had been expecting such a summons at any time, because I had not yet paid my dues. I had to guide a pilgrim along the Milky Way, just as I had once been guided. But I was nervous because it was the first and only time that I would do this, and I did not know how to carry out my mission."

Petrus's words really surprised me. I thought that he had been a guide dozens of times.

"You came here, and I guided you," he continued. "I must confess that in the beginning it was very hard, because you were much more interested in the intellectual implications of the teachings than in the true meaning of the

Road—the Road of the common people. After the encounter with Alfonso, we developed a much stronger, more intense relationship, and I began to believe that I would be able to teach you the secret of your sword. But this did not happen, and now you will have to learn it for yourself during the little time you have left."

This conversation was making me nervous, and I was losing my concentration on the RAM Breathing Exercise. Petrus must have noticed, because he began to sing the song again and stopped only when I was once again relaxed.

"If you discover the secret and find your sword, you will also discover the face of RAM, and you will have the power. But that is not all: in order to achieve total wisdom, you will have to walk the other three Roads, including the secret one, and the secret Road will not be revealed to you, even by someone who has walked it. I am telling you this because we are going to see each other only one more time."

My heart stopped, and involuntarily, I opened my eyes. Petrus was glowing with the kind of brilliance I had only seen around my Master.

"Close your eyes!" he barked, and I immediately obeyed. But I was very upset, and I could not concentrate anymore. My guide started to sing the Italian song again, and only after a while was I able to relax.

"Tomorrow you are going to receive a note telling you where I am. I will be at a group initiation, a ritual of honor in the Tradition. It is a ritual in honor of all of the men and women who, down through the centuries, have helped to keep alive the flame of wisdom, of the good fight, and of agape. You will not be able to speak to me. The place where we will meet is secret. It is bathed in the blood of all those who have walked the road of the Tradition and who, even with their swords sharpened, were unable to brighten the darkness. But their sacrifice was not in vain, and the proof that it was not is that, centuries later, those who have walked different roads will be there to pay them tribute. This is important, and you should never forget it: even if you become a Master, you have to realize that your road is only one of many that lead to God. Jesus once said, 'In my Father's house, there are many mansions.'"

Petrus repeated that after tomorrow, I would not see him again.

"On some future day, you will receive a message from me, asking you to lead someone along the Road to Santiago, just as I have led you. Then you will be able to experience the great secret of the journey—a secret that I am going to reveal to you now, but only through words. It is a secret that has to be experienced to be understood."

There was a prolonged silence. I began to think that he had changed his mind or that he had left the train yard. I felt an enormous desire to open my eyes to see what was happening, but I forced myself to concentrate on the RAM breathing.

"The secret is the following," Petrus said. "You can learn only through teaching. We have been together here on the Road to Santiago, but while you were learning the practices, I learned the meaning of them. In teaching you, I truly learned. By taking on the role of guide, I was able to find my own true path.

"If you succeed in finding your sword, you will have to teach the Road to someone else. And only when that happens—when you accept your role as a Master—will you learn all the answers you have in your heart. Each of us knows the answers, even before someone tells us what they are. Life teaches us lessons every minute, and the secret is to accept that only in our daily lives can we show ourselves to be as wise as Solomon and as powerful as Alexander the Great. But we become aware of this only when we are forced to teach others and to participate in adventures as extravagant as this one has been."

I was hearing the most unexpected farewell in my life. The person with whom I had had the most intense bond was saying good-bye right there in midjourney—in an oily-smelling train yard, with me forced to keep my eyes closed.

"I don't like saying good-bye," Petrus continued. "I am Italian, and I am very emotional. But according to the law of the Tradition, you must find your sword alone. This is the only way that you will believe in your own power. I have passed on to you everything that I have to give. The only thing left is the Dance Exercise, which I am going to teach you now; you should perform it tomorrow at the ritual."

He was silent for a while, and then he spoke:

"May that which is glorified be glorified in the Lord. You may open your eyes."

Petrus was still sitting on the locomotive. I did not want to say anything, because I am Brazilian and also emotional. The mercury lamp providing us with light began to flutter, and a train whistled in the distance, announcing its next stop.

It was then that Petrus taught me the Dance Exercise.

The Dance Exercise

Relax. Close your eyes.

•

Recall the first songs you heard as a child. Begin to sing them in your thoughts. Little by little, let a certain part of your body—your feet, your stomach, your hands, your head, and so on—but only one part, begin to dance to the melody you are singing.

•

After five minutes, stop singing, and listen to the sounds all around you. Compose an internal melody based on them, and dance to it with your whole body. Don't think about anything in particular, but try to memorize the images that spontaneously appear.

•

The dance offers an almost-perfect means of communication with the Infinite Intelligence.

•

This exercise should last fifteen minutes.

•

"One more thing," he said, looking deeply into my eyes. "When I completed my pilgrimage, I painted a beautiful, immense picture that depicted everything that had happened to me here. This is the Road of the common people, and you can do the same thing, if you like. If you don't know how to paint, write something, or create a ballet. Then, regardless of where they are, people will be able to walk the Jacobean route, the Milky Way, the Strange Road to Santiago."

The train that had sounded its whistle began to enter the station. Petrus waved to me and disappeared between the parked railroad cars. I stood there amid the noise of brakes screeching on steel, trying to decipher the mysterious Milky Way over my head, those stars that had guided me here and that had silently watched over the loneliness and destiny of all human beings.

Next day, there was just a note left in my room: 7:00 P.M.—CASTLE OF THE TEMPLARS.

I spent the rest of that afternoon walking around the streets aimlessly. I crossed and recrossed the small city of

Ponferrada, looking from a distance at the castle on the hill where I had been bidden to appear. The Templars had always stirred my imagination, and the castle in Ponferrada was not the only mark made on the Jacobean route by their order. The order had been created by nine knights who had decided not to return from the Crusades. Within a short time, their power had spread throughout Europe, and they had caused a revolution in the values at the beginning of this millennium. While most of the nobility of the time was concerned only with enriching itself through the labor of the serfs, the Knights Templar dedicated their lives, their fortunes, and their swords to one cause only: the protection of the pilgrims that walked the Road to Jerusalem. In the behavior of the Knights, the pilgrims found a model for their own search for wisdom.

In 1118, when Hugh de Payens and eight other knights held a meeting in the courtyard of an old, abandoned castle, they took a vow of love for all humanity. Two centuries later, there were more than five thousand benefices spread throughout the known world; they reconciled two activities that until then had appeared to be incompatible: the military life and the religious one. Donations from the members and from grateful pilgrims allowed the Order of the Knights Templars to accumulate incalculable wealth, which was used more than once to ransom important Christians who had been kidnapped by the Muslims. The honesty of the Knights was such that kings and nobles entrusted their valuables to the Templars and traveled only with a document that attested to the existence of their wealth. This document could be redeemed at any castle of the Order of the Templars for an equivalent sum, giving rise to the letter of credit that is used today.

Their spiritual devotion, in turn, had allowed the Knights Templars to understand the great truth that Petrus had quoted the night before: that the house of the Lord has many mansions. They sought to put an end to religious conflict and to unite the main monotheistic religions of the time: Christian, Jewish, and Islamic. Their chapels were built with the rounded cupola of the Judaic temples of Solomon, the octagonal walls of the Arab mosques, and the naves that were typical of Christian churches.

But as with everything that happens before its time, the Templars came to be viewed with suspicion. The great kings sought to hold economic power, and religious liberalism was regarded as a threat to the Church. On Friday, October 13, 1307, the Vatican and the major European states unleashed one of the most massive police operations of the Middle Ages: during the night, the main leaders of the Templars were seized in their castles and thrown in prison. They were accused of practicing secret ceremonies, including the worship of the devil, of blasphemy against Jesus Christ, of orgiastic rituals, and of engaging in sodomy with their apprentices.

Following a violent sequence of torture, renunciation, and treason, the Order of the Templars was erased from the map of medieval history. Their treasures were confiscated, and their members scattered throughout the world. The last master of the Order, Jacques de Molay, was burned at the stake in the center of Paris, along with a fellow Knight. His last request was that he be allowed "to die looking at the towers of the Cathedral of Notre Dame."

Spain, which was struggling to recapture the Iberian peninsula, welcomed the Knights fleeing from other parts of Europe, and the Spanish kings sought their help in the battles against the Moors. These Knights were absorbed into the Spanish orders, one of which was the Order of San Tiago of the Sword, responsible for protection along the Road.

I was thinking about this history when, exactly at seven in the evening, I passed through the main gate of the old Castle of the Templars of Ponferrada, where I was scheduled for an encounter with the Tradition.

There was no one there. I waited for half an hour and then began to fear the worst: that the ritual must have been at 7:00 A.M. But just as I was deciding to leave, two boys appeared, carrying the flag of Holland and with the scallop shell—the symbol of the Road to Santiago—sewn to their clothing. They came up to me, and we exchanged some words, concluding that we were there for the same purpose. I was relieved that the note had not been wrong.

Every fifteen minutes someone else arrived. There were an Australian, five Spaniards, and another man from Holland. Other than a few questions about the schedule—about which everyone was confused—we did not talk at all. We all sat together in the same part of the castle—a ruined atrium that had served as a storeroom for food in ancient times—and we decided to wait until something happened, even if we had to wait another day and night.

The waiting went on, and we fell to talking about the reasons we were there. It was then that I learned that the Road to Santiago is used by a number of different orders, most of them part of the Tradition. The people who were there had already been through many tests and initiations of the kind that I had gone through long ago in Brazil. Only the Australian and I were expecting to be conferred the highest degree of the first Road. Even without knowing the details, I could see that the process the Australian had gone through was completely different from the RAM practices.

At about 8:45, as we were beginning to talk about our personal lives, a gong rang. We followed the sound to the ancient chapel of the castle.

There we found an impressive scene. The chapel—or what remained of it, since most of it was in ruins—was illuminated only by torches. Where there had once been an altar could be seen seven figures garbed in the secular costumes of the Templars: a hood and steel helmet, a coat of mail, a sword, and a shield. I gasped: it was a scene from the distant past. All that made the situation seem real were our own suits and jeans and our shirts with the scallop shell emblem.

Even with the faint illumination provided by the torches, I could see that one of the Knights was Petrus.

"Approach your Masters," said the Knight who appeared to be the oldest. "Look into the eyes of your Master. Take off your clothes and receive your vestments."

I went to Petrus and looked deeply into his eyes. He was in a kind of trance and seemed not to recognize me. But I could see in his eyes a certain sadness, the same sadness that his voice had conveyed on the previous night. I took all of my clothes off, and Petrus handed me a perfumed black tunic that fell loosely around my body. I surmised that one of the Masters had more than one disciple, but I could not see which he was because of the requirement that I keep my eyes fixed on those of Petrus.

The High Priest directed us to the center of the chapel, and two Knights began to trace a circle around us as they chanted: "Trinitas, Sother, Messias, Emmanuel, Sabahot, Adonai, Athanatos, Jesus . . ."[1]

[1]Since this is an extremely long ritual and can be understood only by those who know the road of the Tradition, I have opted to summarize the incantations used. But this does not change the narrative at all, since this ritual was performed only to establish a reunion with and respect for the ancients. The important element of this part of the Road to Santiago—the Dance Exercise—is described here in its entirety.

The circle was being drawn to provide the protection needed for those within it. I noticed that four of us had white tunics, signifying vows of total chastity.

"Amides, Throdonias, Anitor!" intoned the High Priest. "By the grace of the angels, Lord, I provide the vestment of salvation; I pray that everything I desire be transformed into reality, through thee, O my sacred Adonai, whose kingdom is forever. Amen!"

The High Priest placed over his coat of mail the white mantle with the Templar's Cross outlined in red in the center. The other Knights did the same.

It was exactly nine o'clock, the hour of Mercury, the messenger. And there I was, once again within the circle of the Tradition. There was an incense of mint, basil, and benjamin burning in the chapel, and the grand invocation of the Knights began:

"O great and glorious King, who rules through the power of the Supreme God, EL, over all higher and lower spirits, but especially over the Infernal Order of the Dominion of the East, I invoke you . . . so that I may realize my wish, whatever that may be, so long as it is proper to your labors, through the power of our God, EL, who created and provided all things celestial, of the air, of the earth, and of the infernal realm."

A profound silence followed, and even without being able to see him, we could sense the presence of the being who had been the object of the invocation. This was the consecration of the ritual, a propitious sign that we should continue with our magical activities. I had already participated in hundreds of similar ceremonies, at some of which the results up to this point had been much more surprising. But the Castle of the Templars must have stimulated my imagination a little, because I thought I saw, hovering in the corner of the chapel, a kind of shining bird that I had never seen before.

The High Priest sprinkled water over us without stepping into the circle. Then, with the sacred ink, he wrote in the earth the seventy-two names by which God is known within the Tradition.

All of us—pilgrims and Knights—began to recite the sacred names. The flames of the torches crackled, a sign that the spirit that had been invoked had surrendered.

The moment for the dance had arrived. I knew how to participate because Petrus had taught me on the previous day; it was a different dance from the one I was used to performing at this stage during similar rituals.

No rule was stated, but all of us already knew what it was: no initiate could step outside the protective circle, since we lacked the protection that the Knights had with their suits of mail. I visualized the size of the circle and did exactly as Petrus had taught me.

I thought back to my infancy. A voice, the far-off voice of a woman within me, began to sing a simple melody. I knelt and compressed myself into the seed position and felt that my breast—only my breast—was beginning to dance. I felt at ease, able to enter completely into the ritual of the Tradition. The music within me began to change; my movements became more pronounced, and I entered into a powerful state of ecstasy. Everything around me was darkened, and my body, surrounded by that darkness, felt weightless. I saw myself walking through the flowered fields of Aghata, where I met my grandmother and an uncle who had been important to me when I was a child. I felt the vibration of time in its grid of quadrants, where all roads are joined and mixed, becoming identical despite their being so different from each other. At one point, I saw the Australian flash by me: his body was suffused in a red glow.

The image that followed was of a chalice and paten, and this image lasted for a long time, as if it had a special importance for me. I tried to understand its significance, but nothing came to me, despite my conviction that it had something to do with my sword. Then, after the chalice and paten had vanished, I saw the face of RAM coming toward me out of the darkness. But when the face came closer, it was only the face of N., the spirit that had been invoked, who was well known to me. We did not establish any special kind of communication, and his face dissolved into the darkness that was fluctuating around me.

I don't know how long we continued to dance. But suddenly I heard a voice:

"YAHWEH, TETRAGRAMMATON . . ." and I didn't want to emerge from my trance, but the voice insisted:

"YAHWEH, TETRAGRAMMATON . . ." and I recognized the voice of the High Priest, calling upon everyone to come out of the trance. It irritated me. The Tradition was where I was rooted, and I did not want to come back. But the Master demanded it:

"YAHWEH, TETRAGRAMMATON . . ."

I couldn't maintain the trance. Resentfully, I returned to earth. I was once again within the magic circle there in the ancestral ambiance of the Castle of the Templars.

We pilgrims looked at each other. The sudden interruption seemed to have displeased everyone. I felt a strong urge to tell the Australian that I had seen him in my trance. But when I looked over at him, I saw that it wasn't necessary: he had seen me, too.

The Knights came to us and surrounded us. They began to beat upon their shields with their hands, making a noise that was deafening. Then the High Priest spoke:

"O Spirit N., because thou so diligently responded to my requests, with all due solemnity I allow thee to depart, without injury to man or beast. Go, I command thee, and be ready and anxious to return whenever thou art duly exorcised and conjured by the sacred rites of the Tradition. I conjure thee to go, peacefully and quietly, and may God's peace continue ever to be with thee and me. Amen."

The circle was erased, and we knelt with our heads bowed. A Knight said seven Paternosters and seven Ave Marias with us. The High Priest added seven repetitions of the Apostles' Creed, stating that Our Lady of Medjugorje—whose visitations had been noted in Yugoslavia ever since 1982—had indicated that he should do this. And then we began another of the Christian rituals.

"Andrew, rise and come before me," said the High Priest. The Australian approached the altar, where the seven Knights were standing.

One of the Knights—the one who must have been his guide—spoke:

"Brother, dost thou demand the company of the House?"

"Yes," answered the Australian. And then I understood which of the Christian rituals we were witnessing: the initiation of a Templar.

"Dost thou understand the great severities of the House and its charitable orders?"

"I am ready to support all of them, in God's name, and I desire to be a servant and slave of the House forever, through all the days of my life," answered the Australian.

There followed a series of ritual questions, some of which made no sense in today's world; others were concerned with profound devotion and love. Andrew, with his head bowed, responded to all of them.

"Distinguished brother, thou art asking a great thing of me. But thou art seeing only the outer layer of our religion—the beautiful horses and the elegant vestments," said his guide. "But thou knowest not the hard demands made here within: it will be difficult for thee, who art master of thyself, to serve others; rarely wilt thou be able to do as thou wishest. If thou desirest that thou be here, thou wilt be sent beyond the sea, and if thou desirest that thou be in Acre, thou wilt be sent to Tripoli, or Antioch, or Armenia. And when thou desirest sleep, thou wilt be told to stand guard, and when thou wantest to stand guard, thou wilt be told to sleep in thy bed."

"I desire to enter the House," answered the Australian. It felt as if all of the Templars who had ever lived in the castle were happily attending the initiation ceremony; the torches were crackling in earnest.

Several admonishments followed, and the Australian answered them all by saying that he wanted to enter the House. Finally, his guide turned to the High Priest and repeated all of the answers the Australian had made. The High Priest solemnly asked once more if he was ready to accept all of the rules of the House.

"Yes, Master, God willing. I come before God, before thee, and before the brothers, and I implore and solicit thee, before God and Our Lady, to take me into thy company and into the favors of the House, spiritually and temporally, as one who desires to be servant and slave of the House from now on, for all the days of his life."

"I bid you enter, by God's love," said the High Priest.

With that, all of the Knights unsheathed their swords and pointed them toward heaven. Then they lowered the blades and made of them a crown of steel around Andrew's head. The flames created a golden reflection on the blades, consecrating the moment.

Solemnly his Master came to him. And he gave him his sword.

Someone began to toll a bell, and its notes echoed off the walls of the ancient castle, infinitely repeating themselves. We all bowed our heads, and the Knights disappeared from view. When we looked up, we were only ten; the Australian had left to join the Knights in the ritual banquet.

We changed back into our street clothes and said our good-byes without any further formalities. The dance must have lasted for a long time, because the day was brightening. An immense loneliness invaded my soul.

I was envious of the Australian, who had recovered his sword and had reached the end of his quest. Now I was alone, with no one to guide me; the Tradition—in a distant country in South America—had expelled me without showing me the road back. And I had to continue to walk the Strange Road to Santiago, which was now coming to an end, without knowing the secret of my sword or how to find it.

The bell continued to toll. As I left the castle, with dawn breaking, I noticed that it was the bell of a nearby church, calling the faithful to the first mass of the day. The people of the city were awakening to their work and their unpaid bills, their love affairs and their dreams. But they didn't know that, on the previous night, an ancestral rite had once again taken place, that what had been thought of as dead and gone for centuries had once again been celebrated, and that it continued to demonstrate its awesome power.

El Cebrero

"ARE YOU A PILGRIM?" ASKED THE LITTLE GIRL. SHE WAS the only person in sight on that blazing afternoon in Villafranca del Bierzo.

I looked at her but didn't answer. She was about eight and poorly dressed. She had run to the fountain where I had sat down to rest.

My only concern now was to get to Santiago de Compostela as quickly as possible and put an end to this crazy adventure. I had not been able to forget the sadness in Petrus's voice at the train yard nor the way he had looked at me from a distance when I had met his gaze during the ritual of the Tradition. It was as if all of the effort he had made in helping me had led to nothing. When the Australian had been called to the altar, I was sure that Petrus would have preferred that it had been I who had been called. My sword might very well be hidden in that castle, the repository of legends and ancient wisdom. It was a place that fit perfectly with all of my deductions: deserted, visited only by a few pilgrims who respected the relics of the Order of the Templars, and located on sacred ground.

But only the Australian had been called to the altar. And Petrus must have felt humiliated in the presence of the others because, as a guide, he had not been capable of leading me to my sword.

Besides this, the ritual of the Tradition had aroused in me again a bit of my fascination with occult wisdom, most of which I had forgotten about as I made my way along the Strange Road to Santiago, the Road of the common people. The invocations, the absolute control over the material, the communication with other worlds—all of that was much more interesting to me than the RAM practices. But perhaps the practices had a more objective application in my life; there was no doubt that I had changed a lot since I had begun to walk the Strange Road to Santiago. Thanks to Petrus's help, I had learned that I could pass through waterfalls, win out over enemies, and converse with my messenger about practical matters. I had seen the face of my death and the blue sphere of the love that consumes and floods the entire world. I was ready to fight the good fight and turn my life into a series of triumphs.

Yet a hidden part of me was still nostalgic for the magic circles, the transcendental formulas, the incense, and the sacred ink. The ceremony that Petrus had called an "homage to the ancients" had been for me an intense and healthful encounter with old, forgotten lessons. And the possibility that I might never again have access to that world discouraged me from wanting to go on.

When I had returned to my hotel after the ritual of the Tradition, there in my box, along with my key, was a copy of

The Pilgrim's Guide. This was a book that Petrus had utilized for orientation when the yellow markers were hard to find; it had helped us to calculate the distances between cities. I left Ponferrada that same morning, without having slept, and went out on the Road. By that afternoon, I had discovered that the map was not drawn to scale, and that I had to spend a night out in the open, in a cave in the cliffs.

There, as I meditated on everything that had happened to me since my meeting with Mme Lourdes, I thought about the relentless effort Petrus had made to help me understand that contrary to what we had always been taught, results *were* what counted. One's efforts are salutary and indispensable, but without results, they amount to nothing. And now the only result that I demanded of myself, the only reward for everything I had been through, was to find my sword. That had not happened yet, and Santiago was only a few days away.

"If you are a pilgrim, I can take you to the Gates of Forgiveness," insisted the girl at the fountain in Villafranca del Bierzo. "Whoever passes through those gates need not go all the way to Santiago."

I held out some pesetas to her so that she would go away and leave me alone. But instead she began to splash the water in the fountain, wetting my knapsack and my shorts.

"Come on, come on," she said again. At that moment, I was thinking about one of Petrus's repeated quotations: "He that ploweth should plow in hope. He that thresheth in hope should be partaker of his hope." It was from one of the letters of the apostle Paul.

I had to persevere for a little longer, to continue searching until the end, without being fearful of defeat, to keep alive the hope of finding my sword and understanding its secret.

And—who knows?—was this little girl trying to tell me something that I didn't want to understand? If the Gates of Forgiveness, which were part of a church, had the same spiritual effect as arriving at Santiago, why couldn't my sword be there?

"Let's go," I said to the child. I looked at the mountain that I had just descended; I was going to have to climb part of it again. I had passed by the Gates of Forgiveness with no desire to go to them, since my only goal was to get to Santiago. Now, here was a little girl, the only human being present there on that hot afternoon, insisting that I go back and see something I had decided to ignore. After all, why hadn't that little girl gone away after I had given her some money? Could it be that, in my discouragement and haste, I had walked right past my objective without recognizing it?

Petrus had always said that I liked to fantasize too much about things. But perhaps he was wrong.

As I walked along with the girl, I was remembering the story of the Gates of Forgiveness. They represented a kind of "arrangement" that the Church had made for pilgrims who fell sick. From that point on, the Road became once again difficult and mountainous all the way to Compostela, so during the twelfth century, one of the popes had said that whoever was unable to go further had only to pass through the Gates of Forgiveness to receive the same indulgences as the pilgrims who made it to the end of the Road. With one magic gesture, that pope had resolved the problem posed by the mountains and had inspired an increased number of pilgrimages.

We climbed, following the same route I had traveled earlier in the day: twisting roads, slippery and steep. The girl led, moving along very quickly, and many times I had to ask that she go more slowly. She would do so for a while and then, losing her sense of pace, would begin to run again. Half an hour later, and after much grumbling on my part, we reached the Gates of Forgiveness.

"I have the key to the church," she said. "I will go in and open the gates so you can pass through them."

She went in through the main entrance, and I waited outside. It was a small church, and the gates opened to the north. The door frame was decorated with scallop shells and scenes from the life of San Tiago. As I heard the sound of the key in the lock, an immense German shepherd, appearing out of nowhere, came up to me and stood between the portal and me.

I was immediately prepared for a fight. "Not again," I thought. "Is this story never going to end? Nothing but more and more tests, battles, and humiliations—and still no clue about my sword."

At that moment, though, the Gates of Forgiveness swung open, and the girl appeared. When she saw that the dog was watching me—and that my eyes were already fixed on his—she said some affectionate words to him, and the dog relaxed. Wagging his tail, he followed her toward the back of the church.

Maybe Petrus was right. Maybe I did like to fantasize about things. A simple German shepherd had been transformed in my mind into a threatening supernatural being. That was a bad sign—a sign of the fatigue that leads to defeat.

But there was still hope. The girl signaled to me to enter. With my heart full of expectation, I passed through the Gates of Forgiveness, thereby receiving the same indulgences as the pilgrims who went all the way to Santiago.

My gaze swept over the empty, undecorated church, seeking the only thing I cared about.

"At the top of all the columns you can see shells. The shell is the symbol of the Road," began the girl. "This is Santa Agueda of . . ."

Before long, I could see that it had been useless to come all the way back to this church.

"And this is San Tiago Matamoros, brandishing his sword. You can see dead Moors under his horse's hooves. This statue was made in . . ."

San Tiago's sword was there but not mine. I offered a few more pesetas to the girl, but she would not accept them. A bit offended, she ended her explanations about the church and asked me to leave.

Once again I walked down the mountain and resumed my pilgrimage toward Compostela. As I passed through Villafranca del Bierzo for the second time, a man approached me. He said that his name was Angel and asked if I would be interested in seeing the Church of Saint Joseph the Carpenter. The man's name gave me hope, but I had just been disappointed, and I was beginning to see that Petrus was an expert observer of behavior. People do have a tendency to fantasize about things that do not even exist, while they fail to learn the lessons that are before their very eyes.

But perhaps just to confirm this tendency one more time, I allowed myself to be led by Angel to this other church. It was closed, and he did not have a key. He pointed to the framework of the entrance with its carving of Saint Joseph, his carpentry tools close alongside him. I nodded, thanked him, and offered him some pesetas. He refused them and left me there in the middle of the street—but not before saying, "We are proud of our city. It is not for money that we do this."

I returned to the Road and in fifteen minutes had left Villafranca del Bierzo behind—Villafranca del Bierzo, with its doors, its streets, and its mysterious guides who asked nothing in exchange for their services.

I walked for some time through mountainous terrain; my progress was slow and demanding. As I started out, I thought only about my previous worries—solitude, shame at having disappointed Petrus, my sword and its secret. But soon the images of the little girl and of Angel began insistently to come to mind. While I had been focusing only on what I would gain, they had done the best for me that they could. And they had asked for nothing in return. A vague idea began to surface from deep inside me. It was some sort of link among all the things I was thinking about. Petrus had always insisted that the expectation of reward was absolutely necessary to the achievement of victory. Yet every time that I forgot about the rest of the world and began to think only about my sword, he forced me, through his painful lessons, to return to reality. This was a sequence that had occurred repeatedly during our time together on the Road.

There was some reason for this, and it was somehow connected with the secret of my sword. What was hiding there inside me began to coalesce and come to light. I still was not sure what it was that I was thinking, but something told me that I was looking in the right direction.

I appreciated having run into the little girl and Angel; they had shown something of the love that consumes in the way they spoke about their churches. They had caused me to go over the same ground twice, and because of this, I had forgotten my fascination with the ritual of the Tradition and had returned to the fields of Spain.

I remembered a day long ago when Petrus had told me that we had walked several times over the same part of the Road in the Pyrenees. I remembered that day with nostalgia. It had been a good beginning, and who knew but what this repetition of that event was not an omen of a positive outcome.

That night I arrived at a village and asked for a room at the home of an old lady. She charged me a pittance for my bed and food. We chatted a bit, and she talked about her faith in Jesus of the Sacred Heart and her worries about the olive crop in that drought year. I drank some wine, had some soup, and went to bed early.

I was feeling better about things, mainly because of the concept that was developing in my mind and the fact that it felt ready for expression. I prayed, did some of Petrus's exercises, and decided to invoke Astrain.

I needed to talk to him about what had happened during the fight with the dog. That day he had almost caused me to lose, and then, after his refusal in the episode of the cross, I had decided to do away with him forever. On the other hand, if I had not recognized his voice during the fight, I would have given in to the temptations that had appeared.

"You did everything possible to help Legion win," I said.

"I do not fight against my brothers," Astrain answered. It was the response I had expected. I had already predicted that he would say this, and it didn't make sense to get irritated with the messenger for being himself. I had to seek out in him the ally who had helped me at times like this, for that was his only function. I put my rancor aside and began to tell him animatedly about the Road, about Petrus, and about the secret of the sword, which I felt was beginning to formulate itself in my mind. He had nothing important to say—only that these secrets were not available to him. But at least I had someone to open up with after having spent the entire afternoon in silence. We had been talking for hours when the old lady rapped on my door to tell me that I was talking in my sleep.

I awoke feeling more optimistic and took to the Road early. According to my calculations, that afternoon I would reach Galicia, the region where Santiago de Compostela was located. It was all uphill, and I had to exert myself for almost four hours to keep to the pace I had set for myself. Every time I reached the crest of a hill I hoped that it would mark the point of descent. But this never seemed to happen, and I had to give up any hope of moving along more rapidly. In the distance I could see mountains that were even higher, and I realized that sooner or later I was going to have to cross them. My physical exertions, meanwhile, had made it impossible to think much, and I began to feel more friendly toward myself.

"Come on now, after all, how can you take seriously anyone who leaves everything behind to look for a sword?" I asked myself. What would it really mean to my life if I couldn't find it? I had learned the RAM practices, I had gotten to know my messenger, fought with the dog, and seen my death, I told myself, trying to convince myself that the Road to Santiago was what was important to me. The sword was only an outcome. I would like to find it, but I would like even more to know what to do with it. Because I would have to use it in some practical way, just as I used the exercises Petrus had taught me.

I stopped short. The thought that up until then had been only nascent exploded into clarity. Everything became clear, and a tide of agape washed over me. I wished with all my heart that Petrus were there so that I could tell him what he had been waiting to hear from me. It was the only thing that he had really wanted me to understand, the crowning accomplishment of all the hours he had devoted to teaching me as we walked the Strange Road to Santiago: it was the secret of my sword!

And the secret of my sword, like the secret of any conquest we make in our lives, was the simplest thing in the world: it was what I should do with the sword.

I had never thought in these terms. Throughout our time on the Strange Road to Santiago, the only thing I had wanted to know was where it was hidden. I had never asked myself why I wanted to find it or what I needed it for. All of my efforts had been bent on reward; I had not understood that when we want something, we have to have a clear purpose in mind for the thing that we want. The only reason for seeking a reward is to know what to do with that reward. And this was the secret of my sword.

Petrus needed to know that I had learned this, but I was sure I would never see him again. He had waited so long for this, and he would never know that it had happened.

So I knelt there, took some paper from my notebook, and wrote down what I intended to do with my sword. I folded the sheet carefully and placed it under a stone—one that reminded me of him and his friendship. Time would eventually destroy the paper, but symbolically, I was delivering it to Petrus.

Now he knew that I was going to succeed with my sword. My mission with Petrus had been accomplished.

I climbed the mountain, and the agape flowing through me intensified the colors in the surroundings. Now that I had discovered the secret, I had to find what I was looking for. A faith, an unshakable certainty, took control of my being. I began to sing the Italian song that Petrus had remembered in the train yard. I didn't know the words, so I made them up. There was no one in sight, and I was passing through some deep woods, so the isolation made me sing even louder. Shortly I saw that the words I had used made a kind of absurd sense. They were a way of communicating with the world that only I knew, since now it was the world that was teaching me.

I had experimented with this in a different way during my first encounter with Legion. That day, the gift of tongues had manifested itself in me. I had been the servant of the Spirit, which had used me to save a woman and to create an enemy, and had taught me the cruel version of the good fight. Now everything was different: I was my own Master, and I was learning to communicate with the universe.

I began to talk to everything along the Road: tree trunks, puddles, fallen leaves, and beautiful vines. It was an exercise of the common people, learned by children and forgotten by adults. And I received a mysterious response from those things, as if they understood what I was saying; they, in turn, flooded me with the love that consumes. I went into a kind of trance that frightened me, but I wanted to continue the game until I tired of it.

Petrus was right again: by teaching myself, I had transformed myself into a Master.

It was time for lunch, but I didn't stop to eat. When I passed through the small villages along the Road, I spoke more softly and smiled to myself, and if by chance someone noticed me, they would have concluded that the pilgrims arriving nowadays at the Cathedral of Santiago were crazy. But this didn't matter to me, because I was celebrating the life all around me and because I knew what I had to do with my sword when I found it.

For the rest of the afternoon, I walked along in a trance,

aware of where it was that I wanted to go but more aware of my surroundings and the fact that they had returned agape to me. Heavy clouds began to gather in the sky for the first time in my journey, and I hoped it would rain. After such a long period of hiking and of drought, the rain would be a new, exciting experience. At three in the afternoon, I crossed into Galicia, and I could see on the map that there was one more mountain to climb in order to complete that leg of the pilgrimage. I was determined to climb it and then to sleep in the first town on the other side: Tricastela, where a great king—Alfonso IX—had dreamed of creating an immense city but which, many centuries later, was still a tiny country village.

Still singing and speaking the language I had invented for communicating with the things around me, I began to climb the only remaining mountain: El Cebrero. Its name went back to ancient Roman settlements in the region and was said to mean "February," when something important had presumably happened. In ancient times, this was considered to be the most difficult part of the Jacobean route, but today things have changed. Although the angle of ascent is steeper than in the other mountains, a large television antenna on a neighboring mountain serves as a reference point for pilgrims and prevents their wandering from the Road, a common and fatal event in the past.

The clouds began to lower, and I saw that I would shortly be entering fog. To get to Tricastela, I had to follow the yellow markers carefully; the television antenna was already hidden in the mist. If I got lost, I would wind up sleeping outdoors, and on that day, with the threat of rain, the experience would be quite disagreeable. It is one thing to feel raindrops falling on your face, enjoying the freedom of the life of the Road, and then find a place nearby where you can have a glass of wine and sleep in a bed in preparation for the next day's march. It is quite another to have the raindrops cause a night of insomnia as you try to sleep in the mud, with your wet bandages providing fertile ground for a knee infection.

I had to decide quickly. Either I went forward through the fog—there was still enough light to do so—or I returned to sleep in the small village I had passed through a few hours ago, leaving the crossing of El Cebrero for the next day.

As I realized that I had to make a quick decision, I noticed that something strange was happening. My certainty that I had discovered the secret of my sword was somehow pushing me to go forward into the fog that would shortly engulf me. This feeling was quite different from the one that had made me follow the little girl to the Gates of Forgiveness and made me go with the man to the Church of Saint Joseph the Carpenter.

I remembered that, on the few occasions when I had agreed to put a magic curse on someone in Brazil, I had compared this mystical experience with another very common experience: that of learning to ride a bicycle. You begin by mounting the bicycle, pushing on the pedals, and falling. You try and you fall, try and fall, and you cannot seem to learn how to balance yourself. Suddenly, though, you achieve perfect equilibrium, and you establish complete mastery over the vehicle. It is not a cumulative experience but a kind of "miracle" that manifests itself only when you allow the bicycle "to ride you." That is, you accept the disequilibrium of the two wheels and, as you go along, begin to convert the initial force toward falling into a greater force on the pedal.

At that moment in my ascent of El Cebrero, at four in the afternoon, I saw that the same miracle had occurred. After so much time spent walking the Road to Santiago, the Road to Santiago began to "walk me." I followed what everyone calls one's intuition. And because of the love that consumes that I had experienced all that day, and because my sword's secret had been discovered, and because at moments of crisis a person always makes the right decision, I went forward with no hesitation into the fog.

"This fog has to stop," I thought, as I struggled to see the yellow markers on the stones and trees along the Road. By now the visibility had been very poor for almost an hour, but I continued to sing as an antidote to my fear, while I hoped that something extraordinary would happen. Surrounded by the fog, alone in those unreal surroundings, I began to look at the Road to Santiago as if it were a film; this was the moment when the hero does things that no one else in the film would dare to do, while the audience is thinking that such things only happen in the movies. But there I was, living through a real situation. The forest was growing quieter and quieter, and the fog began to dissipate. I seemed to be reaching the end of the obscurity, but the light confused me and bathed everything in mysterious, frightening colors.

The silence was now complete, and as I noticed this, I heard, coming from my left, a woman's voice. I stopped immediately, expecting to hear it again, but I heard nothing—not even the normal sounds of the forest, with its crickets, its insects, and its animals walking through the dry leaves. I looked at my watch: it was exactly 5:15 P.M. I estimated that I was still about three miles from Tricastela and that there was still time to arrive before dark.

As I looked up from my watch, I heard the woman's voice again. And from that point on, I was to live through one of the most significant experiences of my life.

The voice wasn't coming from somewhere in the woods but from somewhere inside me. I was able to hear it clearly, and it heightened my intuitive sense. It was neither I nor Astrain who was speaking. The voice only told me that I should keep on walking, which I did unquestioningly. It was as if Petrus had returned and was telling me again about giving orders and taking them. At that moment, I was simply an instrument of the Road; the Road was indeed "walking me." The fog grew less and less dense; I seemed to be walking out of it. Around me were the bare trees, the moist and slippery terrain, and ahead of me, the same steep slope I had been climbing for such a long time.

Suddenly, as if by magic, the fog lifted completely. And there before me, driven into the crest of the mountain, was a cross.

I looked around, and I could see both the fog bank from which I had emerged and another above me. Between the two, I could see the peaks of the tallest mountains and the top of El Cebrero, where the cross was. I felt a strong desire to pray. Even though I knew that I would have to detour from the road to Tricastela, I decided to climb to the peak and say my prayers at the foot of the cross. It took forty minutes to make the climb, and I did it in complete silence, within and without. The language I had invented was forgotten; it was not the right language for communicating with other people or with God. The Road to Santiago was "walking me," and it was going to show me where my sword was. Petrus was right again.

When I reached the peak, a man was sitting there, writing something. For an instant I thought he was a supernatural being, sent from elsewhere. Then my intuition told me that he was not, and I saw the scallop shell stitched into his clothing; he was just a pilgrim, who looked at me for a few moments and then walked away, disturbed by my having appeared. Perhaps he had been expecting the same thing as

I—an angel—and we had each found just another person on the Road of the common people.

Although I wanted to pray, I wasn't able to say anything. I stood in front of the cross for some time, looking at the mountains and at the clouds that covered the sky and the land, leaving only the high peaks clear. Thirty yards below me there was a hamlet with fifteen houses and a small church, whose lights were being turned on. At least I had somewhere to spend the night if the Road told me to do so. I was not sure when it would tell me, but even with Petrus gone, I was not without a guide. The Road was "walking me."

An unfettered lamb, climbing the mountain, stopped between the cross and me. He looked at me, a bit frightened. For some time I stood there, looking at the black sky, and the cross, and the white lamb at its foot. All at once, I felt exhausted by all that time spent on tests and battles and lessons and the pilgrimage. I felt a terrible pain in my stomach, and it rose to my throat, where it was transformed into dry, tearless sobs. There I stood, overcome by the scene of the lamb and the cross. This was a cross that I need not set upright, for it was there before me, solitary and immense, resisting time and the elements. It was a symbol of the fate that people created, not for their God but for themselves. The lessons of the Road to Santiago came back to me as I sobbed there, with a frightened lamb as my witness.

"My Lord," I said, finally able to pray, "I am not nailed

to this cross, nor do I see you there. The cross is empty, and that is how it should stay forever; the time of death is already past, and a god is now reborn within me. This cross is the symbol of the infinite power that each of us has. Now this power is reborn, the world is saved, and I am able to perform your miracles, because I trod the Road of the common people and, in mingling with them, found your secret. You came among us to teach us all that we were capable of becoming, and we did not want to accept this. You showed us that the power and the glory were within every person's reach, and this sudden vision of our capacity was too much for us. We crucified you, not because we were ungrateful to the Son of God but because we were fearful of accepting our own capacity. We crucified you fearing that we might be transformed into gods. With time and tradition, you came to be just a distant divinity, and we returned to our destiny as human beings.

"It is not a sin to be happy. Half a dozen exercises and an attentive ear are enough to allow us to realize our most impossible dreams. Because of my pride in wisdom, you made me walk the Road that every person can walk, and discover what everyone else already knows if they have paid the slightest attention to life. You made me see that the search for happiness is a personal search and not a model we can pass on to others. Before finding my sword, I had to discover its secret—and the secret was so simple; it was to know what to do with it. With it and with the happiness that it would represent to me.

"I have walked so many miles to discover things I already knew, things that all of us know but that are so hard to accept. Is there anything harder for us, my Lord, than discovering that we can achieve the power? This pain that I feel now in my breast, that makes me sob and that frightens that poor lamb, has been felt since human beings first existed. Few can accept the burden of their own victory: most give up their dreams when they see that they can be realized. They refuse to fight the good fight because they do not know what to do with their own happiness; they are imprisoned by the things of the world. Just as I have been, who wanted to find my sword without knowing what to do with it."

A god sleeping within me was awakening, and the pain was growing worse and worse. I felt the presence close to me of my Master, and I was able for the first time to turn my sobs into tears. I wept with gratitude for his having made me search for my sword along the Road to Santiago. I wept with gratitude for Petrus, for his having taught me, without saying a word, that I would realize my dreams if I first discovered what I wanted to do with them. I saw the cross, with no one on it, and the lamb at its base, free to go where he wanted in those mountains and to see the clouds above his head and below his feet.

The lamb began to walk away, and I followed him. I already knew where he would lead me; in spite of the clouds, everything had become clear to me. Even if I could not see the Milky Way in the sky, I was certain that it was there, pointing the way along the Road to Santiago. I followed the lamb as he walked in the direction of the hamlet—which was called El Cebrero, like the mountain.

There, at one time, a miracle had happened. It was the miracle of transforming what you do into what you believe in, just like the secret of my sword and of the Strange Road to Santiago. As we descended the mountain, I remembered the story. A farmer from a nearby village had climbed the mountain to attend mass at El Cebrero on a stormy day. The mass was being celebrated by a monk who was almost completely lacking in faith and who ridiculed the farmer for having made such an effort to get there. But at the moment of consecration, the host had actually been transformed into the body of Christ and the wine into his blood. The relics are still there, guarded in that small chapel, a treasure greater than all the riches of the Vatican.

The lamb stopped at the edge of the hamlet, where there was only one street leading to the church. At that moment, I was seized by a terrible fear, and I began to repeat over and over, "Lord, I am not worthy to enter thy house." But the lamb looked at me and spoke to me through his eyes. He said that I should forget forever my unworthiness because the power had been reborn in me, in the same way that it could be reborn in all people who devoted their lives to the good fight. A day would come—said the lamb's eyes—when people would once again take pride in themselves, and then all of nature would praise the awakening of the God that had been sleeping within them.

As the lamb looked at me, I could read all of this in his eyes; now he had become my guide along the Road to Santiago. For a moment everything went dark, and I began to see scenes that were reminiscent of those I had read about in the Apocalypse: the Great Lamb on his throne and people washing his vestments, cleansing them with his blood. This was the moment when the God was awakened in each of them. I also saw the wars and hard times and catastrophes that were going to shake the earth over the next few years. But everything ended with the victory of the Lamb and with every human being on earth awakening the sleeping God and all of God's power.

I followed the lamb to the small chapel built by the farmer and by the monk who had come to believe in what he did. Nobody knows who they were. Two nameless tombstones in the cemetery by the chapel mark the place where they were buried. But it is impossible to tell which is the grave of the monk and which of the farmer. The miracle had occurred because both had fought the good fight.

The chapel was completely lit when I came to its door. Yes, I was worthy of entering, because I had a sword and I knew what to do with it. These were not the Gates of Forgiveness, because I had already been forgiven and had washed my clothing in the blood of the Lamb. Now I wanted only to hold my sword and go out to fight the good fight.

In the small church there was no cross. There on the altar were the relics of the miracle: the chalice and the paten that I had seen during the dance, and a silver reliquary containing the body and blood of Jesus. I once again believed in miracles and in the impossible things that human beings can accomplish in their daily lives. The mountain peaks seemed to say to me that they were there only as a challenge to humans—and that humans exist only to accept the honor of that challenge.

The lamb slipped into one of the pews, and I looked to the front of the chapel. Standing before the altar, smiling—and perhaps a bit relieved—was my Master: with my sword in his hand.

I stopped, and he came toward me, passing me by and going outside. I followed him. In front of the chapel, looking up at the dark sky, he unsheathed my sword and told me to grasp its hilt with him. He pointed the blade upward and said the sacred Psalm of those who travel far to achieve victory:

A thousand fall at your side, and ten thousand to your
right,
but you will not be touched.
No evil will befall you, no curse will fall upon your tent;
your angels will be given orders regarding you,

to protect you along your every way.
I knelt, and as he touched the blade to my shoulders, he said:

Trample the lion and the serpent,
The lion cub and the dragon will make shoes for your feet.

As he finished saying this, it began to rain. The rain fertilized the earth, and its water would return to the sky after having given birth to a seed, grown a tree, brought a flower into blossom. The storm intensified, and I raised my head, feeling the rain for the first time in my entire journey along the Road to Santiago. I remembered the dry fields, and I was joyful that they were being showered upon that night. I remembered the rocks in León, the wheat fields of Navarra, the dryness of Castile, and the vineyards of Rioja that today were drinking the rain that fell in torrents, with all of the force in the skies. I remembered having raised a cross, and I thought that the storm would once again cause it to fall to earth so that another pilgrim could learn about command and obedience. I thought of the waterfall, which now must be even stronger because of the rainfall, and of Foncebadon, where I had left such power to fertilize the soil again. I thought about all of the water I had drunk from so many fountains that were now being replenished. I was worthy of my sword because I knew what to do with it.

The Master held out the sword to me, and I grasped it. I looked about for the lamb, but he had disappeared. But that did not matter: the Water of Life fell from the sky and caused the blade of my sword to glisten.

Epilogue

Santiago de Compostela

From the window of my hotel I can see the Cathedral of Santiago and the tourists at its main gate. Students in black medieval clothing mingle with the townspeople, and the souvenir vendors are setting up their stalls. It is early in the morning, and except for my notes, these are the first lines I have written about the Road to Santiago.

I reached the city yesterday, after having caught the bus that runs from Pedrafita, near El Cebrero, to Compostela. In four hours we covered the 150 kilometers that separate the two cities, and this reminded me of the journey with Petrus. At times, it took us two weeks to cover that distance. In a short while, I am going to the tomb of San Tiago to leave there the image of Our Lady of the Visitation, mounted on the scallop shells. Then, as soon as possible, I am going to catch a plane for Brazil, because I have a lot to do. I remember that Petrus told me once that he had condensed all of his experience into one picture, and the thought occurs to me that I might write a book about everything that has happened to me. But this is still a remote idea; I have so much to do now that I have recovered my sword.

The secret of my sword is mine, and I will never reveal it to anyone. I wrote it down and left it under a stone, but with the rain, the paper has probably been destroyed. It's better that way. Petrus didn't need to know.

I asked my Master whether he had known what day I was going to arrive or whether he had been waiting there for some time. He laughed and said that he had arrived there the morning before and was going to leave the next day, whether I appeared or not.

I asked how that was possible, and he did not answer me. But when we were saying good-bye and he was getting into the rental car that would take him back to Madrid, he gave me a small medal of the Order of San Tiago of the Sword. And he told me that I had already had a great revelation when I had looked into the eyes of the lamb.

And when I think about it, I guess it is true that people always arrive at the right moment at the place where someone awaits them.

By the River Piedra I Sat Down and Wept

For I. C. and S. B., whose loving communion made me see the feminine face of God;

for Monica Antunes, my companion from the beginning, who with her love and enthusiasm spreads the fire all over the world;

for Paulo Rocco, for the joy of the battles we have fought together and for the dignity of the battles we have fought between us;

and for Matthew Lore, for not having forgotten a sage quotation from the I Ching: *"Perseverance is favorable."*

Author's Note

A SPANISH MISSIONARY was visiting an island when he came across three Aztec priests.

"How do you pray?" the missionary asked.

"We have only one prayer," answered one of the Aztecs. "We say, 'God, you are three, we are three. Have pity on us.'"

"A beautiful prayer," said the missionary. "But it is not exactly the one that God heeds. I'm going to teach you one that's much better."

The padre taught them a Catholic prayer and then continued on his path of evangelism. Years later, when he was returning to Spain, his ship stopped again at the island. From the deck, the missionary saw the three priests on the shore and waved to them.

Just then, the three men began to walk across the water toward him.

"Padre! Padre!" one of them called, approaching the ship. "Teach us again that prayer that God heeds. We've forgotten how it goes."

"It doesn't matter," responded the missionary, witnessing the miracle. And he promptly asked God's forgiveness for failing to recognize that He speaks all languages.

This story illustrates just what this book is about. Rarely do we realize that we are in the midst of the extraordinary. Miracles occur all around us, signs from God show us the way, angels plead to be heard, but we pay little attention to them because we have been taught that we must follow certain formulas and rules if we want to find God. We do not recognize that God is wherever we allow Him/Her to enter.

Traditional religious practices are important: they allow us to share with others the communal experience of adoration and prayer. But we must never forget that spiritual experience is above all a *practical* experience of love. And with love, there are no rules. Some may try to control their emotions and develop strategies for their behavior; others may turn to reading books of advice from "experts" on relationships—but this is all folly. The heart decides, and what it decides is all that really matters.

All of us have had this experience. At some point, we have each said through our tears, "I'm suffering for a love that's not worth it." We suffer because we feel we are giving more than we receive. We suffer because our love is going unrecognized. We suffer because we are unable to impose our own rules.

But ultimately there is no good reason for our suffering, for in every love lies the seed of our growth. The more we love, the closer we come to spiritual experience. Those who are truly enlightened, those whose souls are illuminated by love, have been able to overcome all of the inhibitions and preconceptions of their era. They have been able to sing, to laugh, and to pray out loud; they have danced and shared what Saint Paul called "the madness of saintliness." They have been joyful—because those who love conquer the world and have no fear of loss. True love is an act of total surrender.

This book is about the importance of that surrender. Pilar and her companion are fictitious, but they represent the many conflicts that beset us in our search for love. Sooner or later, we have to overcome our fears, because the spiritual path can only be traveled through the daily experience of love.

Thomas Merton once said that the spiritual life is essentially to love. One doesn't love in order to do what is good or to help or to protect someone. If we act that way, we are perceiving the other as a simple object, and we are seeing ourselves as wise and generous persons. This has nothing to do with love. To love is to be in communion with the other and to discover in that other the spark of God.

May Pilar's lament on the bank of the River Piedra guide us toward such communion.

Paulo Coelho

But wisdom is justified
by all her children.

Luke 7:35

By the river Piedra I sat down and wept. There is a legend that everything that falls into the waters of this river—leaves, insects, the feathers of birds—is transformed into the rocks that make the riverbed. If only I could tear out my heart and hurl it into the current, then my pain and longing would be over, and I could finally forget.

By the River Piedra I sat down and wept. The winter air chills the tears on my cheeks, and my tears fall into the cold waters that course past me. Somewhere, this river joins another, then another, until—far from my heart and sight—all of them merge with the sea.

May my tears run just as far, that my love might never know that one day I cried for him. May my tears run just as far, that I might forget the River Piedra, the monastery, the church in the Pyrenees, the mists, and the paths we walked together.

I shall forget the roads, the mountains, and the fields of my dreams—the dreams that will never come true.

I remember my "magic moment"—that instant when a "yes" or a "no" can change one's life forever. It seems so long ago now. It is hard to believe that it was only last week that I had found my love once again, and then lost him.

I am writing this story on the bank of the River Piedra. My hands are freezing, my legs are numb, and every minute I want to stop.

"Seek to live. Remembrance is for the old," he said.

Perhaps love makes us old before our time—or young, if youth has passed. But how can I not recall those moments? That is why I write—to try to turn sadness into longing, solitude into remembrance. So that when I finish telling myself the story, I can toss it into the Piedra. That's what the woman who has given me shelter told me to do. Only then—in the words of one of the saints—will the water extinguish what the flames have written.

All love stories are the same.

By the River Piedra I Sat Down and Wept

WE HAD BEEN CHILDREN TOGETHER. Then he left, like so many young people who leave small towns. He said he was going to learn about the world, that his dreams lay beyond the fields of Soria.

Years passed with almost no news of him. Every now and then he would send me a letter, but he never returned to the paths and forests of our childhood.

When I finished school, I moved to Zaragoza, and there I found that he had been right. Soria *was* a small town, and as its only famous poet had said, roads are made to be traveled. I enrolled in the university and found a boyfriend. I began to study for a scholarship (I was working as a salesgirl to pay for my courses). But I lost the competition for the scholarship, and after that I left my boyfriend.

Then the letters from my childhood friend began to arrive more frequently—and I was envious of the stamps from so many different places. He seemed to know everything; he had sprouted wings, and now he roamed the world. Meanwhile, I was simply trying to put down roots.

Some of his letters, all mailed from the same place in France, spoke of God. In one, he wrote about wanting to enter a seminary and dedicate his life to prayer. I wrote him back, asking him to wait a bit, urging him to experience more of his freedom before committing himself to something so serious.

But after I reread my letter, I tore it up. Who was I to speak about freedom or commitment? Compared to him, I knew nothing about such things.

One day I learned that he had begun to give lectures. This surprised me; I thought he was too young to be able to teach anything to anyone. And then he wrote to me that he was going to speak to a small group in Madrid—and he asked me to come.

So I made the four-hour trip from Zaragoza to Madrid. I wanted to see him again; I wanted to hear his voice. I wanted to sit with him in a café and remember the old days, when we had thought the world was far too large for anyone ever to know it truly.

Saturday, December 4, 1993

THE PLACE where the conference was held was more formal than I had imagined it, and there were more people there than I had expected. How had all this come about?

He must be famous, I thought. He'd said nothing about this in his letters. I wanted to go up to the people in the audience and ask them why they were there, but I didn't have the nerve.

I was even more surprised when I saw him enter the room. He was quite different from the boy I had known—but of course, it had been twelve years; people change. Tonight his eyes were shining—he looked wonderful.

"He's giving us back what was ours," said a woman seated next to me.

A strange thing to say.

"What is he giving back?" I asked.

"What was stolen from us. Religion."

"No, no, he's not giving us anything back," said a younger

woman seated on my right. "They can't return something that has always belonged to us."

"Well, then, what are you doing here?" the first woman asked, irritated.

"I want to listen to him. I want to see how they think; they've already burned us at the stake once, and they may want to do it again."

"He's just one voice," said the woman. "He's doing what he can."

The young woman smiled sarcastically and turned away, putting an end to the conversation.

"He's taking a courageous position for a seminarian," the other woman went on, looking to me for support.

I didn't understand any of this, and I said nothing. The woman finally gave up. The girl at my side winked at me, as if I were her ally.

But I was silent for a different reason. I was thinking, *Seminarian? It can't be! He would have told me.*

When he started to speak, I couldn't concentrate. I was sure he had spotted me in the audience, and I was trying to guess what he was thinking. How did I look to him? How different was the woman of twenty-nine from the girl of seventeen?

I noticed that his voice hadn't changed. But his words certainly had.

By the River Piedra I Sat Down and Wept

YOU HAVE TO take risks, he said. *We will only understand the miracle of life fully when we allow the unexpected to happen.*

Every day, God gives us the sun—and also one moment in which we have the ability to change everything that makes us unhappy. Every day, we try to pretend that we haven't perceived that moment, that it doesn't exist—that today is the same as yesterday and will be the same as tomorrow. But if people really pay attention to their everyday lives, they will discover that magic moment. It may arrive in the instant when we are doing something mundane, like putting our front-door key in the lock; it may lie hidden in the quiet that follows the lunch hour or in the thousand and one things that all seem the same to us. But that moment exists—a moment when all the power of the stars becomes a part of us and enables us to perform miracles.

Joy is sometimes a blessing, but it is often a conquest. Our magic moment helps us to change and sends us off in search of our dreams. Yes, we are going to suffer, we will have difficult times, and we will experience many disappointments—but all of this is transitory; it leaves no permanent mark. And one day we will look back with pride and faith at the journey we have taken.

Pitiful is the person who is afraid of taking risks. Perhaps this person will never be disappointed or disillusioned; perhaps she won't suffer the way people do when they have a dream to follow. But when that person looks back—and at some point everyone looks back—she will hear her heart saying, "What have you done with the miracles that God planted in your days? What have you done with the talents God bestowed on you? You buried yourself in a cave because you were fearful of losing those talents. So this is your heritage: the certainty that you wasted your life."

Pitiful are the people who must realize this. Because when they are finally able to believe in miracles, their life's magic moments will have already passed them by.

❦ ❦ ❦

After the lecture, members of the audience rushed up to him. I waited, worried about what his first impression of me would be after so many years. I felt like a child—insecure, tense because I knew none of his new friends, and jealous that he was paying more attention to the others than to me.

When he finally came up to me, he blushed. Suddenly he was no longer a man with important things to say but was once again the boy who had hidden with me at the hermitage of San Satúrio, telling me of his dream to travel the world (while our parents were calling the police, sure that we had drowned in the river).

"Pilar," he said.

I kissed him. I could have complimented him on his presentation. I could have said I was tired of being around so many people. I could have made some humorous remark about our childhood or commented on how proud I was to see him there, so admired by others.

I could have explained that I had to run and catch the last bus back to Zaragoza.

I could have. What does this phrase mean? At any given moment in our lives, there are certain things that could have happened but didn't. The magic moments go unrecognized, and then suddenly, the hand of destiny changes everything.

That's what happened to me just then. In spite of all the things I could have done or said, I asked a question that has brought me, a week later, to this river and has caused me to write these very lines.

"Can we have coffee together?" I said.

And he, turning to me, accepted the hand offered by fate.

"I really need to talk to you. Tomorrow I have a lecture in Bilbao. I have a car. Come with me."

"I have to get back to Zaragoza," I answered, not realizing that this was my last chance.

Then I surprised myself—perhaps because in seeing him, I had become a child again . . . or perhaps because we are not the ones who write the best moments of our lives. I said, "But they're about to celebrate the holiday of the Immaculate Conception in Bilbao. I can go there with you and then continue on to Zaragoza."

Just then, it was on the tip of my tongue to ask him about his being a "seminarian." He must have read my expression, because he said quickly, "Do you want to ask me something?"

"Yes. Before your lecture, a woman said that you were giving her back what had been hers. What did she mean?"

"Oh, that's nothing."

"But it's important to me. I don't know anything about your life; I'm even surprised to see so many people here."

He just laughed, and then he started to turn away to answer other people's questions.

"Wait," I said, grabbing his arm. "You didn't answer me."

"I don't think it would interest you, Pilar."

"I want to know anyway."

Taking a deep breath, he led me to a corner of the room. "All of the great religions—including Judaism, Catholicism, and

Islam—are masculine. Men are in charge of the dogmas, men make the laws, and usually all the priests are men."

"Is that what the woman meant?"

He hesitated before he answered. "Yes. I have a different view of things: I believe in the feminine side of God."

I sighed with relief. The woman was mistaken; he couldn't be a seminarian because seminarians don't have such different views of things.

"You've explained it very well," I said.

❦ ❦ ❦

THE GIRL WHO HAD winked at me was waiting at the door.

"I know that we belong to the same tradition," she said. "My name is Brida."

"I don't know what you're talking about."

"Of course you do," she laughed.

She took my arm and led me out of the building before I could say anything more. It was a cold night, and I wasn't sure what I was going to do until we left for Bilbao the next morning.

"Where are we going?" I asked.

"To the statue of the Goddess."

"But . . . I need to find an inexpensive hotel where I can stay for the night."

"I'll show you one later."

I wanted to go to some warm café where I could talk to her for a bit and learn as much as I could about him. But I didn't want to argue. While she guided me across the Paseo de Castellana, I looked around at Madrid; I hadn't been there in years.

In the middle of the avenue, she stopped and pointed to the sky. "There She is."

The moon shone brilliantly through the bare branches of the trees on either side of the road.

"Isn't that beautiful!" I exclaimed.

But she wasn't listening. She spread her arms in the form of a cross, turning her palms upward, and just stood there contemplating the moon.

What have I gotten myself into? I thought. I came here to attend a conference, and now I wind up in the Paseo de Castellana with this crazy girl. And tomorrow I'm going to Bilbao!

"O mirror of the Earth Goddess," Brida was saying, her eyes closed. "Teach us about our power and make men understand us. Rising, gleaming, waning, and reviving in the heavens, you show us the cycle of the seed and the fruit."

She stretched her arms toward the night sky and held this position for some time. Several passersby looked at her and laughed, but she paid no attention; I was the one who was dying of embarrassment, standing there beside her.

"I needed to do that," she said, after her long adoration of the moon, "so that the Goddess would protect us."

"What are you talking about?"

"The same thing that your friend was talking about, only with words that are true."

I was sorry now that I hadn't paid closer attention to the lecture.

"We know the feminine side of God," Brida continued as we started to walk on. "We, the women, understand and love the Great Mother. We have paid for our wisdom with persecution and burnings at the stake, but we have survived. And now we understand Her mysteries."

Burnings at the stake? She was talking about witches!

I looked more closely at the woman by my side. She was pretty, with hair that hung to the middle of her back.

"While men were going off to hunt, we remained in the caves, in the womb of the Mother, caring for our children. And it was there that the Great Mother taught us everything.

"Men lived through movement, while we remained close to the womb of the Mother. This allowed us to see that seeds are turned into plants, and we told this to the men. We made the first bread, and we fed our people. We shaped the first cup so that we could drink. And we came to understand the cycle of creation, because our bodies repeat the rhythm of the moon."

She stopped suddenly. "There She is!"

I looked. There in the middle of the plaza, surrounded on all sides by traffic, was a fountain portraying a woman in a carriage drawn by lions.

"This is the Plaza Cybele," I said, trying to show off my knowledge of Madrid. I had seen this fountain on dozens of postcards.

But the young woman wasn't listening. She was already in the middle of the street, trying to make her way through the traffic. "Come on! Let's go over there!" she shouted, waving to me from the midst of the cars.

I decided to try to follow her, if only to get the name of a hotel. Her craziness was wearing me out; I needed to get some sleep.

We made it to the fountain at almost the same time; my heart was pounding, but she had a smile on her lips. "Water!" she exclaimed. "Water is Her manifestation."

"Please, I need the name of an inexpensive hotel."

She plunged her hands into the water. "You should do this, too," she said to me. "Feel the water."

"No! But I don't want to spoil your experience. I'm going to look for a hotel."

"Just a minute."

Brida took a small flute from her bag and began to play. To my surprise, the music had a hypnotic effect; the sounds of the traffic receded, and my racing heart began to slow down. I sat on the edge of the fountain, listening to the noise of the water and the sound of the flute, my eyes on the full moon gleaming above us. Somehow I was sensing—although I couldn't quite understand it—that the moon was a reflection of my womanhood.

I don't know how long she continued to play. When she stopped, she turned to the fountain. "Cybele, manifestation of the Great Mother, who governs the harvests, sustains the cities, and returns to woman her role as priestess . . ."

"Who are you?" I asked. "Why did you ask me to come with you?"

She turned to me. "I am what you see me to be. I am a part of the religion of the earth."

"What do you want from me?"

"I can read your eyes. I can read your heart. You are going to fall in love. And suffer."

"I am?"

"You know what I'm talking about. I saw how he was looking at you. He loves you."

This woman was really nuts!

"That's why I asked you to come with me—because he is important. Even though he says some silly things, at least he recognizes the Great Mother. Don't let him lose his way. Help him."

"You don't know what you're talking about. You're dreaming!" And I turned and rushed back into the traffic, swearing I'd forget everything she had said.

Sunday, December 5, 1993

WE STOPPED for a cup of coffee.

"Yes, life teaches us many things," I said, trying to continue the conversation.

"It taught me that we can learn, and it taught me that we can change," he replied, "even when it seems impossible."

Clearly he wanted to drop the subject. We had hardly spoken during the two-hour drive that had brought us to this roadside café.

In the beginning, I had tried to reminisce about our childhood adventures, but he'd shown only a polite interest. In fact, he hadn't even really been listening to me; he kept asking me questions about things I had already told him.

Something was wrong. Had time and distance taken him away from my world forever? *After all, he talks about "magic moments,"* I reasoned. *Why would he care about an old friend's career? He lives in a different universe, where Soria is only a remote memory—a town frozen in time, his childhood friends still young boys and girls, the old folks still alive and doing the same things they'd been doing for so many years.*

I was beginning to regret my decision to come with him. So when he changed the subject again, I resolved not to insist any further.

The last two hours of the drive to Bilbao were torture. He was watching the road, I was looking out the window, and neither of us could hide the bad feelings that had arisen between us. The rental car didn't have a radio, so all we could do was endure the silence.

"Let's ask where the bus station is," I suggested as soon as we left the highway. "The buses leave from here regularly for Zaragoza."

It was the hour of siesta, and there were few people in the streets. We passed one gentleman and then a couple of teenagers, but he didn't stop to ask them. "Do you know where it is?" I spoke up, after some time had passed.

"Where what is?"

He still wasn't paying attention to what I said.

And then suddenly I understood what the silence was about. What did he have in common with a woman who had never ventured out into the world? How could he possibly be interested in spending time with someone who feared the unknown, who preferred a secure job and a conventional marriage to the life he led? Poor me, chattering away about friends from childhood and dusty memories of an insignificant village—those were the only things I could discuss.

When we seemed to have reached the center of town, I said, "You can let me off here." I was trying to sound casual, but I felt stupid, childish, and irritated.

He didn't stop the car.

"I have to catch the bus back to Zaragoza," I insisted.

"I've never been here before," he answered. "I have no idea where my hotel is, I don't know where the conference is being held, and I don't know where the bus station is."

"Don't worry, I'll be all right."

He slowed down but kept on driving.

"I'd really like to . . . ," he began. He tried again but still couldn't finish his thought.

I could imagine what he would like to do: thank me for the company, send greetings to his old friends—maybe that would break the tension.

"I would really like it if you went with me to the conference tonight," he finally said.

I was shocked. Was he stalling for time so that he could make up for the awkward silence of our trip?

"I'd really like you to go with me," he repeated.

Now, maybe I'm a girl from the farm with no great stories to tell. Maybe I lack the sophistication of women from the big city. Life in the country may not make a woman elegant or worldly, but it still teaches her how to listen to her heart and to trust her instincts.

To my surprise, my instincts told me that he meant what he said.

I sighed with relief. Of course I wasn't going to stay for any conference, but at least my friend seemed to be back. He was even inviting me along on his adventures, wanting to share his fears and triumphs with me.

"Thanks for the invitation," I said, "but I don't have enough money for a hotel, and I do need to get back to my studies."

"I have some money. You can stay in my room. We'll ask for two beds."

I noticed that he was beginning to perspire, despite the chill in the air. My heart sounded an alarm, and all the joy of the moment before turned into confusion.

Suddenly he stopped the car and looked directly into my eyes.

No one can lie, no one can hide anything, when he looks directly into someone's eyes. And any woman with the least bit of sensitivity can read the eyes of a man in love.

I thought immediately of what that weird young woman at the fountain had said. It wasn't possible—but it seemed to be true.

I had never dreamed that after all these years he would still remember. When we were children, we had walked through the world hand in hand. I had loved him—if a child can know what love means. But that was so many years ago—it was another life, a life whose innocence had opened my heart to all that was good.

And now we were responsible adults. We had put away childish things.

I looked into his eyes. I didn't want to—or wasn't able to—believe what I saw there.

"I just have this last conference, and then the holidays of the Immaculate Conception begin. I have to go up into the mountains; I want to show you something."

This brilliant man who was able to speak of magic moments was now here with me, acting as awkward as could be. He was moving too fast, he was unsure of himself; the things he was proposing were confused. It was painful for me to see him this way.

I opened the door and got out, then leaned against the fender, looking at the nearly deserted street. I lit a cigarette. I could try to hide my thoughts, pretend that I didn't understand what he was saying; I could try to convince myself that this was just a suggestion made by one childhood friend to another. Maybe he'd been on the road too long and was beginning to get confused.

Maybe I was exaggerating.

He jumped out of the car and came to my side.

"I'd really like you to stay for the conference tonight," he said again. "But if you can't, I'll understand."

There! The world made a complete turn and returned to where it belonged. It wasn't what I had been thinking; he was no longer insisting, he was ready to let me leave—a man in love doesn't act that way.

I felt both stupid and relieved. Yes, I could stay for at least one more day. We could have dinner together and get a little drunk—something we'd never done when we were younger. This would give me a chance to forget the stupid ideas I'd just had, and it would be a good opportunity to break the ice that had frozen us ever since we left Madrid.

One day wouldn't make any difference. And then at least I'd have a story to tell my friends.

"Separate beds," I said, joking. "And you pay for dinner, because I'm still a student. I'm broke."

We put our bags in the hotel room and came down to see where the conference was to be held. Since we were so early, we sat down in a café to wait.

"I want to give you something," he said, handing me a small red pouch.

I opened it and found inside an old rusty medal, with Our Lady of Grace on one side and the Sacred Heart of Jesus on the other.

"That was yours," he said, noticing my surprise. My heart began to sound the alarm again. "One day—it was autumn, just like it is now, and we must have been ten—I was sitting with you in the plaza where the great oak stood.

"I was going to tell you something, something I had rehearsed for weeks. But as soon as I began, you told me that you had lost your medal at the hermitage of San Satúrio, and you asked me to see if I could find it there."

I remembered. Oh, God, I remembered!

"I did find it. But when I returned to the plaza, I no longer had the courage to say what I had rehearsed. So I promised myself that I would return the medal to you only when I was able to complete the sentence that I'd begun that day almost twenty years ago. For a long time, I've tried to forget it, but it's always there. I can't live with it any longer."

He put down his coffee, lit a cigarette, and looked at the ceiling for a long time. Then he turned to me. "It's a very simple sentence," he said. "I love you."

❦ ❦ ❦

SOMETIMES AN UNCONTROLLABLE *feeling of sadness grips us,* he said. *We recognize that the magic moment of the day has passed and that we've done nothing about it. Life begins to conceal its magic and its art.*

We have to listen to the child we once were, the child who still exists inside us. That child understands magic moments. We can stifle its cries, but we cannot silence its voice.

The child we once were is still there. Blessed are the children, for theirs is the kingdom of heaven.

If we are not reborn—if we cannot learn to look at life with the innocence and the enthusiasm of childhood—it makes no sense to go on living.

There are many ways to commit suicide. Those who try to kill the body violate God's law. Those who try to kill the soul also violate God's law, even though their crime is less visible to others.

We have to pay attention to what the child in our heart tells us. We should not be embarrassed by this child. We must not allow this child to be scared because the child is alone and is almost never heard.

We must allow the child to take the reins of our lives. The child knows that each day is different from every other day.

We have to allow it to feel loved again. We must please this child—even if this means that we act in ways we are not used to, in ways that may seem foolish to others.

Remember that human wisdom is madness in the eyes of God. But if we listen to the child who lives in our soul, our eyes will grow bright. If we do not lose contact with that child, we will not lose contact with life.

THE COLORS AROUND ME were growing vivid; I felt that I was speaking with more intensity and that my glass made a louder sound when I put it down on the table.

A group of about ten of us were having dinner together after the conference. Everyone was speaking at the same time, and I was smiling, for this night was special: it was the first night in many years that I had not planned.

What a joy!

When I'd decided to go to Madrid, I had been in control of my actions and my feelings. Now, suddenly, all that had changed. Here I was in a city where I'd never set foot before, even though it was only three hours from the place where I'd been born. I was sitting at a table where I knew only one person, and everyone was speaking to me as if they'd known me for years. I was amazed that I could enter into the conversation, that I could drink and enjoy myself with them.

I was there because suddenly life had presented me with Life. I felt no guilt, no fear, no embarrassment. As I listened to what he was saying—and felt myself growing closer to him—I was more and more convinced that he was right: there are moments when you have to take a risk, to do crazy things.

I spend day after day with my texts and notebooks, making this superhuman effort just to purchase my own servitude, I thought. *Why do I want that job? What does it offer me as a human being, as a woman?*

Nothing! I wasn't born to spend my life behind a desk, helping judges dispose of their cases.

No, I can't think that way about my life. I'm going to have to return to it this week. It must be the wine. After all, when all is said and done, if you don't work, you don't eat. This is all a dream. It's going to end.

But how long can I make the dream go on?

For the first time I considered going to the mountains with him for the next few days. After all, a week of holidays was about to begin.

"Who are you?" a woman at our table asked me.

"A childhood friend," I answered.

"Was he doing these things when he was a child, too?"

"What things?"

The conversation at the table seemed to fade and then die out.

"You know: the miracles."

"He could always speak well." I didn't understand what she meant.

Everyone laughed, including him. I had no idea what was going on. But—maybe because of the wine—I felt relaxed, and for once I didn't feel like I had to be in control.

I looked around and then said something that I forgot the next moment. I was thinking about the upcoming holiday.

It was good to be here, meeting new people, talking about serious things but always with a touch of humor. I felt like I was really participating in the world. For at least this one night, I was no longer just seeing the real world through television or the newspapers. When I returned to Zaragoza, I'd have stories to tell. If I accepted his invitation for the holidays, I'd have whole years of memories to live on.

He was so right not to pay any attention to my remarks about Soria, I thought. And I began to feel sorry for myself; for so many years, my drawer full of memories had held the same old stories.

"Have some more wine," a white-haired man said, filling my glass.

I drank it down. I kept thinking about how few things I would have had to tell my children and grandchildren if I hadn't come with him.

"I'm counting on our trip to France," he said to me so that only I could hear.

The wine had freed my tongue. "But only if you understand one thing."

"What's that?"

"It's about what you said before the conference. At the café."

"The medal?"

"No," I said, looking into his eyes and doing everything I could to appear sober. "What you said."

"We'll talk about it later," he said, quickly trying to change the subject.

He had said that he loved me. We hadn't had time to talk about it, but I knew I could convince him that it wasn't true.

"If you want me to take the trip with you, you have to listen to me," I said.

"I don't want to talk about it here. We're having a good time."

"You left Soria when you were very young," I went on. "I'm only a link to your past. I've reminded you of your roots, and that's what makes you think as you do. But that's all it is. There can't be any love involved."

He listened but didn't answer. Someone asked him his opinion about something, and our conversation was interrupted.

At least I've explained how I feel, I thought. *The love he was talking about only exists in fairy tales.*

In real life, love has to be possible. Even if it is not returned right away, love can only survive when the hope exists that you will be able to win over the person you desire.

Anything else is fantasy.

From the other side of the table, as if he had guessed what I was thinking, he raised his glass in a toast. "To love," he said.

I could tell that he, too, was a little drunk. So I decided to take advantage of the opening: "To those wise enough to understand that sometimes love is nothing more than the foolishness of childhood," I said.

"The wise are wise only because they love. And the foolish are foolish only because they think they can understand love," he answered.

The others at the table heard him, and in a moment an animated discussion about love was in full swing. Everyone had a strong opinion and was defending their position tooth and nail; it took more wine to calm things down. Finally someone said it was getting late and that the owner of the restaurant wanted to close.

"We have five days of vacation," someone shouted from

another table. "If the owner wants to close, it's just because you were getting too serious."

Everyone laughed—except me.

"Then where can we talk about serious things?" someone asked the drunk at the other table.

"In church!" said the drunk. And this time all of us laughed.

My friend stood up. I thought he was going to start a fight, because we were all acting like adolescents, and that's what adolescents do. Fighting is as much a part of being a teenager as the kisses, the secret embraces, the loud music, and the fast pace.

But instead he took my hand and moved toward the door. "We should go," he said. "It's getting late."

❧ ❧ ❧

IT WAS RAINING in Bilbao. Lovers need to know how to lose themselves and then how to find themselves again. He was able to do both well. Now he was happy, and as we returned to the hotel he sang:

Son los locos que inventaron el amor.

The song was right: it must have been the lunatics who invented love.

I was still feeling the effects of the wine, but I was struggling to think clearly. I had to stay in control of the situation if I wanted to make the trip with him.

But it will be easy to be in control because I'm not too emotional, I thought. *Anyone who can conquer her heart can conquer the world.*

Con un poema y un trombón
a develarte el corazón

To lose my heart to you with a poem and a trombone. I wish I didn't have to control my heart. If I could surrender, even if only for a weekend, this rain falling on my face would feel different. If love were easy, I would be embracing him now, and the words of his song would be our story. If Zaragoza weren't waiting for me after the holidays, I'd want to stay drunk and be free to kiss him, caress him, say the things and hear the things that lovers say and do to each other.

But no! I can't. I don't want to.

Salgamos a volar, querida mia, *the song says.*

Yes, let's fly away. But under my *conditions.*

He still didn't know that I was going to say yes to his invitation. Why did I want to take this risk?

Because I was drunk, because I was tired of days that were all the same.

But this weariness will pass. I'm going to want to get back to Zaragoza, where I have chosen to live. My studies are waiting for me. The husband I'm still looking for is waiting for me—a husband who won't be as difficult to find.

An easier life waits for me, with children and grandchildren, with a clear budget and a yearly vacation. I don't know what his fears are, but I know my own. I don't need new fears—my own are enough.

I was sure I could never fall in love with someone like him. I knew him too well, all his weaknesses and fears. I just couldn't admire him as the others seemed to.

But love is much like a dam: if you allow a tiny crack to form through which only a trickle of water can pass, that trickle will quickly bring down the whole structure, and soon no one will be able to control the force of the current.

For when those walls come down, then love takes over, and it no longer matters what is possible or impossible; it doesn't even matter whether we can keep the loved one at our side. To love is to lose control.

No, no, I cannot allow such a crack to form. No matter how small.

"Hey, hold up a minute!"

He stopped singing immediately. Quick steps echoed on the damp pavement behind us.

"Let's get out of here," he said, grabbing my arm.

"Wait!" a man shouted. "I need to talk to you!"

But he moved ahead even more rapidly. "This has nothing to do with us," he said. "Let's get to the hotel."

Yet it did have to do with us—there was no one else on the street. My heart was beating fast, and the effects of the wine disappeared altogether. I remembered that Bilbao was in Basque country and that terrorist attacks were common. The man's footsteps came closer.

"Let's go," he said, hurrying along.

But it was too late. A man's figure, soaked from head to foot, stepped in front of us.

"Stop, please!" the man said. "For the love of God."

I was frightened. I looked around frantically for a means of escape, hoping that by some miracle a police car would appear. Instinctively, I clutched at his arm—but he pulled away.

"Please!" said the man. "I heard that you were in the city. I need your help. It's my son." The man knelt on the pavement and began to weep. "Please," he said, "please!"

My friend gasped for breath; I watched as he lowered his head and closed his eyes. For a few minutes the silence was broken only by the sound of the rain and the sobs of the man kneeling on the sidewalk.

"Go to the hotel, Pilar," he said finally. "Get some sleep. I won't be back until dawn."

Monday, December 6, 1993

LOVE IS A TRAP. When it appears, we see only its light, not its shadows.

"Look at the land around here!" he said. "Let's lie down on the ground and feel the planet's heart beating!"

"But I'll get my coat dirty, and it's the only one I have with me."

We were driving through hills of olive groves. After yesterday's rain in Bilbao, the morning sun made me sleepy. I hadn't brought sunglasses—I hadn't brought anything, since I'd expected to return to Zaragoza two days ago. I'd had to sleep in a shirt he loaned me, and I'd bought a T-shirt at a shop near the hotel in Bilbao so that at least I could wash the one I was wearing.

"You must be sick of seeing me in the same clothes every day," I said, trying to make a joke about something trivial to see if that would make all this seem real.

"I'm glad you're here."

He hadn't mentioned love again since he had given me the

medal, but he had been in a good mood; he seemed to be eighteen again. Now he walked along beside me bathed in the clear morning light.

"What do you have to do over there?" I asked, pointing toward the peaks of the Pyrenees on the horizon.

"Beyond those mountains lies France," he answered with a smile.

"I know—I studied geography, too, you know. I'm just curious about why we have to go there."

He paused, smiling to himself. "So you can take a look at a house you might be interested in."

"If you're thinking about becoming a real estate agent, forget it. I don't have any money."

It didn't matter to me whether we visited a village in Navarra or went all the way to France. I just didn't want to spend the holidays in Zaragoza.

You see? I heard my brain say to my heart. *You're happy that you've accepted his invitation. You've changed—you just haven't recognized it yet.*

No, I hadn't changed at all. I was just relaxing a little.

"Look at the stones on the ground."

They were rounded, with no sharp edges. They looked like pebbles from the sea. But the sea had never been here in the fields of Navarra.

"The feet of laborers, pilgrims, and explorers smoothed these stones," he said. "The stones were changed—and the travelers were too."

"Has traveling taught you all the things you know?"

"No. I learned from the miracles of revelation."

I didn't understand, but I didn't pursue it. For now, I was content to bask in the beauty of the sun, the fields, and the mountains.

"Where are we going now?" I asked.

"Nowhere. Let's just enjoy the morning, the sun, and the countryside. We have a long trip ahead of us." He hesitated for a moment and then asked, "Do you still have the medal?"

"Sure, I've kept it," I said, and began to walk faster. I didn't want to talk about the medal—I didn't want to talk about anything that might ruin the happiness and freedom of our morning together.

A VILLAGE APPEARED. Like most medieval cities, it was situated atop a mountain peak; even from a distance, I could see the tower of a church and the ruins of a castle.

"Let's drive to that village," I suggested.

Although he seemed reluctant, he agreed. I could see a chapel along the road, and I wanted to stop and go in. I didn't pray anymore, but the silence of churches always attracted me.

Don't feel guilty, I was saying to myself. *If he's in love, that's his problem.* He had asked about the medal. I knew that he was hoping we'd get back to our conversation at the café. But I was afraid of hearing something I didn't want to hear. *I won't get into it, I won't bring up the subject.*

But what if he really did love me? What if he thought that we could transform this love into something deeper?

Ridiculous, I thought to myself. *There's nothing deeper than love. In fairy tales, the princesses kiss the frogs, and the frogs become princes. In real life, the princesses kiss princes, and the princes turn into frogs.*

After driving for another half hour, we reached the chapel. An old man was seated on the steps. He was the first person we'd seen since our drive began.

It was the end of fall, and, in keeping with tradition, the fields had been returned once more to the Lord, who would fertilize the land with his blessings and allow human beings to harvest his sustenance by the sweat of their brows.

"Hello," he said to the man.

"How are you?"

"What is the name of this village?"

"San Martín de Unx."

"Unx?" I said. "It sounds like the name of a gnome."

The old man didn't understand the joke. Disappointed, I walked toward the entrance to the chapel.

"You can't go in," warned the old man. "It closed at noon. If you like, you can come back at four this afternoon."

The door was open and I could look inside, although it was so bright out that I couldn't see clearly.

"Just for a minute?" I asked. "I'd like to say a prayer."

"I'm very sorry. It's already closed."

He was listening to my conversation with the old man but didn't say anything.

"All right, then, let's leave," I said. "There's no point in arguing."

He continued to look at me, his gaze empty, distant. "Don't you want to see the chapel?" he asked.

I could see he didn't approve of my decision. *He thinks I'm weak, cowardly, unable to fight for what I want. Even without a kiss, the princess is transformed into a frog.*

"Remember yesterday?" I said. "You ended our conversation in the bar because you didn't want to argue with me. Now when I do the same thing, you criticize me."

The old man watched our discussion impassively. He was probably happy that something was actually happening, there in a place where all the mornings, all the afternoons, and all the nights were the same.

"The door to the church is open," he said, speaking to the old man. "If you want some money, we can give you some. But she wants to see the church."

"It's too late."

"Fine. We'll go in anyway." He took my arm and we went in.

My heart was pounding. The old man could get nasty, call the police, ruin the trip.

"Why are you doing this?"

"Because you wanted to see the chapel."

I was so nervous I couldn't even focus on what was inside. The argument—and my attitude—had ruined our perfect morning.

I listened carefully for any sounds from outside. *The old man might call the village police,* I thought. *Trespassers in the chapel! Thieves! They're breaking the law!* The old man had said the chapel was closed, that visiting hours were over. *He's a poor old man, unable to keep us from going in. And the police will be tough on us because we offended a feeble old man.*

I stayed inside the chapel just long enough to show that I'd really wanted to see it. As soon as enough time had passed for an imaginary Ave Maria, I said, "Let's go."

"Don't be frightened, Pilar. Don't just fall into playing a role."

I didn't want my problem with the old man to become a

problem with him, so I tried to stay calm. "I don't know what you mean by 'playing a role.'"

"Some people always have to be doing battle with someone, sometimes even with themselves, battling with their own lives. So they begin to create a kind of play in their head, and they write the script based on their frustrations."

"I know a lot of people like that. I know just what you mean."

"But the worst part is that they cannot present the play by themselves," he continued. "So they begin to invite other actors to join in.

"That's what that fellow outside was doing. He wanted revenge for something, and he chose us to play a part. If we had accepted his restrictions, we'd be regretting it now. We would have been defeated. We would have agreed to participate in his miserable life and in his frustrations.

"The man's aggression was easy to see, so it was easy for us to refuse the role he wanted us to play. But other people also 'invite' us to behave like victims, when they complain about the unfairness of life, for example, and ask us to agree, to offer advice, to participate."

He looked into my eyes. "Be careful. When you join in that game, you always wind up losing."

He was right. But I still wasn't happy about being inside the chapel. "OK, but I've already said my prayer. I've done what I wanted to do. Let's go."

The contrast between the darkness inside the chapel and the strong sunlight blinded me for a few moments. When my eyes adjusted, I saw that the old man was no longer there.

"Let's have some lunch," he said, walking in the direction of the village.

ʚ ʚ ʚ

I DRANK TWO GLASSES of wine at lunch. I'd never done that in my life.

He was speaking to the waiter, who told him that there were several Roman ruins in the area. I was trying to listen to their conversation, but I was having trouble stifling my bad mood.

The princess had turned into a frog. So what? Who do I have to prove anything to? I wasn't looking for anything—not for a man and certainly not for love.

I knew it, I said to myself. *I knew he was going to turn my world upside down. My brain warned me, but my heart didn't want to take its advice.*

I've paid a considerable price for the little I have gained. I've been forced to deny myself many things I've wanted, to abandon so many roads that were open to me. I've sacrificed my dreams in the name of a larger dream—a peaceful soul. I didn't want to give up that peace.

"You're tense," he said, breaking off his conversation with the waiter.

"Yes, I am. I think that old man went for the police. I think this is a small place, and they know where we are. I think this boldness of yours about having lunch here could wind up ruining our holiday."

He twirled his glass of water. Surely he knew that this was not the problem—that I was actually ashamed. Why do we always do this? Why do we notice the speck in our eye but not the mountains, the fields, the olive groves?

"Listen, that's not going to happen," he said. "The old man

has gone home and has already forgotten the whole thing. Trust me."

That's not why I'm so tense, you idiot.

"Listen to your heart more," he went on.

"That's just it! I *am* listening to it," I said. "And I feel that we should leave. I'm not enjoying this place."

"You shouldn't drink during the day. It doesn't help anything."

Up to that point, I'd controlled myself. Now it was time to say what I thought.

"You think you know everything," I said, "that you know all about magic moments, the inner child . . . I don't know what you're doing here with me."

He laughed. "I admire you. And I admire the battle you're waging with your heart."

"What battle?"

"Never mind," he said.

But I knew what he was talking about.

"Don't kid yourself," I said. "We can talk about it if you like. You're mistaken about my feelings."

He stopped fooling with his glass and looked at me. "No, I'm not mistaken. I know you don't love me."

This confused me even more.

"But I'm going to fight for your love," he continued. "There are some things in life that are worth fighting for to the end."

I was speechless.

"You are worth it," he said.

I turned away, trying to pretend that I was interested in the restaurant's decor. I had been feeling like a frog, and suddenly I was a princess again.

I want to believe what you're saying, I thought to myself. *It won't change anything, but at least I won't feel so weak, so incapable.*

"I apologize for my outburst," I said.

He smiled, signaled to the waiter, and paid the check.

On the way back to the car, I became confused again. Maybe it was the sun—but no, it was autumn, and the sun was weak. Perhaps the old man—but he disappeared a while ago.

All this was so new to me. Life takes us by surprise and orders us to move toward the unknown—even when we don't want to and when we think we don't need to.

I tried to concentrate on the scenery, but I couldn't focus on the olive groves, the village atop the mountain, the chapel with the old man at the gate. All of it was so unfamiliar.

I remembered how much I'd drunk the day before and the song he had sung:

Las tardecitas de Buenos Aires tienen este no sé . . .
¿Qué sé yo?
Viste, salí de tu casa, por Arenales . . .

Why sing of the nights of Buenos Aires, when we were in Bilbao? I didn't live on a street called Arenales. What had gotten into him?

"What was that song you were singing yesterday?" I asked.

"*Balada para un loco,*" he said. "Why do you ask about it now?"

"I don't know."

But I had a reason: I knew he'd sung the song as a kind of snare. He'd made me memorize the words, just as I would memorize course work for an examination. He could have sung a song I was familiar with—but he'd chosen one I'd never heard before.

It was a trap. Later, if I heard the song played on the radio or at a club, I'd think of him, of Bilbao, and of a time in my life when autumn turned to spring. I'd recall the excitement, the adventure, and the child who was reborn out of God knows where.

That's what he was thinking. He was wise, experienced; he knew how to woo the woman he wanted.

I'm going crazy, I told myself. *I must be an alcoholic, drinking so much two days in a row. He knows all the tricks. He's controlling me, leading me along with his sweetness.*

"I admire the battle you are waging with your heart," he had said at the restaurant.

But he was wrong. Because I had fought with my heart and defeated it long ago. I was certainly not going to become passionate about something that was impossible. I knew my limits; I knew how much suffering I could bear.

"Say something," I demanded, as we walked back to the car.

"What?"

"Anything. Talk to me."

So he began to tell me about the visions of the Virgin Mary at Fátima. I don't know why he came up with that, but the story of the three shepherds who had spoken to the Virgin distracted me.

My heart relaxed. *Yes, I know my limits, and I know how to stay in control.*

❦ ❦ ❦

WE ARRIVED AT NIGHT in a fog so dense we could hardly see where we were. I could make out only a small plaza, a lamppost, some medieval houses barely illuminated by the yellow light, and a well.

"The fog!" he exclaimed.

I couldn't understand why he was so excited.

"We're in Saint-Savin," he explained.

The name meant nothing to me. But we were in France, and that in itself thrilled me.

"Why this place?" I asked.

"Because the house I want you to see is here," he answered, laughing. "Also, I promised that I would come back here on the day of the Immaculate Conception."

"Here?"

"Well, near here."

He stopped the car. When we stepped out, he took my hand, and we began to walk through the fog.

"This place became a part of my life quite unexpectedly," he said.

You too? I thought.

"When I first came here, I thought I was lost. But I wasn't—actually, I was just rediscovering it."

"You talk in riddles sometimes," I said.

"This is where I realized how much I needed you in my life."

I looked away; I couldn't understand him. "But what does that have to do with losing your way?"

"Let's find someone who'll rent us a room, because the two hotels in this village are only open during the summer. Then we'll have dinner at a good restaurant—no tension, no fear of the police, no need to think about running back to the car! And when the wine loosens our tongues, we'll talk about many things."

We both laughed. I already felt more relaxed. During the drive here, I had looked back over the wild things I'd been thinking. And as we crossed over the top of the mountains that separate France from Spain, I'd asked God to cleanse my soul of tension and fear.

I was tired of playing the child and acting the way many of my friends did—the ones who are afraid that love is impossible without even knowing what love is. If I stayed like that, I would miss out on everything good that these few days with him might offer.

Careful, I thought. *Watch out for the break in the dam. If that break occurs, nothing in the world will be able to stop it.*

"May the Virgin protect us from here on," he said.

I remained silent.

"Why didn't you say 'amen'?" he asked.

"Because I don't think that's important anymore. There was a time when religion was a part of my life, but that time has passed."

He turned around and began to walk back to the car. "I still pray," I went on. "I prayed as we were crossing the Pyrenees. But it's something automatic, and I'm not even sure I still believe in it."

"Why?"

"Because I've suffered, and God didn't listen to my prayers. Because many times in my life I have tried to love with all my heart, and my love has wound up being trampled or betrayed. If God is love, he should have cared more about my feelings.

"God *is* love. But the one who understands this best is the Virgin."

I burst out laughing. When I turned to look at him, I saw that he was serious—this was not a joke.

"The Virgin understands the mystery of total surrender," he went on. "And having loved and suffered, she freed us from pain. In the same way that Jesus freed us from sin."

"Jesus was the son of God. They say that the Virgin was merely a woman who happened to receive him into her womb," I said. I was trying to make up for my laughter and let him know that I respected his faith.

He opened the car door and took out our bags. When I tried to take mine from his hand, he smiled. "Let me carry your bag."

No one's done that for me in a long time, I thought.

We knocked on the door of the first house, but the woman said she didn't rent rooms. At the second door, no one answered. At the third, a kind old man greeted us—but when we looked at the room, there was only a double bed. I turned it down.

"Maybe we should head for a larger city," I suggested as we left.

"We'll find a room," he said. "Do you know the exercise of the Other? It's part of a story written a hundred years ago, whose author . . ."

"Forget the author, and tell me the story," I interrupted. We were once more walking along the only street in Saint-Savin.

❦ ❦ ❦

MAN RUNS INTO an old friend who had somehow never been able to make it in life. "I should give him some money," he thinks. But instead he learns that his old friend has grown rich and is actually seeking him out to repay the debts he had run up over the years.

They go to a bar they used to frequent together, and the friend buys drinks for everyone there. When they ask him how he became so successful, he answers that until only a few days ago, he had been living the role of the "Other."

"What is the Other?" they ask.

"The Other is the one who taught me what I should be like, but not what I am. The Other believes that it is our obligation to spend our entire life thinking about how to get our hands on as much money as possible so that we will not die of hunger when we are old. So we think so much about money and our plans for acquiring it that we discover we are alive only when our days on earth are practically done. And then it's too late."

"And you? Who are you?"

"I am just like everyone else who listens to their heart: a person who is enchanted by the mystery of life. Who is open to miracles, who experiences joy and enthusiasm for what they do. It's just that the Other, afraid of disappointment, kept me from taking action."

"But there is suffering in life," one of the listeners said.

"And there are defeats. No one can avoid them. But it's better to lose some of the battles in the struggle for your dreams than to be defeated without ever even knowing what you're fighting for."

"That's it?" another listener asked.

"Yes, that's it. When I learned this, I resolved to become the person I had always wanted to be. The Other stood there in the corner of my room, watching me, but I will never let the Other into myself again—even though it has already tried to frighten me, warning me that it's risky not to think about the future.

"From the moment that I ousted the Other from my life, the Divine Energy began to perform its miracles."

❦ ❦ ❦

In spite of the fact that my friend had long ago expelled the Other from his life, he still wasn't having much luck finding us lodging for the night. But I knew he hadn't told me that story for his own sake—he had told it for mine. He seemed to be talking about my fears, my insecurity, and my unwillingness to see what was wonderful because tomorrow it might disappear and then I would suffer.

The gods throw the dice, and they don't ask whether we want to be in the game or not. They don't care if when you go, you leave behind a lover, a home, a career, or a dream. The gods don't care whether you have it all, whether it seems that your every desire can be met through hard work and persistence. The gods don't want to know about your plans and your hopes. Somewhere they're throwing the dice—and you are chosen. From then on, winning or losing is only a question of luck.

The gods throw the dice, freeing love from its cage. And love can create or destroy—depending on the direction of the wind when it is set free.

For the moment, the wind was blowing in his favor. But the wind is as capricious as the gods—and deep inside myself, I had begun to feel some gusts.

AT LAST, as if fate wanted to show me that the story of the Other was true—and the universe always conspires to help the dreamer—we found a house to stay in, with a room with separate beds. My first move was to bathe, wash my clothes, and put on the shirt I had bought. I felt refreshed, and this made me feel more secure.

After having dinner with the couple who owned the house—the restaurants were also closed during the autumn and winter—he asked for a bottle of wine, promising to replace it the next day. We put on our coats, borrowed two glasses, and went out.

"Let's sit on the edge of the well," I suggested.

And there we sat, drinking to keep the cold and the tension away.

"It looks like the Other has gotten to you," I joked. "Your good mood seems to have disappeared."

He laughed. "I knew we were going to find a room, and we did. The universe always helps us fight for our dreams, no matter how foolish they may be. Our dreams are our own, and only we can know the effort required to keep them alive."

In the fog, which hung yellow under the glow of the street lamp, we couldn't see even as far as the other side of the plaza.

I took a deep breath. We couldn't avoid the subject any longer.

"We have to talk about love," I said. "You know how I've been these last few days. If it had been up to me, the subject would never have come up. But ever since you brought it up, I haven't been able to stop thinking about it."

"It's risky, falling in love."

"I know that," I answered. "I've been in love before. It's like a narcotic. At first it brings the euphoria of complete surrender. The next day, you want more. You're not addicted yet, but you like the sensation, and you think you can still control things. You think about the person you love for two minutes, and forget them for three hours.

"But then you get used to that person, and you begin to be completely dependent on them. Now you think about him for three hours and forget him for two minutes. If he's not there, you feel like an addict who can't get a fix. And just as addicts steal and humiliate themselves to get what they need, you're willing to do anything for love."

"What a horrible way to put it," he said.

It really was a horrible way to put it; my analogy didn't go with the romance of the evening—the wine, the well, and the medieval houses in the plaza. But it was true. If he was going to base so many of his actions on love, he needed to know what the risks were.

"So we should love only those who can stay near us," I said.

He looked out at the fog. Now he no longer seemed interested in whether we negotiated the dangerous waters of a conversation about love. I was being tough, but there was no other way.

Subject closed, I thought. *Our being together for these three days has been enough to change his mind.* My pride was a bit wounded, but my heart was relieved. *Do I really want this?* I asked myself. I realized that I was already beginning to sense the storms brought on by the winds of love. I had already begun to feel the break in the dam.

We drank for some time without bringing up anything serious. We talked about the couple who owned the house and the saint for whom the town had been named. He told me some of the legends about the church across the square, which I could barely see in the fog.

"You're upset," he said at one point.

Yes, my mind was wandering. I wished I were there with someone who could bring peace to my heart—someone with whom I could spend a little time without being afraid that I would lose him the next day. With that reassurance, the time would pass more slowly. We could be silent for a while because we'd know we had the rest of our lives together for conversation. I wouldn't have to worry about serious matters, about difficult decisions and hard words.

❦ ❦ ❦

WE SAT THERE in silence—and that in itself was a sign. For the first time, we had nothing to say, although I only noticed this when he stood up to go find us another bottle of wine.

Silence. Then I heard the sound of his footsteps returning to the well where we'd been sitting for more than an hour, drinking and staring at the fog.

This was the first time we'd been silent for so long. It was not the awkward silence of the trip from Madrid to Bilbao. And not the silence of my fearful heart when we were in the chapel near San Martín de Unx.

This was a silence that spoke for itself. A silence that said we no longer needed to explain things to each other.

The sound of his footsteps halted. He was looking at me—and what he saw must have been beautiful: a woman seated on the edge of a well, on a foggy night, in the light of the street lamp.

The ancient houses, the eleventh-century church, and the silence.

The second bottle of wine was half empty when I decided to speak.

"This morning, I convinced myself that I was an alcoholic. I've been drinking from morning to night. In these past three days, I've drunk more than in the entire past year."

He reached out and stroked my hair without saying anything. I absorbed his touch without trying to pull away.

"Tell me about your life since I last saw you," I asked.

"There are no great mysteries to tell. My path is always there, and I do everything I can to follow it in a dignified way."

"What is your path?"

"The path of someone seeking love."

He hesitated for a moment, fiddling with the near-empty bottle.

"And love's path is really complicated," he concluded.

"Because on that path we can go either to heaven or to hell?" I wasn't sure whether he was referring to us or not.

He didn't respond. Perhaps he was still deep in the ocean of silence, but the wine had loosened my tongue again, and I had to speak.

"You said that something here in this city altered your course."

"Yes, I think it did. I'm still not absolutely sure, and that's why I wanted to bring you here."

"Is this some kind of test?"

"No. It's a surrender. So that She will help me to make the right decision."

"Who will?"

"The Virgin."

The Virgin! I should have known. I was surprised that all his years of travel, of learning, of new horizons hadn't freed him from the Catholicism of his childhood. In at least this respect, my friends and I had come a long way—we no longer lived under the weight of guilt and sin.

"I'm surprised that after all you've been through, you still keep the faith."

"I haven't kept it. I lost it and recovered it."

"But a faith in virgins? In impossible things and in fantasies? Haven't you had an active sex life?"

"Well, normal. I've been in love with many women."

To my surprise, I felt a stab of jealousy. But my inner battle seemed already to have subsided, and I didn't want to start it up again.

"Why is she 'The Virgin'? Why isn't She presented to us as a normal woman, like any other?"

He drained the few drops remaining in the bottle and asked if I wanted him to go for another. I said no.

"What I want is an answer from you. Every time we start to speak about certain things, you try to talk about something else."

"She *was* normal. She had already had other children. The Bible tells us that Jesus had two brothers. Virginity, as it relates to Jesus, is based on a different thing: Mary initiated a new generation of grace. A new era began. She is the cosmic bride, Earth, which opens to the heavens and allows itself to be fertilized.

"Because of the courage She showed in accepting her destiny, She allowed God to come down to earth—and She was transformed into the Great Mother."

I didn't understand exactly what he was telling me, and he could see that.

"She is the feminine face of God. She has her own divinity."

He spoke with great emotion; in fact, his words almost sounded forced, as if he felt he was committing a sin.

"A goddess?" I asked.

I waited for him to explain, but he couldn't say anything more. I thought about his Catholicism and about how what he had just said seemed blasphemous.

"Who is the Virgin? What is the Goddess?"

"It's not easy to explain," he said, clearly growing more and more uncomfortable. "I have some written material with me. If you want, you can read it."

"I don't want to read right now; I want you to explain it to me," I insisted.

He looked around for the wine bottle, but it was empty. Neither of us could remember why we had come to the well in the first place. Something important was in the air—as if what he was saying were part of a miracle.

"Go on," I urged him.

"Her symbol is water—like the fog all around us. The Goddess uses water as the means to manifest Herself."

The mist suddenly seemed to take on a life of its own, becoming sacred—even though I still didn't understand what he was trying to say.

"I don't want to talk to you about history. If you want to learn about the history, you can read the books I brought with me. But you should know that this woman—the Goddess, the Virgin

Mary, the Shechinah, the Great Mother, Isis, Sofia, slave and mistress—is present in every religion on the face of the earth. She has been forgotten, prohibited, and disguised, but Her cult has continued from millennium to millennium and continues to survive today.

"One of the faces of God is the face of a woman."

I studied his face. His eyes were gleaming, and he was staring into the fog that enveloped us. I could see that I no longer needed to prompt him.

"She is present in the first chapter of the Bible—when the spirit of God hovered over the waters, and He placed them below and above the stars. It was the mystic marriage of earth and heaven. She is present in the final chapter of the Bible, when

the Spirit and the bride say, "Come!"
And let him who hears say, "Come!"

And let him who thirsts come.
Whoever desires, let him take the
water of life freely."

"Why is water the symbol of the feminine face of God?"

"I don't know. But She normally chooses that medium to manifest Herself. Maybe because She is the source of life; we are generated in water, and for nine months we live in it. Water is the symbol of the power of woman, the power that no man—no matter how enlightened or perfect he may be—can capture."

He paused for a moment and then began again.

"In every religion and in every tradition, She manifests Herself in one form or another—She always manifests Herself. Since I am a Catholic, I perceive Her as the Virgin Mary."

He took me by the hand, and in less than five minutes, we had walked out of Saint-Savin. We passed a column by the side of the road that had something strange at the top: it was a cross with an image of the Virgin in the place where Jesus ought to have been.

Now the darkness and the mist completely enveloped us. I began to imagine I was immersed in water, in the maternal womb—where time and thought do not exist. Everything he had been saying to me was beginning to make sense. I remembered the woman at the conference. And then I thought of the girl who had led me to the plaza. She too had said that water was the symbol of the Goddess.

"Twenty kilometers from here there's a grotto," he was telling me. "On the eleventh of February, 1858, a young girl was baling hay near the grotto with two other children. She was a fragile, asthmatic girl who lived in miserable poverty. On that winter's day, she was afraid of crossing a small stream, because if she got wet she might fall ill. And her parents needed the little money she made as a shepherd.

"A woman dressed in white, with two golden roses on her feet, appeared. The woman treated the child as if she were a princess, asked if she might return to that place a certain number of times, and then vanished. The two other girls, who were entranced by what had happened, quickly spread the story.

"This brought on a long ordeal for the girl. She was imprisoned, and the authorities demanded that she deny the whole story. Others offered her money to get her to ask the apparition for special favors. Within days, her family began to be insulted in the plaza by people who thought that the girl had invented the story in order to get attention.

"The girl, whose name was Bernadette, had no understanding of what she had seen. She referred to the lady who had appeared as 'That,' and her parents, concerned as they were, went to the village priest for assistance. The priest suggested that when the apparition next appeared, Bernadette should ask the woman's name.

"Bernadette did as she was asked, but received only a smile in response. 'That' appeared before her a total of eighteen times and, for the most part, said nothing. During one of her appearances, though, she asked the girl to kiss the ground. Without understanding why, Bernadette did as she was asked. During another visitation, she asked the girl to dig a hole in the floor of the grotto. Bernadette obeyed, and there immediately appeared a hole filled with filthy water, because swine were kept there.

"'Drink the water,' the woman said.

"The water was so dirty that although Bernadette cupped it in her hands, she threw it away three times, afraid to bring it to her mouth. Finally she did, despite her repugnance. In the place where she had dug, more water began to come forth. A man who was blind in one eye applied several drops of the water to his face and recovered his vision. A woman, desperate because her newborn child appeared to be dying, dipped the child in the spring—on a day when the temperature had fallen below zero. And the child was cured.

"Little by little, the word spread, and thousands of people began to come to the place. The girl repeatedly asked the woman her name, but the woman merely smiled.

"Until one day, 'That' turned to Bernadette, and said, 'I am the Immaculate Conception.'

"Satisfied at last, the girl ran to tell the parish priest.

"'That cannot be,' he said. 'No one can be the tree and the fruit at the same time, my child. Go there, and throw holy water on her.'

"As far as the priest was concerned, only God could have

existed from the very beginning—and God, as far as anyone could tell, was a man."

He paused for a long time.

"Bernadette threw holy water on 'That,' and the apparition smiled tenderly, nothing more.

"On the sixteenth of July, the woman appeared for the last time. Shortly after, Bernadette entered a convent, not knowing that she had changed forever the destiny of that small village near the grotto. The spring continued to flow, and miracles followed, one after the other.

"The story spread, first throughout France and later the world. The city grew and was transformed. Businesses sprang up everywhere. Hotels opened. Bernadette died and was buried in a place far from there, never knowing what had occurred.

"Some people who wanted to put the church in a bad light—and who knew that the Vatican was now acknowledging apparitions—began to invent false miracles that were later unmasked. The church reacted strongly: from a certain date on, it would accept as miracles only those phenomena that passed a rigorous series of examinations performed by medical and scientific commissions.

"But the water still flows, and the cures continue."

I heard something nearby; it frightened me, but he didn't seem to notice. The fog now had a life and a story of its own. I was thinking about everything he had told me, and I wondered how he knew all of this.

I thought about the feminine face of God. The man at my side had a soul filled with conflict. A short time ago, he had written to me that he wanted to enter a Catholic seminary, yet now he was thinking that God has a feminine face.

He was silent. I still felt as if I were in the womb of the Earth Mother, beyond time and place.

"There were two important things that Bernadette didn't know," he finally said. "The first was that prior to the arrival of the Christian religion in these parts, these mountains were inhabited by Celts—and the Goddess was their principal object of devotion. Generations and generations had understood the feminine face of God and shared in Her love and Her glory."

"And the second thing?"

"The second was that a short time before Bernadette experienced her visions, the authorities at the Vatican had met in secret. Virtually no one knew what had occurred at those meetings—and there's no question but that the priest in the small village didn't have the slightest idea. The highest council of the Catholic Church was deciding whether they should ratify the dogma regarding the Immaculate Conception.

"The dogma wound up being ratified, through the papal bull known as *Ineffabilis Deus*. But the general public never knew exactly what this meant."

"And what do you have to do with all this?" I asked.

"I am Her disciple. I have learned through Her." He seemed to be saying that She was the source of all his knowledge.

"You have seen Her?"

"Yes."

ɩ̃ ɩ̃ ɩ̃

WE RETURNED to the plaza and walked toward the church. I saw the well in the lamplight, with the bottle of wine and two glasses on its wall. *A couple of sweethearts must have been here,* I think. *Silent, allowing their hearts to speak to each other. And after their hearts had said all they had to say, they began to share the great mysteries.*

I felt that I was facing something quite serious and that I needed to learn everything I could from my experiences. For a few moments, I thought about my studies, about Zaragoza, and about the man I was hoping to find in my life—but all that seemed far away, clouded by the mists over Saint-Savin.

"Why did you tell me the story of Bernadette?" I asked.

"I don't know why exactly," he answered, without looking at me directly. "Maybe because we're not too far from Lourdes. Maybe because the day after tomorrow is the day of the Immaculate Conception. Or maybe it was because I wanted to show you that my world is not so solitary and mad as it may appear. There are others who are part of that world, and they believe in what they say."

"I never said that your world is mad. Maybe it's mine that's crazy. I mean, here I am, spending the most crucial time of my life concentrating on textbooks and courses that won't help me at all to escape from the place I already know too well."

I sensed that he was relieved that I understood him. I expected him to say something more about the Goddess, but instead he turned to me and said, "Let's get some sleep. We've had a lot to drink."

Tuesday, December 7, 1993

He went straight to sleep, but I was awake for a long time, thinking about the fog, the wine, and our conversation. I read the manuscript he gave me, and what was in it thrilled me: God—if God really existed —was both Father and Mother.

Later, I turned out the light and lay there thinking. When we were quiet with each other, I was able to see how close I felt to him.

Neither of us had said anything. Love doesn't need to be discussed; it has its own voice and speaks for itself. That night, by the well, the silence had allowed our hearts to approach each other and get to know each other better. My heart had listened closely to what his had said, and now it was content.

Before I fell asleep, I decided I would do what he called the "exercise of the Other."

I am here in this room, I thought, *far from everything familiar to me, talking about things that have never interested me and sleeping in a city where I've never set foot before. I can pretend—at least for a few minutes—that I am different.*

I began to imagine how I would like to be living right at that moment. I wanted to be happy, curious, joyful—living every moment intensely, drinking the water of life thirstily. Believing again in my dreams. Able to fight for what I wanted.

Loving a man who loved me.

Yes, that was the woman I wanted to be—the woman who was suddenly presenting herself and becoming me.

I felt that my soul was bathed in the light of a god—or of a goddess—in whom I had lost faith. And I felt that at that moment, the Other left my body and was standing in the corner of that small room.

I observed the woman I had been up until then: weak but trying to give the impression of strength. Fearful of everything but telling herself it wasn't fear—it was the wisdom of someone who knew what reality was. Putting up shutters in front of windows to keep the joy of the sun from entering—just so the sun's rays wouldn't fade my old furniture.

I looked at the Other, there in the corner of the room—fragile, exhausted, disillusioned. Controlling and enslaving what should really be free: her emotions. Trying to judge her future loves by the rules of her past suffering.

But love is always new. Regardless of whether we love once, twice, or a dozen times in our life, we always face a brand-new situation. Love can consign us to hell or to paradise, but it always takes us somewhere. We simply have to accept it, because it is what nourishes our existence. If we reject it, we die of hunger, because we lack the courage to stretch out a hand and pluck the fruit from the branches of the tree of life. We have to take love where we find it, even if that means hours, days, weeks of disappointment and sadness.

The moment we begin to seek love, love begins to seek us.

And to save us.

When the Other left me, my heart once again began to speak to me. It told me that the breach in the dike had allowed the waters to pour through, that the wind was blowing in all directions at once, and that it was happy because I was once again willing to listen to what it had to say.

My heart told me that I was in love. And I fell asleep with a smile on my lips.

When I awoke, the window was open and he was gazing at the mountains in the distance. I watched him without saying anything, ready to close my eyes if he turned toward me.

As if he knew, he turned and looked at me.

"Good morning," he said.

"Good morning. Close the window—it's so cold."

The Other had appeared with no warning. It was still trying to change the direction of the wind, to detect shortcomings, to say, No, that's impossible. But it knew it was too late.

"I have to get dressed," I said.

"I'll wait for you downstairs."

I got up, banished the Other from my thoughts, opened the window again, and let the sun in. Its light bathed everything—the mountains with their snow-covered peaks, the ground blanketed in dry leaves, and the river, which I could hear but not see.

The sun shone on me, warming my nude body. I was no longer cold—I was consumed by a heat, the heat of a spark becoming a flame, the flame becoming a bonfire, the bonfire becoming an inferno. I knew.

I wanted this.

I also knew that from this moment on I was going to experience heaven and hell, joy and pain, dreams and hopelessness; that I would no longer be capable of containing the winds that blew from the hidden corners of my soul. I knew that from this moment on love would be my guide—and that it had waited to lead me ever since childhood, when I had felt love for the first time. The truth is, I had never forgotten love, even when it had deemed me unworthy of fighting for it. But love had been difficult, and I had been reluctant to cross its frontiers.

I recalled the plaza in Soria and the moment when I had asked him to find the medal I had lost. I had known what he was going to tell me, and I hadn't wanted to hear it, because he was the type who would someday go off in search of wealth, adventure, and dreams. I needed a love that was possible.

I realized that I had known nothing of love before. When I saw him at the conference and accepted his invitation, I'd thought that I, as a mature woman, would be able to control the heart of the girl who had been looking for so long for her prince. Then he had spoken about the child in all of us—and I'd heard again the voice of the child I had been, of the princess who was fearful of loving and losing.

For four days, I had tried to ignore my heart's voice, but it had grown louder and louder, and the Other had become desperate. In the furthest corner of my soul, my true self still existed, and I still believed in my dreams. Before the Other could say a word, I had accepted the ride with him. I had accepted the invitation to travel with him and to take the risks involved.

And because of that—because of that small part of me that had survived—love had finally found me, after it had looked for me everywhere. Love had found me, despite the barricade that the Other had built across a quiet street in Zaragoza, a barricade of preconceived ideas, stubborn opinions, and textbooks.

I opened the window and my heart. The sun flooded the room, and love inundated my soul.

❦ ❦ ❦

We wandered for hours, through the snow and along the roads. We breakfasted in a village whose name I never found out but in whose central plaza a dramatic fountain sculpture displayed a serpent and a dove combined into a single fabulous creature.

He smiled when he saw it. "It's a sign—masculine and feminine joined in a single figure."

"I'd never thought before about what you told me yesterday," I said. "But it makes sense."

"'And God created man and woman,'" he quoted from Genesis, "because that was his image and simulacrum: man and woman."

I noted a new gleam in his eye. He was happy and laughed at every silly thing. He fell into easy conversation with the few people we met along the way—workers dressed in gray on their way to the fields, adventurers in colorful gear, preparing to climb a mountain peak. I said little—my French is awful—but my soul rejoiced at seeing him this way.

His joy made everyone who spoke with him smile. Perhaps his heart had spoken to him, and now he knew that I loved him—even though I was still behaving like just an old friend.

"You seem happier," I said at one point.

"Because I've always dreamed of being here with you, walking through these mountains and harvesting the 'golden fruits of the sun.'"

The golden fruits of the sun—a verse written ages ago, repeated by him now, at just the right moment.

"There's another reason you're happy," I said, as we left the small village with the strange statue.

"What's that?"

"You know that I'm happy. You're responsible for my being here today, climbing the mountains of truth, far from my mountains of notebooks and texts. You're making me happy. And happiness is something that multiplies when it is divided."

"Did you do the exercise of the Other?"

"Yes. How did you know?"

"Because you've changed too. And because we always learn that exercise at the right time."

The Other pursued me all through the morning. Every minute, though, its voice grew fainter, and its image seemed to dissolve. It reminded me of those vampire films where the monster crumbles into dust.

We passed another column with an image of the Virgin on the cross.

"What are you thinking about?" he asked me.

"About vampires. Those creatures of the night, locked inside themselves, desperately seeking company. Incapable of loving."

"That's why legend has it that only a stake through the heart can kill them; when that happens, the heart bursts, freeing the energy of love and destroying the evil."

"I never thought of that before. But it makes sense."

I had succeeded in burying the stake. My heart, freed of all its curses, was aware of everything. The Other no longer had a place to call its own.

A thousand times I wanted to take his hand, and a thousand times I stopped myself. I was still confused—I wanted to tell him I loved him, but I didn't know how to begin.

We talked about the mountains and the rivers. We were lost in a forest for almost an hour, but eventually we found the path again. We ate sandwiches and drank melted snow. When the sun began to set, we decided to return to Saint-Savin.

THE SOUND of our footsteps echoed from the stone walls. At the entrance to the church, I instinctively dipped my hand in the font of holy water and made the sign of the cross. I recalled that water was the symbol of the Goddess.

"Let's go in," he suggested.

We walked through the dark, empty building. Saint Savin, a hermit who had lived at the start of the first millennium, was buried below the main altar. The walls of the place were crumbling and had clearly been reconstructed several times.

Some places are like that: they can suffer through wars, persecutions, and indifference, but they still remain sacred. Finally someone comes along, senses that something is missing, and rebuilds them.

I noticed an image of the crucified Christ that gave me a funny feeling—I had the impression that his head was moving, following me.

"Let's stop here."

We were before an altar of Our Lady.

"Look at the image."

Mary, with her son in her lap. The infant Jesus pointing to the heavens.

"Look more carefully," he said.

I studied the details of the wooden carving: the gilt paint, the pedestal, the perfection with which the artist had traced the folds of the robe. But it was when I focused on the finger of the child Jesus that I understood what he meant.

Although Mary held him in her arms, it was Jesus who was supporting her. The child's arm, raised to the sky, appeared to be lifting the Virgin toward heaven, back to the place of Her Groom's abode.

"The artist who created this more than six hundred years ago knew what he wanted to convey," he commented.

Footsteps sounded on the wooden floor. A woman entered and lit a candle in front of the main altar.

We remained silent for a while, respecting her moment of prayer.

Love never comes just a little at a time, I thought, as I watched him, absorbed in contemplation of the Virgin. The previous day, the world had made sense, even without love's presence. But now we needed each other in order to see the true brilliance of things.

When the woman had gone, he spoke again. "The artist knew the Great Mother, the Goddess, and the sympathetic face of God. You've asked me a question that up until now I haven't been able to answer directly. It was 'Where did you learn all this?'"

Yes, I had asked him that, and he had already answered me. But I didn't say so.

"Well, I learned in the same way that this artist did: I accepted love from on high. I allowed myself to be guided," he went on. "You must remember the letter I wrote you, when I spoke of wanting to enter a monastery. I never told you, but I did in fact do that."

I immediately remembered the conversation we'd had before the conference in Bilbao. My heart began to beat faster, and I tried to fix my gaze on the Virgin. She was smiling.

It can't be, I thought. *You entered and then you left. Please, tell me that you left the monastery.*

"I had already lived some pretty wild years," he said, not guessing my thoughts this time. "I got to see other peoples and other lands. I had already looked for God in the four corners of the earth. I had fallen in love with other women and worked in a number of different jobs."

Another stab. I would have to be careful that the Other didn't return. I kept my gaze on the Virgin's smile.

"The mysteries of life fascinated me, and I wanted to understand them better. I looked for signs that would tell me that someone knew something. I went to India and to Egypt. I sat with masters of magic and of meditation. And finally I discovered what I was looking for: that truth resides where there is faith."

Truth resides where there is faith! I looked around again at the interior of the church—the worn stones, fallen and replaced so many times. What had made human beings so insistent? What had caused them to work so hard at rebuilding this small temple in such a remote spot, hidden in the mountains?

Faith.

"The Buddhists were right, the Hindus were right, the Muslims were right, and so were the Jews. Whenever someone follows the path to faith—sincerely follows it—he or she is able to unite with God and to perform miracles.

"But it wasn't enough simply to know that—you have to make a choice. I chose the Catholic Church because I was raised in it, and my childhood had been impregnated with its mysteries. If I had been born Jewish, I would have chosen Judaism. God is the same, even though He has a thousand names; it is up to us to select a name for Him."

Once again, steps sounded in the church.

❦ ❦ ❦

A MAN APPROACHED and stared at us. Then he turned to the center altar and reached for the two candelabra. He must have been the one responsible for guarding the church.

I remembered the watchman at the other chapel, the man who wouldn't allow us to enter. But this man said nothing.

"I have a meeting tonight," he said when the man left.

"Please, go on with what you were saying. Don't change the subject."

"I entered a monastery close to here. For four years, I studied everything I could. During that time, I made contact with the Clarifieds and the Charismatics, the sects that have been trying to open doors that have been closed for so long to certain spiritual experiences. I discovered that God was not the ogre that had frightened me as a child. There was a movement afoot for a return to the original innocence of Christianity."

"You mean that after two thousand years, they finally understood that it was time to allow Jesus to become a part of the church?" I said with some sarcasm.

"You may think you're joking, but that was exactly it. I began to study with one of the superiors at the monastery. He taught me that we have to accept the fire of revelation, the Holy Spirit."

The Virgin continued to smile, and the infant Jesus kept his joyful expression, but my heart stopped when he said that. I too had believed in that once—but time, age, and the feeling that I was a logical and practical person had distanced me from religion. I realized how much I wanted to recover my childhood faith, when I had believed in angels and miracles. But I couldn't possibly bring it back simply through an act of will.

"The superior told me that if I believed that I knew, then I would in fact eventually know," he continued. "I began to talk to myself when I was in my cell. I prayed that the Holy Spirit would manifest itself and teach me what I needed to know. Little by little, I discovered that as I talked to myself, a wiser voice was saying things for me."

"That's happened to me, too," I interrupted him.

He waited for me to go on. But I couldn't say anything else.

"I'm listening," he said.

Something had stopped my tongue. He was speaking so beautifully, and I couldn't express myself nearly as well.

"The Other wants to come back," he said, as if he had guessed what I was thinking. "The Other is always afraid of saying something that might sound silly."

"Yes," I said, struggling to overcome my fear. "OK, sometimes when I'm talking with someone and get excited about what I'm saying, I find myself saying things I've never said before. It seems almost as if I'm 'channeling' an intelligence that isn't mine—one that understands life much better than me. But this is rare. In most conversations I prefer to listen. I always feel as if I'm learning something new, even though I wind up forgetting it all."

"We are our own greatest surprise," he said. "Faith as tiny as a grain of sand allows us to move mountains. That's what I've learned. And now, my own words sometimes surprise me.

"The apostles were fishermen, illiterate and ignorant. But they accepted the flame that fell from the heavens. They were not ashamed of their own ignorance; they had faith in the Holy Spirit. This gift is there for anyone who will accept it. One has only to believe, accept, and be willing to make mistakes."

The Virgin smiled down on me. She had every reason to cry—but She was joyful.

"Go on."

"That's all," he answered. "Accept the gift. And then the gift manifests itself."

"It doesn't work that way."

"Didn't you understand me?"

"I understand. But I'm like everyone else: I'm scared. It might work for you or for my neighbor, but never for me."

"That will change someday—when you begin to see that we are really just like that child there."

"But until then, we'll all go on thinking we've come close to the light, when actually we can't even light our own flame."

He didn't answer.

"You didn't finish your story about the seminary," I said.

"I'm still there."

Before I could react, he stood up and walked to the center of the church.

I stayed where I was. My head was spinning. *Still in the seminary?*

Better not to think about it. Love had flooded my soul, and there was no way I could control it. There was only one recourse:

the Other, with whom I had been harsh because I was weak, and cold because I was afraid—but I no longer wanted the Other. I could no longer look at life through its eyes.

A sharp, sustained sound like that of an immense flute interrupted my thoughts. My heart jumped.

The sound came again. And again. I looked behind me and saw a wooden staircase that led up to a crude platform, which didn't seem to fit with the frozen beauty of the church. On the platform was an ancient organ.

And there he was. I couldn't see his face because the lighting was bad—but I knew he was up there.

I stood up, and he called to me.

"Pilar!" he said, his voice full of emotion. "Stay where you are."

I obeyed.

"May the Great Mother inspire me," he said. "May this music be my prayer for the day."

And he began to play the Ave Maria. It must have been about six in the evening, time for the Angelus—a time when light and darkness merge. The sound of the organ echoed through the empty church, blending in my mind with the stones and the images laden with history and with faith. I closed my eyes and let the music flow through me, cleansing my soul of all fear and sin and reminding me that I am always better than I think and stronger than I believe.

For the first time since I had abandoned the path of faith, I felt a strong desire to pray. Although I was seated in a pew, my soul was kneeling at the feet of the Lady before me, the woman who had said,

"Yes,"

when She could have said "no." The angel would have sought out someone else, and there would have been no sin in the eyes of the Lord, because God knows His children's weakness.

But She had said,

"Thy will be done,"

even though She sensed that She was receiving, along with the words of the angel, all the pain and suffering of Her destiny; even though Her heart's eyes could see Her beloved son leaving the house, could see the people who would follow Him and then deny Him; but

"Thy will be done,"

even when, at the most sacred moment in a woman's life, She had to lie down with the animals in a stable to give birth, because that was what the Scriptures required;

"Thy will be done,"

even when, in agony, She looked through the streets for Her son and found Him at the temple. And He asked that She not interfere because He had other obligations and tasks to perform;

"Thy will be done,"

even when She knew that She would search for Him for the rest of Her days, Her heart filled with pain, fearing every moment for His life, knowing that He was being persecuted and threatened;

"Thy will be done,"

even when, finding Him in the crowd, She was unable to draw near Him;

"Thy will be done,"

even when She asked someone to tell Him that She was there and the son sent back the response, "My mother and my brothers are those who are here with me";

"Thy will be done,"

even when at the end, after everyone had fled, only She, another woman, and one of them stood at the foot of the cross, bearing the laughter of His enemies and the cowardice of His friends;

"Thy will be done."

Thy will be done, my Lord. Because you know the weakness in the heart of your children, and you assign each of them only the burden they can bear. May you understand my love—because it is the only thing I have that is really mine, the only thing that I will be able to take with me into the next life. Please allow it to be courageous and pure; please make it capable of surviving the snares of the world.

The organ stopped, and the sun went into hiding behind the mountains—as if both were ruled by the same Hand. The music had been his prayer, and his prayer had been heard. I opened my eyes and found the church in complete darkness, except for the solitary candle that illuminated the image of the Virgin.

I heard his footsteps again, returning to where I sat. The light of that single candle gleamed on my tears, and my smile—a smile that wasn't perhaps as beautiful as the Virgin's—showed that my heart was alive.

He looked at me, and I at him. My hand reached out for his and found it. Now it was his heart that was beating faster—I could almost hear it in the silence.

But my soul was serene, and my heart at peace.

I held his hand, and he embraced me. We stood there at the feet of the Virgin for I don't know how long. Time had stopped.

She looked down at us. The adolescent girl who had said "yes" to her destiny. The woman who had agreed to carry the son of God in Her womb and the love of God in Her heart. She understood.

I didn't want to ask for anything. That afternoon in the church had made the entire journey worthwhile. Those four days with him had made up for an entire year in which so little had happened.

We left the church hand in hand and walked back toward our room. My head was spinning—seminary, Great Mother, the meeting he had later that night.

I realized then that we both wanted to unite our souls under one destiny—but the seminary and Zaragoza stood in the way. My heart felt squeezed. I looked around at the medieval homes and the well where we had sat the previous night. I recalled the silence and the sadness of the Other, the woman I had once been.

God, I am trying to recover my faith. Please don't abandon me in the middle of this adventure, I prayed, pushing my fears aside.

HE SLEPT A LITTLE, but I stayed awake, looking out the darkened window. Later, we got up and dined with the family—they never spoke at the table. He asked for a key to the house.

"We'll be home late tonight," he said to the woman.

"Young people should enjoy themselves," she answered, "and take advantage of the holidays as best they can."

"I have to ask you something," I said, when we were back in the car. "I've been trying to avoid it, but I have to ask."

"The seminary," he said.

That's right. I don't understand. Even though it's no longer important, I thought.

"I have always loved you," he began. "I kept the medal, thinking that someday I would give it to you and that I'd have the courage to tell you that I love you. Every road I traveled led back to you. I wrote the letters to you and opened every letter of yours afraid that you would tell me you had found someone.

"Then I was called to the spiritual life. Or rather, I accepted the call, because it had been with me since childhood—just as it was for you. I discovered that God was extremely important to my life and that I couldn't be happy if I didn't accept my vocation. The face of Christ was there in the face of every poor soul I met on my travels, and I couldn't deny it."

He paused, and I decided not to push him.

Twenty minutes later, he stopped the car and we got out.

"This is Lourdes," he said. "You should see it during the summer."

What I saw now were deserted streets, closed shops, and hotels with bars across their entrances.

"Six million people come here in the summer," he went on enthusiastically.

"It looks like a ghost town to me."

We crossed a bridge and arrived at an enormous iron gate with angels on either side. One side of the gate was standing open, and we passed through it.

"Go on with what you were saying," I said, in spite of my decision not to pursue it. "Tell me about the face of Christ on the people you met."

I could see that he didn't want to continue the conversation. Perhaps this wasn't the right time or place. But having begun, he had to complete it.

We were walking down a broad avenue, bordered on both sides by snow-covered fields. At its end, I could see the silhouette of a cathedral.

"Go on," I repeated.

"You already know. I entered the seminary. During the first year, I asked that God help me to transform my love for you into a love for all people. In the second year, I sensed that God had heard me. By the third year, even though my longing for you was still strong, I became certain that my love was turning toward charity, prayer, and helping the needy."

"Then why did you seek me out? Why rekindle the flame in me? Why did you tell me about the exercise of the Other and force me to see how shallow my life is?" I sounded confused and tremulous. From one minute to the next, I could see him drawing closer to the seminary and further from me. "Why did you come back? Why wait until today to tell me this story, when you can see that I am beginning to love you?"

He did not answer immediately. Then he said, "You'll think it's stupid."

"I won't. I'm not worried anymore about seeming ridiculous. You've taught me that."

"Two months ago, my superior asked me to accompany him to the house of a woman who had died and left all her wealth to the seminary. She lived in Saint-Savin, and my superior had to prepare an inventory of what was there."

We were approaching the cathedral at the end of the avenue. My intuition told me that as soon as we reached it, any conversation we were having would be interrupted.

"Don't stop," I said. "I deserve an explanation."

"I remember the moment I stepped into that house. The windows looked out on the Pyrenees, and the whole scene was filled with the brightness of the sun, intensified by the snow's glare. I began to make a list of the things in the house, but after just a few minutes, I had to stop.

"I had discovered that the woman's taste was exactly the same as mine. She owned records that I would have purchased, the same music that I would have enjoyed listening to as I looked out on that beautiful landscape. Her bookshelves were filled with books I had already read and others that I would have loved to read. Looking at the furnishings, the paintings, and all her other possessions, I felt as if I had chosen them myself.

"From that day on, I couldn't forget that house. Every time I went to the chapel to pray, I realized that my renunciation had not been total. I imagined myself there with you, looking out at the snow on the mountaintops, a fire blazing in the hearth. I pictured our children running around the house and playing in the fields around Saint-Savin."

Although I had never been near the house, I knew exactly what it looked like. And I hoped he'd say nothing else so that I could fantasize.

But he went on.

"For the past two weeks, I haven't been able to stand the sadness in my soul. I went to my superior and told him what was happening to me. I told him about my love for you and what had begun when we were taking the inventory."

A light rain began to fall. I bowed my head and gathered the front of my coat. I suddenly didn't want to hear the rest of the story.

"So my superior said, 'There are many ways to serve our Lord. If you feel that's your destiny, go in search of it. Only a man who is happy can create happiness in others.'

"'I don't know if that's my destiny,' I told my superior. 'Peace came into my heart when I entered this seminary.'

"'Well, then, go there and resolve any doubts you may have,' he said. 'Remain out there in the world, or come back to the seminary. But you have to be committed to the place you choose. A divided kingdom cannot defend itself from its adversaries. A divided person cannot face life in a dignified way.'"

He pulled something from his pocket and handed it to me. It was a key.

"The superior loaned me the key to the house. He said that he would hold off for a while on selling the possessions. I know that he wants me to return to the seminary. But he was the one who arranged the presentation in Madrid—so that we could meet."

I looked at the key in my hand and smiled. In my heart, bells were ringing, and the heavens had opened to me. He could serve God in a different way—by my side. Because I was going to fight for that to happen.

I put the key in my bag.

❦ ❦ ❦

THE BASILICA LOOMED in front of us. Before I could say anything, someone spotted him and came toward us. The light rain continued, and I had no idea how long we would be there; I couldn't forget that I had only one set of clothes, and I didn't want them to get soaked.

I concentrated on that problem. I didn't want to think about the house—that was a matter suspended between heaven and earth, awaiting the hand of destiny.

He introduced me to several people who had gathered around. They asked where we were staying, and when he said Saint-Savin, one of them told us the story of the hermit saint who was buried there. It was Saint Savin who had discovered the well in the middle of the plaza—and the original mission of the village had been to create a refuge for religious persons who had left the city and come to the mountains in search of God.

"They are still living there," another said.

I didn't know if the story was true, nor did I have any idea who "they" were.

Other people began to arrive, and the group began to move toward the entrance of the grotto. An older man tried to tell me something in French. When he saw that I didn't understand, he switched to an awkward Spanish.

"You are with a very special man," he said. "A man who performs miracles."

I said nothing but remembered that night in Bilbao when a desperate man had come looking for him. He had told me nothing about where he had gone, and I hadn't asked. Right now, I preferred to think about the house, which I could picture perfectly—its books, its records, its view, its furniture.

Somewhere in the world, a home awaited us. A place where we could care for daughters or sons who would come home from school, fill the house with joy, and never pick up after themselves.

We walked in silence through the rain until finally we reached the place where the visions of Mary had occurred. It was exactly as I had imagined: the grotto, the statue of Our Lady, and the fountain—protected by glass—where the miracle of the water had taken place. Some pilgrims were praying; others were seated silently inside the grotto, their eyes closed. A river ran past the entrance, and the sound of the water made me feel at peace. As soon as I saw the image, I said a quick prayer, asking the Virgin to help me—my heart needed no more suffering.

If pain must come, may it come quickly. Because I have a life to live, and I need to live it in the best way possible. If he has to make a choice, may he make it now. Then I will either wait for him or forget him.

Waiting is painful. Forgetting is painful. But not knowing which to do is the worst kind of suffering.

In some corner of my heart, I felt that she had heard my plea.

Wednesday, December 8, 1993

BY THE TIME the cathedral's clock struck midnight, the group around us had grown considerably. We were almost a hundred people—some of them priests and nuns—standing in the rain, gazing at the statue.

"Hail, Our Lady of the Immaculate Conception," someone close to me said, as soon as the tolling of the bells ceased.

"Hail," everyone answered, with some applause.

A guard immediately came forward and asked that we be quiet. We were bothering the other pilgrims.

"But we've come a long way," said one of the men in our group.

"So have they," answered the guard, pointing to the others who were praying in the rain. "And they are praying silently."

I wanted to be alone with him, far from this place, holding his hand and telling him how I felt. We needed to talk more about the house, about our plans, about love. I wanted to reassure him, to make clear how strong my feelings were, and to let him know that his dream could come true—because I would be at his side, helping him.

The guard retreated, and one of the priests began to recite the rosary in a low voice. When we reached the creed that closes the series of prayers, everyone remained silent, their eyes closed.

"Who are these people?" I asked.

"Charismatics," he answered.

I had heard of them before but didn't know exactly what their name meant. He could see that I didn't understand.

"These are people who accept the fire of the Holy Spirit," he said, "the fire that Jesus left but that is used by so few people to light their candles. These people are very close to the original truth of Christianity, when everyone was capable of performing miracles.

"They are guided by the Woman Dressed by the Sun," he said, pointing with his eyes to the Virgin.

The group began to chant quietly, as if in response to an invisible command.

"You're shivering from the cold. You don't have to take part in this," he said.

"Are you going to stay?"

"Yes. This is my life."

"Then I'm going to participate," I answered, even though I would have preferred to be far from there. "If this is your world, I want to learn to be a part of it."

The group continued to sing. I closed my eyes and tried to

follow the words, even though I couldn't speak French. I repeated the words without understanding them. But their sound helped the time to pass more quickly.

It would end soon. And we could return to Saint-Savin, just the two of us.

I went on singing mechanically—but little by little, I began to feel the music taking hold of me, as if it had a life of its own. It was hypnotizing. The cold seemed less bitter, and the rain no longer bothered me. The music made me feel better. It transported me back to a time when God had felt closer to me and had helped me.

Just as I was about to surrender completely to the music, it stopped.

I opened my eyes. This time, instead of a guard, there was a priest. He approached one of the other priests in our group. They whispered to one another for a few moments, and the padre left.

Our priest turned to us. "We have to say our prayers on the other side of the river," he said.

❧ ❧ ❧

SILENTLY, WE WALKED across the bridge directly in front of the grotto and moved to the other bank. It was a prettier place, on the bank of the river, surrounded by trees and an open field. The river now separated us from the grotto. From there, we could clearly see the illuminated image, and we could sing loudly without disturbing others' prayers.

The people around me began to sing louder, raising their faces to the sky and smiling as the raindrops coursed down their cheeks. Some raised their arms, and soon everyone joined in, waving their arms from side to side in rhythm to the music.

I wanted to give in to the moment, but at the same time I wanted to pay close attention to what they were doing. One priest near me was singing in Spanish, and I tried to repeat the words. They were invocations to the Holy Spirit and the Virgin, requesting their presence and asking that they rain down their blessings and their powers on each of us.

"May the gift of tongues befall us," said another priest, repeating the phrase in Spanish, Italian, and French.

What happened next was incomprehensible. Each of the many people present began to speak a language that was different from any I had ever heard. It was more sound than speech, with words that seemed to come straight from the soul, making no sense at all. I recalled our conversation in the church, when he had spoken about revelations, saying that all wisdom was the result of listening to one's own soul. *Perhaps this is the language of the angels,* I thought, trying to mimic what they were doing—and feeling ridiculous.

Everyone was looking at the statue of the Virgin on the other side of the river; they all seemed to be in a trance. I looked around for him and found him standing at some distance from me. His hands were raised to the heavens and he was speaking rapidly, as if in conversation with Her. He was smiling and nodding his head as if in agreement; occasionally he looked surprised.

This is his world, I thought.

The whole scene began to scare me. The man I wanted at my side was telling me that God is also female, he was speaking an incomprehensible language, he was in a trance, and he seemed closer to the angels than to me. The house in the mountains began to seem less real, as if it were part of a world that he had already left behind.

All of our days together—starting with the conference in Madrid—seemed to be part of a dream, a voyage beyond the space and time of my life. At the same time, though, the dream had the flavor of the world, of romance, and of new adventures. I had tried to resist; now I knew how easily love could set fire to the heart. I had tried to stay unreceptive to all of this in the beginning; now I felt that since I had loved before, I would know how to handle it.

I looked around again, and it dawned on me that this was not the Catholicism I had been taught at school. And this was not the way I had pictured the man in my life.

A man in my life! How strange! I said to myself, surprised at the thought.

There on the bank of the river, looking across at the grotto, I felt both fear and jealousy. Fear because it was all new to me, and what is new has always scared me. Jealousy because, bit by bit, I could see that his love was greater than I'd thought and spread over places where I'd never set foot.

Forgive me, Our Lady. Forgive me if I'm being selfish or small-minded, competing with you for this man's love.

But what if his vocation wasn't to be with me but was to retreat from the world, locking himself in a seminary and conversing with angels? How long would he resist before he fled from our house to return to his true path? Or even if he never went back to the seminary, what price would I have to pay to keep him from returning to that path?

Everyone there, except me, seemed to be concentrating on what they were doing. I was staring at him, and he was speaking the language of the angels.

Suddenly, fear and jealousy were replaced by calm and solitude. The angels had someone to talk with, and I was alone.

I had no idea what pushed me into trying to speak that strange language. Perhaps it was my strong need to connect with him, to tell him what I was feeling. Perhaps I needed to let my soul speak to me—my heart had so many doubts and needed so many answers.

I didn't know exactly what to do, and I felt ridiculous. But all around me were men and women of all ages, priests and laypeople, novices and nuns, students and old-timers. They gave me the courage to ask the Holy Spirit for the strength to overcome my fear.

Try, I said to myself. *All you have to do is open your mouth and have the courage to say things you don't understand. Try!*

I prayed that this night—the night following a day that had been so long that I couldn't even remember how it had begun—would be an epiphany. A new beginning for me.

God must have heard me. The words began to come more easily—and little by little they lost their everyday meanings. My embarrassment diminished, my confidence grew, and the words began to flow freely. Although I understood nothing of what I was saying, it all made sense to my soul.

Simply having the courage to say senseless things made me euphoric. I was free, with no need to seek or to give explanations for what I was doing. This freedom lifted me to the heavens—where a greater love, one that forgives everything and never allows you to feel abandoned, once again enveloped me.

It feels as if my faith is coming back, I thought, surprised at the miracles that love can perform. I sensed that the Virgin was holding me in her lap, covering me and warming me with her mantle. The strange words flew more rapidly from my lips.

Without realizing it, I began to cry. Joy flooded my heart—a joy that overpowered my fears and was stronger than my attempts to control every second of my life.

I realized that my tears were a gift; at school, the sisters had taught me that the saints wept with ecstasy. I opened my eyes, gazed at the darkness of the heavens, and felt my tears blending with the raindrops. The earth was alive and the drops from above brought the miracles of heaven with them. We were all a part of that same miracle.

How wonderful that God may be a woman, I said to myself, as the others continued to chant. *If that's true, then it was certainly God's feminine face that taught us how to love.*

"Let us pray in tents of eight," said the priest in Spanish, Italian, and French.

Once again, I was confused. What was happening? Someone came over to me and put his arm around my shoulders. Another person did the same on my other side. We formed a circle of eight people, arms around each other's shoulders. Then we leaned forward, our heads touching.

We looked like a human tent. The rain fell harder, but no one cared. The position we had taken concentrated all our energies and heat.

"May the Immaculate Conception help my child find his way," said the man embracing me from the right. "Please, let's say an Ave Maria for my child."

"Amen," everyone said. And we eight prayed an Ave Maria.

"May the Immaculate Conception enlighten me and arouse in me the gift of curing," said a woman from our circle. "Let us say an Ave Maria."

Again, all of us said "Amen" and we prayed. Each person

made a petition, and everyone participated in the prayers. I was surprised at myself, because I was praying like a child—and like a child, I believed that our prayers would be answered.

The group fell silent for a fraction of a second. I realized that it was my turn to make a petition. Under any other circumstances, I would have died of embarrassment and been unable to say a word. But I felt a presence, and that presence gave me confidence.

"May the Immaculate Conception teach me to love as she loves," I finally said. "May that love grow in me and in the man to whom it is dedicated. Let us say an Ave Maria."

We prayed together, and again I felt a sense of freedom. For years, I had fought against my heart, because I was afraid of sadness, suffering, and abandonment. But now I knew that true love was above all that and that it would be better to die than to fail to love.

I had thought that only others had the courage to love. But now I discovered that I too was capable of loving. Even if loving meant leaving, or solitude, or sorrow, love was worth every penny of its price.

I have to stop thinking of these things. I have to concentrate on the ritual.

The priest leading the group asked that we disband the tents and pray for the sick. Everyone continued to pray, sing, and dance in the rain, adoring God and the Virgin Mary. Now and then, people went back to speaking strange languages, waving their arms, and pointing to the sky.

"Someone here . . . someone who has a sick daughter-in-law . . . must know that she is being cured," cried one woman.

The prayers resumed, along with chants of joy. From time to time, we would hear the voice of this woman again.

"Someone in this group who lost her mother recently must have faith and know that she is in the glory of heaven."

Later, he would tell me that she had the gift of prophecy, that certain individuals can sense what is happening at some distant place or what will happen in the future.

Secretly, I too believed in the power of that voice that was speaking of miracles. I hoped that voice would speak of the love between two of those present. I hoped to hear that voice proclaim that this love was blessed by all the angels and saints—and by God and by the Goddess.

I'M NOT SURE how long the ritual lasted. People continued to speak in tongues and to chant; they danced with their arms held up to the sky, prayed for the people around them, and petitioned for miracles.

Finally, the priest who was conducting the ceremony said, "Let us chant a prayer for all of those here who are participating for the first time in a Charismatic renewal."

Apparently I was not the only one. That made me feel better.

Everyone chanted a prayer. This time I just listened, asking that favors be granted to me.

I needed many.

"Let us receive the blessing," said the priest.

The crowd turned toward the illuminated grotto across the river. The priest said several prayers and blessed us all. Then everyone kissed, wished each other a "Happy Day of the Immaculate Conception," and went their separate ways.

He came to me. His expression was happier than usual.

"You're soaked," he said.

"So are you!" I laughed.

We walked back to the car and drove to Saint-Savin. I'd been so eager for this moment to arrive—but now that it was here, I didn't know what to say. I couldn't even bring myself to talk about the house in the mountains, the ritual, the strange languages, or the tent prayers.

He was living in two worlds. Somewhere, those two worlds intersected—and I had to find where that was.

But at that moment, words were useless. Love can only be found through the act of loving.

"I've only got one sweater left," he said when we reached the room. "You can have it. I'll buy another for myself tomorrow."

"We'll put our wet things on the heater. They'll be dry by tomorrow. Anyway, I've got the blouse that I washed yesterday."

Neither of us said anything for a few minutes.

Clothing. Nakedness. Cold.

Finally, he took another shirt out of his bag. "You can sleep in this," he said.

"Great," I answered.

I turned out the light. In the dark, I took off my wet clothes, spread them over the heater, and turned it to high.

By the light from the lamppost outside the window, he must have been able to make out my silhouette and known that I was naked. I slipped the shirt on and crawled under the covers.

"I love you," I heard him say.

"I'm learning how to love you."

He lit a cigarette. "Do you think the right moment will come?" he asked.

I knew what he meant. I got up and sat on the edge of his bed.

The light from his cigarette illuminated our faces. He took my hand and we sat there for some time. I ran my fingers through his hair.

"You shouldn't have asked," I said. "Love doesn't ask many questions, because if we stop to think we become fearful. It's an inexplicable fear; it's difficult even to describe it. Maybe it's the fear of being scorned, of not being accepted, or of breaking the spell. It's ridiculous, but that's the way it is. That's why you don't ask—you act. As you've said many times, you have to take risks."

"I know. I've never asked before."

"You already have my heart," I told him. "Tomorrow you may go away, but we will always remember the miracle of these few days. I think that God, in Her infinite wisdom, conceals hell in the midst of paradise—so that we will always be alert, so that we won't forget the pain as we experience the joy of compassion."

He took my face in his hands. "You learn quickly," he said.

I had surprised myself. But sometimes if you think you know something, you do wind up understanding it.

"I hope you won't think I'm being difficult," I said. "I have been with many men. I've made love to some I've barely known."

"Same here," he said.

He was trying to sound natural, but from his touch, I could tell that he hadn't wanted to hear this from me.

"But since this morning, I feel as if I'm rediscovering love. Don't try to understand it, because only a woman would know what I mean. And it takes time."

He caressed my face. Then I kissed him lightly on the lips and returned to my bed.

I wasn't sure why I did. Was I trying to bind him even closer to me, or was I trying to set him free? In any case, it had been a long day, and I was too tired to think about it.

For me, that was a night of great peace. At one point, I seemed to be awake even though I was still sleeping. A feminine presence cradled me in Her lap; I felt as if I had known Her a long time. I felt protected and loved.

I woke at seven, dying of the heat. I remembered having turned the heater to high in order to dry my clothes. It was still dark, and I tried to get up without making a sound so that I wouldn't disturb him.

But as soon as I stood, I could see that he wasn't there.

I started to panic. The Other immediately awoke and said to me, "See? You agreed, and he disappeared. Like all men do."

My panic was increasing by the minute, but I didn't want to lose control. "I'm still here," the Other said. "You allowed the wind to change direction. You opened the door, and now love is flooding your life. If we act quickly, we'll be able to regain control."

I had to be practical, to take precautions.

"He's gone," said the Other. "You have to get away from this place in the middle of nowhere. Your life in Zaragoza is still intact; get back there quickly—before you lose everything you've worked so hard to gain."

He must have had some good reason, I thought.

"Men always have their reasons," said the Other. "But the fact is that they always wind up leaving."

Well, then, I had to figure out how to get back to Spain. I had to keep my wits about me.

"Let's start with the practical problem: money," the Other said.

I didn't have a cent. I would have to go downstairs, call my parents collect, and wait for them to wire me the money for a ticket home.

But it was a holiday, and the money wouldn't arrive until the next day. How would I eat? How would I explain to the owners of the house that they would have to wait for several days for their payment? "Better not to say anything," said the Other.

Right, she was the experienced one. She knew how to handle situations like this. She wasn't the impassioned girl who loses control of herself. She was the woman who always knew what she wanted in life. I should simply stay on there, as if he were expected to return. And when the money arrived, I would pay the bill and leave.

"Very good," said the Other. "You're getting back to how you were before. Don't be sad. One of these days, you'll find another man—one you can love without taking so many risks."

I gathered my clothes from the heater. They were dry. I needed to find out which of the surrounding villages had a bank, make a phone call, take steps. If I thought carefully about all of that, there wouldn't be time for crying or regrets.

Then I saw his note:

I've gone to the seminary. Pack up your things, because we're going back to Spain tonight. I'll be back by late afternoon. I love you.

I clutched the note to my breast, feeling miserable and relieved at the same time. I noticed that the Other had retreated.

I loved him. With every minute that passed, my love was growing and transforming me. I once again had faith in the future, and little by little, I was recovering my faith in God. All because of love.

I will not talk to my own darkness anymore, I promised myself, closing the door on the Other. *A fall from the third floor hurts as much as a fall from the hundredth.*

If I have to fall, may it be from a high place.

❦ ❦ ❦

"DON'T GO OUT hungry again," said the woman.

"I didn't realize you spoke Spanish," I answered, surprised.

"The border isn't far from here. Tourists come to Lourdes in the summer. If I couldn't speak Spanish, I couldn't rent rooms."

She made me some toast and coffee. I was already trying to prepare myself to make it through the day—each hour was going to seem like a year. I hoped that this snack would distract me for a while.

"How long have you two been married?" she asked.

"He was the first person I ever loved," I said. That was enough.

"Do you see those peaks out there?" the woman continued. "The first love of my life died up in those mountains."

"But you found someone else."

"Yes, I did. And I found happiness again. Fate is strange: almost no one I know married the first love of their lives. Those who did are always telling me that they missed something important, that they didn't experience all that they might have."

She stopped talking suddenly. "I'm sorry," she said. "I didn't mean to offend you."

"I'm not offended."

"I always look at that well there in the plaza. And I think to myself that before, no one knew where there was water. Then Saint Savin decided to dig and found it. If he hadn't done that, this village would be down there by the river."

"But what does that have to do with love?" I asked.

"That well brought many people here, with their hopes and dreams and conflicts. Someone dared to look for water, water was found, and people gathered where it flowed. I think that when we look for love courageously, it reveals itself, and we wind up attracting even more love. If one person really wants us, everyone does. But if we're alone, we become even more alone. Life is strange."

"Have you ever heard of the book called the *I Ching?*" I asked her.

"No, I haven't."

"It says that a city can be moved but not a well. It's around the well that lovers find each other, satisfy their thirst, build their homes, and raise their children. But if one of them decides to leave, the well cannot go with them. Love remains there, abandoned—even though it is filled with the same pure water as before."

"You speak like a mature woman who has already suffered a great deal, my dear," she said.

"No. I've always been frightened. I've never dug a well. But I'm trying to do that now, and I don't want to forget what the risks are."

I felt something in the pocket of my bag pressing at me. When I realized what it was, my heart went cold. I quickly finished my coffee.

The key. I had the key.

"There was a woman in this city who died and left everything to the seminary at Tarbes," I said. "Do you know where her house is?"

The woman opened the door and showed me. It was one of the medieval houses on the plaza. The back of the house looked out over the valley toward the mountains in the distance.

"Two priests went through the house about two months ago," she said. "And . . ." She stopped, looking at me doubtfully. "And one of them looked a lot like your husband."

"It was," I answered. The woman stood in her doorway, puzzled, as I quickly left. I felt a burst of energy, happy that I had allowed the child in me to pull a prank.

I soon stood in front of the house, not knowing what to do. The mist was everywhere, and I felt as if I were in a gray dream where strange figures might appear and take me away to places even more peculiar.

I toyed nervously with the key.

With the mist as thick as it was, it would be impossible to see the mountains from the window. The house would be dark; there would be no sun shining through the curtains. The house would seem sad without him at my side.

I looked at my watch. Nine in the morning.

I had to do something—something that would make the time pass, that would help me wait.

Wait. This was the first lesson I had learned about love. The day drags along, you make thousands of plans, you imagine every possible conversation, you promise to change your behavior in certain ways—and you feel more and more anxious until your loved one arrives. But by then, you don't know what to say. The hours of waiting have been transformed into tension, the tension has become fear, and the fear makes you embarrassed about showing affection.

I didn't know whether I should go in. I remembered our conversation of the previous day—the house was the symbol of a dream.

But I couldn't spend the whole day just standing there. I gathered up my courage, grasped the key firmly, and walked to the door.

PILAR!"

The voice, with a strong French accent, came from the midst of the fog. I was more surprised than frightened. I thought it might be the owner of the house where we had rented the room—although I didn't recall having told him my name.

"Pilar!" I heard again, nearer this time.

I looked back at the plaza shrouded in mist. A figure was approaching, walking hurriedly. Perhaps the ghosts that I had imagined in the fog were becoming a reality.

"Wait," the figure said. "I want to talk to you."

When he had come closer, I could see that it was a priest. He looked like a caricature of the country padre: short, on the heavy side, with sparse white hair on a nearly bald head.

"Hola," he said, holding out his hand and smiling.

I answered him, a bit astonished.

"Too bad the fog is hiding everything," he said, looking toward the house. "Since Saint-Savin is in the mountains, the view from this house is beautiful; you can see the valley down below and the snow-covered peaks. But you probably already knew that."

I decided that this must be the superior from the monastery.

"What are you doing here?" I asked. "And how do you know my name?"

"Do you want to go in?" he said, trying to change the subject.

"No! I'd like you to answer my questions."

Rubbing his hands together to warm them, he sat down on

the curb. I sat down next to him. The fog was growing thicker by the minute. The church was already hidden from sight, and it was only sixty feet away from us.

All I could see was the well. I remembered what the young woman in Madrid had said.

"She is present," I said.

"Who?"

"The Goddess," I answered. "She is this mist."

"So, he must have talked to you about that," he laughed. "Well, I prefer to refer to Her as the Virgin Mary. That's what I'm used to."

"What are you doing here? How do you know my name?" I repeated.

"I came here because I wanted to see you two. A member of the Charismatic group last night told me you were both staying in Saint-Savin. And it's a small place."

"He went to the seminary."

The padre's smile disappeared, and he shook his head. "Too bad," he said, as if speaking to himself.

"You mean, too bad he went to the seminary?"

"No, he's not there. I've just come from the seminary."

For a moment, I couldn't say anything. I thought back to the feeling I'd had when I woke up: the money, the arrangements I needed to make, the call to my parents, the ticket. But I'd made a vow, and I wasn't going to break it.

A priest was sitting beside me. As a child, I used to tell everything to our priest.

"I'm exhausted," I said, breaking the silence. "Less than a week ago, I finally learned who I am and what I want in life. Now I feel like I've been caught in a storm that's tossing me around, and I can't seem to do anything about it."

"Resist your doubts," the padre said. "It's important."

His advice surprised me.

"Don't be frightened," he continued, as if he knew what I was feeling. "I know that the church is in need of new priests, and he would be an excellent one. But the price he would have to pay would be very high."

"Where is he? Did he leave me here to return to Spain?"

"To Spain? There's nothing for him to do in Spain," said the priest. "His home is at the monastery, only a few kilometers from here. He's not there. But I know where we can find him."

His words brought back some of my joy and courage—at least he hadn't gone away.

But the priest was no longer smiling. "Don't let that encourage you," he went on, again reading my mind. "It would be better if he *had* gone back to Spain."

He stood and asked me to go with him. We could see only a few yards in front of us, but he seemed to know where he was going. We left Saint-Savin by the same road along which, two nights before—or could it have been five years before?—I had heard the story of Bernadette.

"Where are we going?" I asked.

"To find him," he answered.

"Padre, you've confused me," I said, as we walked along together. "You seemed sad when you said he wasn't at the seminary."

"Tell me what you know about the religious life, my child."

"Very little. Only that the priests take a vow of poverty, chastity, and obedience." I wondered whether I should go on and decided that I would. "And that they judge the sins of others, even though they may commit the same sins themselves. That they know all there is to know about marriage and love, but they never marry. That they threaten us with the fires of hell for mistakes that they themselves make. And they present God to us as a vengeful being who blames man for the death of His only Son."

The padre laughed. "You've had an excellent Catholic education," he said. "But I'm not asking you about Catholicism. I'm asking about the spiritual life."

I didn't respond for a moment. "I'm not sure. There are people who leave everything behind and go in search of God."

"And do they find Him?"

"Well, you would know the answer to that, Padre. I have no idea."

The padre noticed that I was beginning to gasp with exertion, and he slowed his pace.

"You had that wrong," he said. "A person who goes in search of God is wasting his time. He can walk a thousand roads and join many religions and sects—but he'll never find God that way.

"God is here, right now, at our side. We can see Him in this mist, in the ground we're walking on, even in my shoes. His angels keep watch while we sleep and help us in our work. In order to find God, you have only to look around.

"But meeting Him is not easy. The more God asks us to participate in His mysteries, the more disoriented we become, because He asks us constantly to follow our dreams and our hearts. And that's difficult to do when we're used to living in a different way.

"Finally we discover, to our surprise, that God wants us to be happy, because He is the father."

"And the mother," I said.

The fog was beginning to clear. I could see a small farmhouse where a woman was gathering hay.

"Yes, and the mother," he said. "In order to have a spiritual life, you need not enter a seminary, or fast, or abstain, or take a vow of chastity. All you have to do is have faith and accept God. From then on, each of us becomes a part of His path. We become a vehicle for His miracles."

"He has already told me about you," I interrupted, "and he has taught me these ideas."

"I hope that you accept God's gifts," he answered. "Because it hasn't always been that way, as history teaches us. Osiris was drawn and quartered in Egypt. The Greek gods battled because of the mortals on earth. The Aztecs expelled Quetzalcoatl. The Viking gods witnessed the burning of Valhalla because of a woman. Jesus was crucified. Why?"

I didn't have an answer.

"Because God came to earth to demonstrate His power to us. We are a part of His dream, and He wants His dream to be a happy one. Thus, if we acknowledge that God created us for happiness, then we have to assume that everything that leads to sadness and defeat is our own doing. That's the reason we always kill God, whether on the cross, by fire, through exile, or simply in our hearts."

"But those who understand Him . . ."

"They are the ones who transform the world—while making great sacrifices."

The woman carrying the hay saw the priest and came running in our direction. "Padre, thank you!" she said, kissing his hands. "The young man cured my husband!"

"It was the Virgin who cured your husband," he said. "The lad is only an instrument."

"It was he. Come in, please."

I recalled the previous night. When we arrived at the cathedral, a man had told me I was with a man who performed miracles.

"We're in a hurry," the padre said.

"No! No, we're not," I said, in my halting French. "I'm cold, and I'd like some coffee."

The woman took me by the hand, and we entered the house. It was simple but comfortable: stone walls, wood floors, and bare rafters. Seated in front of the fireplace was a man of about sixty.

As soon as he saw the padre, he stood to kiss his hand.

"Don't get up," said the priest. "You still need to convalesce a bit."

"I've already gained twenty-five pounds," he answered. "But I'm still not able to be of much help to my wife."

"Not to worry. Before long, you'll be better than ever."

"Where is the young man?" the husband asked.

"I saw him heading toward where he always goes," the wife said. "Only today, he went by car."

The padre eyed me but didn't say anything.

"Give us your blessing, Père," the woman asked. "His power . . ."

"The Virgin's power," the priest corrected.

"The Virgin Mother's power is also your power, Père. It was you who brought it here."

This time, he didn't look my way.

"Pray for my husband, Père," the woman insisted.

The priest took a deep breath. "Stand in front of me," he said to the man.

The old man did as he was told. The padre closed his eyes and said an Ave Maria. Then he invoked the Holy Spirit, asking that it be present and help the man.

He suddenly began to speak rapidly. It sounded like a prayer of exorcism, although I couldn't understand what he was saying. His hands touched the man's shoulders and then slid down his arms to his fingertips. He repeated this gesture several times.

The fire began to crackle loudly in the fireplace. This may have been a coincidence, yet it seemed that the priest was entering into territory I knew nothing about—and that he was affecting the very elements.

Every snap of the fire startled the woman and me, but the padre paid no attention to it; he was completely involved in his task—an instrument of the Virgin, as he had said. He was speaking a strange language, and the words came forth at great speed. He was no longer moving his hands; they simply rested on the man's shoulders.

The ritual stopped as quickly as it had started. The padre turned and gave a conventional blessing, making the sign of the cross with his right hand. "May God be ever here in this house," he said.

And turning to me, he asked that we continue our walk.

"But you haven't had coffee," the woman said, as she saw that we were about to leave.

"If I have coffee now, I won't be able to sleep," the padre answered.

The woman laughed and murmured something like "It's still morning." But we were already on our way.

"Padre, the woman spoke of a young man who cured her husband. Was it he?"

"Yes, it was."

I began to feel uneasy. I remembered the day before, and Bilbao, and the conference in Madrid, and people speaking of miracles, and the presence that I had sensed as we embraced and prayed.

I was in love with a man who was capable of performing cures. A man who could help others, bring relief to suffering, give health to the sick and hope to their loved ones. Was I distracting him from his mission just because it was at odds with my image of a house with white curtains, cherished records, and favorite books?

"Don't blame yourself, my child," the padre said.

"You're reading my mind."

"Yes, I am," the padre said. "I have that gift too, and I try to be worthy of it. The Virgin taught me to penetrate the turmoil of human emotions in order to control them as well as possible."

"Do you perform miracles, too?"

"I am not able to cure. But I have one of the gifts of the Holy Spirit."

"So you can read my heart, Padre. And you know I love him, with a love that is growing every minute. We discovered the world together, and together we remain in it. He has been present every day of my life—whether I wanted him there or not."

What could I say to this priest who was walking beside me? He would never understand that I had had other men, that I had been in love, and that if I had married, I would be happy. Even as a child, I had found and forgotten love in the plaza of Soria.

But the way things looked now, I hadn't forgotten that first love very well. It had taken only three days for all of it to come rushing back.

"I have a right to be happy, Padre. I've recovered what was lost, and I don't want to lose it again. I'm going to fight for my happiness. If I give up the fight, I will also be renouncing my spiritual life. As you said, I would be putting God aside, along with my power and my strength as a woman. I'm going to fight for him, Padre."

I knew what that little man was doing here. He had come to convince me to leave him, because he had a more important mission to accomplish.

No, I couldn't believe that the padre walking at my side wanted us to marry and live in a house like the one in Saint-Savin. The priest had said that to trick me. He wanted me to lower my defenses and then—with a smile—he would convince me of the opposite.

He read my thoughts without saying a word. Or perhaps he was trying to fool me. Maybe he didn't know what others were thinking. The fog was dissipating rapidly, and I could now see the path, the mountain peak, the fields, and the snow-covered trees. My emotions were becoming clearer, as well.

Damn! If it's true that he can read someone's thoughts, then let him read mine and know everything! Let him know that yesterday he wanted to make love to me—that I refused and that now I regret it.

Yesterday I had thought that if he had to leave, I would still at least have the memory of my childhood friend. But that was nonsense. Even though he hadn't entered me, something even more profound had, and it had touched my heart.

"Padre, I love him," I repeated.

"So do I. And love always causes stupidity. In my case, it requires that I try to keep him from his destiny."

"That won't be easy, Padre. And it won't be easy in my case, either. Yesterday, during the prayers at the grotto, I discovered that I too can bring forth these gifts that you were talking about. And I'm going to use them to keep him with me."

"Good luck," said the padre, with a smile. "I hope you can."

He stopped and took a rosary from his pocket. Holding it, he looked into my eyes. "Jesus said that we should not take oaths, and I am not doing so. But I'm telling you, in the presence of all that is sacred to me, that I would not like him to adopt the conventional religious life. I would not like to see him ordained a priest. He can serve God in other ways—at your side."

It was hard for me to believe that he was telling me the truth. But he was.

"He's up there," the padre said.

I turned. I could see a car parked a bit further ahead—the same car we had driven from Spain.

"He always comes on foot," he said, smiling. "This time he wanted to give us the impression that he'd traveled a long way."

THE SNOW WAS SOAKING my sneakers. But the padre was wearing only open sandals with woolen socks. I decided not to complain—if he could stand it, so could I. We began to hike toward the top of the mountains.

"How long will it take us?"

"Half an hour at the most."

"Where are we going?"

"To meet with him. And others."

I could see that he didn't want to say any more. Maybe he needed all of his energy for climbing. We walked along in silence—the fog had by now disappeared almost completely, and the yellow disk of the sun was coming into view.

For the first time I had a view of the entire valley; there was a river running through it, some scattered villages, and Saint-Savin, looking as though it were pasted against the slope of the mountain. I could make out the tower of the church, a cemetery I had not noticed before, and the medieval houses looking down on the river.

A bit below us, at a point we had already passed, a shepherd was tending his flock of sheep.

"I'm tired," the padre said. "Let's stop for a while."

We brushed the snow from the top of a boulder and rested against it. He was perspiring—and his feet must have been frozen.

"May Santiago preserve my strength, because I still want to walk his path one more time," said the padre, turning to me.

I didn't understand his comment, so I decided to change the subject. "There are footsteps in the snow."

"Some are those of hunters. Others are of men and women who want to relive a tradition."

"Which tradition?"

"The same as that of Saint Savin. Retreat from the world, come to these mountains, and contemplate the glory of God."

"Padre, there's something I need to understand. Until yesterday, I was with a man who couldn't choose between the religious life and marriage. Today, I learn that this same man performs miracles."

"We all perform miracles," he said. "Jesus said, 'If our faith is the size of a mustard seed, we will say to the mountain, "Move!" And it will move.'"

"I don't want a lesson in religion, Padre. I'm in love with a man, and I want to know more about him, understand him, help him. I don't care what everyone else can do or can't do."

The padre took a deep breath. He hesitated for a moment and then said, "A scientist who studied monkeys on an island in Indonesia was able to teach a certain one to wash bananas in the river before eating them. Cleansed of sand and dirt, the food was more flavorful. The scientist—who did this only because he was studying the learning capacity of monkeys—did not imagine what would eventually happen. So he was surprised to see that the other monkeys on the island began to imitate the first one.

"And then, one day, when a certain number of monkeys had learned to wash their bananas, the monkeys on all of the other islands in the archipelago began to do the same thing. What was most surprising, though, was that the other monkeys learned to do so without having had any contact with the island where the experiment had been conducted."

He stopped. "Do you understand?"

"No," I answered.

"There are several similar scientific studies. The most common explanation is that when a certain number of people evolve, the entire human race begins to evolve. We don't know how many people are needed—but we know that's how it works."

"Like the story of the Immaculate Conception," I said. "The vision appeared for the wise men at the Vatican and for the simple farmer."

"The world itself has a soul, and at a certain moment, that soul acts on everyone and everything at the same time."

"A feminine soul."

He laughed, without saying just what he was laughing about.

"By the way, the dogma of the Immaculate Conception was not just a Vatican matter," he said. "Eight million people signed a petition to the pope, asking that it be recognized. The signatures came from all over the world."

"Is that the first step, Padre?"

"What do you mean?"

"The first step toward having Our Lady recognized as the incarnation of the feminine face of God? After all, we already accept the fact that Jesus was the incarnation of His masculine side."

"And so . . . ?"

"How much time must pass before we accept a Holy Trinity that includes a woman? The Trinity of the Holy Spirit, the Mother, and the Son?"

"Let's move on. It's too cold for us to stand here," he said. "A little while ago, you noticed my sandals."

"Have you been reading my mind?" I asked.

"I'm going to tell you part of the story of the founding of our religious order," he said. "We are barefoot Carmelites, according to the rules established by Saint Teresa of Avila. The sandals are a part of the story, for if one can dominate the body, one can dominate the spirit.

"Teresa was a beautiful woman, placed by her father in a convent so that she would receive a pure education. One day, when she was walking along a corridor, she began to speak with Jesus. Her ecstasies were so strong and deep that she surrendered totally to them, and in a short time, her life had been completely changed. She felt that the Carmelite convents had become nothing more than marriage brokerages, and she decided to create an order that would once again follow the original teachings of Christ and the Carmelites.

"Saint Teresa had to conquer herself, and she had to confront the great powers of her day—the church and the state. But she was determined to press on, because she was convinced that she had a mission to perform.

"One day—just when Teresa felt her soul to be weakening—a woman in tattered clothing appeared at the house where she was staying. The woman wanted to speak with Teresa, no matter what. The owner of the house offered the woman some alms, but the woman refused them; she would not go away until she had spoken with Teresa.

"For three days, the woman waited outside the house, without eating or drinking. Finally Teresa, out of sympathy, bade the woman come in.

"'No,' said the owner of the house. 'The woman is mad.'

"'If I were to listen to everyone, I'd wind up thinking that I'm the crazy one,' Teresa answered. 'It may be that this woman has the same kind of madness as I: that of Christ on the cross.'"

"Saint Teresa spoke with Christ," I said.

"Yes," he answered. "But to get back to our story: the woman was brought to Teresa. She said that her name was María de Jesus Yepes and that she was from Granada. She was a Carmelite novice, and the Virgin had appeared and asked that she found a convent that followed the primitive rules of the order."

Like Saint Teresa, I thought.

"María de Jesus left the convent on the day of her vision and began walking barefoot to Rome. Her pilgrimage lasted two years—and for that entire period, she slept outdoors, in the heat and the cold, living on alms and the charity of others. It was a miracle that she made it. But it was an even greater miracle that she was received by Pope Pius IV. Because the pope, just like María de Jesus, Teresa, and many others, was thinking of the same thing," he finished.

Just as Bernadette had known nothing of the Vatican's decision and the monkeys from the other islands couldn't have known about the experiment that was being conducted, so María de Jesus and Teresa knew nothing of what the other was planning.

Something was beginning to make sense to me.

We were now walking through a forest. With the fog all but gone, the highest tree branches, covered with snow, were receiving the first rays of the sun.

"I think I know where you're going with this, Padre."

"Yes. The world is at a point when many people are receiving the same order: 'Follow your dreams, transform your life, take the path that leads to God. Perform your miracles. Cure. Make prophecies. Listen to your guardian angel. Transform yourself. Be a warrior, and be happy as you wage the good fight. Take risks.'"

Sunshine was everywhere. The snow was glistening, and the glare hurt my eyes. Yet at the same time, it seemed to support what the priest was saying.

"And what does all this have to do with him?"

"I've told you the heroic side of the story. But you don't know anything about the soul of these heroes."

He paused.

"The suffering," he picked up again. "At moments of transformation, martyrs are born. Before a person can follow his dream, others have to make sacrifices. They have to confront ridicule, persecution, and attempts to discredit what they are trying to do."

"It was the church that burned the witches at the stake, Padre."

"Right. And Rome threw the Christians to the lions. But those who died at the stake or in the sand of the arena rose quickly to eternal glory—they were better off.

"Nowadays, warriors of the light confront something worse than the honorable death of the martyrs. They are consumed, bit by bit, by shame and humiliation. That's how it was with Saint Teresa—who suffered for the rest of her life. That's how it was for María de Jesus, too. And for the happy children who saw Our Lady in Fátima, Portugal—well, Jacinta and Francisco died just a few months later; Lucia entered a convent from which she never emerged."

"But that's not how it was for Bernadette."

"Yes, it was. She had to live through prison, humiliation, and discredit. He must have described that to you. He must have told you the words of the visitation."

"Some of them."

"In the visitations at Lourdes, the phrases uttered by Our Lady wouldn't fill half a page of a notebook, but one of the things the Virgin said clearly to the girl was *'I do not promise you happiness in this world.'* Why did she warn Bernadette? Because she knew the pain that awaited Bernadette if she accepted her mission."

I looked at the sun, the snow, and the bare branches of the trees.

"He is a revolutionary," he continued, sounding humble. "He has the power, and he converses with Our Lady. If he is able to concentrate his forces well, he can be one of the leaders in the spiritual transformation of the human race. This is a critical point in the history of the world.

"But if he chooses this path, he is going to go through a great deal of suffering. His revelations have come to him before their time. I know the human soul well enough to know what he can expect."

The padre turned to me and held me by the shoulders. "Please," he said. "Keep him from the suffering and tragedy that lie in store for him. He will not be able to survive them."

"I understand your love for him, Padre."

He shook his head. "No, no. You don't understand anything. You are still too young to know the evils of the world. At this point, you see yourself as a revolutionary too. You want to change the world with him, open new paths, see the story of your love for each other become legend—a story passed down through the generations. You still think that love can conquer all."

"Well, can't it?"

"Yes, it can. But it conquers at the right time—after the celestial battles have ended."

"But I love him. I don't have to wait for the celestial battles to end for my love to win out."

He gazed into the distance.

"On the banks of the rivers of Babylon, we sat down and wept," he said, as if talking to himself. "On the willows there, we hung up our harps."

"How sad," I answered.

"Those are the first lines of one of the psalms. It tells of exile and of those who want to return to the promised land but cannot. And that exile is still going to last for a long time. What can I do to try to prevent the suffering of someone who wants to return to paradise before it is time to do so?"

"Nothing, Padre. Absolutely nothing."

❦ ❦ ❦

"THERE HE IS," said the padre.

I saw him. He was about two hundred yards from me, kneeling in the snow. He was shirtless, and even from that distance, I could see that his skin was red with the cold.

His head was bowed and his hands joined in prayer. I don't know if I was influenced by the ritual I had attended the night before or by the woman who had been gathering hay, but I felt that I was looking at someone with an incredible spiritual force. Someone who was no longer of this world—who lived in communion with God and with the enlightened spirits of heaven. The brilliance of the snow seemed to strengthen this perception.

"At this moment, there are others like him," said the priest. "In constant adoration, communing with God and the Virgin. Hearing the angels, the saints, the prophecies and words of wisdom, and transmitting all of that to a small gathering of the faithful. As long as they continue in this way, there won't be a problem.

"But he is not going to remain here. He is going to travel the world, preaching the concept of the Great Mother. The church is not yet ready for that. And the world has stones at hand to hurl at those who first introduce the subject."

"And it has flowers to throw on those who come afterward."

"Yes. But that's not what will happen to him."

The priest began to approach him.

"Where are you going?"

"To bring him out of his trance. To tell him how much I like you. To say that I give my blessing to your union. I want to do that here, in this place, which for him is sacred."

I began to feel sick with an inexplicable fear.

"I have to think, Padre. I don't know if this is right."

"It's not right," he answered. "Many parents make mistakes with their children, thinking they know what's best for them. I'm not his father, and I know I'm doing the wrong thing. But I have to fulfill my destiny."

I was feeling more and more anxious.

"Let's not disturb him," I said. "Let him finish his contemplation."

"He shouldn't be here. He should be with you."

"Maybe he's communicating with the Virgin."

"He may be. But even so, we have to go to him. If I approach him with you at my side, he will know that I have told you everything. He knows what I think."

"Today is the day of the Immaculate Conception," I insisted. "A very special day for him. I saw his happiness last night at the grotto."

"The Immaculate Conception is special for all of us," the padre answered. "But now I'm the one who doesn't want to discuss religion. Let's go to him."

"Why now, Padre? Why at this moment?"

"Because I know that he is deciding his future. And he may make the wrong choice."

I turned away and began to walk down the same path we had just come up. The padre followed me.

"What are you doing? Don't you see that you're the only one who can save him? Don't you see that he loves you and would give up everything for you?"

I hurried my steps, and it was difficult for him to keep up. Yet he fought to stay at my side.

"At this very moment, he is making his decision! He may be deciding to leave you! Fight for the person you love!"

But I didn't stop. I walked as fast as I could, trying to escape the mountains, the priest, and the choices behind me. I knew that the man who was rushing along behind me was reading my thoughts and that he understood that it was useless to try to make me go back. Yet he insisted; he argued and struggled to the end.

Finally, we reached the boulder where we had rested a half hour earlier. Exhausted, I threw myself down.

I tried to relax. I wanted to run from there, to be alone, to have time to think.

The padre appeared a few minutes later, as exhausted as I was.

"Do you see these mountains surrounding us?" he started in. "They don't pray; they are already a part of God's prayers. They have found their place in the world, and here they will stay. They were here before people looked to the heavens, heard thunder, and wondered who had created all of this. We are born, we suffer, we die, and the mountains endure.

"There is some point at which we have to wonder whether all our effort is worth it. Why not try to be like those mountains—wise, ancient, and in their place? Why risk everything to transform a half-dozen people who will immediately forget what they've been taught and move on to the next adventure? Why not wait until a certain number of monkeys learn, and then the knowledge will spread, with no suffering, to all the other islands?"

"Is that what you really think, Padre?"

He was silent for a few moments.

"Are you reading my thoughts now?"

"No. But if that's the way you feel, you wouldn't have chosen the religious life."

"I've tried many times to understand my fate," he said. "But I haven't yet. I accepted that I was to be a part of God's army, and everything I've done has been in an attempt to explain to people why there is misery, pain, and injustice. I ask them to be good Christians, and they ask me, 'How can I believe in God when there is so much suffering in the world?'

"And I try to explain something that has no explanation. I try to tell them that there is a plan, a battle among the angels, and that we are all involved in the battle. I try to say that when a certain number of people have enough faith to change the scenario, all of the others—everywhere on the planet—will benefit. But they don't believe me. They do nothing."

"They are like the mountains," I said. "The mountains are beautiful. Anyone who beholds them has to think about the grandness of creation. They are living proof of the love that God feels for us, but their fate is merely to give testimony. They are not like the rivers, which move and transform what is around them."

"Yes. But why not be like the mountains?"

"Maybe because the fate of mountains is terrible," I answered. "They are destined to look out at the same scene forever."

The padre said nothing.

"I was studying to become a mountain," I continued. "I had put everything in its proper place. I was going to take a job with the state, marry, and teach the religion of my parents to my children, even though I no longer accepted it. But now I have decided to leave all that behind me in order to be with the man I love. And it's a good thing I decided not to be a mountain—I wouldn't have lasted very long."

"You say some very wise things."

"I'm surprising myself. Before, all I could talk about was my childhood."

I stood and started back down the trail. The padre seemed to respect my silence and did not try to speak to me until we reached the road.

I took his hands and kissed them. "I'm going to say good-bye. But I want you to know that I understand you and your love for him."

The padre smiled and gave me his blessing. "And I understand your love for him, too," he said.

I spent the rest of the day walking through the valley. I played in the snow, visited a village near Saint-Savin, had a sandwich, and watched some boys playing soccer.

At the church in the village, I lit a candle. I closed my eyes and repeated the invocations I had learned the previous night. Then, concentrating on a crucifix that hung behind the altar, I began to speak in tongues. Bit by bit, the gift took over. It was easier than I had thought.

Perhaps this all seems silly—murmuring things, saying words that have no meaning, that don't help us in our reasoning. But when we do this, the Holy Spirit is conversing with our souls, saying things the soul needs to hear.

When I felt that I was sufficiently purified, I closed my eyes and prayed.

Our Lady, give me back my faith. May I also serve as an instrument of your work. Give me the opportunity to learn through my love, because love has never kept anyone away from their dreams.

May I be a companion and ally of the man I love. May we accomplish everything we have to accomplish—together.

When I returned to Saint-Savin, night had almost fallen. The car was parked in front of the house where we were staying.

"Where have you been?" he asked.

"Walking and praying," I answered.

He embraced me.

"At first, I was afraid you had gone away. You are the most precious thing I have on this earth."

"And you are for me," I answered.

❦ ❦ ❦

IT WAS LATE when we stopped in a small village near San Martín de Unx. Crossing the Pyrenees had taken longer than we'd thought because of the rain and snow of the previous day.

"We need to find someplace that's open," he said, climbing out of the car. "I'm hungry."

I didn't move.

"Come on," he insisted, opening my door.

"I want to ask you a question—a question I haven't asked since we found each other again."

He became serious, and I laughed at his concern.

"Is it an important question?"

"Very important," I answered, trying to look serious. "It's the following: where are we going?"

We both laughed.

"To Zaragoza," he said, relieved.

I jumped out of the car, and we went looking for a restaurant that was open. It was going to be almost impossible at that hour of the night.

No, it's not impossible. The Other is no longer with me. Miracles do happen, I said to myself. "When do you have to be in Barcelona?" I asked him. He'd told me he had another conference there.

He didn't answer, and his expression turned serious. *I shouldn't ask such questions,* I thought. *He may think I'm trying to control his life.*

We walked along without speaking. In the village plaza, there was an illuminated sign: *Mesón el Sol.*

"It's open—let's have something to eat" was all he said.

The red peppers with anchovies were arranged on the plate in the shape of a star. On the side, some *manchego* cheese, in slices that were almost transparent. In the center of the table, a lighted candle and a half-full bottle of Rioja wine.

"This was a medieval wine cellar," our waiter told us.

There was no one in the place at that time of night. He went off to make a telephone call. When he came back to the table, I wanted to ask him whom he had called—but this time I controlled myself.

"We're open until two-thirty in the morning," the man said. "So if you like, we can bring you some more ham, cheese, and wine, and you can go out in the plaza. The wine will keep you warm."

"We won't be here that long," he answered. "We have to get to Zaragoza before dawn."

The man returned to the bar, and we refilled our glasses. I felt the same sense of lightness I had experienced in Bilbao—the smooth inebriation that helps us to say and hear things that are difficult.

"You're tired of driving, and we've been drinking," I said. "Wouldn't it be better to stay the night? I saw an inn as we were driving."

He nodded in agreement.

"Look at this table," he said. "The Japanese call it *shibumi,* the true sophistication of simple things. Instead, people fill their bank accounts with money and travel to expensive places in order to feel they're sophisticated."

I had some more wine.

The inn. Another night at his side.

"It's strange to hear a seminarian speak of sophistication," I said, trying to focus on something else.

"I learned about it at the seminary. The closer we get to God through our faith, the simpler He becomes. And the simpler He becomes, the greater is His presence.

"Christ learned about his mission while he was cutting wood and making chairs, beds, and cabinets. He came as a carpenter to show us that—no matter what we do—everything can lead us to the experience of God's love."

He stopped suddenly.

"But I don't want to talk about that," he said. "I want to talk about the other kind of love."

He reached out to caress my face. The wine made things easier for him. And for me.

"Why did you stop so suddenly? Why don't you want to talk about God and the Virgin and the spiritual world?"

"I want to talk about the other kind of love," he said again. "The love that a man and a woman share, and in which there are also miracles."

I took his hands. He might know of the great mysteries of the Goddess, but he didn't know any more than I did about love—even though he had traveled much more than I had.

We held hands for a long time. I could see in his eyes the deep fears that true love tests us with. I could see that he was remembering the rejection of the night before, as well as the long time we had been separated, and his years in the monastery, searching for a world where such anxieties didn't intrude.

I could see in his eyes the thousands of times that he had imagined this moment and the scenes he had constructed about us. I wanted to say that yes, he was welcome, that my heart had won the battle. I wanted to tell him how much I loved him and how badly I wanted him at that moment.

But I was silent. I witnessed, as if in a dream, his inner conflict. I could see that he was wondering whether I'd reject him again, that he was thinking about his fear of losing me, and about the hard words he had heard at other, similar times—because we all have such experiences, and they leave scars.

His eyes gleamed. He was ready to surmount any barrier.

I took one of my hands from his and placed my glass of wine at the edge of the table.

"It's going to fall," he said.

"Exactly. I want you to tip it over the edge."

"Break the glass?"

Yes, break the glass. A simple gesture, but one that brings up fears we can't really understand. What's wrong with breaking an inexpensive glass, when everyone has done so unintentionally at some time in their life?

"Break the glass?" he repeated. "Why?"

"Well, I could give you lots of reasons," I answered. "But actually, just to break it."

"For you?"

"No, of course not."

He eyed the glass on the edge of the table—worried that it might fall.

It's a rite of passage, I wanted to say. It's something prohibited. Glasses are not purposely broken. In a restaurant or in our home, we're careful not to place glasses by the edge of a table. Our universe requires that we avoid letting glasses fall to the floor.

But when we break them by accident, we realize that it's not very serious. The waiter says, "It's nothing," and when has anyone been charged for a broken glass? Breaking glasses is part of life and does no damage to us, to the restaurant, or to anyone else.

I bumped the table. The glass shook but didn't fall.

"Careful!" he said, instinctively.

"Break the glass," I insisted.

Break the glass, I thought to myself, *because it's a symbolic gesture. Try to understand that I have broken things within myself that were much more important than a glass, and I'm happy I did. Resolve your own internal battle, and break the glass.*

Our parents taught us to be careful with glasses and with our bodies. They taught us that the passions of childhood are impossible, that we should not flee from priests, that people cannot perform miracles, and that no one leaves on a journey without knowing where they are going.

Break the glass, please—and free us from all these damned rules, from needing to find an explanation for everything, from doing only what others approve of.

"Break the glass," I said again.

He stared at me. Then, slowly, he slid his hand along the tablecloth to the glass. And with a sudden movement, he pushed it to the floor.

The sound of the breaking glass caught the waiter's attention. Rather than apologize for having broken the glass, he looked at me, smiling—and I smiled back.

"Doesn't matter," shouted the waiter.

But he wasn't listening. He had stood, seized my hair in his hands, and was kissing me.

I clutched at his hair, too, and squeezed him with all my strength, biting his lips and feeling his tongue move in my mouth. This was the kiss I had waited for so long—a kiss born by the rivers of our childhood, when we didn't yet know what love meant. A kiss that had been suspended in the air as we grew, that had traveled the world in the souvenir of a medal, and that had remained hidden behind piles of books. A kiss that had been lost so many times and now was found. In the moment of that kiss were years of searching, disillusionment, and impossible dreams.

I kissed him hard. The few people there in the bar must have been thinking that all they were seeing was just a kiss. They didn't know that this kiss stood for my whole life—and his life, as well. The life of anyone who has waited, dreamed, and searched for their true path.

The moment of that kiss contained every happy moment I had ever lived.

ɕ ɕ ɕ

HE TOOK OFF MY CLOTHES and entered me with strength, with fear, and with great desire. I ran my hands over his face, heard his moans, and thanked God that he was there inside me, making me feel as if it were the first time.

We made love all night long—our lovemaking blended with our sleeping and dreaming. I felt him inside me and embraced him to make sure that this was really happening, to make sure that he wouldn't disappear, like the knights who had once inhabited this old castle-hotel. The silent walls of stone seemed to be telling stories of damsels in distress, of fallen tears and endless days at the window, looking to the horizon, looking for a sign of hope.

But I would never go through that, I promised myself. I would never lose him. He would always be with me—because I had heard the tongues of the Holy Spirit as I looked at a crucifix behind an altar, and they had said that I would not be committing a sin.

I would be his companion, and together we would tame a world that was going to be created anew. We would talk about the Great Mother, we would fight at the side of Michael the Archangel, and we would experience together the agony and the ecstasy of pioneers. That's what the tongues had said to me—and because I had recovered my faith, I knew they were telling the truth.

Thursday, December 9, 1993

I AWOKE WITH HIS arm across my breast. It was already mid-morning, and the bells of a nearby church were tolling.

He kissed me. His hands once again caressed my body.

"We have to go," he said. "The holiday ends today, and the roads will be jammed."

"I don't want to go back to Zaragoza," I answered. "I want to go straight to where you're going. The banks will be open soon, and I can use my bank card to get some money and buy some clothes."

"You told me you didn't have much money."

"There are things I can do. I need to break with my past once and for all. If we go back to Zaragoza, I might begin to think I'm making a mistake, that the exam period is almost here and we can stand to be separated for two months until my exams are over. And then if I pass my exams, I won't want to leave Zaragoza. No, no, I can't go back. I need to burn the bridges that connect me with the woman I was."

"Barcelona," he said to himself.

"What?"

"Nothing. Let's move on."

"But you have a presentation to make."

"But that's two days from now," he said. His voice sounded different. "Let's go somewhere else. I don't want to go straight to Barcelona."

I got out of bed. I didn't want to focus on problems. As always after a first night of love with someone, I had awakened with a certain sense of ceremony and embarrassment.

I went to the window, opened the curtains, and looked down on the narrow street. The balconies of the houses were draped with drying laundry. The church bells were ringing.

"I've got an idea," I said. "Let's go to a place we shared as children. I've never been back there."

"Where?"

"The monastery at Piedra."

As we left the hotel, the bells were still sounding, and he suggested that we go into a church nearby.

"That's all we've done," I said. "Churches, prayers, rituals."

"We made love," he said. "We've gotten drunk three times. We've walked in the mountains. We've struck a good balance between rigor and compassion."

I'd said something thoughtless. I had to get used to this new life.

"I'm sorry," I said.

"Let's just go in for a few minutes. The bells are a sign."

He was right, but I wouldn't know that until the next day.

Afterward, without really understanding the meaning of the sign we had witnessed in the church, we got the car and drove for four hours to get to the monastery at Piedra.

❦ ❦ ❦

THE ROOF HAD FALLEN in, and the heads were missing from the few images that were still there—all except for one.

I looked around. In the past, this place must have sheltered strong-willed people, who'd seen to it that every stone was cleaned and that each pew was occupied by one of the powerful individuals of the time.

But all I saw now were ruins. When we had played here as children, we'd pretended these ruins were castles. In those castles I had looked for my enchanted prince.

For centuries, the monks of the monastery at Piedra had kept this small piece of paradise to themselves. Situated on a valley floor, it enjoyed a plentiful supply of what the neighboring villages had to beg for—water. Here the River Piedra broke up into dozens of waterfalls, streams, and lakes, creating luxuriant vegetation all around.

Yet one had only to walk a few hundred yards to leave the canyon and find aridity and desolation. The river itself once again became a narrow thread of water—as if it had exhausted all of its youth and energy in crossing the valley.

The monks knew all this, and they charged dearly for the water they supplied to their neighbors. An untold number of battles between the priests and the villagers marked the history of the monastery.

During one of the many wars that shook Spain, the monastery at Piedra had been turned into a barracks. Horses rode through the central nave of the church, and soldiers slept in its pews, telling ribald stories there and making love with women from the neighboring villages.

Revenge—although delayed—finally came. The monastery was sacked and destroyed.

The monks were never able to reconstruct their paradise. In one of the many legal battles that followed, someone said that the inhabitants of the nearby villages had carried out a sentence pronounced by God. Christ had said, "Give drink to those who thirst," and the priests had paid no heed. For this, God had expelled those who had regarded themselves as nature's masters.

And it was perhaps for this reason that although much of the monastery had been rebuilt and made into a hotel, the main church remained in ruins. The descendants of the local villagers had never forgotten the high price that their parents had paid for something that nature provides freely.

"Which statue is that? The only one with its head?" I asked him.

"Saint Teresa of Avila," he answered. "She is powerful. And even with the thirst for vengeance that the wars brought about, no one dared to touch her."

He took my hand, and we left the church. We walked along the broad corridors of the monastery, climbed the wooden staircases, and marveled at the butterflies in the inner gardens. I recalled every detail of that monastery because I had been there as a girl, and the old memories seemed more vivid than what I was seeing now.

Memories. The months and years leading up to that week seemed to be part of some other incarnation of mine—an era to which I never wanted to return, because it hadn't been touched by the hand of love. I felt as if I had lived the same day over and over for years on end, waking up every morning in the same way, repeating the same words, and dreaming the same dreams.

I remembered my parents, my grandparents, and many of my old friends. I recalled how much time I had spent fighting for something I didn't even want.

Why had I done that? I could think of no explanation. Maybe because I had been too lazy to think of other avenues to follow. Maybe because I had been afraid of what others would think. Maybe because it was hard work to be different. Perhaps because a human being is condemned to repeat the steps taken by the previous generation until—and I was thinking of the padre—a certain number of people begin to behave in a different fashion.

Then the world changes, and we change with it.

But I didn't want to be that way anymore. Fate had returned to me what had been mine and now offered me the chance to change myself and the world.

I thought again of the mountain climbers we had met as we traveled. They were young and wore brightly colored clothing so as to be easily spotted should they become lost in the snow. They knew the right path to follow to the peaks.

The heights were already festooned with aluminum pins; all they had to do was attach their lines to them, and they could climb safely. They were there for a holiday adventure, and on Monday they would return to their jobs with the feeling that they had challenged nature—and won.

But this wasn't really true. The adventurous ones were those who had climbed there first, the ones who had found the routes to the top. Some, who had fallen to their death on the rocks, had never even made it halfway up. Others had lost fingers and toes to frostbite. Many were never seen again. But one day, some of them had made it to the summit.

And their eyes were the first to take in that view, and their hearts beat with joy. They had accepted the risks and could now honor—with their conquest—all of those who had died trying.

There were probably some people down below who thought, "There's nothing up there. Just a view. What's so great about that?"

But the first climber knew what was great about it: the acceptance of the challenge of going forward. He knew that no single day is the same as any other and that each morning brings its own special miracle, its *magic moment* in which ancient universes are destroyed and new stars are created.

The first one who climbed those mountains must have asked, looking down at the tiny houses with their smoking chimneys, "All of their days must seem the same. What's so great about that?"

Now all the mountains had been conquered and astronauts had walked in space. There were no more islands on earth—no matter how small—left to be discovered. But there were still great adventures of the spirit, and one of them was being offered to me now.

It was a blessing. The padre didn't understand anything. These pains are not the kind that hurt.

Fortunate are those who take the first steps. Someday people will realize that men and women are capable of speaking the language of the angels—that all of us are possessed of the gifts of the Holy Spirit and that we can perform miracles, cure, prophesy, and understand.

❧ ❧ ❧

WE SPENT THE afternoon walking along the canyon, reminiscing about our childhood. It was the first time he had done so; during our trip to Bilbao, he had seemed to have lost all interest in Soria.

Now, though, he asked me about each of our mutual friends, wanting to know whether they were happy and what they were doing with their lives.

Finally, we arrived at the largest waterfall of the Piedra, where a number of small, scattered streams come together and the water is thrown to the rocks below from a height of almost one hundred feet. We stood at the edge of the waterfall, listening to its deafening roar and gazing at the rainbow in its mist.

"The Horse's Tail," I said, surprised that I still remembered this name from so long ago.

"I remember . . . ," he began.

"Yes! I know what you're going to say!"

Of course I knew! The waterfall concealed a gigantic grotto. When we were children, returning from our first visit to the monastery at Piedra, we had talked about that place for days.

"The cavern," he said. "Let's go there."

It was impossible to pass through the torrent of water. But ancient monks had constructed a tunnel that started at the highest point of the falls and descended through the earth to a place at the rear of the grotto.

It wasn't difficult to find the entrance. During the summer, there may even have been lights showing the way, but now the tunnel was completely dark.

"Is this the right way?" I asked.

"Yes. Trust me."

We began to descend through the hole at the side of the falls. Although we were in complete darkness, we knew where we were going—and he asked me again to trust him.

Thank you, Lord, I was thinking, as we went deeper and deeper into the earth, *because I was a lost sheep, and you brought me back. Because my life was dead, and you revived it. Because love wasn't alive in my heart, and you gave me back that gift.*

I held on to his shoulder. My loved one guided my steps through the darkness, knowing that we would see the light again and that it would bring us joy. Perhaps in our future there would be moments when the situation was reversed—when I would guide him with the same love and certainty until we reached a safe place and could rest together.

We walked slowly, and it seemed as if we would never stop descending. Maybe this was another rite of passage, marking the end of an era in which there had been no light in my life. As I walked through the tunnel, I was remembering how much time I had wasted in one place, trying to put down roots in soil where nothing could grow any longer.

But God was good and had given me back my lost enthusiasm, directing me toward the adventures I had always dreamed about.

And toward the man who—without my knowing it—had waited for me all my life. I felt no remorse over the fact that he was leaving the seminary—there were many ways to serve God, as the padre had said, and our love only multiplied the number of them. Starting now, I would also have the chance to serve and help—all because of him.

We would go out into the world, bringing comfort to others and to each other.

Thank you, Lord, for helping me to serve. Teach me to be worthy of that. Give me the strength to be a part of his mission, to walk with him on this earth, and to develop my spiritual life anew. May all our days be as these have been—going from place to place, curing the sick, comforting those in sorrow, speaking of the Great Mother's love for all of us.

SUDDENLY, THE SOUND of water could be heard again and light flooded our path. The dark tunnel was transformed into one of the most beautiful spectacles on earth. We were in an immense cavern, the size of a cathedral. Three of its walls were of stone, and the fourth was the Horse's Tail, with its water falling into the emerald-green lake at our feet.

The rays of the setting sun passed through the waterfall, and the moist walls glittered.

We leaned back against the stone wall, saying nothing.

When we were children, this place was a pirates' hideout, where the treasures of our childhood imagination were kept. Now, it was the miracle of Mother Earth; I knew she was there and felt myself to be in her womb. She was protecting us with her walls of stone and washing away our sins with her purifying water.

"Thank you," I said in a loud voice.

"Whom are you thanking?"

"Her. And you, because you were an instrument in restoring my faith."

He walked to the edge of the water. Looking out, he smiled. "Come over here," he said.

I joined him.

"I want to tell you something you don't know about yet," he said.

His words worried me a little. But he looked calm and happy, and that reassured me.

"Every person on earth has a gift," he began. "In some, the gift manifests itself spontaneously; others have to work to discover what it is. I worked with my gift during the four years I was at the seminary."

Now I would have to "play a role," as he had taught me when the old man had barred us from the church. I would have to feign that I knew nothing. *There's nothing wrong with doing this,* I told myself. *This is a not a script based on frustration but on happiness.*

"What did you do at the seminary?" I asked, trying to stall for time in order to play my role better.

"That doesn't matter," he said. "The fact is that I developed a gift. I am able to cure, when God so wills it."

"That's wonderful," I answered, acting surprised. "We won't have to spend money on doctors!"

He didn't laugh. I felt like an idiot.

"I developed my gift through the Charismatic practices that you saw," he went on. "In the beginning, I was surprised. I would pray, asking that the Holy Spirit appear, and then, through the laying on of my hands, I would restore many of the sick to good health. My reputation began to spread, and every day people lined up at the gates of the seminary, seeking my help. In every infected, smelly laceration, I saw the wounds of Jesus."

"I'm so proud of you," I said.

"Many of the people at the monastery opposed me, but my superior gave me his complete support."

"We'll continue this work. We'll go out together into the world. I will clean and bathe the wounds, and you will bless them, and God will demonstrate His miracles."

He looked away from me, out at the lake. There seemed to be a presence in the cavern similar to the one I had sensed that night in Saint-Savin when we had gotten drunk at the well in the plaza.

"I've already told you this, but I'll say it again," he continued. "One night I awoke, and my room was completely bright. I saw the face of the Great Mother; I saw Her loving look. After that, She began to appear to me from time to time. I cannot make it happen, but every once in a while, She appears.

"By the time of my first vision, I was already aware of the work being done by the true revolutionaries of the church. I knew that my mission on earth, in addition to curing, was to smooth the way for this new acceptance of God as a woman. The feminine principle, the column of Misericordia, would be rebuilt—and the temple of wisdom would be reconstructed in the hearts of all people."

I was staring at him. His face, which had grown tense, now relaxed again.

"This carried a price—which I was willing to pay."

He stopped, as if not knowing how to go on with his story.

"What do you mean when you say you *were* willing?" I asked.

"The path of the Goddess can only be opened through words and miracles. But that's not the way the world works. It's going to be very hard—tears, lack of understanding, suffering."

That padre, I thought to myself. *He tried to put fear in his heart. But I shall be his comfort.*

"The path isn't about pain; it's about the glory of serving," I answered.

"Most human beings still cannot trust love."

I felt that he was trying to tell me something but couldn't. I wanted to help him.

"I've been thinking about that," I broke in. "The first man who climbed the highest peak in the Pyrenees must have felt that a life without that kind of adventure would lack grace."

"What do you mean when you use the word *grace?*" he asked me, and I could see that he was feeling tense again. "One of the names of the Great Mother is Our Lady of the Graces. Her generous hands heap Her blessings on those who know how to receive them. We can never judge the lives of others, because each person knows only their own pain and renunciation. It's one thing to feel that you are on the right path, but it's another to think that yours is the only path.

"Jesus said, 'The house of my Father has many mansions.' A gift is a grace, or a mercy. But it is also a mercy to know how to live a life of dignity, love, and work. Mary had a husband on earth who tried to demonstrate the value of anonymous work. Although he was not heard from very much, he was the one who provided the roof over their heads and the food for their mouths, who allowed his wife and son to do all that they did. His work was as important as theirs, even though no one ever gave him much credit."

I didn't say anything, and he took my hand. "Forgive me for my intolerance."

I kissed his hand and put it to my cheek.

"This is what I'm trying to explain to you," he said, smiling again. "I realized, from the moment I found you again, that I couldn't cause you to suffer because of my mission."

I began to feel worried.

"Yesterday I lied to you. It was the first and last lie I've ever told you," he continued. "The truth is that instead of going to the monastery, I went up on the mountain and conversed with the Great Mother. I said to Her that if She wanted, I would leave you and continue along my path. I would go back to the gate where the sick gathered, to the visits in the middle of the night, to the lack of understanding of those who would deny the idea of faith, and to the cynical attitude of those who cannot believe that love is a savior. If She were to ask me, I would give up what I want most in the world: you."

I thought again of the padre. He had been right. A choice had been made that morning.

"But," he continued, "if it were possible to resolve this awful predicament in my life, I would promise to serve the world through my love for you."

"What are you saying?" I asked, frightened now.

He seemed not to hear me.

"It's not necessary to move mountains in order to prove one's faith," he said. "I was ready to face the suffering alone and not share it. If I had continued along that path, we would never have our house with the white curtains and the view of the mountains."

"I don't care about that house! I didn't even want to go in!" I said, trying not to shout. "I want to go with you, to be with you in your struggle. I want to be one of those who does something for the first time. Don't you understand? You've given me back my faith!"

The last rays of the sun illuminated the walls of the cavern. But I couldn't see its beauty.

God hides the fires of hell within paradise.

"You're the one who doesn't understand," he said, and I could see his eyes begging me to comprehend. "You don't see the risks."

"But you were willing to accept those risks!"

"I *am* willing. But they are *my* risks."

I wanted to interrupt him, but he wasn't listening.

"So yesterday, I asked a miracle of the Virgin," he continued. "I asked that She take away my gift."

I couldn't believe what I was hearing.

"I have a little money and all the experience that years of traveling have given me. We'll buy a house, I'll get a job, and I'll serve God as Saint Joseph did, with the humility of an anonymous person. I don't need miracles in my life anymore to keep the faith. I need you."

My legs were growing weak, and I felt as if I might faint.

"And just as I was asking that the Virgin take away my gift, I began to speak in tongues," he went on. "The tongues told me, 'Place your hands on the earth. Your gift will leave you and return to the Mother's breast.'"

I was in a panic. "You didn't . . ."

"Yes. I did as the inspiration of the Holy Spirit bade. The fog lifted, and the sun shone on the mountains. I felt that the Virgin understood—because She had also loved so greatly."

"But She followed Her man! She accepted the path taken by Her son!"

"We don't have Her strength, Pilar. My gift will be passed on to someone else—such gifts are never wasted.

"Yesterday, from that bar, I phoned Barcelona and canceled my presentation. Let's go to Zaragoza—you know the people there, and it's a good place for us to start. I'll get a job easily."

I could no longer think.

"Pilar!" he said.

But I was already climbing back through the tunnel—this time without a friendly shoulder to lean on—pursued by the multitude of the sick who would die, the families that would suffer, the miracles that would never be performed, the smiles that would no longer grace the world, and the mountains that would remain in place.

I saw nothing—only the darkness that engulfed me.

Friday, December 10, 1993

On the bank of the River Piedra I sat down and wept. My memory of that night is confused and vague. I know that I almost died, but I can't remember his face nor where he took me.

I'd like to be able to remember all of it—so that I could expel it from my heart. But I can't. It all seems like a dream, from the moment when I came out of that dark tunnel into a world where darkness had already fallen.

There was not a star in the sky. I remember vaguely walking back to the car, retrieving my small bag, and beginning to wander at random. I must have walked to the road, trying to hitch a ride to Zaragoza—with no success. I wound up returning to the gardens at the monastery.

The sound of water was everywhere—there were waterfalls on all sides, and I felt the presence of the Great Mother following me wherever I walked. Yes, She had loved the world; She loved it as much as God did—because She had also given Her son to be sacrificed by men. But did She understand a woman's love for a man?

She may have suffered because of love, but it was a different kind of love. Her Groom knew everything and performed miracles. Her husband on earth was a humble laborer who believed everything his dreams told him. She never knew what it was to abandon a man or to be abandoned by one. When Joseph considered expelling Her from their home because She was pregnant, Her Groom in heaven immediately sent an angel to keep that from happening.

Her son left Her. But children always leave their parents. It's easy to suffer because you love a person, or the world, or your son. That's the kind of suffering that you accept as a part of life; it's a noble, grand sort of suffering. It's easy to suffer for a cause or a mission; this ennobles the heart of the person suffering.

But how to explain suffering because of a man? It's not explainable. With that kind of suffering, a person feels as if they're in hell, because there is no nobility, no greatness—only misery.

That night, I slept on the frozen ground, and the cold anesthetized me. I thought I might die without a covering—but where could I find one? Everything that was most important in my life had been given so generously to me in the course of one week—and had been taken from me in a minute, without my having a chance to say a thing.

My body was trembling from the cold, but I hardly noticed. At some point, the trembling would stop. My body's energy would be exhausted from trying to provide me with heat and would be unable to do anything more. It would resume its customary state of relaxation, and death would take me in its arms.

I shook for another hour. And then peace came.

Before I closed my eyes, I began to hear my mother's voice. She was telling a story she had often told me when I was a child, not realizing it was a story about me.

"A boy and a girl were insanely in love with each other," my mother's voice was saying. "They decided to become engaged. And that's when presents are always exchanged.

"The boy was poor—his only worthwhile possession was a watch he'd inherited from his grandfather. Thinking about his sweetheart's lovely hair, he decided to sell the watch in order to buy her a silver barrette.

"The girl had no money herself to buy him a present. She went to the shop of the most successful merchant in the town and sold him her hair. With the money, she bought a gold watchband for her lover.

"When they met on the day of the engagement party, she gave him the wristband for a watch he had sold, and he gave her the barrette for the hair she no longer had."

❧ ❧ ❧

I WAS AWAKENED by a man shaking me.

"Drink this!" he was saying. "Drink this quickly!"

I had no idea what was happening nor the strength to resist. He opened my mouth and forced me to drink a hot liquid. I noticed that he was in his shirtsleeves and that he had given me a wrap.

"Drink more!" he insisted.

Without knowing what I was doing, I obeyed. Then I closed my eyes.

I awoke in the convent, and a woman was tending me.

"You almost died," she said. "If it weren't for the watchman, you wouldn't be here."

I stood up dizzily. Parts of the previous day came back to me, and I wished that the watchman had never passed my way.

But apparently this was not the time for me to die. I was to go on living.

The woman led me to the kitchen and prepared some coffee, biscuits, and bread for me. She asked me no questions, and I explained nothing. When I had finished eating, she gave me my bag.

"See if everything's still there," she said.

"I'm sure it is. I didn't really have anything much."

"You have your life, my child. A long life. Take better care of it."

"There's a city near here where there's a church," I said, wanting to cry. "Yesterday, before I came here, I went into that church with . . ."

I couldn't explain.

"... with a friend from my childhood. I had already had enough of the churches around here, but the bells were ringing, and he said it was a sign—that we should go in."

The woman refilled my cup, poured some coffee for herself, and sat down to hear my story.

"We entered the church," I continued. "There was no one there, and it was dark. I tried to look for the sign, but I saw only the same old altars and the same old saints. Suddenly, we heard a movement above, where the organ was.

"It was a group of boys with guitars, who began to tune their instruments. We decided to sit and listen to the music for a while before continuing our trip. Shortly a man came in and sat down next to us. He was happy and shouted to the boys to play a *paso doble*."

"Bullfight music?" the woman said. "I hope they didn't do that!"

"They didn't. But they laughed and played a flamenco melody instead. My friend and I felt as if heaven had descended on us; the church, the surrounding darkness, the sound of the guitars, and the man's delight—it was all a miracle.

"Little by little, the church began to fill. The boys continued to play the flamenco, and everyone who came in smiled, infected by the joy of the musicians.

"My friend asked if I wanted to attend the mass that was about to begin. I said no—we had a long ride ahead of us. So we decided to leave—but before we did, we thanked God for yet another beautiful moment in our lives.

"As we arrived at the gate, we saw that many people—perhaps the entire population of the town—were walking to the church. I thought it must have been the last completely Catholic town in Spain—maybe because the crowds seemed to be having so much fun.

"As we got into the car, we saw a funeral procession approaching. Someone had died; it was a mass for the dead. As soon as the cortege reached the gates of the church, the musicians stopped the flamenco music and began to play a dirge."

"May God have mercy on that soul," said the woman, crossing herself.

"May He have mercy," I said, repeating her gesture. "But our having gone into that church really had been a sign—that every story has a sad ending."

The woman said nothing. Then she left the room and returned immediately with a pen and paper.

"Let's go outside," she said.

We went out together, and the sun was rising.

"Take a deep breath," she said. "Let this new morning enter your lungs and course through your veins. From what I can see, your loss yesterday was not an accident."

I didn't answer.

"You also didn't really understand the story you told me, about the sign in the church," she went on. "You saw only the sadness of the procession at the end. You forgot the happy moments you spent inside. You forgot the feeling that heaven had descended on you and how good it was to be experiencing all of that with your . . ."

She stopped and smiled.

". . . childhood friend," she said, winking. "Jesus said, 'Let the dead bury the dead' because he knew that there is no such thing as death. Life existed before we were born and will continue to exist after we leave this world."

My eyes filled with tears.

"It's the same with love," she went on. "It existed before and will go on forever."

"You seem to know everything about my life," I said.

"All love stories have much in common. I went through the same thing at one point in my life. But that's not what I remember. What I remember is that love returned in the form of another man, new hopes, and new dreams."

She held out the pen and paper to me.

"Write down everything you're feeling. Take it out of your soul, put it on the paper, and then throw it away. Legend says that the River Piedra is so cold that anything that falls into it—leaves, insects, the feathers of birds—is turned to stone. Maybe it would be a good idea to toss your suffering into its waters."

I took the pages. She kissed me, and said I could come back for lunch if I wanted to.

"Don't forget!" she shouted as she walked away. "Love perseveres. It's men who change."

I smiled, and she waved good-bye.

I looked out at the river for some time. And I cried until there were no more tears.

Then I began to write.

Epilogue

I WROTE FOR AN ENTIRE DAY, AND then another, and another. Every morning, I went to the bank of the River Piedra. Every afternoon, the woman came, took me by the arm, and led me back to the old convent.

She washed my clothes, made me dinner, chatted about trivial things, and sent me to bed.

One morning, when I had almost finished the manuscript, I heard the sound of a car. My heart leaped, but I didn't want to believe it. I felt free again, ready to return to the world and be a part of it once again.

The worst had passed, although the sadness remained.

But my heart was right. Even without raising my eyes from my work, I felt his presence and heard his footsteps.

"Pilar," he said, sitting down next to me.

I went on writing, without answering. I couldn't pull my thoughts together. My heart was jumping, trying to free itself from my breast and run to him. But I wouldn't allow it.

He sat there looking at the river, while I went on writing. The entire morning passed that way—without a word—and I recalled the silence of a night near a well when I'd suddenly realized that I loved him.

When my hand could write no longer, I stopped. Then he spoke.

"It was dark when I came up out of the cavern. I couldn't find you, so I went to Zaragoza. I even went to Soria. I looked everywhere for you. Then I decided to return to the monastery at Piedra to see if there was any sign of you, and I met a woman. She showed me where you were, and she said you had been waiting for me."

My eyes filled with tears.

"I am going to sit here with you by the river. If you go home to sleep, I will sleep in front of your house. And if you go away, I will follow you—until you tell me to go away. Then I'll leave. But I have to love you for the rest of my life."

I could no longer hold back the tears, and he began to weep as well.

"I want to tell you something . . . ," he started to say.

"Don't say a thing. Read this." I handed him the pages.

❦ ❦ ❦

I GAZED AT THE RIVER PIEDRA all afternoon. The woman brought us sandwiches and wine, commented on the weather, and left us alone. Every once in a while, he paused in his reading and stared out into space, absorbed in his thoughts.

At one point I went for a walk in the woods, past the small waterfalls, through the landscape that was so laden with stories and meanings for me. When the sun began to set, I went back to the place where I had left him.

"Thank you" was what he said as he gave the papers back to me. "And forgive me."

On the bank of the River Piedra, I sat down and wept.

"Your love has saved me and returned me to my dream," he continued.

I said nothing.

"Do you know Psalm 137?" he asked.

I shook my head. I was afraid to speak.

"On the banks of the rivers of Babylon . . ."

"Yes, yes, I know it," I said, feeling myself coming back to life, little by little. "It talks about exile. It talks about people who hang up their harps because they cannot play the music their hearts desire."

"But after the psalmist cries with longing for the land of his dreams, he promises himself,

If I forget you, O Jerusalem,
let my right hand forget its skill.
Let my tongue cling to the roof of my mouth,
if I do not exalt Jerusalem."

I smiled again.

"I had forgotten, and you brought it back to me."

"Do you think your gift has returned?" I asked.

"I don't know. But the Goddess has always given me a second chance in life. And She is giving me that with you. She will help me to find my path again."

"Our path."

"Yes, ours."

He took my hands and lifted me to my feet.

"Go and get your things," he said. "Dreams mean work."